RANCHO SANTIAGO COLLEGE

3 3065 00204 0578

Rancho Santiago College
Orange Campus Library

D0872227

ETHNIC CLEANSING

Andrew Bell-Fialkoff

ST. MARTIN'S PRESS
NEW YORK

Rancho Santiago College
Orange Campus Library

JV 6091
B45 1996

ETHNIC CLEANSING

Copyright © Andrew Bell-Fialkoff, 1996. All rights reserved. Printed in the United States of America. No part of this book may be used or reproduced in any manner whatsoever without written permission except in the case of brief quotations embodied in critical articles or reviews. For information, address St. Martin's Press, 175 Fifth Avenue, New York, N.Y. 10010.

ISBN 0-312-10792-7

Library of Congress Cataloging-in-Publication Data

Bell-Fialkoff, Andrew
    Ethnic Cleansing / Andrew Bell-Fialkoff.
        p.   cm.
    Includes bibliographical references and index.
    ISBN 0-312-10792-7
    1. Population transfers. 2. Forced migration. I. Title.
JV6091.B45 1996
304.8—dc20   96-19400
                                                         CIP

Design by Milton Heiberg Studios

First edition: October 1996
10 9 8 7 6 5 4 3 2 1

TABLE OF CONTENTS

LIST OF FIGURES, MAPS, AND TABLES

ACKNOWLEDGMENTS

I would like to thank everybody who taught and assisted me during the course of my studies. My special thanks go to Professor Walter Clemens, Jr., who made this book possible; Professor Robert Hefner, who shared many insights into the intricacies of cultural change and ethnic boundaries; Professor William Keylor, who taught me the techniques of historical research and supervised my progress; Professor Murray Melbin, who introduced me to the techniques of sociological research; and Professor Uri Ra'anan, who shared his vast knowledge of the problems of Eastern Europe and the Middle East. My special thanks go to Anne Bell, whose unfailing support sustained me during the long years of study; and William B. Meyer, whose friendship and erudition have been a source of wonder and inspiration. Many other teachers, assistants, and librarians, too numerous to be mentioned in this brief acknowledgment, have also been extremely helpful throughout these years. They have earned my deepest gratitude. Many thanks to them all.

Throughout the book, I have translated the French, Czech, and occasional German, Latin, and Russian into English. Needless to say, all errors and oversights in this book are entirely mine.

To Vera, Too Late

Introduction:
What Is Population Cleansing?

Population cleansing, not unlike pornography, defies easy definition. It covers a wide range of phenomena from genocide at one end to subtle pressure to emigrate at the other. Between these extremes lie expulsion and mass population transfers. Common to them all is the removal of an undesirable population from a given territory.

The term "cleansing" itself is ambiguous. In everyday use it has positive connotations of cleanliness and purification, evoking soap and water. But when applied to human populations it refers to refugees, deportation, and detention. It spells suffering. And that is why the term is widely used: it is a euphemism that hides the ugly truth.

An enemy, real or imagined, is often perceived as unclean, as a contamination or a cancer that must be eliminated or excised. An example of this was the German Association for the Extermination of Vermin (DEGESCH), which supplied poison gas to Nazi extermination camps.

Cleansing applies not only to ethnic groups. In fact, I deliberately omit the term "ethnic" from our discussion since cleansing can be applied to many other kinds of groups, such as those characterized by religion, race, or class. And while all types of cleansing involve population removal, not all forms of removal constitute cleansing.

Like "cleansing," "removal" is also a vague term. After all, genocide also implies removal of a population. The Holocaust is a case in point: areas that had been cleared of Jews were designated *Judenrein* ("clean of the Jews").

But what about milder forms of population removal, such as putting pressure on a certain category of people to emigrate by making their life so uncomfortable that they decide to leave? Wouldn't that amount to a kind of cleansing?

For the purposes of this book I will leave both extremes out of our discussion. Genocide, because in its scope and horror the mass murder of our time deserves to be treated as a separate category; the not always subtle pressure to leave, because it may grade imperceptibly into pressure by economic necessity. In this case much, if not most, emigration from Europe in the nineteenth century (and from elsewhere in the twentieth) would have to be included as well. This would make the concept unwieldy and, ultimately, too broad to be useful.

However, in our future discussions, we should keep in mind that the lines that separate population cleansing from genocide at one extreme of the continuum and emigration under pressure at the other extreme are often imprecise and should be regarded as guidelines rather than clear indicators.

So, to qualify as cleansing, a population removal must be forced and deliberate. This, however, may not be easily identifiable either. Take, for example, the slow annihilation, expulsion, and assimilation of the American Indians in the United States. In 250 years, roughly from 1630 until 1880, Indians were effectively cleansed from most of North America. And yet, there was no grand design, no planned policy of destruction directed by the government, except for a few mass expulsions in the nineteenth century. Rather, there was a slow spread of white settlement; "European" diseases ravaged the native population; and countless skirmishes pushed the Indians farther and farther west.

Or take the effects of the slave trade in many parts of Black Africa. Although it removed a large portion of racially distinct population, there was no desire to cleanse per se, only greed driven by the economic forces of supply and demand.

Finally, the revocation of the Edict of Nantes in 1685 sent thousands of Huguenots fleeing to Protestant countries. The French government clearly wanted to rid France of a religious minority. And yet, aside from the revocation and subsequent discrimination, virtually no measures were taken toward actual expulsion comparable to the expulsion of Jews from Spain in 1492.

These three examples—the North American Indians, the African slaves, and the Huguenots—illustrate an important point: not every expulsion, even if it is deliberate and removes an undesirable population from a given territory, qualifies as cleansing. We could, of course, distinguish between deliberate and nondeliberate cleansing, but then the latter category would inevitably include virtually any population removal. To avoid confusion, I suggest that we add one more caveat to our definition: not only must the population be undesirable but the removal itself must be based on the trait(s) that make(s) it undesirable. Thus, the removal of Africans through slave trade, cruel and reprehensible though it was, does not qualify as cleansing because the motive was purely economic. The population was not removed because it was African or Black. The slave trader did not aim at removing Blacks, Africans, members of certain tribes, or any other specific category of people from a specific territory. Rather, his goal was to make a profit by selling merchandise, in this case people. (Race was not an integral element in justifying the slave trade, at least not everywhere. Slave trade in Whites, mostly Christians, flourished in the Ottoman empire until the end of the eighteenth century. The main slave traders were Crimean Tatars who raided Russian, Ukrainian, Polish, Romanian, and Hungarian territories and sent thousands of captives to the main market in Constantinople. The last major raid against Russia occurred in 1769 [John A. Armstrong, *Nations before Nationalism,* Chapel Hill: University of North Carolina Press, 1982, p. xxxv]. Only Russian annexation of the Crimea put an end to Tatar depredations. But the slave trade in Constantinople continued, although on a smaller scale. The main factor, it seems, was availability, not race. For example, Russian serfs, White and Christian, could be sold by their masters, also White and Christian, until 1861.)

Nor does the slow push-back of American Indians qualify as cleansing, according to our definition, except in those cases when the Indians were removed through an organized expulsion, only because they were Indian.

So far we have discussed the removal only of unwanted populations. But valued populations can also be removed in what may be called "reverse cleansing." Such was the recall of German minorities from the Baltic states in 1941, as well as the resettlement of other groups of ethnic Germans in Nazi Germany in an effort to save every ounce of valuable German blood.

Nor should we leave out temporary cleansing, which aims at removing a certain population for a period of time only, like the internment of Japanese in the United States after Pearl Harbor. The problem with temporary cleansing is that it may seem indistinguishable from internment or evacuation. We may, of course, relegate the temporary removal of an undesirable population to the category of cleansing while the temporary removal of desirable populations could be classified as evacuation. But this is hair-splitting; and since cases of temporary cleansing are extremely rare—if the population is undesirable enough, why not make the resettlement permanent?—we will not encounter many instances.

To summarize, let us define population cleansing as follows:

Population cleansing is a planned, deliberate removal from a certain territory of an undesirable population distinguished by one or more characteristics such as ethnicity, religion, race, class, or sexual prefer-

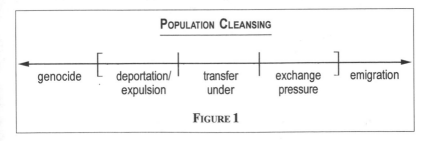

POPULATION CLEANSING

genocide — deportation/expulsion — transfer under — exchange pressure — emigration

FIGURE 1

ence. These characteristics must serve as the basis for removal for it to qualify as cleansing.

We may reiterate that cleansing so defined is a part of a wider continuum of population removal ranging from genocide at one extreme to voluntary emigration under pressure at another. Figure 1 elucidates this continuum:

PART I

Chapter 1

CLEANSING:
A HISTORICAL OVERVIEW

Cleansing as a state policy was probably initiated by the Assyrians. Up to 4.5 million people in conquered territories were forcibly resettled in the reigns of Assurnasirpal II (883-859 B.C.) and Assurbanipal (669-627 B.C.).[1] The Assyrians used forced resettlement of the vanquished as a means of crushing resistance. Usually, it was the elites that were resettled. For example, most of the 27,290 Israelites sent to Gozan and Media (modern Kurdistan) in 721 B.C. belonged to the upper classes.[2] This made perfect sense in terms of policy objectives and ease of execution, since the elites were more urbanized and, therefore, easier to collect and also because a leaderless mass of peasants and artisans was less likely to rise in revolt. Complete population removal has always been much more expensive.

Such massive population removals indicate that the people of the conquered territories were regarded as dangerous, which in itself is an indicator that they shared a collective identity. Whether the Israelites who were resettled in 721 B.C. defined themselves primarily as worshippers of Yahweh or as inhabitants of the land of Israel, or both, it is clear that loyalty toward Assyria could not be expected. Nowadays, they might be said to be "politically unreliable."

The Neo-Babylonian Empire, which supplanted Assyria as the major power in the Middle East, continued Assyrian policies. After Nebuchadnezzar captured Jerusalem in 597 B.C., some 10,000 state and military officials, along with skilled craftsmen and other leading citizens, were sent to Babylon.[3]

The cleansing was repeated on a wider scale in 586 B.C., after the suppression of an unsuccessful anti-Babylonian uprising.[4] Thanks to the Bible we know more about Hebrews than other ethnies, but Hebrews were by no means unique in this respect. Cleansing was applied to other conquered peoples as well: it seems to have been the most effective way of making the conquered populations docile.

These early instances of cleansing suggest two things. One, wars of ethnic resistance and liberation are by no means an exclusively modern phenomenon. We have additional proof of this in incidents such as the resistance that the Persians encountered in Greece and the anti-Hyksos uprisings in Egypt. Second, the transfer of the elites suggests that, much like in later feudal societies such as Poland or Hungary, it was the elites who were considered the bearers of collective identity. Eliminate the elites, and the leaderless population would be subdued.

Ancient Greeks of the classical period did not build empires, although Athens, in the fifth century B.C., did aspire to transform the Athenian League into its obedient instrument. Rather, Greek unity was based on ethno-cultural ties and a sense of ethnic community. In many ways Greek collectivity was similar to medieval Germany and Italy, with their numerous political entities within a larger cultural continuum. But even in Greece instances of politically inspired population removal occurred.

The earliest incidents resulted from struggles that were purely internal and lacked any ethnic component, struggles between monarchy and "democracy" (represented by the local oligarchy) within the Greek polis. This was a Panhellenic phenomenon and was a major feature of Greek political history in the eighth through sixth centuries B.C. The party that lost—the monarchy and its allies, more often than not—was forced to emigrate. And since other existing poleis could not absorb, for economic and political reasons, large numbers of refugees, the emigres had to look elsewhere. Usually, they were forced to found a new polis on virgin land. This was the driving force behind the planting of many Greek colonies throughout the Mediterranean and beyond.[5]

Intrapolis political cleansing characterized population removal in preclassical Greece. Interpolis cleansing spread in the postclassical period with incidents such as the destruction of Olynthos by Philip of Macedon, the father of Alexander the Great, in August 348 B.C.[6] All the inhabitants who did not escape were sold into slavery, and the city itself was destroyed.

On the one hand, it may seem dubious to classify as ethnic cleansing the enslavement of the Olynthians: after all, they were indisputably Greek, and the massive sale implies a strong economic, rather than political, motive.

On the other hand, Olynthos, the leading city in the Chalcidic League, was a political thorn in Macedon's side. And the fact that some former Olynthians, those who could be traced, were later bought out and the city rebuilt, all at considerable expense (as an inducement to Alexander's famous mentor, Aristotle, who came from Olynthos), indicates that political considerations predominated. In any case, the inhabitants were removed as Olynthians.

We should keep in mind that in the world of city-states, people of each statelet developed a strong sense of local identity reinforced by differences in dialect, custom, and culture, as later Bavarians and Venetians differed from other Germans and Italians. So one may argue that the destruction and depopulation of Olynthos, and other similar episodes of Greek history, were indeed an instance of ethnic, or perhaps subethnic, cleansing.

The tragedy of Olynthos was by no means an isolated episode. In fact, Greeks had a special term for it: *andrapodismos*,[7] which combines notions of deportation and enslavement, and which comes close to the modern concept of cleansing. One instance of *andrapodismos* occurred in Thebes in September 335 B.C. It was carried out by Alexander the Great. Thebes had been a major center of resistance to the Macedonian drive for hegemony in Greece. It was a powerful city-state, which spearheaded a revolt against Alexander and encouraged others to join. It had to be brought to heel if Macedon were to establish a firm grip on Greece.

When the city, after a fierce resistance, was captured, some 6,000 Thebans lay slaughtered and another 30,000 were prisoners.[8] The city was destroyed and the prisoners sold for the enormous profit of 440 talents.[9] Here again, as was typical of the ancient world, political and economic motivation went hand in hand: the destruction of the demographic base of a political enemy brought in substantial revenues.

The economic motive already discernible in Greece gained further impetus in Rome. Virtually every Roman conquest sent thousands of captives to the slave markets throughout the republic and later the empire. Thus, the capture of Agrigentum in Sicily in 202 B.C. produced some 25,000 captives, and the war in Greece in 167 B.C. generated 150,000 slaves. Marius enslaved some 90,000 captive Teutons and 60,000 Cymbrians, while Caesar wrote in his *De Bello Gallico* that he had sold 53,000 into slavery.[10] At a time when few tribes exceeded 100,000 this was ethnic cleansing par excellence.

The economic motivation was reinforced by the expansion of *latifundia* (large estates) in the second century B.C. The wars with Carthage required mass conscription; male citizens between the ages of 17 and 46 served 16 or even 20 years in the army. Between 200 and 168 B.C., about 47,000 Romans were drafted for prolonged periods of time. And if Italics and south Italian

Greeks are included, the total easily reaches 130,000.[11] Since a great many of these men were farmers and small holders, the land they owned often fell into disuse and was eventually bought up by rich land owners or other small holders who managed to avoid military service. This led to the amalgamation of small plots into large *latifundia*, which required slave labor on a grand scale. Thus, the emergence and expansion of *latifundia* created an insatiable demand for slaves.

It would be a mistake, however, to think that at this stage economic motives can be clearly divorced from political concerns. Most often both went together. When an obstinate enemy such as Carthage or a rebellious province such as Judea had to be brought to heel, dispersing the population was the most effective method. And since enslavement not only dispersed enemy population but was also highly profitable, it is not surprising that mass enslavement was a frequent occurrence in Rome. Such dual motivation was at work in the annihilation of Corinth and Carthage in 146 B.C. and the suppression of Judea in A.D. 66-70 and 132-35, which resulted in the displacement and enslavement of thousands of Carthaginians, Hebrews, and Greeks and effectively cleansed these countries of a large proportion of their original inhabitants.

Corinth was the capital of the Achaean League, an important port and fortress guarding the passage to the Peloponnesus. By 150 B.C. it found itself at the head of the anti-Roman resistance in Greece. Upon capturing the city in 146 B.C., Romans destroyed it and sold all surviving inhabitants into slavery.[12]

In that same year, Rome destroyed another major foe: Carthage. Since its defeat in the Second Punic War, Carthage had made a substantial recovery. However, it suffered repeated encroachments from neighboring Numidia, a client of Rome. Eventually, the conflict escalated into open warfare during which Rome stepped in on the side of its client. The siege of Carthage lasted three years. When it ended, the city was razed and the survivors sold into slavery.[13]

Similar cleansing, but on a vaster scale, occurred in Judea after the Great Jewish War of A.D. 66-70 and the suppression of the Bar Kochba revolt in A.D. 132-35. In suppressing this last flicker of Hebrew independence, the Romans destroyed 985 towns and villages, 50 forts, and killed some 580,000 people. Countless others died from disease and starvation, and so many were sold into slavery that the price of a slave fell below that of a horse.[14] The ultimate result was a drastic depopulation of the country, in effect a major cleansing on a scale that dwarfed all previous cleansings.

But Romans were not only cleansers; occasionally, as in the First Mithridatic War in Asia Minor in 88 B.C., they were the cleansed. During his invasion of Roman territory, King Mithridates VI of Pontus encouraged Asian debtors to kill their Roman creditors. In the massacres that followed some 80,000 Romans, Italics, and Italian Greeks, many of them trade representatives, were massacred.[15] And although massacres technically fall outside ethnic cleansing, in this instance they were carried out on the basis of ethnic origin and thus qualify as such, or at least as a borderline case.

The major instances of population cleansing in antiquity—Assyrian, Greek, Roman—demonstrate that cleansing was either strategic and political aimed at securing the hold on newly conquered territories; economically motivated (aimed at realizing profits from the sale of slaves); or, usually, both.

***

With the onset of the Middle Ages the pattern of cleansing drastically changed: it was now applied to religious minorities rather than conquered populations. Earlier, ethnicity and religion had formed an organic whole: most tribes and ethnic groups had a religion of their own. Empires of antiquity had destroyed that link. Greek-speaking Alexandrians worshipping Isis were granted Roman citizenship and probably considered themselves Roman. The identification was so persistent that when the Osmanli Turks established their state in Asia Minor at the end of the thirteenth century they found themselves fighting "Rum" (Rome), a striking testimony to the lingering identification with Rome on the part of Greek-speaking Byzantines. Even today, the area around Istanbul is still known as "Rumelia" (the Roman country). What's more, Greeks of today call themselves *romeios* (literally, Romans).

After the collapse of Rome, Christianity remained the most important binding element in Western civilization. Religion supplanted the state. A person could be a subject of the king of France or the emperor of the Holy Roman Empire, but he was first and foremost a Christian; if not, he was beyond the pale of citizenship, community, or even humanity.

The division of Europe, the Mediterranean, and the Middle East between competing cultural and religious blocs—Latin and Byzantine Christianity and Islam—brought about a shift toward civilizational and religious conflict. Civilizational conflict had not been entirely absent in the ancient world: the struggle of the Greeks against Persia can be interpreted as a struggle between two civilizations. However, with the advent of the Middle Ages this kind of conflict became more prevalent: first when Muslim Arabs tried to subjugate Christian Europe, then when Christians counterattacked in the Crusades, and finally when the Muslim Turks attacked Europe in the fourteenth through seventeenth centuries. In a confrontation of this kind it was natural that religious minorities, especially those belonging to the other side, would be feared and suspected of being a fifth column. Such dangerous minorities became prime candidates for cleansing. In a sense, this was a variety of political cleansing, since politicized religion threatened the security of the state. But it was also a qualitatively new phenomenon, since religion now determined a person's loyalty to the state. (Isolated instances of this phenomenon can be found in antiquity, such as when Jewish religious precepts precluded deification of Antiochus Epiphanes in the early second century B.C. and thus precluded Jewish loyalty to the Seleucid Empire. But in the Middle Ages this became the rule, not an exception.)

Ethnic enmity had not completely disappeared. Each religious bloc experienced many internal conflicts, often accompanied by massacre and cleansing. A massacre of Danes occurred in Anglo-Saxon England on November 13, 1002, when "in pursuance of secret instructions sent by the King over the whole country, the inhabitants of every town and city armed, and murdered all the Danes who were their neighbors. Young and old, babies and soldiers, men and women, every Dane was killed."[16] The Anglo-Danes, whose families had been living in the country for generations, some since the ninth century, were clearly murdered as Danes. And this was not an isolated case; exactly 300 years later, in 1302, Flemings of Bruges massacred all Frenchmen living or stationed in the city.[17] Frenchmen were also massacred throughout Sicily in 1282 in a revolt against the Anjou dynasty known as Sicilian Vespers.[18] Flemings themselves repeatedly came under fire in England. In 1344 the king had to issue a special proclamation against attacks on foreign clothmakers, most of them Flemish;[19] and in 1381, during the Wat Tyler uprising, rebels beheaded a number of Flemings and lawyers(!) in one of the earliest attempts at ethnic and social cleansings.[20]

All of these examples involved mass murder and, at least in the case of the Danes in England, can be classified as genocide, putting them outside our definition. However, there are other examples of pure cleansing, such as repeated attempts to expel Germans from the Czech lands. As early as the eleventh century, according to the chronicler Cosmas, Prince Spytihnev "earned everyone's admiration because he ordered the expulsion within three days of all Germans from Bohemia wherever they are found."[21] Sporadic pogroms and expulsions of Germans reached a peak during the Hussite period in the fifteenth century, were discontinued when the Czech Lands came under Austrian rule, and then were successfully implemented after World War II on a massive scale.

And yet, despite these numerous examples, ethnicity played a secondary role in medieval cleansing; religion was clearly preponderant. This was a natural development in a civilization suffused with religious feeling, where God was felt to be ever present and daily life was organized around the rituals of prayer. In such a civilization the world was divided between believers and nonbelievers, with the assumption that nonbelievers were not completely acceptable and had to be either converted or cleansed. We can glimpse this mindset in the Muslim division of the world into the "Realm of Islam" and the "Realm of War." It is implied that eventually the Realm of War will be converted, by force of arms, into the Realm of Islam.

Indeed, from the very beginning, Arabs, unlike Christians, practiced what they preached. During the great Arab expansion of the seventh and eighth centuries, pagans who refused conversion were massacred. Christians and Jews were usually spared (though not always, as in the massacres of Jews in and around Medina), but were relegated to the status of second-class minorities whose fortunes depended on the good will of Muslim rulers. Constant wars with Christians in Iberia and Byzantium put strain on Arab relations with such minorities.

Arabs were not alone in trying to impose religious orthodoxy. Their conquest divided the Mediterranean, until then the area of a unified civilization, into two large religious blocs, not unlike the ideological blocs of the cold war. As we know from recent Soviet experience, dissidents are not tolerated in such orthodoxies. Persecutions of religious minorities also occurred outside the Christian and Muslim blocs, such as the massive persecutions of non-Zoroastrians in Sassanian Persia in the fourth century.[22]

In what came to be the West, early instances of religious intolerance include Antiochus Epiphanes' campaign against observant Jews in the second century B.C. and attempts to suppress Christians in imperial Rome.

As paganism in Europe receded, the Jews remained the only sizable religious minority in Christendom. It is hardly surprising that major attempts at religious cleansing in medieval Europe were directed against them.

Although restrictions on Jews were imposed as early as the sixth century in Visigothic Spain, the first major instance of mass murder with the intent to cleanse dates from the First Crusade of 1096-99. That campaign included a series of massacres perpetrated by the Crusaders on their way to Jerusalem, starting in Rouen and then, in a trail of blood and destruction, throughout the Rhine and the Moselle valleys, as well as in Prague and Hungary. Entire communities, perhaps tens of thousands of people in all, were wiped out. The Crusade culminated in a wholesale massacre of all non-Christians in Jerusalem. The city was emptied of its Jewish and Muslim inhabitants.

Expulsion was a more frequently used method of cleansing than massacre, and here as well Jews were the prime target. Its first major occurrence in medieval Christendom was probably the expulsion of Jews from the Crimea when the Byzantine armies captured the peninsula (most of it under Khazar rule until then) in 1016. In the West, the pioneer in the expulsion of Jews was the city of Paris, in 1182.[23]

Jews were relatively easy to cleanse since they were a small and highly urbanized population. Even with Jews, however, it was difficult to cleanse an entire country, especially in decentralized feudal polities. Only a relatively centralized government could organize an eviction on such a scale. Hence, it is not surprising that England, which achieved centralization earlier than most other European states, led the way. It expelled its entire Jewish population of some 16,000 in 1290. The English example was soon followed by France in 1306 and Provence in 1394 and 1490.

In central and eastern Europe cleansing started even earlier, with various German principalities leading the way in the twelfth century. Silesia (not yet German, strictly speaking) expelled its Jews in 1159. Other countries and cities, such as Hungary in 1349-60, Austria in 1421, Lithuania in 1445 and 1495, and Cracow in 1494, also carried out major expulsions.[24]

Perhaps the best known and largest expulsions were those from Spain in 1492 and Portugal in 1497, which sent a multitude of Jewish refugees (estimates vary from 50,000 to 250,000) in all directions.[25] Iberian cleansings set an important example in the sense that Spain, unlike other European countries, had a large Muslim population as well. The harsh treatment meted out to Spain's Muslim minority proves that attempts at purification were directed at any religious minority, not just the Jews.

Another significant feature of the Iberian cleansing is the long history of animosity that predated the expulsion. The animosity was a natural consequence of the Reconquista, which saw the gradual liberation of the Iberian peninsula from Muslim rule in the eighth through fifteenth centuries. Paradoxically, real pressure on Muslim and Jewish minorities in Christian-ruled areas did not start in earnest until the balance had decisively shifted in favor of the Christians, as if they were too busy to harass religious minorities in the heat of battle. The pressure manifested itself in riots and mob action that culminated in Jewish massacres throughout Iberia in 1391.

With the establishment of the Inquisition in 1481-83 the state took over, and in the first 12 years of its existence condemned about 13,000 *conversos* (converts) for the secret practice of Judaism.[26] In 1492, all Jews who refused conversion were expelled. Thus, the year 1492 was not a sudden explosion of bigotry and religious intolerance but was the culmination of a long period of gestation and development.

Ten years later the same fate befell Spanish Muslims.[27] That expulsion, however, was not as complete as the cleansing of Jews in 1492 had been because Muslims were not as highly urbanized. The Muslim expulsion affected mostly urban elites and the middle class (if we can apply such terms to merchants and artisans of late medieval Spain). Rural Muslims, especially in isolated areas, were allowed to stay but those who remained were forcibly Christianized in 1526. Like Jews, the *Moriscos* (converted Muslims) were not deemed completely reliable and were eventually expelled en masse in 1609-14. About 275,000 of the 300,000 still living in Spain at that time had to leave.[28]

Marranos (converted Jews), although never expelled en masse like the Moriscos, perhaps because they were a highly dispersed population sometimes blended with the "old" Christian majority, also came under close scrutiny: they were closely watched by the Inquisition. "New Christians" were distrusted. Occasionally, they were attacked, as for example in the great pogrom during Easter week of 1507 in Lisbon.[29] Many *Marranos* were burned at the stake, the last such auto-da-fe taking place in Lisbon in 1755 (burning at the stake for other offenses continued until 1790).[30]

Forced conversion often played an important role in religious cleansings. And no wonder, for it achieved the same result: it eliminated religious minorities. Widely practiced by Arabs at the time of the initial conquests in the seventh and eighth centuries, forced conversions of infidels periodically occurred throughout the Muslim world, as in Tunis in 1146.[31]

Persia also has a long tradition of forced conversions, the earliest going back to 430 (when it was still Zoroastrian), the latest in 1838. And if we count persecutions of the Bahais in contemporary Iran, we can say that in Persia attempts at purification have never ceased.

Byzantium in its heyday also experienced several major conversion campaigns, in 640, 721, 873, and 930. And in Europe, where they were directed mostly against the Jews, such conversions were numerous: 591 in Marseilles and Arles, 629 in Paris, 1010 in Limoges, 1146 in Spain, 1407 in Cracow, 1431 in Toulouse, and 1543 and 1783 in Rome only begin the list.

Religious cleansing was directed not only outward, against other religions, but also inward, against heretics who had somehow deviated from the "right path". The defensive mechanism based on religion seems to function like a rampart surrounding the collective identity, protecting it both from the enemies on the outside and the subversives inside.

Not every religious persecution can be classified as cleansing, of course. To qualify, it has to remove a well-defined population from a certain territory, and the removal itself must be motivated by some ideologically objectionable characteristic(s) of the removed population. Not every pogrom leads to massacre, and not every persecution results in cleansing. The suppression of the

Albigensian heresy in what is now southern France in the thirteenth century, accompanied by massacres, fits the parameters of cleansing as previously defined. On the other hand, the infamous witch hunts of the sixteenth and seventeenth centuries probably don't because we don't have conclusive proof that a well-defined population of witches actually existed. For the most part, victims were innocent women, often elderly, who were caught up in antiwitch hysteria. Although there is no doubt that individuals did practice witchcraft, witches as a category existed only in popular imagination. And while witch hunts do show certain parallels with the weeding out of *Marranos* and *Moriscos* in Spain and Portugal, the persecution of individuals belonging to a nonexistent community does not constitute a cleansing, even though there was clear intent to cleanse on the part of religious authorities.

With the onset of the Reformation, the basis for cleansing in Europe began to shift to denomination. Religious wars in France (1562-98) and Germany (1544-52 and 1618-48) led to massacres and displacements of Catholics and Protestants alike. The best known instance is probably the St. Bartholomew's Day massacre of Huguenots in France on August 23-24, 1572,[32] although the sack of Protestant Magdeburg in May 1631, during which some 20,000 Protestants lost their lives, was much worse. At the other end of Europe, Bogdan Khmelnytsky's Cossacks, mostly Orthodox Ukrainians, carried out extensive massacres of Catholic Poles and Jews during the anti-Polish campaigns of 1648-54.

These examples clearly demonstrate that there was a strong tendency to impose religious orthodoxy and homogeneity in the Christian and Muslim world throughout the Middle Ages. This tendency was not politically articulated, however, although the language of religion and religious concepts were used in political struggles and discourse, such as to justify Czech resistance to German penetration. It was not until 1555 that the Peace of Augsburg established the principle of religious homogeneity as the basis for political order.[33] The principle was enunciated in the formula *cuius regio eius religio* (the ruler determines [the subjects'] religion). In other words, the ruler had the final say in the religious matters of his state, and every subject had to accept his religion or leave.

It was the Peace of Augsburg that established the principle of religious homogeneity of a political entity. As such, it is the cornerstone of modern totalitarianism and all subsequent drives to impose orthodoxy. Those who would not accept had to leave or be cleansed. Thus, the Peace of Augsburg is the mother of modern cleansing.

One could argue that the modern notion of cleansing derives from the medieval dichotomy of religious purity/impurity. The impure, by the very logic of such a Manichaean dichotomy, have to be banished. It was therefore natural that nationalism, with its strong religious and messianic components (noted by Carlton Hayes, Salo Baron, and many others), would display the same tendency toward (self-)cleansing and (self-)purification. It is highly significant, however, that this principle was not elaborated until the beginning of the sixteenth century, that is soon after the consolidation of the increasingly centralized states of Western Europe—England, France, Spain, Portugal—in the second half of the fifteenth century.

Organized religion has always been highly politicized. It is hardly surprising then that the early modern states would try to use religion to their advantage. Since religion provided the primary identity of society and individual, it was deemed imperative to ensure compliance of the population with state religion. Thus, the medieval notions of religious purity/impurity were transformed, under the impact of political struggle and religious wars, into a political principle. And modern cleansing was born.

***

In the first stage, roughly between 1530 and 1730, cleansing remained either religious or, if it had a significant ethnic component, couched in religious terms. In this early phase was Spanish persecution of the Protestants in the Low Countries at the end of the sixteenth century, which sent some 175,000 Protestants fleeing for their lives; and Catholic counterreformation in Bohemia half a century later, which displaced some 150,000 Protestants (in a population of 2.5 million).[34] Perhaps the best known among the first type, the purely religious kind, is the revocation of the Edict of Nantes in 1685,[35] which removed legal protection and toleration from French Protestants and sent thousands of Huguenots fleeing in all directions. Although expulsion per se was not the goal, the royal government clearly wanted to suppress and eliminate the non-Catholic faith. The revocation was an act of self-cleansing.

A more clearly discernible ethnic component can be found in the mass expulsions of the Irish Catholics from Ulster. Although the beginnings of the Ulster Plantation—the settlement of Protestants on land confiscated from the Catholics—go back to 1609, the turning point was not reached until after the rebellion of 1641. The rebellion, its suppression, and the plagues that followed destroyed about half of the total population of Ireland.[36] Most of the remaining Irish Catholics were expelled from Ulster, and English and Scottish settlers, all of them Protestant, were brought in. By 1688, about 80 percent of Irish land was owned by Protestants.

The reason for such harsh treatment was not only ideological but also strategic: Catholic Ireland could offer Catholic Spain and France a base of operations against England. And there were other factors as well, such as the

Cromwellian struggle against the royalists and the economic advantages of acquiring valuable land for a very good price. Whatever the motivations, the fact remains that the expelled were Catholic and Irish while the newcomers who took their place were Protestants of English and Scottish stock. Thus, although still a religious expulsion, it can also qualify as the first ethnic cleansing of modern times.

The last large-scale cleansing based on purely religious considerations (in the West; elsewhere, religious expulsions never ceased) occurred on October 31, 1731, in the Catholic Bishopric of Salzburg, in what is now Austria, where over 20,000 Protestants, mostly Lutherans, were ordered to leave.[37]

***

A quarter of a century later the second phase began with the purely ethnic cleansing of the francophone Acadians in Canada. That expulsion resulted from the resumption of war between England and France in North America. Initially, things did not go well for England: it suffered defeat in the summer of 1755. As the situation became critical, the English turned on the French Acadians, who, they were afraid, would stab them in the back. The Acadian delegates were summoned before the Council of Halifax to give an oath of loyalty to the English crown. When they refused, the council decided to deport them.[38]

That decision seems to have been based mostly on strategic grounds and was greatly influenced by the unfavorable military situation. And technically, Acadians were expelled only because of their refusal to give the oath. We should also note that their loyalties probably lay with the French crown, not the French nation as such, although the crown, in this case, symbolized the French state and nation. Nevertheless, the fact remains that the Acadians were expelled as Frenchmen or, at the very least, as French sympathizers.

Deportations continued until 1763, by which time only about 2,300 to 4,700 of the original 13,000 *habitants* remained in their homeland.[39] While Acadia was being emptied, English and American settlers whose loyalty was not in doubt were brought in. By 1763, when the deportations ceased, about 12,000 English speakers had been settled in Acadia.[40]

The expulsion of the Acadians was the opening salvo in the second period of cleansing, which lasted approximately from 1750 to 1900. In this period cleansing was practiced mainly by Europeans in the colonies and was applied, most often, to non-White populations. Deportations of Indians in the United States are a case in point.

Although the dispossession of Native Americans had been going on since the arrival of Europeans in the New World, it had involved mostly unorganized or locally sponsored migration onto new, sparsely populated lands. The government took little or no part in this process, and the British government even tried to protect the Indians, to the irritation of colonials. This began to change after the United States gained independence. The first major government-sponsored removal of the Indian population was the result of a complex deal between Georgia and the federal government in April 1802.[41] In it, Georgia ceded its western land claims to the federal government, and in return, the government agreed to cancel Indian title to land ownership within the state.

Aside from straightening Georgia's irregular frontier, which was deeply indented by Indian-held territories (although this shouldn't have mattered, since it was an internal frontier and thus no strategic considerations could have applied), the main concern of the signatories was to put an end to the close cohabitation of the two races by which "the civilized man was not improved while the savage was depraved."[42]

The crisis came to a head in the late 1820s when settlement pressure on the Indians intensified. Alarmed, the Cherokee nation made a desperate bid to ward off further encroachments. On July 26, 1827, it adopted a written constitution, modeled on that of the United States, which declared the Cherokees a sovereign and independent nation and thus not subject to agreements between third parties.[43] But a piece of paper could not protect the now defenseless Indians. The next year Georgia added Indian lands to its territory and in 1830 extended its jurisdiction over them.[44] And then the Federal Removal Act of May 1830 provided the legal framework for the cleansing.[45] Internal feuds between various factions within the doomed tribes sowed discord, prevented organized resistance, and facilitated the removal. The feuds even allowed the Jackson administration to regard the removal as a voluntary migration since turncoats willing to cooperate in the destruction of their own people could always be found.

The removal itself was brutal. The deportees were often relocated under harsh conditions. And when they arrived at their destination they often found that no accommodations had been prepared for them. Although the removal was dressed up as a legal sale, later investigations of Choctaw claims during the Van Buren administration uncovered major fraud perpetrated against the Indians.[46] Even worse, the deportation served as a model for further removals of Indian populations from Kansas in 1854 and of the Civilized Tribes then living in Oklahoma in the 1880s.[47]

Indians were not the only victims of cleansing in North America. There were also scattered incidents of anti-Chinese violence that sometimes ended in wholesale expulsions and thus amounted to cleansing, although on a much smaller scale. Such was the expulsion of the Chinese from Humboldt County,

California, in 1885.[48] The Chinese were also expelled en masse from several towns on the Pacific coast at the end of the 1870s.[49] These expulsions were repeated in 1885 in Tacoma, Seattle, and many smaller towns. These incidents, though brutal and painful for the Chinese, were limited in scope and were directed mainly against cheap Chinese labor. In a way, this was as much a labor cleansing as it was a racial one.

Finally, one should also mention several religiously motivated expulsions of Mormon communities in the early 1830s. These cleansings differ from the prevalent type of this period and can be regarded as the last echoes of religious cleansings in medieval Europe.

Having first established themselves in Jackson County, Missouri, the Mormons faced increasing hostility from their neighbors and the state. Incompatibility in philosophies, general outlooks, and ways of life often led to violent clashes between Mormons and their non-Mormon neighbors.

By the summer of 1836 Mormons were "asked" to leave Clay County, Missouri. They disregarded the "request." Mounting tensions and recurrent intercommunal violence prompted Missouri Governor Lilburn Boggs to issue an order, on October 26, 1838, which stipulated that the Mormons should be "exterminated" or driven out. Indeed, 17 were killed four days later at Haun's Mill.[50] At this point the Mormons finally gave up and moved to Illinois in the winter-spring of 1838-39.[51]

North America was by no means the only continent where expansionist Europeans practiced the art of cleansing. Australia, more compact and with smaller indigenous population, was also the scene of some major population removals (although most cases were probably closer to genocide). As in America, the first contacts between Europeans and the Aborigines were for the most part friendly. The relations soured when the newcomers started to spread out from the areas of initial settlement. "Shooting abos" became a sport, often practiced on Saturdays, in which local police also took part.[52] These massacres were called dispersals. Sometimes, if the Aborigines stole sheep from the farms built on their land, they were given food laced with arsenic.

An even more thorough genocide occurred in Tasmania, where between 2,000 and 3,000 Aborigines were hunted down and killed. Some 200 who remained were deported to Flinders Island, where most of them died out. The last 16 were later returned to Tasmania, where the last one died in 1876.

Although efforts to protect the Aborigines started fairly early—seven white men were hanged in 1838 for killing Aborigines at Myall Creek[53]—it was not until the 1870s that various Australian states began to offer legal protection to the Aborigines. It took another 70 years, until 1951, for the Australian Government to create the Department of Native Welfare. In 1964 the Aborigines finally became de facto citizens when the Social Welfare Act was extended to them. But only in 1967 were census takers instructed to include them with the rest of the human population.[54]

Things were very different in New Zealand, where the Treaty of Waitangi, signed in 1840 between Maori chiefs and Queen Victoria, guaranteed the tribes of New Zealand the "full, exclusive and undisputed possession of their lands."[55] The Treaty, however, failed to prevent a war between the Maori and the British. When it ended, in 1865, the government confiscated about 3 million acres of Maori land (some of which was later returned)[56] and evicted some Maori tribes, but this was more of a punitive dispossession than ethnic cleansing per se.

The cleansings of this period, with some notable exceptions in Australia, did not aim at annihilation. Complete destruction of an ethnic group did not become a stated—or unstated—goal until the end of the nineteenth century. The native colonial populations were either far away from the metropole or too numerically insignificant to be perceived as a major threat. The Great Famine in Ireland in 1845-48 and the great migration it engendered might seem to be an exception to this. But despite the fact that the calamity killed up to a million Irish and sent another million across the ocean, it does not qualify as a cleansing. First, it was not planned. Although some Englishmen, including those in government circles and at the *Times,* expressed satisfaction that soon there would be no Irish left in Ireland, no organized effort was made to depopulate the country. Rather, natural calamity and unequal land distribution were allowed to take their toll, without government interference. Second, as in other (British) colonies and the United States, the native population was allowed to recoup its losses. This was true of Australia and New Zealand, Ireland and North America. In Ireland, for example, after the initial drop from about 8 million to fewer than 5 million, the total population stabilized and remained stationary until the 1960s.

***

It is only after 1900, in the third, contemporary phase, that enormously destructive cleansings aimed not only at removal but at complete annihilation of the unwanted populations began.

The first country that tried to implement a complete cleansing was Ottoman Turkey. This was a sprawling empire founded by the Osmanli Turks at the end of the thirteenth century. It reached its zenith in the sixteenth and seventeenth centuries, but by the nineteenth century it had fallen into decline and had become the "sick man of Europe."

The multiethnic populations of old Turkey were subdivided into various "millets." The division was based on religion, each religion and denomination constituting a millet. This system gave a tremendous advantage to the established minorities, such as the Greeks, whose clergy monopolized the Orthodox Christian establishment not only in Greek areas but also among Bulgarians, Romanians, and other Orthodox peoples. So successful were the Greeks, even in the higher echelons of Turkish administration, that by the end of the eighteenth century it looked as though they might take over the entire state apparatus of the Ottoman Empire and perhaps re-establish the Byzantine Empire in a new form.

This, by the way, goes to show that Turkey around 1800 was a relatively tolerant society that accepted the religious and ethnic diversity of its populations. Why then, a hundred years later, did it launch successive cleansing campaigns against Armenians, Christian Lebanese, Nestorian Christians, Anatolian and Pontic Greeks, Kurds, and several other minorities?

We should seek the answer in the transition from multiethnic empire to a national state in the age of nationalism. Turkey was by no means alone in this painful process. Austria, Germany, and Russia all followed the same path. When the dominant imperial ethny, previously defined in dynastic and/or religious terms, redefines itself as a national entity, as an ethnic group in the context of a multiethnic empire, it embarks on a path of ethnic competition with other ethnies in a zero-sum game. It is compelled, by the very logic of the game, to eliminate or at least neutralize its competitors: in short, to seek purity.

It is a mutually reinforcing process. The effort to suppress other ethnies and to maintain the empire provokes a response from the oppressed, which increases tensions. As hatred on both sides grows, the other ethnies come to be perceived as the enemies, as fifth columns that must be eliminated to preserve the sacred homeland. As the cycle of repression and revolt intensifies, there occurs a fatal polarization and permanent estrangement. Sooner or later, the empire falls apart.

The two European (Austrian and German) and two Eurasian (Russian and Turkish) empires that survived until 1900 came crashing down in 1917-18. The paths of each imperial ethny subsequently diverged. Austria imploded, to re-emerge as a small, ethnically and religiously homogeneous republic. In the process, it also "produced" Hitler and Nazism (this, of course, should be viewed within the larger German context).

Germany collapsed, attempted to redefine itself as a racial entity, made another bid for world hegemony, collapsed again, and was reorganized by the Allies as a democracy.

Russia also redefined itself, as a class-based entity, and even rebuilt the empire by embracing a new faith, messianic Communism. The new empire lasted for another 70 years and then also fell apart in 1989-91. Only now

Russia is trying to complete the transition to a nation-state that other empires completed years ago.

Turkey, not unlike Austria, was relatively successful among this group because it was the weakest among the empires and could not aspire to another bid for empire building like Germany or Russia. Nor could it hope to rebuild the empire as a Pan-Turkic entity despite a strong Pan-Turkic component in Turkish nationalism: its path toward the outlying Turkic areas was blocked by Russia. For that reason, the imperial and the pan-Turanian ideas had to be discarded; only the "little Turkey" idea could be implemented. Thus, from very early on, the new Turkey had to redefine itself as a new ethnic nation on the narrow Osman ethnic base. Unexpectedly, among the four empires, Turkey's transformation was probably the most successful and the most complete. However, it was achieved largely through a painful process of self-cleansing directed against troublesome ethnoreligious minorities. These minorities were perceived as particularly dangerous since, except for the Kurds, they were all Christians, like Turkey's main adversary. They could be used—and occasionally were willing participants—in Russian and European meddling in Turkish affairs. It is not surprising that they came to be seen, by Turkish elites and masses alike, as a treacherous fifth column.

Not all massacres or expulsions in Ottoman Turkey were organized by the government. The partridge massacres[57] (so called because they arose from a dispute over a partridge) of Arab Christians by the Druze in 1841 in what is now Lebanon were purely local intercommunal clashes. But the massacres of 1860 had a very strong cleansing component to them, not least because they were carried out with the connivance of the local Turkish administration. Within a month at least 11,000 Christians were killed, 4,000 died in flight, and about 100,000 were made homeless.[58] Many towns and villages were completely denuded of their former Christian inhabitants.

As the government did nothing to prevent the massacres (in fact, the troops sometimes joined in), Muslims throughout the region came to the conclusion that the sultan had issued a secret order to rid the country of the infidel. Encouraged, the Muslims of Damascus fell upon local Christians on July 9, 1860, and quickly dispatched nearly 5,500 of them. As reverberations from the massacres spread throughout the region whole villages in Palestine embraced Islam as the only way of escaping death.[59]

The idea of exterminating the infidels was later applied to Armenians. A Christian population divided between Turkey and Russia, Armenians were perceived as particularly problematic. This impression was reinforced by the fact that Russia had traditionally played the role of the protector of Orthodox Christian peoples in the Balkans and in the Middle East. And although relations between Russian Armenians and the Russian government were sometimes tense, their position in Russia was incomparably better than that of Armenians in Turkey. Hence, it is fair to say that Armenian sympathies lay almost exclusively with Russia. And the Turks knew that.

As ties with Europe grew closer and ideas of freedom and self-determination penetrated the remotest corners of the empire, unrest spread throughout the Armenian community. To rein in their Armenian subjects the Turkish governments encouraged Kurdish settlement in Armenian areas. This was dangerous for the Armenians since they, unlike the Kurds, were prohibited from bearing arms and thus were utterly defenseless.

As the Armenian community in Turkey grew restless, the authorities incited the Kurds against Armenians. By 1894-96 hostilities between the two communities, surreptitiously instigated and encouraged by the authorities, grew into a veritable war. Turkish troops were sent into the area, ostensibly to separate the combatants but in reality to help the Kurds (who were then mistakenly seen as more reliable because they were Muslim). The total Armenian death toll in this period is estimated at around 200,000 or 8 percent of the total Armenian population in Turkey.[60] And this was but a prelude to later cleansings.

The facts of the cleansing of 1915-16 are well known, and need not be detailed here. It was conducted with the utmost brutality in the middle of a desperate war. In Armenia, deportation (mostly into the Syrian desert), death marches, starvation, and outright murder resulted in as many as 1.5 million Armenian deaths and the cleansing about 90 percent of the Armenian ethnic territory of its Armenian inhabitants. More anti-Armenian pogroms occurred in Baku, Shusha, and elsewhere in Azerbaijan under Turkish occupation in 1918. In Baku alone about 30,000 were killed; another 32,000 died in Shusha, the main town of Karabakh.[61]

By the early 1920s the situation in Transcaucasia was stabilized by the reimposition of the Russian (now Soviet) rule. After 1923 Armenians felt sufficiently secure within the new empire to settle anywhere they chose, including in Muslim areas such as Azerbaijan. Eventually, about half a million settled among Azeri Turks, many even in Baku, the site of a major massacre.

When the Soviet empire began to crumble in the late 1980s and the tottering central apparatus loosened the reins, the old animosities, long dormant, were reawakened. This new round of unrest was sparked by the dispute over Nagorno-Karabakh, a predominantly Armenian enclave within Azerbaijan. The dispute led to a brutal anti-Armenian pogrom in Sumgait in February 1988, which sent 7,000 Armenian refugees fleeing for their lives.[62] This was followed by mass expulsions of 157,000 Azeris from Armenia,[63] and then another anti-Armenian pogrom in Baku in January 1990 (with the active participation of Azeri refugees from Armenia).

When the Soviet army reasserted control over the Azeri capital thousands of Armenians and Russians were evacuated. A de facto population exchange followed that sent thousands of Armenians and Azeris to their ethnic homelands. And then a major thrust of the Armenian army deep into Azerbaijan uprooted up to a million Azeris, who fled farther east. As of this writing, an uneasy truce is holding, but there is no end in sight to the conflict. One thing is clear: the new Armenia and Azerbaijan will be ethnically homogeneous states with very few, if any, ethnic or religious minorities.

The history of the Azeri-Armenian conflict exemplifies the cyclical nature of many ethnic conflicts. Unresolved ethnic conflicts, like volcanic eruptions, are often interspersed with long periods of quiescence, only to explode again and again until mixed populations are separated.

Armenians were not the only victims of ethnic cleansing in the Ottoman Turkey during World War I. Nestorian and Jacobite Christians,[64] as well as the Maronites of Lebanon, were also massacred and evicted during the war. This indicates that the Turkish government saw the minority problem in ethnoreligious terms, rather than as a purely ethnic issue. After the war, most of these Christian minorities found themselves outside Turkey, under the more or less benevolent jurisdictions of colonial powers. But when Arab countries with large Christian populations—Egypt, Iraq, Lebanon, Syria—gained independence, the Muslim majority in these countries subjected all minorities, not just Christians, to various forms of pressure and discrimination. Tired of being second-class citizens, many Christians emigrated—a good example of leaving under pressure—further weakening the strength of their communities. This was particularly evident among the Lebanese Christians, who lost out in the civil war of 1975-93 and are now confined to a small sliver of land north of Beirut.

Minority cleansings in Turkey did not stop there. Anatolian and Pontic Greeks were yet another ethnoreligious minority that was subjected to cleansing. Most Greek communities escaped the kinds of major massacres that befell Christians in Armenia, Lebanon, and Mesopotamia in 1915-16. Their time came in the early 1920s, after Greece sent an expeditionary corps (in May 1919) to occupy the predominantly Greek Smyrna and its hinterland.[65] The expedition was prompted by a mistaken belief that Turkey had been fatally weakened by the war and would not fight back, and also by a desire to preempt Italy, which had designs on Turkish territory populated by Anatolian Greeks. Still another factor was an erroneous impression that the Western Allies would rescue Greece if things turned sour.

The expedition was a disaster; Ataturk rallied the Turks, and their counteroffensive, launched in August 1922, brought the Turkish forces to the gates of Smyrna. The city fell on September 8, and in the massacre that ensued the following day about 30,000 Christians, mostly Greeks, lost their lives.[66] The Allied ships, safely anchored offshore, did not intervene.

A compulsory exchange of population between Greece and Turkey followed the debacle at Smyrna and completed the cleansing. It sent approximately 1.1 million Anatolian Greeks who still remained in Turkey to Greece and some 380,000 Muslims from Greece, mostly Turks, to Turkey.[67] Some 300,000 Greeks were allowed to remain in and around Constantinople, but their numbers gradually declined due to emigration and, possibly, assimilation. Fierce anti-Greek riots in Istanbul in 1955 dealt a major blow to the Greek community in the city; at present it has dwindled to some 130,000.[68]

No matter how painful it was for all parties concerned, the cleansing and the compulsory exchange of the populations seem to have prevented large-scale military conflicts later. The only time Greece and Turkey came close to blows was in 1974, over ethnically mixed Cyprus. There, years of ethnic tensions and nationalistic agitation culminated in an unsuccessful pro-Greek coup, Turkish invasion, and the partition of the island into a Greek south and Turkish north. In the process, some 180,000 Greeks fled south,[69] while thousands of Turkish Cypriots fled north. As might be expected, thousands were stranded on the wrong side of the divide, notably the 9,390 Turkish refugees camping at the Episcopi (British) base.[70] To solve the problem, both sides agreed to an exchange (or regrouping, as they called it) at the third round of talks in Vienna (July 31-August 2, 1975). The relocation was to be carried out on a purely voluntary basis and initially several thousand Greeks chose to stay in the north. But living in a hostile ethnic environment proved too much of a challenge for most: by May 1987, only 678 remained. A similar process occurred among Turkish Cypriots stranded in the south: ultimately, only 130 chose to stay.[71]

Most of the Cypriot cleansing was self-inflicted: it occurred through fright and flight. One may even argue that there was no cleansing at all since most displacement was effected by refugee outflow. Does it count as a case of cleansing? Only to the extent of leaving under pressure; it is a borderline case.

The only cohort of the Pontic Greeks who escaped cleansing and population exchange in the 1920s were the Greeks living on the northern shore of the Black Sea in the Russian-held areas. But history caught up with them even there: most of them were rounded up in the late 1940s and sent east, to Siberia and Central Asia. And half a century later, after Abkhazia's capital Sukhumi fell to Abkhazian insurgents in September 1993, the Greek government evacuated some 12,000 of the 15,000 local Greeks.

The last Ottoman minority to be mentioned is the Kurds. In the nineteenth century successive Turkish governments used Muslim Kurds to destroy the ethnic cohesiveness of Armenian territories. Once the Armenians were gone and Turkey was redefined as a nation-state, Kurds were no longer Muslim allies but a troublesome ethnic minority that had to be either assimilated or somehow gotten rid of. In the 1920s there were several anti-Kurdish campaigns. Until very recently their language was not taught in the schools, their ethnicity was denied, and even their official name was changed to "mountain Turks."

This drastic change in the fortunes of Turkish Kurds illustrates a number of things. First, the switch from one collective identity to another can be quickly accomplished, often within just a few years. Second, ethnic alliances, not unlike political or military ones, are strategic in nature. They are determined by considerations of security and the balance of power in a given area. And third, switches of collective identity are potentially reversible: if the resurgence of Islamic fundamentalism switches the focus of Turkish collective identity back to religion, it would be quite possible to see the reintegration of a significant portion of the Kurdish community into the Turkish polity as Muslims, much as the Azeri community in Iran is fully integrated within the Iranian society. In this case, much will depend on whether the Kurdish majority will desecularize itself. If it does so, by embracing some form of fundamentalist Islam, it will have a good chance of reintegrating within the Turkish community (provided the Turkish community is also desecularized, of course); if it does not, it will go down the path of ethnic nationalism and separatism, and the conflict in Turkey will be exacerbated.

Secular, socialist Iraq offers an example of this alternative: secular ethnic nationalism. Indeed, it is in Iraq that the Kurds experienced several classical ethnic cleansings during their long insurgency, the last time in 1991, during the final stages of the Persian Gulf War. The Iraqi predicament offers no escape: secular nationalism pits the Arab against the Kurd. But a desecularized, fundamentalist Iraq would set the Sunni against the Shi'a. In either case, the minority community can count on support from across the border: Kurds from their ethnic cousins abroad, the Shi'a from Iran. It is a no-win situation typical of artificial states with borders that were drawn by colonial powers.

Thus, within the 30 years between 1894 and 1924 Turkey successfully cleansed itself of most of its ethnic and religious minorities. But the Kurds, the only large minority remaining, are the source of never-ending and increasingly embarrassing troubles. Will Turkey engage in one more cleansing?

***

While the Ottoman Turkish elites chose to redefine Turkish collective identity along ethnic lines, their Russian counterparts reached out in several directions.

Russian nationalism made its first appearance in the eighteenth century when Russian backwardness, compared to the West, became glaringly apparent.[72] When Dmitriy Uvarov, the minister of education, defined Russianness in 1832, he chose a formula inspired by the medieval French dictum *un roi, une foi, une loi* (one king, one faith, one law; a sort of *e pluribus unum*). In Russian, it became *samoderzhaviie, pravoslaviie, narodnost'* (autocracy, orthodoxy, nationality), where *narodnost'* is equivalent to German *volksgeist*.[73] ("Nationality"[74] is close but inexact. Incidentally, the same formula later inspired Hitler's *ein Volk, ein Reich, ein Fuhrer* [one people, one empire, one leader] somewhat reversing the order of priorities.[75] It is interesting that the absolutist state puts the political principle first, ahead of religion.)

Until 1917 Orthodoxy played a major role in the official definition of Russianness: non-Orthodox peoples, even Christians of other denominations, were generally denied advancement into the higher echelons of the state apparatus (although this varied with time and place; Baltic barons, for example, most of them Protestants, did very well in St. Petersburg and the imperial bureaucracy). Jews, in particular, were singled out for discrimination. The infamous dictum of Pobedonostsev, director general of the Synod, that one-third of Russian Jews should (be made to) emigrate, one-third should assimilate, and one-third would die out[76] already envisions a cleansing to be carried out in several stages. However, the discrimination against Jews was predominantly religious in nature; converts escaped legal discrimination.

Toward the end of the nineteenth century Russian nationalism began to acquire a purely ethnic character. This was preceded by a major rift within the ranks of Russian intelligentsia, between the cosmopolitan Westernizers and the inward-looking Slavophiles, with the latter winning the struggle to define Russian nationalism.

When the Russian empire collapsed it was the Marxists, an offshoot of the Westernizer tradition, who emerged victorious. They, of course, strove to redefine Russian collective identity in terms of class. It was a momentous choice because it allowed Russia to reconstitute its empire on the basis of an internationalist, antinationalist movement, which, paradoxically, became an effective instrument of imperial expansion. This unusual reversal was made possible by Russian intellectual susceptibility to messianic ideas. This trait has been pointed out by many observers, including Nicolas Berdyaev.[77] The messianism of the new faith, its claim to universality, and the use of proletarian internationalism as a justification for expansionism, allowed Russian nationalism to reconstruct and re-establish the empire on a new foundation. But the creation of a new collective identity based on

Marxist premises created a new kind of minority that had to be eradicated: the class enemy. It is not surprising, therefore, that class served as the criterion of the first cleansings in the new empire.

Actually, isolated instances of class cleansing can be found long before Marxism, such as when the Wallachian princeling Vlad the Devil (Dracul in Romanian, hence Dracula) invited all beggars of his principality to a feast and then set the hall on fire. However, this early cleansing of the lumpenproletariat was nonideological; it was enacted for the perverse pleasure of a sadistic despot who also wanted to rid his country of beggars. This was not the case in early Soviet Russia. There the destruction of the "parasitic" classes, especially the bourgeoisie, was prescribed by Communist ideology. The expropriations of wealth and mass shootings of the bourgeois during the Red Terror were the first stage in the liquidation of this class. But, unlike his ethnic counterpart, the bourgeois who had been stripped of his property and thus proletarianized was no longer bourgeois. He and his descendants could be allowed to continue their physical existence; hence the decline in ideological cleansing in later Soviet years. In a sense, the proletarianization of the bourgeois was akin to a religious conversion of a persecuted religious minority.

Other undesirable categories could not disappear so conveniently. Unlike the bourgeoisie, most of the aristocracy had inherited their title. A pauperized aristocrat was still an aristocrat, hence the expulsion of the *dvoriane* (gentry) from Leningrad and elsewhere well after the Soviet rule had been firmly established.[78]

The destruction of the kulaks was conducted on a vaster scale. The category of the kulak, though ill-defined and varying by time period and location, basically included members of the rural bourgeoisie, small holders, and independent farmers. Altogether, several million people were exiled to Siberia in 1929-32 or died from starvation. Within three years, the wealthier and more productive part of the peasantry was sacrificed on the altar of ideological purity and forced industrialization.

The destruction of the kulaks, later duplicated on a much larger scale in China (in 1949-56) shows how easy it is to reify almost any group of people into a new category. It also demonstrates how easily collective identities can be manufactured, by inclusion or exclusion. And it does not matter whether they are "imagined communities" or not; that certainly did not matter to the persecuted kulaks.

In Ukraine, the anti-kulak campaign was also used to destroy Ukrainian nationalism and resistance to Russification. Already in April 1929 the OGPU had begun persecuting small groups on charges of Ukrainian nationalism. In July some 5,000 members of the Union for the Liberation of Ukraine

were arrested.[79] Other trials targeted members of the Ukrainian intelligentsia. But Stalin realized that "decapitating" a nation would not be enough.
"Only a mass terror," wrote Robert Conquest, "throughout the body of the
nation—that is, the peasantry—could really reduce the country to submission."[80] As Stalin himself put it, "The nationality problem is, in its very
essence, a problem of the peasantry."[81] (This assertion is, of course, un-
Marxist, since only the urban sector, particularly the bourgeoisie, is supposed to be the carrier of the nationalist bacilli.) The artificially created
famine that accompanied the collectivization thus killed two birds (one ethnic and one ideological) with one stone. By starving about five million
people,[82] Stalin destroyed a large segment of the Ukrainian peasantry and blunted
the will to resist throughout the republic.

Similar devastating purges were also carried out in Kazakhstan and elsewhere. The total number of Kazakh households, for example, declined from
1,233,000 in 1929 to 565,000 by 1936, mostly due to the excesses of collectivization, although some of the decrease resulted from a mass exodus to
Uzbekistan and Turkmenistan.[83]

Newly acquired non-Russian areas, such as the Baltic states annexed by
Russia in 1940, also suffered ideological cleansing that crushed nationalist resistance. In Estonia alone a mass deportation in June 1941, on the eve of the
war, sent 10,157 people to Siberia; another roundup, in 1949, disposed of 20,702
people in one swoop.[84] Altogether 85,000 Balts were deported or executed during the first year of Russian occupation in 1940-41; 150,000 were deported
immediately upon Russian reoccupation in 1944-45.[85] They were followed by
440,000 more during 1946-53, at the height of the anti-Russian guerrilla movement.[86] The total for 1940-53 comes to 675,000, out of a prewar population of
5.7 million. However, most of the surviving deportees were allowed to return
home in the late 1950s, which makes it clear that cleansing, not genocide, as is
sometimes claimed, had been the objective.[87]

Ideological cleansing peaked in 1937, the year of the Great *Chistka,*
usually translated as purge, but *chistka* also means cleaning, cleansing,
expurgation. The German invasion of 1941 brought ideological purges
to a halt. The emphasis of collective identity shifted to the Great Russian (and Soviet) people; soldiers were encouraged to fight for *Rodina-
mat'* (Motherland). But the Marxist symbolism was not entirely
abandoned: it was grafted onto the older patriotic and nationalistic themes
that were hurriedly resurrected. In addition to defending Russia-the-
Mother, Soviet soldiers were also called upon to fight for Stalin, a char-
ismatic ideological leader with strong religious overtones whose image
invoked the Father. In fact, camp inmates called him *bat'ko* (father),

and among the KGB personnel his nickname was Papa. This harked back to the paternal image of Russian tsars and priests *(batiushka,* or dear father) and created a complex symbolism of mother Russia and father Stalin. The Great Russian people were called upon to fight *Za Rodinu, za Stalina!* (for Motherland and Stalin), and soldiers were encouraged to join the Party before the battle and die as Communists, as a few centuries earlier they would have been called upon to die as Christians.

It is often asserted that in 1941 Russia switched from sterile proletarian internationalism to a reawakened Russian nationalism. One can argue that it did not switch but rather resurrected an important part of its heritage, adding it to the extant collective identity at a time of mortal danger. Thus, Russia in 1941 offers an interesting example of how identities are accumulated.

The new national-Communist (actually, it should be called ethno-Communist) identity was not static; the balance gradually shifted to the ethnic end of the spectrum.

The first instances of purely ethnic cleansing (divorced from the ideological component that characterized the anti-kulak campaign in Ukraine and the cleansings in Baltic area) go back to the prewar era. These cleansings were largely strategic, such as the deportation of 25,000 to 30,000 Finns from the border area with Finland in 1935.[88] So was the cleansing directed against Soviet Germans after the outbreak of World War II. Immediately after the outbreak of the war most Germans, except some in Siberia, were sent east. This cleansing can be compared to the internment of Japanese in the United States except that it was carried out with greater brutality and the deportees were not allowed to return after the war. Altogether, 400,000 Volga Germans, 60,000 from North Caucasus, and 40,000 from the Crimea and Ukraine were sent to Kazakhstan, Siberia, and the Far East.[89]

After the German retreat, the Soviet government, in the time-honored imperial tradition, decided to cleanse out former and potential unreliables. Greeks and Bulgarians, accused of collaboration with Germans, were the first to go (by decree of the Supreme Soviet of April 19, 1943).[90] Most of the Greek and Bulgarian population of Ukraine and the Crimea were deported. Those who remained followed in 1949, such as the 40,000 Greeks in Georgia who were rounded up on June 14, 1949.[91] But the cleansing did not seem to affect members of these ethnies living in other areas, such as Bulgarians in Bessarabia (perhaps because Slav Bulgarians were considered allies in non-Slav Moldavia).

Kalmyks were probably the first indigenous ethny to be cleansed in its entirety. They were deported on December 27, 1943.[92] The Karachai suffered the same fate at this time. Next came the other peoples of North

Caucasus: the Chechen and the Ingush in March 1944 and the Balkars in April 1944.[93]

It is generally assumed that these peoples were punished for their willing cooperation with the invading Germans, and in some cases this assumption is not unfounded. We know, for example, what the Crimean Tatars were accused of: during the occupation the Tatar Council of the Crimea had petitioned the Romanian authorities (Romania was the occupying power) to exterminate all Russians remaining in the peninsula. When the request was denied the Council organized a mass slaughter on its own in which between 70,000 and 120,000 Russians died.[94] In other cases, however, other factors must have guided the imperial Russian hand. The Germans never reached the Chechen and the Ingush lands; although there were some anti-Russian uprisings when the German armies approached the area, Wixman suggests that the deportation of these peoples may be explained by Russia's future designs on Turkey: pro-Turkish Muslims within Soviet Russia would be a dangerous and unreliable fifth column.[95] This view is supported by the subsequent expulsion of Meshkhetian Turks (Muslim Georgians) from Ajaria. However, this theory does not explain extensive deportations of Greeks and Bulgarians. Perhaps, Stalin had simply decided to get rid of all the troublesome minorities at once. Or maybe cleansings, once started, generated their own momentum. Robert Conquest estimates the total number of the deportees at 1.6 million.[96] (He includes Meshkhetian Turks but does not count non-Volga Germans.) Altogether, about 540,000 Germans, 400,000 Chechens, 200,000 Crimean Tatars, and thousands of other victims were forcibly displaced.

Cleansing was also reintroduced with a vengeance in the re-annexed areas of the Baltic, as well as in western Ukraine and Bessarabia, but here it is impossible to separate ethnic motives from strategic and ideological ones. The same applies to many other small ethnic groups. They offer a good example of the combined effects of ideological and ethnic cleansing since they were subjected to both. For example, between 160,000 and 170,000 Crimean Tatars were ideologically cleansed (as kulaks and other class enemies or political unreliables) in 1921-41.[97] The final and total cleansing in April-July 1944 was merely the coup de grace to an ethny already bled white by previous cleansings.

Both trends, ethnic and ideological, fused in the cleansing of Jews that seems to have been planned for 1953-54 but was unexpectedly cancelled by Stalin's death. The resurgence of the ethnic component in the Russian collective identity brought forth the anti-Semitism of the Russian masses. The Jew, in his reincarnation as a footloose, rootless cosmopolitan, turned into an ideological foe or at least an ideological misfit. Hence, the ever present anti-Semitism of the Khrushchev and Brezhnev years, usually concealed behind rabid anti-Zionism. Whatever the ideology, the Jew was always conveniently there, fit for any ideological or ethnic "othering."

Whatever the motivation in each particular case, the postwar period, until Stalin's death in 1953, saw a rare interplay of ethnic and ideological cleansings. Since there were no longer enemy classes to be purged, the ideological pogrom concentrated on the intelligentsia, which was suspected of harboring anti-Soviet, or at least insufficiently Soviet, sentiments. Akhmatova and Zoshchenko, like Mandelshtam before the war, were placed beyond the circle of the Soviet "us." Others, less fortunate, were incarcerated and sent to camps. Others still, like Mikhoels, were simply assassinated.

The fusion of ideology and ethnicity shows the emergence of an interesting hybrid, an ethnoideological identity, not unlike the ethnoreligious identities of Armenians or Jews.

The lack of ideological cleansings after 1953 indicates that Russian (but not Chinese) Communism, as an ideology, was a spent force by then. It may be argued that it died with Stalin in 1953. The years that followed, the period of stagnation, were a slow agony. As ideology withered and died, the Russian collective identity had to fill the void, hence the resurgence of ethnic nationalism and the Orthodox faith. But this newly resurrected Orthodoxy is a different faith, stripped of its ecumenical appeal. This is a Russian faith, a newly ethnicized faith that serves as an emblem of the Russian spirit.

In a sense, nationalism had corroded the Communist cocoon from within; it had destroyed it from the inside and then slithered out in 1989-90, leaving the dead ideological skin behind. In the process, Russia had to reinvent its collective identity yet again, this time in purely ethnic terms. But this is not a process limited to Russia alone, for we are witnessing an explosion of ethnic nationalisms everywhere in Eastern Europe. For Russia, the process of redefinition is particularly painful since even the new Russia contains numerous ethnic minorities, about 25 million in a population of 150 million. A solution is thus out of sight, as the daily confrontations with minority nationalisms stoke the fires of Russian extremism. And the problem is there to stay, unless Russia contracts to its ethnic heartland west of the Volga or reverts to the totalitarian suppression of ethnic dissent.

***

The third ethny that faced the problem of the transformation from an imperial entity into a nation was the German ethny of Germany and Austria. I will here speak of *the* German ethny because the Austrian segment of the German ethny did not complete its psychological separation from the rest of the German-speaking entity until after World War II, toward the late 1960s.[98]

In Germany, unlike Turkey and Russia, the transformation went along the "racial" lines. At first glance it may seem that this was probably inevitable in an ethny that had slowly expanded eastward, colonizing the eastern plains. However, the Russians, historically, display a similar pattern of eastward expansion into Siberia and the Far East. Like the Germans, they had a profound disregard for their eastern and southern neighbors, especially if they belonged to the Mongol race (which did not prevent considerable racial and ethnic intermixture). The similarities do not end there.

Like Russians, Germans chose a transcendental ideology with a wide international appeal, an ideology that was profoundly totalitarian. In many ways, both ideologies were a mirror image of each other, which is not surprising since both derive from German philosophy.

The gestation of German ethnoracial nationalism can be traced through Judeophobia. In medieval Germany Jews were regarded as an alien religious minority antithetical to Christianity ("Christ killers," "enemies of Christ"). Toward the end of the nineteenth century, under the influence of Houston Stewart Chamberlaine and Count de Gobineau (who regarded race as the foundation of advanced civilization), Jews were redefined as a racial contaminant, a danger to the racial purity of the German race. This was a time—the middle and the second half of the nineteenth century—of Jewish assimilation and integration, when thousands of Jews entered the mainstream of German economic and intellectual life. The boundary maintenance mechanism between the two groups crumbled; another one had to be erected if the Germans were to retain their distinctiveness (which raises the question, why did it have to be erected at all? Why was the German ethny, like so many others, unable to lower the barrier and simply let the Jews dissolve in the German melting pot?). In an increasingly secular world where religion had ceased to command allegiance, ethnicity and race were useful alternatives.

The Russian example shows that it was not the only alternative. But it is interesting that Russian ideology was no less anti-Semitic than German. It is quite possible that the anti-Judaism inherent in Marxism made this ideology more easily digestible, first by the Russian intelligentsia, then by the masses.

Marx took the Christian rejection of the Jew and applied it to class, with Jews acquiring a new demonology, that of a parasitic class (noted by Paul Johnson in his masterful *History of the Jews*). But that does not explain why progressive and technologically advanced Germany latched on to the more primitive organicism of blood and race.

It seems that the answer to this paradox should be sought in Austria. Even after 1870, the German empire did not have many ethnic minorities, only Poles and a few Danes, Frenchmen, and Lithuanians. These minorities lived at the fringes of the empire, were not very conspicuous, and played a limited role in the life of the Reich. The situation was vastly different in Austria, where, by 1914, German speakers numbered only 12 million in a population of 50 million. There they felt beleaguered and vulnerable, under the assault of the *tschusch* (eastern rabble). Russia, secure in its vast territory and its Slavic multitudes, could adopt class as an ideology. German Austrians could not; hence the spectacular growth of rabid German and Pan-German nationalism in Austria, which ultimately brought forth Hitler and Nazism. Had it not been for Austria's nationality problems, Germany might well have followed—or led—Russia into the realm of class.

Hitler's meteoric rise and fall are very well-known, and we need not recount them here. He interests us only because under his rule cleansing reached its final and logical conclusion: complete physical annihilation. Although Nazis regarded all non-Germanic peoples as racially inferior they did not have much time, barely 12 years, to implement their program of "purification." That is why only four groups were slated for immediate eradication: Jews, Gypsies, gays, and political undesirables, such as Communists (we should also mention mental patients, but that program was quickly discontinued).

The German pattern, like the Russian, also shows a multiplicity of cleansings—by ethnicity, by ideology, and sexual preference—despite the fact that the German ethny was defined largely in racial terms. The multiplicity of cleansings bespeaks the multiplicity of collective identities accumulated through the centuries.

There is no need to recount the horrors of the Holocaust: they are very well known. About 6 million European Jews perished.[99] As noted in the introduction, the Nazis actually introduced the word "cleansing" into their vocabulary, as in *Judenrein* (Jew-free), to designate areas from which all Jews had been deported. The destruction of European Jewry was also complete in the sense that it combined all methods of cleansing: deportation, expulsion, population transfer, and massacre.

Among the other victims were Gypsies (the estimates range from 219,700 to 1.5 million;[100] the wide range is not surprising in a nomadic, difficult to track population); thousands of gays; and a large number of Communists and other ideological opponents such as Jehovah's Witnesses from all over occupied Europe. (Like Jews, Jehovah's Witnesses were banned from all civil service jobs [in April 1935].[101] A year later they were subjected to mass arrests and incarceration in concentration camps; only those who renounced their faith were released. But at least they had this option because they were not a racial minority.)

There were many homosexuals among Hitler's early supporters, notably SA leader Ernst Rohm. When Hitler and Rohm parted ways, Rohm's homosexuality was used as a weapon in discrediting the SA and its leader. In 1935 the antihomosexual provisions of Paragraph 175 were strengthened and extended (by coincidence, 1934 saw the recriminalization of homosexuality in the Soviet Union). From then on the number of convictions rose rapidly, from 2,319 in 1931-33 to 24,450 in 1937-39.[102] The low point was reached in the decree of September 4, 1941, which stipulated that "deviant criminals . . . [who] threatened the health of the German people" were to be put to death.[103] Conservative estimates put the number of gays convicted and incarcerated in concentration camps during the 12 years of Nazi rule at 5,000 to 15,000.[104] Himmler gave specific instructions on what to do with SS men caught in homosexual acts: they were to be shipped to concentration camps and then shot while trying to escape.[105] This elaborate charade is incomprehensible unless we keep in mind that the SS were considered the crème de la crème of the German nation. Even the existence of homosexuality within their ranks could not be acknowledged.

Finally, one should not forget that approximately 70,000 mentally retarded people were eliminated before the program was discontinued due to protests. Their annihilation was meant to preserve the health of racial Supermen and thus to reinforce the racial aspect of German collective identity. (Here we hear echoes of Sparta.)[106]

Aside from these four categories only Poles experienced annihilation on a large scale (approximately 3 million). Other groups would have joined them had not Hitler run out of time; he planned, for example, to ship most Czechs east, cleansing Bohemia and Moravia. We should also mention the starvation of Russian POWs in various camps, but as this was a nonideological annihilation, it cannot be considered a cleansing.

Germans practiced "pure" cleansing as well: cleansing through deportation and expulsion of ethnically and racially undesirable populations without immediate extermination (which was sometimes merely postponed). One such instance was the Germanization of Warthegau and West Prussia, Polish territories incorporated into the Reich after the occupation of Poland. The expulsions and deportations of Poles and Jews started in October 1939 at Gdynia.[107] The expulsion orders were often issued without warning and implemented at night; the deportees were given between 20 minutes and 2 hours to collect their belongings; they were usually limited to one suitcase of 40 to 100 pounds, to contain personal items only. All valuables such as jewelry, gold, and stocks and bonds had to be left behind. German authorities made no provisions for the deportees either on the road or in nonincorporated occupied Poland, where they were dumped. During the first two years of German occupation about 1.2 million Poles and 300,000 Jews were cleansed from the incorporated territories.[108] This was the largest, but not the only, cleansing implemented by Germans in occupied Europe. In Alsace-Lorraine approximately 200,000 French speakers were also cleansed by the end of 1941.[109]

Nazi Germany also practiced what I would call reverse cleansing. In his desire to create a compact and powerful German Reich, Hitler recalled and collected people of German language, culture, and ancestry (the so-called Volksdeutsche) from all over Eastern Europe. By the spring of 1942 over 700,000 Germans (including many non-Germans who claimed German ancestry in order to escape harsh conditions at home) had been transferred to Germany from the Baltic states, Bukovina, South Tyrol, and elsewhere.[110] Most of them were resettled in the territories Hitler wanted to Germanize, particularly in western Poland. This cleansing in reverse served the same purpose as standard cleansing: to strengthen the ethny, to create ethnically homogeneous areas, and to lay the ground for further expansion. Like the German war effort, the recall and resettlement of German minorities proved ephemeral: many of the Volksdeutsche fled before the advancing Russian armies, while those who stayed behind were either slaughtered or evicted.

***

This brings us to the largest and most sweeping cleansing in history: the removal of between 10 million and 14 million Germans from eastern Europe. Various proposals to that effect had been floated among the Allies during the war. As appeasement at Munich had failed to secure "peace in our time," the only option that remained was the transfer of the intransigent minority.

The Czechoslovak government-in-exile submitted a plan of expulsion to the Allies as early as November 23, 1944.[111] The final decision was taken by the Big Three—the United Kingdom, the United States, and the USSR—on August 2, 1945, at Potsdam.[112] Three months later, on November 20, 1945, the Inter-Allied Control Council authorized the transfer of 2.5 million Germans from Czechoslovakia (presumably leaving approximately 1 million in place),[113] and 3.5 million Germans from Poland. Each person was allowed to take up to 70 kilograms of personal possessions and 1,000 marks.[114]

The transfers from Czechoslovakia started in January 1946 and were officially terminated in October 1947. Although up to 1 million ethnic Germans were supposed to have been left in place, the Czech authorities, with tacit—and sometimes vocal—Russian support proceeded to expel nearly all Germans. Their goal was to rid their country of the German menace once and for all.

By the end of 1946 there were 2,380,000 Sudeten Germans in the American zone of occupation and 840,000 in the Soviet, for a total of 3,220,000. By the time the compulsory transfers finally ended only 241,000 Germans had been allowed to stay.[115] However, the imposition of Communist rule and Russian domination made life in Czechoslovakia less attractive. At the same time the feelings of "racial loneliness" that struck the dwindling minority in an ethnically alien state made emigration increasingly attractive. Ironically, those who stayed behind came to be pitied. Further migration, mostly to West Germany, reduced the remaining German population to about 60,000 at present.

An even larger cleansing of the remaining Germans was carried out in Poland, which in its new borders included provinces—Silesia, East Pomerania, and Prussia—that had had a large, compact German population (Silesia alone numbered about 6 million before the war). Of the 3.5 million who were to be expelled,[116] 2 million were to be admitted to the Soviet zone of occupation while 1.5 million were destined for the British zone. About 900,000 Silesians who could prove Slav ancestry were allowed to stay; often, a name ending in "ski" sufficed. But here, as in Czechoslovakia, the entitlement to West German citizenship and the hardships of Polish life soon generated a constant stream of emigres and refugees. At present only about 300,000 ethnic Germans, or at least people who claim German ancestry, remain.[117]

It is impossible to give an exact figure of the expelled Germans: thousands of Germans and non-Germans claiming German ancestry were recalled and resettled in various German-occupied areas, especially western Poland; then thousands fled before the advancing Russian armies; some returned only to be expelled later, while others still passed themselves off as Slavs and remained, only to emigrate to West Germany in the years to come. Altogether, as previously noted, it is estimated that between 10 million and 14 million Germans were cleansed from Czechoslovakia, Hungary, Poland, Romania, the USSR, and Yugoslavia after World War II. Joseph Schechtman puts the number of transferees at 11.73 million plus 2.1 million who died from starvation and exposure during the period of expulsions—for a total of 13.83 million.[118]

Germans were not the only people slated for cleansing by the Allies. Hungarian minorities outside Hungary, particularly those in Slovakia, were also prime candidates. During his visit to Moscow in March 1945, Czechoslovak President Benes procured Stalin's consent for the expulsion of two-thirds of Czechoslovakia's 600,000 Hungarians. In the event, however, most of the Hungarians were spared. Hungary actively opposed any population transfers involving Hungarian minorities across the border because it wanted to retain its claims to southern areas of Slovakia (and still hoped for border rectifications with Romania). The Czech government, for its part, may have needed a trump card against Slovak demands for autonomy. By the end of 1945 only 25,000 to 30,000 Hungarians had been expelled,[119] and most of these were political extremists and their families; it was more a de-Nazification program than an ethnic cleansing. Then both governments reached an agreement (on February 27, 1946) to exchange an equal number of Slovak Hungarians and Hungarian Slovaks. Eventually, 31,000 Magyars from Slovakia were exchanged for 33,000 Slovaks from Hungary.[120] But this was a population exchange rather than pure cleansing; and when both countries were communized the exchange ceased.

A similar exchange, but on a much larger scale, occurred between Poland and the Soviet Union. It involved Poles living in Belarus, Lithuania, and Ukraine, and members of these nationalities living in Poland. However, the agreement between Poland and the USSR offered potential transferees a choice, so the exchange itself did not involve an outright cleansing.

Meanwhile, at the other end of the Soviet Union, cleansing was applied to the approximately 400,000 Japanese inhabitants of southern Sakhalin, which had been annexed by the victorious Soviets. They were repatriated in 1946-47.[121] (But thousands of Koreans forcibly brought in by the Japanese were not, probably because they were not considered enemy aliens. On the contrary, Koreans were made to stay, often against their will. Only in the last few years were some of them allowed to travel or even settle in South Korea.)

This was not the first time that the Japanese were subjected to cleansing. Earlier, in 1941, about 100,000 Japanese-Americans were methodically gathered by the American government and placed in detention camps. This detention was temporary; it lasted only as long as the Japanese were deemed to pose a danger to national security. After the war the detainees were released and allowed to reintegrate into the American society. One may even question whether this case fits within our definition of cleansing. I believe it does, not least because population removal was applied to an ethnoracial group as a group; Germans and Italians, although presumably no less dangerous on grounds of national security, were not affected.

The difference between a detention that is cleansing and one that is not can be seen in the contrast between the detention of Japanese-Americans and the arrest of approximately 2,000 of labor activists in Bisbee, Arizona on July 12, 1917, and the subsequent deportation of 1,186 of them.[122] This action was carried out in response to a strike that brought Bisbee, a copper mining town, to a standstill. It removed a certain number of people who shared a set of characteristics from a given territory, but the activists did not comprise a "population." Unless we are willing to introduce a new category called labor cleansing, the detention and deportation at Bisbee were just a police action. Nor do they fit the model of class cleansing as later practiced in Soviet Russia and other Communist countries since the removal was not directed at the working class as such, only against union activists.

***

Since World War II the world has witnessed a proliferation of all types of cleansing: ethnic, religious, racial, class, and so on. All of them can be subdivided into cleansings that accompanied the process of decolonization and those that were generated by local ethnic conflicts. Of course, the two can and do occur together.

Among the postcolonial cleansings, a distinction should be made between those that involved the expulsion of former colonial masters and those that involved indigenous populations. The first type, the elimination of colonial masters, has a history that goes back at least to the massacres of the French in Haiti in January-March 1804. These were particularly gruesome: men, women, and children were killed with the utmost cruelty. In fact, these massacres qualify as racial genocide but, since they were organized by the state and aimed at eliminating the White minority from Haiti, they also fit the category of a racial cleansing.[123]

More recent examples of this type of cleansing are provided by the expulsion of Belgians from the Belgian Congo, now known as Zaire, and by the emptying of Algeria of French settlers.

The Belgians, about 100,000, were brutally expelled from Zaire when the country achieved independence in June 1960. Mistreatment, especially rapes of White women, recurred on a large scale during the attempted Katanga secession. Although the expulsion itself was largely motivated by political hatred of the former colonial masters, it was directed against a racially distinct population within a certain territory, and thus fits within our general definition of cleansing. (This case was actually more complicated: when the White population started to flee some Black leaders realized that, in the short run, the country could not do without their expertise. Some of the Black leaders tried to prevent a mass exodus by coercion and roadblocks, which sowed panic and an ardent desire to flee among the increasingly nervous Whites.)[124]

The expulsion of about a million *pieds noirs* from Algeria in 1962 was less brutal[125] and also less clearly identifiable as an outright cleansing. Rather, it was a flight under pressure, but the pressure was real, so it can probably be classified as a borderline case or self-cleansing.

The other type of postcolonial cleansings involved expulsions of and by indigenous peoples. One such was the gigantic exchange of populations, accompanied by massacre and flight, between India and Pakistan in 1947. The partition of India caught millions of people on the wrong side of the border. Muslims, for example, were concentrated in the west and east of the country with large pockets in between. The partition lines cut across mixed-population Bengal and Punjab. And the conflict over Jammu and Kashmir later divided that territory as well.

The first intercommunal massacres started in 1946 in Bihar and reached their peak in August-October 1947 in the immediate aftermath of the partition. The Sikhs of east Punjab were particularly ferocious, although other combatants were not far behind. At least half a million people lost their lives and 12 million—7 million Muslims and 5 million Hindus and Sikhs—fled to their ethnic homelands.[126]

Compared to the staggering dimensions of India, the bloodletting in Palestine pales. There, the partition of the country and the birth of Israel also generated massive population outflows (some of them self-inflicted, like the flight from Algeria). A preview of such outflows had occurred a decade earlier, during the fierce anti-Jewish riots of 1936-39, when life was so dangerous, even for the Arabs, that about 40,000 of them left.[127] The postwar flight was on a greater scale; by 1950, when the dust settled, there were 726,000 Arab refugees living outside Israel plus 31,000 inside the country.[128]

It was not only the Arabs who fled the hostilities. There were also thousands of Jewish refugees from areas occupied by Jordan, such as Old Jerusalem and Judea. This, of course, was a continuation of an old pattern: the Jewish population of Hebron had been massacred and expelled in 1929 and there had been earlier pogroms in 1921 and 1920.

On the whole, the Arab stance was the more uncompromising: Jews who could not flee were massacred. On the Jewish side, the attitudes were more complex, running the gamut from slaughter in Deir Yassin in April 1948,[129] which was an exception, to appeals to remain, as happened in Haifa, also in April 1948.[130] Finally, to the overall number of Jewish refugees within Palestine we should also add Jews from other Arab countries who were forced to flee in the 1950s, for a total of approximately 800,000.

***

After decolonization, cleansing spread throughout the world. Until the collapse of Yugoslavia it seems to have been concentrated exclusively in the Third World. During that period it was tempting to conclude that cleansing was somehow connected with the end of colonial rule. Presumably, colonial rule diverted the attention of the indigenous peoples from their age-old animosities to the struggle against colonialism. When colonial rule was re-moved the old animosities flared up.

Although this is indeed what happened in many cases, cleansing had not been unknown even before decolonization, and in countries that had not been colonies. One such instance was the cleansing of Haitians from the border areas of the Dominican Republic in early October 1937.

The border between Haiti and the Dominican Republic had been delim-ited only in 1936.[131] During the previous 80 years there had been a continu-ous migration flow from impoverished, overpopulated Haiti.[132] Although the border areas had always had a mixed population and there had been considerable intermarriage and interpenetration of the two cultures, ten-sions between the two populations had also been increasing, not least due to economic competition in a tight labor market. When the border between the two countries was finally delimited, the Dominican government suddenly found itself with large strips of border territory inhabited either by Haitians or by a mixed population whose Hispanic character had been diluted. Fears aroused by the presence of an alien population sympathetic to the neighbor-ing state and memories of brutal Haitian invasions led to state-sponsored and state-organized massacres and expulsions. The orders were given by Dominican dictator Trujillo and were carried out by the army and the Policia Nacional. From 15,000 to 20,000 Haitians were butchered and thousands more fled or were expelled.[133] The expulsions were probably more racial in character than might have initially appeared since many Black Spanish-speakers were also expelled to Haiti, where one could still encounter them in 1960.[134] Eventually, a settlement between the two countries was reached. The Dominican Republic paid $550,000 to the victims' families (a large portion of the money ended up in the coffers of various government offi-cials in Port-au-Prince).[135]

In general, however, aside from the dispossession of the autochthonous Indian populations, the history of Latin America offers few examples of cleansing. The only other one of note was the expulsion of thousands of Salvadorans from neighboring Honduras in July 1969.

As in many similar situations the crisis had deep roots in the history of both countries. Tiny Salvador could not support a quickly growing population. Land hunger, lack of birth control, and general impoverishment led to the mass emi-gration of some 300,000 Salvadorans to neighboring Honduras.[136]

On the Honduran side, earlier immigration of West Indians, which had cre-ated tensions, was curtailed in 1903 and fully prohibited in 1929.[137] This made the banana industry, a major industry in Honduras, turn to the importation of Salvadoran labor. As the alien population in Honduras grew, so did xenopho-bia. In 1959 some 300 Salvadoran families fled harassment in Honduras.[138]

Tensions worsened with the introduction of agrarian reform in 1962 and the demarcation of the border between the two countries, also begun in 1962. The agrarian reform, which allocated land only to native-born Hondurans, whipped up anti-Salvadoran passions. When expulsions started, the Honduran newspaper *El Cronista* announced "Salvadorans Cleansed From Ten Towns In Yoro,"[139] years before the term "cleansing" appeared in common usage.

Although expulsions had started in the spring of 1969, the crisis erupted when the Honduran soccer team was defeated by the Salvadoran team on June 29, 1969. This mundane occurrence led to assaults on Salvadorans living in Honduras, allegedly including rape, lynching, and sexual mutilation.[140] The Salvadoran retaliation—a surprise air attack on July 14, 1969, and a four-day war that followed—ended in the largest ethnic cleansing in Latin America in modern times, the expulsion and flight of about 130,000 people,[141] although at least 100,000 people of Salvadoran origin stayed in Honduras throughout the war and after.

Other parts of the developing world were not immune to cleansing. One of the largest instances was the bloodletting in Indonesia in September-October 1965, which combined elements of an ideological anti-Communism with purely ethnic anti-Chinese hysteria. The merging of the two strands was the result of a link between the Peking-leaning Communist Party of Indonesia and the local Chinese, which in turn was a classical case of a vulnerable diaspora minority seeking support from powerful ethnic cousins in the historic homeland. As non-Muslims in an increasingly self-conscious Muslim society, many of them better off than the indigenous ethnic groups, the Chinese had often attracted envy and hostility. Ironically, even wealthy Chinese came to be seen, in Indonesia at that time, as instruments of Chinese Communist penetration. The Indonesian conflagration was also the result of complex internal political divisions; an army takeover and riots that accompanied it were used by various factions in the government and the population to settle old scores.

In the chaos that erupted in 1965, hundreds of thousands were slaughtered. It is impossible to separate with any degree of precision the number of Communist and Chinese victims (they were often the same), but it seems that certain elements in the army protected their Chinese business partners. For that reason, the cleansing was more political than ethnic. However, even the most modest estimates start at 87,000; the highest end at 1 million. The most reliable range is probably 200,000 to 500,000.[142]

The occupation of East Timor in 1974 and the subsequent attempts to suppress the liberation movement also resulted in massive population movements, but it is closer to genocide because it involved mass murder.[143]

The enmity between the Indonesians and the minorities is of a fairly recent origin. A much more ancient hatred led to similar genocidal cleansings in Cambodia and Sri Lanka.

In the last several centuries Cambodia has been steadily losing ground to the Vietnamese, who came to be perceived as the hereditary enemy of the Cambodian nation. Many of the Vietnamese living in Cambodia (estimated at 300,000 to 700,000, few of them assimilated)[144] were suspected of supporting the Viet Cong. The coup d'etat by General Lon Nol against Prince Sihanouk in March 1970 was accompanied by numerous attacks on the Vietnamese (especially in Phnom Penh with its 100,000 to 150,000 ethnic Vietnamese) and at least three massacres in April.[145] When Pol Pot's fanatically ideological and nationalistic regime came to power in April 1975, one of its first actions was the wholesale expulsion of 2 million people from Phnom Penh (an urban cleansing?) and the slaughter of intellectuals, middle-class people, and ethnic Vietnamese.[146] Thousands were annihilated, their bodies floating down the Mekong into Vietnam. Before it was defeated and overthrown by the invading Vietnamese, the regime killed no fewer than 1 million (up to 3 million according to some estimates)[147] ideologically unreliable Cambodians in one of the worst ideological cleansings of our time. In June 1978 170,000 persons of Vietnamese origin (plus an estimated 150,000 Cambodians) fled or were forced to flee to Vietnam.[148] The mass murder in Cambodia is yet another proof of the lethal combination of ideological and ethnic hatreds.

Another example of ethnic cleansing in Asia involves the Sinhalese and the Tamils in Sri Lanka. But this case, along with that of Cyprus, will be dealt with in greater detail in later chapters, so I will not delve into it here.

In Africa there are many examples of ethnic and racial cleansings in the postcolonial period. The largest and probably best known was the expulsion of thousands of Igbos in Nigeria. The anti-Igbo pogroms with a strong anti-Christian undercurrent started in the Hausa areas of Nigeria in the summer of 1967. Thousands of Igbos fled to their ancestral homeland in the east, where retaliatory pogroms against Muslim northerners were already in progress. In July, the eastern area (also known as Biafra) tried to secede, starting a war that lasted until January 1970. In the course of this conflict there was a de facto exchange of population between east and north and a major population cleansing in the east as the government forces fought their way across the rebel areas. In the process, thousands of Igbos also died of starvation.

Much more vicious, if smaller in scale, were various cleansings perpetrated by Idi Amin in Uganda. Most of these, especially in the initial period, were little more than political persecutions that resulted from political struggles within the country's ruling apparatus. At the time, Amin was trying to eliminate all opposition to his dictatorship, and members of the Acholi and Langi tribes, both prominent in the security forces, the army, and the police, were the prime target. In just one instance, 167 Acholi officers and soldiers were hacked to death at Mbarara Barracks (other sources indicate 258 deaths).[149] Catholics were another target for Idi Amin (who was a Muslim Kakwa). Amin had claimed that he had a mission to convert the predominantly Christian Uganda to Islam[150] and did not spare efforts to staff the administration and the armed forces with his people,[151] preferably Muslims.

But the Asians, descendants of various east Indian nationalities who had settled in Uganda when it was still a British colony, were by far Idi Amin's favorite target. In this he was fully supported by the majority of the Black population, which envied the Asians' business acumen and hated them for their alleged reluctance to intermarry. The Asians were expelled en masse after Amin signed an expulsion decree on August 5, 1972. The expulsion of Asians involved 71,000 people and was a pure example of racial cleansing.[152]

Other instances of population cleansings and expulsions in postcolonial Africa include those of non-Muslim Black Africans by government armies in Sudan, and, recently, ethnically motivated expulsions in West Africa.

Until 1991 it looked as though population cleansing was confined to the new states of the Third World. Europe, it seemed, had found a tolerable modus vivendi for its numerous minorities. The fall of Yugoslavia disproved that idea.

The cycle of mutual destruction—for that is what it is—was started in 1941 by Croatian extremists (the so-called Ustashe). The puppet state of Croatia, established after the German invasion and dismemberment of Yugoslavia in April 1941, included about 2 million Serbs within its borders (about one-third of the population). The huge Serbian minority was regarded as a mortal threat to Croatia.

From the very beginning there was a widespread idea, particularly in the Croat ruling circles, that there was no place for Serbs in Croatia. Resentments against Croatia's Serbs go back to the nineteenth century when they were seen as allies of Hungary and thus inimical to Croatia. In 1941, the old antagonism, combined with "German" ideas, led to a complete rejection. For example, Milan Budak, Croatia's minister of education, speaking at a banquet in June 1941, said that "one-third of the Serbs we shall kill, another third we shall deport and the last third we shall force to embrace the Roman Catholic religion and thus meld them into Croats."[153] (This was probably an echo of Pobedonostsev's infamous dictum regarding Russian Jews.) Later that month, Viktor Gutich, governor of Western Bosnia, speaking at Banya Luka, urged that the city and all of Croatia be "thoroughly cleansed of Serbian dirt."[154]

An orgy of destruction followed in which almost 300,000 Serbs in Croat-controlled territory were killed (164,000 in Bosnia-Hercegovina and 131,000 in Croatia proper);[155] many more were driven out into rump Serbia, which was itself in dire straits due to destruction inflicted by the invading Germans.

Bulgaria and Hungary, which were awarded chunks of former Yugoslavia, also cleansed their territory through expulsion and, in a few instances, massacre. About 70,000 Yugoslav citizens, mostly Serbs who had settled in (formerly Hungarian) Vojevodina after World War I, were evicted. They were given a 24-hour notice (generous by contemporary German standards) and were allowed to take one suitcase and the equivalent of six dollars in cash. Another 120,000 Yugoslav citizens in Bulgarian-annexed Macedonia were also expelled.[156]

After the war Serbs refrained from massive retaliation (except against the personnel of the Croatian armed forces). But the legacy of mutual hatred, fear, and distrust remained very much alive by the time Yugoslavia began to crumble in the late 1980s.

As the dissolution gained momentum, the media began discussing large-scale population transfers. In March 1991 the popular Serbian magazine *Nin* featured an article about the possibility of a voluntary population exchange between Serbia and Croatia. It suggested that Serbs from Croatia be resettled in Vojevodina while Bosnian Croats would move into houses abandoned by Croatia's Serbs.

When fighting between Serbia and Croatia broke out in the beginning of March 1991, thousands fled. Initially, most refugees were Serbs fleeing Croatia, such as the 20,000 who flocked into Vojevodina in March of that year. By the beginning of 1992 there were 158,000 refugees, mostly Serbs, in Serbia.

As the fighting spread and the Serbs scored major victories—and started to pay back for past injustices—Croats and Muslims began to leave their homes in ever increasing numbers. Within one month of Bosnia's declaration of independence on March 3, 1992, 420,000 people had escaped from the region. By the end of July 1992, according to the High Commissioner for Refugees, the number of displaced persons was approaching 2.5 million.[157] By August, about one-third of Croatian Serbs had fled; the number of ethnic Croat refugees in Croatia was approaching half a million, or 12 percent of the country's Croat population.

As the fighting intensified, the warring factions began expelling enemy populations. Here there is a fine and indefinite line separating "voluntary" refugees who were afraid to stay in captured territory (such as the 25,000 remaining inhabitants of Jajce who fled the town when it fell in October

1992) and others who were terrorized into leaving, such as the 70,000 Muslims from Sanjak. Often, the victors would surround a village, cut off all communications, and set it on fire. If the inhabitants were lucky, they were allowed to flee; if not, they were raped and/or killed. Several features characterized these cleansing campaigns. The most unusual was the mass rape of some 30,000 to 50,000 predominantly Muslim women (others were by no means immune). Economic gain was also a strong motive in many expulsions since abandoned houses were either looted or given to the victors' local co-ethnics, or allocated to co-ethnic refugees. Another unusual method of cleansing utilized in the Balkan war was the detention of men (usually) whose families were then forced to sign affidavits of "voluntary" emigration and property transfer as a condition of their release.[158] About 5,000 Muslim families in the Bihac area "expressed a desire" to sign such affidavits and emigrate. As of August 1992, Bosnian reports estimated that 260,000 had passed through 105 Serbian-run camps; 17,000 had died and 130,000 were still in detention. Serbs asserted that Muslims and Croats ran 40 camps where more than 6,000 Serbs had died.[159] At present, large areas of Bosnia and Croatia have been cleansed.

The cleansing in Bosnia is the most spectacular and best known among recent cases, but there are many more that have received scant attention from the world media. One was the expulsion of approximately 350,000 Yemenis from Saudi Arabia in October 1990.[160] They were expelled because Yemen supported Saddam Hussein, and the Yemenis came to be perceived as a potential fifth column by the Saudi authorities.

Another major expulsion, that of the Palestinians from Kuwait, occurred in the aftermath of the Gulf War. Most Palestinians sided with Iraq during the occupation of Kuwait, and many collaborated with the occupation authorities. After the liberation of the country virtually the entire Palestinian community of 380,000 then living in Kuwait was expelled in the spring and summer of 1991 (most went to Jordan).[161]

And approximately 200,000 Georgians were forced out and/or fled Abkhazia in September-October 1993 after Abkhazian separatists wrested control over the province from the Georgian government.[162] About 12,000 Greeks living there before the conflict have also been evacuated.

Another cleansing catastrophe has taken place in Rwanda (it will be dealt with in a later chapter) and is threatening to spill over into neighboring Burundi. And the recapture of Krajina by Croatian forces in early August 1995 sent the entire Serbian population still remaining in the region fleeing to Bosnia and Serbia.

***

As the century draws to a close we may see more and more cleansing campaigns in many parts of the world. Why?

There is a common misconception that democracy decreases intolerance and prejudice. This is not true. "There is apparently no reason to believe that with increasing democratic organization of society there will be a correlative decrease in social intolerance," wrote Oliver Cromwell Cox. "The focus of intolerance may change—that is to say, Jews may be tolerated [especially if they had been reduced to a few thousand Holocaust survivors]—but, since we may expect that even in an advanced democracy social values will be jealously defended, no group regarded as alien and disruptive of social harmony and solidarity could be assured a peaceful, tolerated existence. As Lord Acton observes: 'The true democratic principle, that the people shall not be made to do what it does not like, is taken to mean that it shall never tolerate what it does not like.' . . . it is only necessary that the dominant group believes in the menace of the cultural tenets and practices of the other group; whether they are actually harmful or not is not the crucial circumstance."[163]

Modernity is yet another panacea. A steadily increasing economic and cultural integration of the global village is supposed to decrease "primordial" attachments. Eventually, "membership in ethnic groups must become increasingly irrelevant."[164] This assumption fails to take into account that the individualistic ethos of a mobile society leads to fierce competition. In the Hobbesian free-for-all any weapon, including ethnic, racial, and religious differences, lends itself to effective use. In this situation increased mobility and greater ethnic and racial mixing lead to an increased awareness of differences, which then can be blamed for any real or imagined grievances. "Railways are the greatest breeder of national hatreds," wrote Kautsky a hundred years ago.[165] Airlines are even more lethal.

It is fashionable to blame nationalism and ancient hatreds, and they do bear much of the blame. But nationalism is merely a symptom, not the cause, of the malaise. The real culprits are the ideals of freedom, self-determination, and representative democracy based on the one man/one vote principle.

Ever since Locke enunciated the consent of the governed as a fundamental principle of a legitimate political system, the idea of representative government has inexorably gained ground. It is an admirable principle. The problem is that it was enunciated before the rise of nationalism, at a time when religion was still the focus of collective identity. It applied to monoethnic societies, or rather to societies that were still unaware of their multiethnicity. God and King were still the cornerstones of the political order.

The French revolution expanded the principle of freedom from individual to nation, but it defined the nation in the Western sense, as an entity based on *jus soli.* Things changed when the new ideology and ideals reached central and eastern Europe where nationhood was defined ethnically, through *jus sanguinis.* In these societies freedom and representation were redefined in collective terms, shifting legitimacy from the individual to the ethnic group.

It is the holy trinity of freedom, self-determination, and representative democracy that push each collectivity, but especially ethnies, toward sovereignty and independence. In a world of nation-states, sovereignty and statehood are the ultimate measure of maturity. An ethny without a state is not a complete ethny. It is also a vulnerable ethny because it lacks the protective carapace of the state. Even a weak state is better than none. Latvians and Estonians could not withstand Germany or Russia, but they fared incomparably better than stateless Jews and Gypsies. Ultimately, statehood is a guarantee of survival.

But a stable statehood is possible only where the majority of citizens can agree on some basic issues, where they share a way of life and a philosophy of living. Diversity, especially territorially entrenched multiethnicity, introduces a disruptive element into a political equation (compare Quebec nationalism, for example, with nonterritorial Black or Indian nationalist movements). And since power, in a democracy, ultimately resides with the majority, a minority will always be subjected to the will, or at best the good graces, of the majority.

Until 1789 hierarchy and subservience were accepted; in the contemporary world the ideal of liberty beckons to individuals and groups alike. And, as more and more ethnies reach out for statehood, the reluctance to share one's home with an alien group will continue to increase. Thus, the tendency toward homogeneity will also become more prominent. One need only compare the multiethnic empires prevalent in 1900 and the increasingly monoethnic states of 1920, 1950, and 1990. (Here I am talking about indigenous ethnies, not about immigrant minorities, most of whom will be integrated into their new homelands as individual migrants.) Translated into the language of political action, this tendency will manifest itself in many more cleansings in the years to come.

Chapter 2

A Typology of Cleansing

At this point it will be useful to set forth a short typology of cleansing. First, to classify is to understand. By listing major kinds of cleansing we will be able to understand the phenomenon better. Second, classification will enable us to explore the complex interrelationships between various types of cleansing. It will help us to trace its evolution. Ultimately, a typology may clarify trends in cleansing, for classification often has a predictive value. And prediction takes us halfway to prevention.

Building a typology of cleansing is complicated by the fact that the group's view of itself may differ from the way others view it. It is the difference between ascription and self-ascription, and the two do not always match. For example, there were hundreds of thousands of Jewish converts to Christianity all over Europe in the 1930s. In Hungary alone their number reached about 100,000. They regarded themselves as Christians, but when the Germans occupied Hungary the converts were reclassified as racially Jewish, and many of them perished along with other Jews.

Even where the difference in ascription and self-ascription is absent the motivation of the cleanser is not always clear. We cannot say, for example, whether Armenians were cleansed for their ethnicity or religion. Both aspects of their collective identity were fused together and separating them is impossible. One thing is certain: the Turkish government and most ethnic Turks perceived Armenians, both as Christians and non-Turks, as a major threat to their collectivity and state, a threat that had to be eliminated.

Another complicating factor is the diachronic changes in ascription and self-ascription. Jews, for example, in their long history in the diaspora, changed from a religious minority in medieval Europe to an ethnic group in the nineteenth century central and eastern Europe to, of all things, a racial contaminant in Nazi ideology.

At the same time, Jewish self-ascription has also changed significantly. Actually, there was not one but many self- ascriptions, since Orthodox Jews, assimilated Jews, Zionists, and all other ideological strands in between view "the Jew" differently. The oldest self-ascription, and also the one with the most continuity, is that of the Orthodox Jews, who see themselves as a people united by their covenant with God and separated, by the same covenant, from all other people. Although cleansing affected all kinds of Jews the criteria applied to cleansing changed from one epoch to another.

The overview of cleansing in the previous chapter revealed that historically cleansing went through three phases. In antiquity it was used as a political tool to ensure control over alien, recently conquered, populations and as a source of slaves. It was the economic aspect of cleansing that was probably the most salient characteristic of that period. The conqueror not only weakened the enemy and diminished the likelihood of future resistance, he could also make a profit and procure a steady supply of manpower for the economy back home. Cleansing was thus virtually devoid of any ideological component (inasmuch as ideology is an abstract system of belief in the modern sense rather than something that is implied in the pattern of one's culture).

During the Middle Ages cleansing acquired a mostly religious character although ethnic and political cleansing did not entirely disappear. But economic cleansing had virtually died out since money could no longer be made off slavery. Uprooted serfs from an enemy state could be resettled on a conqueror's land if there was a labor shortage, but that kind of settlement was sporadic. Even on the German-Slav frontier in the twelfth and thirteenth centuries peasants from as far away as Flanders were usually invited, not forced, to settle. They were often enticed by wide-ranging privileges. Slavery continued to flourish in the Middle East, through capture of Christians from the northern shores of the Mediterranean and Africans, but this was a purely for-profit exercise, like the later trade in African slaves, not cleansing as defined in this book.

In the early modern period cleansing gradually lost its religious character and acquired the ethnic orientation we are familiar with today. It was superseded by colonial cleansing of indigenous peoples carried out by European settlers. Finally, in this century we have witnessed a proliferation of various types of cleansing—ideological, postcolonial, and, of course, purely ethnic—which, I believe, shows the accumulation of different types of collective identities. This accumulation is manifested in the addition of "outer rings" or boundary maintenance mechanisms to the existing core. Geographically, cleansing in the Old World differed from cleansing in the New World. The first kind was practiced by states, often empires, in their struggle for territorial control and/or expansion. The second type comprised a slow push-back of the indigenous populations by colonial powers in the Americas and Australia. The difference was partly determined by the absence of political structures that could organize effective resistance in most new territories of the New World and Australia. Another factor was the profound difference in technological development of the autochthonous peoples and the invading Europeans, which made the conquest easy and the subsequent mass immigration and settlement possible.

In addition to historical and geographical divisions, there is also what I would call, for lack of a better term, paradigmatic cleansing: cleansing based on certain (undesirable) characteristics of a segment of the population. This is a varied collection.

First, there is cleansing by physical characteristics. This type includes cleansing by race, which occurs when a certain group is cleansed because of its genetic makeup. Such was the cleansing of Indians in the Americas, Aborigines in Australia, Whites in Haiti, and Asians in Uganda. Racial cleansing was often presented as a civilizational imperative due to the incompatibility of two civilizations and the impossibility of their peaceful coexistence. There is also what I would call a pseudoracial cleansing, such as the cleansing of Jews by the Nazis, who conceived it as a racial cleansing even though Jews do not constitute a distinct race and are, in fact, often indistinguishable from the general population among whom they live.

A rare variety of this type of cleansing is the elimination of people with physical deformities. Such was the murder of weaklings and malformed babies in Sparta. Perhaps, in this instance we should call it preemptive cleansing. I would classify it as a borderline case since deformed babies did not constitute a group or a population. But the desire to weed out a certain kind of people in a given population—to cleanse—was definitely there.

Probably the most common kind of cleansing is that by cultural markers, which has proliferated in the last 200 years. Here we have ethnic cleansing based on culture, language, and ascription. Examples include the mass expulsion of Germans from Eastern Europe in 1945-47 and that of the Salvadorans from Honduras. Another subdivision is religious cleansing, which was prevalent in the Middle Ages. It has by no means disappeared in our time although it is now usually combined with ethnicity. In this century alone, Armenians and Greeks in Turkey, Hindus and Muslims in the Indian subcontinent and, right before our eyes, Christians of various denominations and Muslims in Bosnia and Croatia, all provide examples of religious and ethnoreligious cleansing. Where ethnicity and religion are fused we may call a cleansing civilizational, since the adversaries often represent two distinct civilizations.

As civilizations became more complex, new social categories were created, and this in turn resulted in new forms of what may be called ideological cleansing. Thus, the introduction of the concept of class led to the cleansing of undesirable classes in Marxist states. Here Soviet Russia was the pioneer, later followed by other Communist states in Europe and Asia. Class cleansing affected the bourgeoisie, the aristocracy, and, in Russia and China, rural bourgeoisie known in Russian as the kulaks. Class cleansing was a characteristic of early Communist societies: by the time they reached maturity all "parasitic" classes slated for annihilation had been eliminated.

Another variety of ideological cleansing is political cleansing directed against political opponents and, on occasion, against politically unreliable populations as a whole. Like so many other phenomena, political cleansing originated in the poleis of preclassical Greece in the eighth to sixth centuries B.C. during a period of acute political struggle between the monarchy and "democracy." (This was discussed in chapter 1.)

Such cleansing was merely a matter of expediency. As a clearly enunciated political principle, the modern variety grew out of religious cleansing. As a political principle it was first formulated by the Peace of Augsburg in 1555 (see chapter 1).

Strategic cleansing is often closely linked with political persecution. To distinguish the two we must keep in mind that strategic cleansing is more limited in scope and is usually applied to sensitive military areas.

Here we can also distinguish two subvarieties: first, external cleansing directed against alien populations or opponents in the newly acquired territories, and second, internal cleansing, or self-cleansing, focused on the elimination of internal political opponents. This kind of cleansing is often practiced against political foes, especially after a civil war (in which case it falls into the category of political cleansing). For example, the suppression of the Paris Commune in 1871 led to the shooting of 20,000 to 25,000 communards and the deportation of about 5,000 to New Caledonia.[1] Seventy years later, in the Spanish civil war of 1936-39, the Republicans killed about 20,000 opponents while the Nationalists eliminated about 400,000.[2] Tellingly, the mass executions were called *limpia* (cleanup).[3]

To this category we may add (political) refugees who fled in anticipation of persecution based on certain characteristics. The Russian Civil war of

1919-22 generated 1.5 million White refugees, the Spanish war of 1936-39 about 300,000 Republicans.[4] Or the flow can be generated by a politically motivated invasion, such as the suppression of the Hungarian revolution in 1956, which sent some 200,000 political refugees from Hungary,[5] or the invasion of Czechoslovakia in 1968, which generated an outflow of over 120,000. But this type of anticipatory self-cleansing is hard to distinguish from flight under pressure or forced emigration. It is another borderline case.

An altogether different kind of cleansing is a cleansing whose goal is making a profit. This type can be called economic cleansing. It was particularly widespread in antiquity, when selling newly enslaved populations could bring enormous profits to slave traders. However, we must distinguish between this type of enslavement as an instrument of cleansing and simple enslavement for profit only, which was common in Africa in the sixteenth to nineteenth centuries. (This refers to the slave trade practiced by Europeans; slavery by Arab traders had been going on much longer. Both were purely economic enterprises.) Only when enslavement was directed at the population of a given polity, as in Thebes, and was combined with political goals can we speak of an economic cleansing. In other words, this kind of cleansing does not exist independently; it must include political goals, such as destruction of the adversary's political power and demographic base.

A much rarer type is cleansing by gender, as when the entire male population of a conquered tribe was slaughtered or enslaved, or when young women were taken by conquerors as concubines. Here we should apply the same test that we applied to economic cleansing: if the elimination of the male or female population was done expressly for the purpose of destroying the community then it would qualify as cleansing. Otherwise, it will simply be a matter of greed, status, and lust. The recent rape of thousands of mostly Muslim women in Bosnia had clear ideological overtones and thus can serve as an example of cleansing by gender. The perpetrators were aiming at destroying the honor and integrity of the Muslim population (they actually dishonored themselves, but that is another matter).

Even rarer is cleansing by sexual preference. We know of several attempts to suppress (male) homosexuality in Byzantium. In most civilizations such campaigns were extremely rare, partly because not every civilization regarded homosexuality as a sin, partly because homosexuals were not regarded as a community (a homosexual was acting as an individual, to be punished on an individual basis), and partly because gays were usually closeted and led a clandestine existence that attracted little attention. Only the totalitarian states of the twentieth century, especially Nazi Germany and Soviet Russia (although Soviet Russia does not seem to have practiced it on the same scale) put cleansing by sexual preference on the map.

Cleansing by age is also very rare. We know of the cleansing of babies ordered by Herod. Sparta killed weak and malformed babies as a matter of course, but this was an elimination of individuals, not a population cleansing per se. Still, such babies were weeded out as a class of individuals, and the goal was to make sure that Sparta's population stayed healthy.

At the other end of the age spectrum we have cleansing by old age. In some technologically primitive societies old people past a certain age were abandoned to the elements, particularly in lean years. However, this was not a regular occurrence and, as with babies, the elimination was carried out on an individual basis rather than as a campaign affecting the whole community. In neither case was the destruction of a population pursued as a goal. So, cleansing by age is another borderline case.

There are several more categories of elimination and persecution that defy easy definition. One such was the burning of witches in medieval Europe. Like the cleansing of the aged or gays, it was usually applied to individuals; on the other hand, the elimination of the entire witch population, presumed in existence, was clearly the aim. The fact that the witch population was probably an "imagined community" does not invalidate the elimination of this category as cleansing. So this would be yet another borderline case.

Other types include the killing of approximately 70,000 mentally ill patients in Nazi Germany in 1939, soon discontinued;[6] the mass removal of prostitutes occasionally practiced by various states in different epochs; and the elimination of beggars in medieval Wallachia by Vlad the Dracul. The last probably qualifies as social cleansing although this was a bizarre and isolated incident.

Finally, virtually all types of cleansing can be either permanent (as is usually the case) or temporary (such as the internment of the Japanese in the United States during World War II). (See the Appendix, "Typology of Cleansing," pp. 287-288.) Temporary cleansing is often practiced in strategically sensitive military areas (the expulsion of some 600,000 Jews from the Russian frontier zone in 1914-15, for example)[7] although examples of permanent expulsions in these areas are also fairly well known (such as the resettlement of approximately 60,000 Armenian families from Old Julfa in Isfahan in 1604).[8]

Chapter 3

CLEANSING AS A METONYM OF COLLECTIVE IDENTITY

The brief history of cleansing presented in chapter 1 clearly shows a substantial change in the pattern of cleansing throughout recorded history. Let us now focus on this process.

Cleansing is directed against an enemy that is deemed to be a threat to a collectivity and the integrity of its institutions. Often, the enemy is a minority that conspicuously differs from the rest of the population. Such a minority is perceived as a fifth column that can either rebel against central authorities or ally itself with an external enemy. Minorities that belong to ethnic majorities in adjacent states, particularly large and expansionist states, are the most suspect. Populations in recently acquired territories are also often untrustworthy. It is not surprising, therefore, that cleansing has often been applied to newly conquered territories, especially by sprawling multiethnic empires in which the loss of one segment threatens the dissolution of the entire empire. In antiquity, this tendency is most evident in the history of aggressive, expansionist polities such as Assyria and Rome. In the Greek world it was expansionist Macedon that practiced cleansing on a scale until then unencountered in Greek history.

Three features characterize cleansing in the early phase of its development (which roughly corresponds to the period of antiquity in the Mediterranean and the Middle East, that is, from the eighth century B.C. until the fourth to sixth centuries A.D.). One is the economic component in Greek and

Roman cleansing. The second is the incomplete or partial character of the cleansing usually directed against the elites in the newly acquired territories. And the third is the "total" character of many, if not most, cleansed groups.

The economies, particularly the agriculture-based economies, of most ancient societies needed slave labor. This was the case in Ancient Egypt, Babylon, Persia, and especially Rome from the third century B.C. on. The reliance of Roman latifundia on slave labor created an insatiable demand for slaves. Stripping the newly conquered or rebellious territories of their population was a convenient way of supplying thousands of slaves. Thus, slavery promoted cleansing.

However, we should distinguish the purely economic aspect of slavery from enslavement as an instrument of cleansing. As stated earlier, even mass enslavement of a population does not, in itself, constitute a cleansing. According to our definition, only the politically or ideologically motivated removal of population constitutes a cleansing. Most other instances of mass enslavement are simply an economic activity. In practice, this means that economic cleansing cannot exist in a pure form but must be part of a solution to a political problem.

Among major historical periods in the Old World only antiquity experienced the symbiosis of the political and the economic in cleansing, the economic gain often being the driving force behind forced population removals. The contrast with a purely economic mass enslavement that did not have political connotations and therefore does not qualify as cleansing can be seen in the enslavement of Africans in the sixteenth through nineteenth centuries. Thousands of Africans were sold into slavery, but for purely economic reasons. There was no desire either on the part of the Europeans or local and Arab slave traders to cleanse Africa of unwanted population.

Another important feature of these early cleansings is the incomplete character of the population removal. The expulsions pursued very practical purposes: crushing resistance, preventing future unrest, weakening the demographic base of the enemy. They were largely devoid of ideological content; ideological "total" cleansings lay in the distant future. Thus, it was not necessary to remove the entire population. Removing the elites decapitated the rebels, eliminated potential leaders, and achieved basically the same results at lower costs. Hence, the cleansings of elites practiced by the Assyrians and, to a smaller degree, the Romans. (However, with its most stubborn foes, such as Carthage and Judea, Rome showed an increasing tendency toward total cleansing.)

The third characteristic of early cleansings is the "total" character of many of the cleansed ethnies. At this stage, many, if not most, ethnic groups were still characterized by a specific language, religion, and set of customs. In a sense, each major ethny—Egyptians, Hebrews, Greeks, Romans—was a complete civilization. Empires of antiquity broke the link between ethny and its cultural attributes. Already Assyria and Persia had witnessed and promoted a substantial mixing of peoples, including large scale migrations and population transfers. The conquests of Alexander the Great and the spread of Hellenism reinforced this trend. It became even more pronounced in the later Roman Empire, which experienced something close to "panmixia." Thus, by late antiquity, there were Greek-speaking Jews living in Alexandria and Latinized Celts worshipping Isis in Rome. Before the third century B.C., however, and in many areas well beyond this point, each major ethny was still a separate civilization. And the cleansing of such an ethny can be called civilizational or, perhaps, intercivilizational, since it is applied by bearers of one civilization to another.

Numerous instances of intracivilizational cleansing also occurred, especially in those areas where a cultural continuum was split into city-states, such as in early Mesopotamia, Phoenicia, and classical Greece. However, major cleansings of this epoch, such as those of the Jews in 597-587 B.C. and A.D. 70 and of Carthagenians and Corinthians in 146 B.C., were clearly intercivilizational in nature.

To sum up, cleansings of the early phase were inter- and intracivilizational, often incomplete and, in postclassical Greece and the late Roman Empire, with strong economic motivation. The unfocused nature of these early cleansings, their lack of a major unifying parameter, bespeak the diffuse character of most collective identities.

The spread of Christianity and Islam provided collective identity with a unifying element. Sometime between the fourth and sixth centuries, the focal point of collective identity in Europe and the Middle East had shifted to religion, and the change in the patterns of cleansing reflected this shift: it was now redirected against religious minorities. Other forms of cleansing, including ethnic, did not entirely disappear: the elimination of Danes in England is a case in point. But the major frontlines of this time pitted Christians against Muslims in Iberia, Russia, and the Middle East (especially during the Crusades); they also separated Christians of the Western and Eastern rite in the Balkans and elsewhere in eastern Europe. Even in purely interstate conflicts, such as the Hundred Years' War between England and France, the enemy was often (mis)represented by using religious imagery. Thus, the French often depicted the English as devils with horns; some Frenchmen and Scots thought that the English had tails artfully concealed

in their pants ("Engloiz couez" in the *Ballade contre les anglais* of 1429).[1]
And "Jewish" faces grace many a devil in churches all over Europe.

The tendency to define collective identity by religion probably reached
its high point in the religious wars between Catholics and Protestants after
the Reformation. Earlier conflicts dressed in religious garb, even the intercivilizational Reconquista, do not give us many examples of religious cleansing (there were notable exceptions, of course, such as the massacres of Jews
and Muslims perpetrated by the Crusaders in 1096-99). Judging by the cre-
scendo in religious cleansing in the sixteenth and seventeenth centuries,
religion, as the focus of collective identity, reached its climax in this period
after a long gestation and development stretching over a thousand years. The
high point was probably reached in 1550-1650 (the French Wars of Religion,
the Thirty Years' War, and the Khmelnytsky massacres) to be followed by a
hundred years of decline and then the switch to the next phase. In the process,
cleansing lost the partial, incomplete character it had had earlier and acquired
the totality that has characterized it ever since. This is a natural development:
religion is the bearer of the Absolute, and compromise is not possible. Tolerance blossoms when religion loses its inner conviction. As long as religion
provides the basis for collective identity and retains its strength, coexistence
with other religious groups is not to be expected. It is feasible only when one
religious group subordinates all others, as did Islam in India and the Balkans, in
a hierarchy of religions. In Germany of the sixteenth and seventeenth centuries, where a clear predominance could not be established, separation was
the only solution. Hence the Peace of Augsburg, and the principle of *cuius
regios eius religio.* In France, where the Catholic side gained the upper
hand, an experiment in unequal coexistence—"toleration"—lasted for close
to a hundred years but ultimately failed with the revocation of the Edict of
Nantes and the emigration of some 200,000 Huguenots. Anti-Huguenot
violence, incidentally, was cyclical, with the long peaceful interludes
typical of many ethnic and ethnoreligious conflicts.

The waning of religion as a political force in the eighteenth century
coincided with the rise of modern nationalism. It is no accident that nationalism, a new religion worshiping ethnos and nation, supplanted the old
religion that worshipped God. In the new world that came into being in the
eighteenth century—and is still with us—the Divine died, and Man was
orphaned. The increasingly lonely, atomized individual sought solace in the
superfamily of the nation.

But this change did not simply involve the shedding of the old religious
identity and the acquisition of a new ethnic one, like the shedding of a snake's
skin. Rather, the new national/ethnic identity was superimposed on the old
one, adding a concentric circle to the old religious core.

Perhaps even this analogy is not completely satisfactory. After all, ethnicity marked by religion, language, and custom has always been with us. With the development of nationalism, however, it acquired a new significance and a new importance.

Ethnies in which ethnonational identity is inextricably linked with religion are often found at civilizational divides: Armenians, Greeks, and Maronites at the Christian/Muslim front, the Irish astride the Catholic/Protestant frontier in Ulster, Catholic Poles hemmed in between Orthodox Russia and Protestant Prussia, and finally the explosive mixture of Orthodox Serbs, Catholic Croats, and Bosnian Muslims in a tight little corner of the Balkans where three religions meet. It is not surprising that cleansing has been visited on all of the above.

However, extreme nationalism was possible even where the religious factor played a secondary role: witness Germany. Perhaps, this exaggerated sense of ethnonational allegiance was the only way to overcome deep religious and regional divisions that had always plagued Germany and its "tribes." (The same should apply to other countries with strong regionalist traditions, such as Italy or Spain. Unlike Germany, neither one developed a comparably obsessive nationalism. But both displayed strong totalitarian tendencies, which helped to overcome internal divisions. The reason for this difference could be that although Italy and Spain display strong regionalism neither one experienced a deep religious split like Germany or, to a lesser extent, France. In other words, it is possible that religion encourages totalitarian tendencies but curbs nationalism).

German nationalism did not abate with unification. Toward the end of the nineteenth century (ironically, with some help from foreigners such as Houston Stewart Chamberlaine, an Englishman, and Count de Gobineau, a Frenchman), German *kulturtrager* redefined ethnic nationalism in racial terms. Confusion of race with ethnicity was fairly common during this period. In fact, well into the 1920s and 1930s numerous monographs were published on racial conflict, where ethnic conflict was meant. For example, a well-known book on ethnic problems in Hungary by R. W. Seton-Watson was titled *Racial Problems in Hungary*. This delusion of seeing ethnicity in racial terms, determined by "blood," later showed up as a basic component in Nazi ideology. It may be called a pseudoracial identity, because it was erroneously premised on the existence of the Aryan race. No matter, even if the Aryan race was only a figment of Nazi imagination, "Aryanism" was yet another identity "ring" that defined Germanness and set it apart from other, supposedly lesser people.

After the horrors of World War II race temporarily fell out of fashion, at least in Western academic circles. In fact, many social scientists, such as

Ashley Montagu, refused to acknowledge the existence of race, preferring to see a collection of clines where laymen see racial characteristics. From their point of view, it is absurd even to speak of racialism and racial identity since race does not exist. But these esoteric views left barely a dent in the perceptions of the man in the street, to whom race is self-evident. It is manifested in skin color and certain facial features. If we limit race to visible markers we get racial nationalisms such as negritude and various American groups known as Black separatists and White supremacists.

Although racial identity on the individual level is very common, especially in areas where members of several races live together, very few states ever made racial identity an official social category (South Africa in the period of apartheid was a prominent exception). One of the main reasons for this is that, in the long run, racial identity is difficult to maintain. It is relatively easy to do in multiracial, hierarchical (openly or not) societies in which there is a strong correlation between status and race (usually defined by color). Elsewhere, race includes too many ethnies to serve as a focus of collective identity. It's almost as if Serbs, Croats, and Bosnians hate each other for religious and/or ethnic reasons because they cannot hate each other racially, since they all belong to the same race.

If racial identity is usually too diffuse to command lasting allegiance, at least it is perceived by most people as a natural phenomenon. Such is not the case with class. Class as an ideological (in contrast to a socioeconomic) category is a man-made fiber, spun in its modern form by Marx's fertile imagination.

As a major element of collective identity, "ideological" class was incorporated into the ideology of all Marxist states from Russia to Cuba. Of course communists were not the first to use class as an instrument of social engineering. Vlad the Dracul's class cleansing in medieval Wallachia mentioned earlier is a case in point. But the communist regimes in this century were much more professional. Rulers of Stalinist Russia and Maoist China shot thousands of class enemies in the early stages of the communist takeover. They then "de-classed" the entire strata of urban bourgeoisie and the aristocracy by the wholesale confiscation of their wealth and the abolition of titles. Later still they deported and starved to death millions of kulaks who were the rural bourgeoisie (more often than not, the rural middle class).

Such wholesale destruction of enemy classes shows that the focus of collective identity in these societies had shifted to class. Or rather an attempt was made to effect such a shift. Like ethnos and race in ethnic and racial nationalism, class was elevated to the status of collective identity through the indoctrination of the masses by a segment of the intellectuals (the children and grandchildren of Dostoyevsky's "demons"). But whereas nationalism of any type is based on a natural phenomenon, class as an ideology is artificial. That is why it failed to "stick"; its sudden downfall shows shallow roots. But before it fell, the relative ease with which the class doctrine spread and acquired adherents demonstrates the great malleability of collective identity.

The application of class cleansing in Stalinist Russia (and later in China) was so successful that soon the goal of eliminating the "parasitic" classes was achieved. The Soviet Union turned into a "mature" socialist society with only two classes: workers and peasants. This does not mean that Soviet society lacked an elite or that all social stratification based on differences in income and education had been eliminated. But the old propertied classes, as defined by Marx through ownership of the means of production, had been destroyed. And there lay the great conundrum: once the "significant other" had been eliminated, the boundary maintenance mechanism based on class was no longer operational. In a society of workers and peasants, class identity as such became obsolete. (The same applies to monoethnic societies. But here the "other" is just across the border.)

The elimination of the "parasitic" classes is one of the main reasons that mature communist societies have to look for another ideology and collective identity. The very logic of success creates an identity vacuum in mature socialism, a vacuum that has to be filled by another identity. And nationalism is conveniently close at hand; in fact, it has never left.

In Russia it was reignited by the German attack in 1941. The war came at a time when the classless society had been achieved and class identity was already on the wane. In a war with another nation only nationalism could provide an adequate ideological response. So the war hastened the re-emergence of Russian nationalism as the focus of Russian—and Soviet— collective identity. (This is not to say that purely ideological components were entirely absent on either the German or Russian side. Ideology and messianism were a strong undercurrent in both. In fact, the reason Russia was so successful in adopting socialism is that messianism was inherent in Russian ethnic identity, and socialism, messianic to its core, was a shoe that fit the Russian soul well.)

Did Communist Russians reject or abandon their ethnicity? Hardly. Trotsky did, but then he was Jewish and had different identities to shed and for different reasons. After the first 10 or 20 years of socialism, Russian ethnic identity and nationalism gradually reasserted themselves. Russians turned into radishes: red on the outside, white (that is, nationalistic) on the inside. After 1945 one could encounter many Russians who saw their country as a socialist empire. Later still, with a change in the intellectual fashion to, for example, the ultra-Russian "village" school of literature, which hailed Slavic roots and healthy indigenous peasantry, they redefined Russian *dukhovnost'* (spirituality), a major component of Russian identity, in religious terms. They preferred to see the Russian man as racially (vis-a-vis the Asians) and spiritually (vis-a-vis the Westerners) superior. In such people all four identities—religious, ethnonational, class, and racial—came together.

It was striking to see just how easily the class element was shed in the unfolding drama of perestroika. This is yet another proof of its artificiality. (One can acquire or discard an ideology, but how does one discard one's ethnicity—one's language and culture? It might be argued that one's sociological—as opposed to ideological—class cannot be discarded either. But in postmodern society, in which the greater part of the population is middle-class, class loses its significance. It becomes a "non-binder," much like ethnicity in a monoethnic society.)

In both 1917 and 1990 Russia shed its religious identity. But in 1917 one religion—messianic socialism—supplanted another, while in 1990 there was simply no substitute. Russia, so used to the Russian Idea, lost its bearings. It became, in the phrase of a Russian academic, "just another Brazil" (that is, a country without a mission). The current explosion of nationalism is a desperate attempt to hold on to at least one form of collective identity. (It can be argued that the class identity was not cast aside, but rather regressed from the "for itself" to the "in itself" state. Will the reappearance of the bourgeoisie and the pauperization of large segments of Russian population re-emphasize the class-as-an-identity binder once again?)

There are several more collective categories that have been vocal in asserting their identity in the last twenty or so years: women, gays and, to some extent, older people.

Actually, the roots of today's feminism go back to the nineteenth century and the struggle for suffrage. In our own time radical feminism redefined women and womanhood as an oppressed class, often in Marxist terms, and sought to awaken and raise women's consciousness in a Marxist transition from the *an sich* to the *fur sich* stage. The *fur sichness* does not come easily, though: most women are bound to men through family and sexual ties and are not open to extreme radicalization. In other words, they do not erect and maintain collective defense mechanisms based on gender. This failure is the direct result of the impossibility of constituting a full collectivity based on one gender, if only because the inability to procreate would doom such an entity to extinction. On the other hand, the fact that relatively few women succumb to gender extremism does not in itself disqualify womanhood as a collective identity: a proletarian who does not define himself as such is still a proletarian and a Jew who thinks he is a Christian is still a Jew, as was demonstrated during the Holocaust.

Much the same applies to gays. But in this case the radicalization is both easier and more difficult. It is easier because gays enjoy less acceptance and, as a discriminated-against minority, are more open to radicalism. It is more difficult because, with the exception of large concentrations of gays in a few major urban centers, they are scattered and, often, closeted (that is, clandestine).

We may even argue that gays, scattered and isolated throughout the general population, display a pattern common to diaspora minorities. If the rejection of an alien ethny signifies the existence of a defensive boundary maintenance mechanism protecting one's own ethnic group, the rejection of gays and lesbians points to a similar defensive mechanism on the part of the heterosexual community defined by sexual preference. Gays are seen as a dangerous sexual minority that has to be eliminated.

However, there is a serious definitional problem that we encounter only with gays: in some individuals homosexual activity may be a passing phase. This adds a fluidity to the gay identity lacking in all others. One is a woman or a Black forever; one may be gay for only a few years. (Actually, with the increasing availability of sex change operations, gender is beginning to acquire a certain degree of fluidity as well.)

This element of inconstancy, of passing, is even more pronounced in age. But here it is a natural given, fully accepted by society. Also, age progresses in a linear sequence absent in gayness. Is there a collective identity based on age?

We will try to answer this and other questions concerning diverse collective identities later in this chapter, in sections devoted to each collective identity. But now let us look at all the collective identities we have so far (un)covered. They are, chronologically, the total, if diffuse, identity of the early phase (largely cotemporal with antiquity), the religious identity prevalent during the Middle Ages and the Renaissance, and, since the end of the eighteenth century, an accumulation of ethnic, racial, class, gender, and gay identities. (Here we mean ideological, as opposed to sociological, identities; class, for example, has always existed as social category, but it was Marxism that turned class into a social entity. The new, ideological conception of class made it the foundation of a class-based collective identity. We should also mention caste, but in its classical form, as it exists in the Indian subcontinent, it is a purely local phenomenon that cannot be translated into a universal. On the other hand, if it is defined as a status category with some economic underpinnings, caste has a universal validity and should be placed somewhere between class and ethny on the continuum of collective identities.)

The various kinds of collective identities can be subdivided into two major groups. The first five—ethnic, religious, racial, class, and caste—can reproduce themselves and can exist as discrete social entities (although this does not fully apply to class since a proletarian needs a peasant unless he can grow his own food). The rest—age, gender, and sexual preference—cannot function as independent entities and cannot reproduce by themselves. This may change as advances in science make it possible for women of 90 to conceive and give birth or enable lesbian separatists and gay males to have children without recourse to the opposite sex. Until then, however, all three categories will depend, for their reproduction and replenishment, on society in general.

As shifts in the focus of collective identity manifest themselves in the changing patterns of cleansing, it becomes clear that collective identities are accumulated. From the original state of one tribe, one language, and one religion (we will, of course, find many irregularities in this pattern in the earliest epochs) religion took precedence during the Middle Ages, to be superseded by other identities in successive waves of identity formation. In the process, the old identities were not shed and discarded; instead, each new one was added to the existing ones, like rings on a tree.

One may even postulate that the more identities a group has the more difficult it is to change its affiliation. The Religious Man or Woman of the Middle Ages could effect a major change by converting to another religion. In the multiple-identity man of today the sheer number of identities makes a major switch much more problematic. Of course, one can change only one identity at a time, but even such a limited switch will call for a major rearrangement in the complex interrelationship of other identities. Thus, an assimilation into another ethnic culture with different patterns of gender roles will affect one's gender identity. A Cuban assimilating into the Anglo-American mainstream will have to adjust his or her gender role as well. He or she may also discover that the line dividing races in America is stricter than the one in Cuba. Someone who was considered White in Cuba may be classified as Black in the United States. In this case, a readjustment of one's racial identity will also be called for. With multiple identities, the relative importance of each one declines, although for most people their ethnic identity is probably the first among equals.

There is one more distinction that splits identities into two subsets. Until the appearance of class, identities were natural and self-evident in the sense that they developed in the process of long-term sociopolitical and cultural evolution. A person who was born in France and spoke French was French; a Black person was a Negro; a person who believed in Christ was a Christian. Ideological class, as opposed to a purely sociological class, marks the appearance and advancement of a qualitatively new kind of identity: an identity created, defined, and reified by people. Of course, proletarians had existed long before Marx, but it took Marxism to create the proletariat.

It may be argued, however, that religion, ethnicity, and race also require reification to function as identity-forming agents. A peasant who considers himself a *hiesiger* or a *tutejshy* (both mean "local" in German and Belorussian, respectively) does not have an ethnic identity per se. He has to be awakened to his identity, nationalized or ethnicized, so to say. That is precisely what happened during the process of mobilization of the masses that accompanied nation-building in Europe in the nineteenth and twentieth centuries (even in France, according to Eugen Weber, the peasantry did not join the mainstream of national life until the interwar period). In other words, a *hiesiger* peasant who learns to consider himself German is an equivalent of a worker who is taught to consider himself a member of the proletariat. In that sense, Marx did for class what Herder had done for ethnicity: he created an ideology that helped to mobilize proletarians, transforming them into the proletariat, just as nationalism had mobilized ethnos and reorganized and restructured it into a nation. In the process, existing categories were reified into new entities with collective identities.

This is precisely what has been happening in the last three hundred years, first in Europe, then elsewhere. The process of identity creation that has been unfolding since the Reformation is a story of successive reifications. It can be applied to many groups. In principle, little prevents computer programmers from developing programmer class consciousness or even ethnicity, complete with its own dialect (they already have slang), customs, and initiation rights. And if Unix programmers separate from Cobol programmers we may have the beginnings of a programmer ethnic conflict.

For programmers—or any other group—to achieve a collective identity, they must be able to form a durable group. To do that, they must be able to reproduce themselves as a group. For example, by programmers' marrying only or mainly other programmers and their children following in their profession and existing independently as an economic and political entity. This latter requirement, in turn, presupposes the division of labor (of which programmers, like any other purely professional grouping, are incapable) and an erection of a boundary maintenance mechanism, without which no distinct group is possible. These requirements are absolutely indispensable for a durable group formation.

The concept of boundary maintenance mechanism was introduced by Norwegian anthropologist Fredrik Barth in 1969. Until then, the consensus among anthropologists—Clifford Geertz being, perhaps, the most prominent—regarded ethnicity in terms of "givens" and "primordial attachments," that is, of traits inherited from ancestors. This approach developed in the context of state building in former colonies, which faced the task of integrating disparate ethnies into nation-states. Accordingly, each ethny was deemed to be distinguished from all others by the sum total of these traits. This approach emphasized the "content" of each culture. However, it did not pay sufficient attention to the interaction between various ethnies. It was too static to adequately deal with dynamic aspects of ethnic processes.

Barth shifted the emphasis from the static content of each ethny to the dynamic interaction between ethnies. He pointed out that it was not unusual to find two or more ethnies living in close proximity, often sharing the same space, their members crossing the line through matrimony and constant interaction, yet maintaining their internal cohesiveness. Clearly, the interaction between these groups was contained and regulated by an invisible barrier, which Barth called the "boundary maintenance mechanism."

We will return to the concept of the boundary maintenance mechanism later, in the section on ethnic identity. But for now let us continue with our examination of collective identities. Our survey of collective identities shows that there are two types of identity: entity-forming (let's call them "positive") and entity-nonforming (let's call them "neutral," not "negative"; I will explain why shortly).

Positive identities—ethnic, religious, racial—allow members to form complex, structured social entities that may function socially and politically as independent agents. Neutral identities—class, gender, sexual preference—do not. They may generate political movements, but their members cannot form fully independent social entities (even a worker needs a peasant and, possibly, a teacher). If they do—if gays, for example, acquire the capacity to reproduce unisexually (they already have the capacity for the division of labor and a boundary maintenance mechanism)—then the identity will be rendered positive.

Identities may also play a destructive role when one identity displaces and destroys another one. Such entity-destructive identities may be called "negative." The negativity of such an identity is not inherent in the identity itself but rather resides in its destructive potential. Assimilation (a switch from one ethnic identity to another), is an example of this destructive capacity within one level of identity, the ethnic. If a Polish immigrant gradually becomes fully Americanized, his Polish identity has been supplanted by the American one. In this case the American identity is negative because it has destroyed the other, Polish, identity. At the same time, it does not cease being positive, in the sense that it is still entity-forming. This kind of a switch often occurs where a status difference between the two identities is present, that is, when one community looks down on the other. When the difference in status is less pronounced, identities of the same order are simply accumulated as nested identities, such as Scotch and British or Catalan and Spanish.

Such a switch or accumulation of identities is also possible on different levels when an identity of one order—ethnic, for example—is supplanted or rendered secondary by an identity of another order, let's say class. Since class is not an entity-forming identity (it is neutral), we can say that the original ethnic identity has been neutralized. This is what happened to the Russian ethnic identity in the first decade of communist rule, before Russian nationalism returned with a vengeance in the 1940s. At the same time, even a neutralized Russian identity retained its destructive capacity vis-a-vis other ethnic identities in the Soviet Union, since the assimilation of non-Russians continued. (The terms "positive" and "negative," recall, refer only to the entity-forming or entity-destructive capacity of a collective identity, not to any positive or negative value judgment being applied to it.)

One of the most fascinating aspects of identity interaction is that an identity may "pull" its adherents through a series of transformations into an entirely new configuration of identities. The spread of the Bogomil heresy in Bosnia prepared the ground for the acceptance of Islam after the Turkish conquest. In the process, Bosnia was definitively torn away from Croatia, which eventually led to the creation of a new ethnic group. Another example is how the adoption of the Belorussian language by eastern Lithuanians in the Vilna and Grodno areas later facilitated their Polonization, which redrew the ethnic and religious borders in the whole region. The heresy of the Bogomils and the Belorussification of eastern Lithuanians acted as "relays" for further identity creation and transformations.

In principle, this kind of transformation is possible on more than one level. If, for example, an aristocracy adopts Protestantism while the commoners stay Catholic, and then the Catholic workers and peasants redefine themselves in class terms, a religious conflict may be transformed into a class or a religious/class conflict. But such complicated permutations, although interesting, are relatively rare.

So far, we have been talking about collective identity without a workable definition. Like many other phenomena that seem self-evident, it is hard to come up with a satisfactory definition.

Everyone is a member of numerous groups: one's family, the company one works for, an ethny to which one belongs. These groups vary in size and longevity, from a few individuals in a nuclear family to hundreds of millions in large ethnic groups, from a tribe that may exist for centuries to a department in a company that may be created and dismantled within a few years. Whatever its size or longevity, each group tries to induce a certain degree of homogeneity. Each one creates a set of rules, explicit and implicit, that members are expected to follow. The very existence of a group depends on its ability to retain members within the structured continuum of intragroup relationships. The longer a group exists, the likelier it is to develop intragroup solidarity, a system of symbols, and sets of rules governing relationships between group members and outsiders: in short, binders that keep the group together. Inevitably, groups develop what may be called a group mentality and a group personality, such as a collection of customs and ceremonies such as initiation and/or induction ceremonies.

I have already mentioned problems of definition, unsurprising in a phenomenon that is so diverse, complex, and all-encompassing. Definitions of a group are legion, yet a completely satisfactory one remains elusive. Almost a hundred years ago, Albion Small, for example, defined a group as "any number of people between whom relations are such that they must be thought of together."[2] Half a century later George Homans wrote that "a group is defined by the interactions of its members."[3] (I should point out that in this particular case Homans was referring to small groups where every member knew everyone else.) Among contemporary sociologists, George De Vos put the emphasis on the "common cause," which he defined broadly as "common origin, common beliefs and values" and even a "common sense of survival."[4]

We can come up with many more definitions that stress commonality and common interest (in voluntary associations, of course). The important thing is that each person belongs to numerous groups and that group memberships are defined in terms of their difference from and opposition to nonmembers.[5] (For that reason this phenomenon is sometimes called "segmented oppositionalism" or, somewhat misleadingly, "nested identities.") That is, Signor Spumante may be an inhabitant of Florence, a man of Tuscany, an Italian, an Italian speaker, a West European, a White male, and a Catholic, in a complex system of ever expanding circles. His identity as an inhabitant of Florence (where he may well have a subidentity if he is identified with a certain neighborhood) matters only in relation to neighboring towns and, perhaps, to Tuscans outside of Florence. In an encounter with Italians from other parts of the country he will be a Tuscan; to an

Austrian or Hungarian he will be Italian; to other Europeans a Mediterranean, to Protestants a Catholic, and so on. His adherence to Roman Catholicism will usually be of little import to a French or Spanish Catholic, just as the fact that he is White will be of little interest to other Whites but may be important to some Blacks. In short, groups and collective identities usually acquire significance only in reference to other groups and collectivities on the same level.

Although the importance of any identity varies with each encounter, one or two identities usually take precedence. For example, that same Signor Spumante may usually think of himself as an engineer, since profession is a major determinant of status in a modern society. While he remains at home, in Florence, his Italian and Catholic "tags" are likely to be less prominent, since the vast majority of his fellow Florentines are also Italian and Catholic. Once he ventures outside, however, to England or Albania, the Italian and Catholic identities will most likely come to the fore.

In much of Eastern Europe, however, profession, as a status marker, is less important than ethnic affiliation. A West European (and even more so an American), to the question "Who are you?" will probably say "I am an engineer" or whatever. An Eastern European will most likely answer this question with "I am Polish" or "Ukrainian." This shows that the emphasis on specific components in the total complex of collective identities has a spatial dimension.

There is another feature of collective identity we may want to cover, its rigidity. In Europe, especially in ethnically mixed areas of Eastern and Central Europe, ethnicity is quite rigid: if one was born of German parents one is always a German, even if one does not speak a word of German (only intermarriage can change the children's affiliation). In other parts of the world, as in some societies of southeast Asia such as Malaysia and Thailand, ethnic affiliation is much more fluid, and people of mixed origin who feel equally at ease within two or more ethnic groups often choose their public persona depending on the situation. This gives rise to the situational or optional ethnicity that is quite baffling to Westerners. (This fascinating phenomenon was masterfully described by Judith Nagata; I will return to it later.)

Interrelationships of various collectivities can be vertical or lateral (horizontal). Groups of the same order, such as tribes, may coexist side by side on terms of equality ("vertically"). Others may form complex stratified systems, like castes in India or classes elsewhere (in horizontal layers, or "laterally"). Both types of group order, vertical and lateral, may coexist within the same society: several castes may have similar status while several other castes are above and below them. (In other words, castes A, B, and C may have similar status. Their relationship is vertical. If caste D is above and caste E is below A, B, and C, we have a lateral relationship.) Both types are expressed through cultural markers that, in a rich variety and in any number of possible combinations, define a collectivity and help to maintain boundaries between various groups.

In the contemporary world incorporation into a group and the maintenance of group boundaries have evolved into a highly politicized process, especially if groups of unequal status share a limited economic and political space. In Grillo's words, this entails "the elaboration of an ideological and symbolic system through which the concept of 'Us' is projected in such a way that it becomes part of the predominant mode of discourse, an aspect of everyone's everyday experience."[6] In other words, the complex social, political, and economic reality is interpreted in terms of group conflict, whether the group be ethnic, religious, or class-based. Such a society is suffused with struggle and enmity between groups, and most, if not every, encounter between members of various groups is ethnicized or racialized.

This is not an entirely modern phenomenon. In the medieval world group differences were often dressed in religious garb, so that ethnicization or racialization of group differences in the contemporary world merely transposed group conflict onto another plane by using other markers. Groups and markers change, group conflict is eternal.

In the modern world (from the eighteenth century on) the process of collective identity formation goes through several stages. In Stage 1 people of common origin, occupation, or orientation have to be mobilized. A perceived injustice is the best way to mobilize the masses, and the language of liberty, equality, and fraternity provides a ready-made vocabulary and a set of symbols and goals for virtually any group suffering from any disparity between its status and aspirations. The creation of a political movement aimed at eliminating the injustice signifies the end of Stage 1. Most groups never advance any further.

However, if the group can reproduce itself as a closed system and develop the division of labor, as well as a boundary maintenance mechanism, its members can be "tribalized." That is, they will coalesce into a discrete social entity, which may erect a boundary maintenance mechanism and may become an independent actor on the political, social, economic, or cultural scene. This is Stage 2 (and the most difficult stage at that).

At Stage 3 the group may reach out for statehood. This process is facilitated by the ideals of self-determination and representative democracy: whatever people want they are entitled to, as long as they express their will in free elections. Paradoxically, the requirements in Stage 3 are less stringent.

Basically, any tribe can acquire statehood as long as its geopolitical situation allows it. That is one of the main reasons why states have proliferated since the French Revolution. In principle, almost any group can be tribalized through a political movement and subsequently acquire statehood. Ethnic groups are the most versatile and thus the most successful at this. In a world of ethnies any group is potentially an ethny, even if its membership is bound by race and class. If it aspires to become one, it has to ethnicize itself by creating markers of its own. This has been done successfully by the newly settled countries of the New World. And recently we have witnessed the creation, virtually from nothing, of gay ethnicity, resembling diaspora ethnicities, which created cultural symbols and markers as it went along.

The relative ease of group creation (and the category reification it sometimes involves) adds an additional hurdle to any attempt at group definition. On the one hand, it makes it easier, since new groups and categories can be created *ex nihilo*. On the other hand, if almost any collection of individuals can be a group, then what is not a group?

For the purposes of this book let us define a collectivity not just as a permanent collection of people who have developed a collective identity but as a permanent collection that in addition is part of a larger system of similar collectivities. It is understood that each permanent group develops a system of symbols we call cultural markers, maintains a boundary in regards to other groups of the same kind, and elaborates rules of inclusion and exclusion that regulate the transfer of group membership across its boundaries.

With the above definition in mind, what does it mean, we may ask, to be Austrian? For most Austrians, and probably most outsiders as well, it means to have been born (or at least raised) in Austria, speak German, be a Catholic, possess certain historical memories, eat schnitzel and sacher torte and, in the not so distant past, dance waltzes in the Vienna Woods.

Thus, at first glance, one's identity seems to be defined by "primordial attachments" that "stem from the 'givens,'" that is, kin, culture, class, language, and religion.[7] This approach, of which Clifford Geertz was probably the best-known proponent, focused on identity "contents." I have already mentioned Fredrik Barth, who redirected attention to the contact area between two societies, the "boundary maintenance mechanism." Both concepts, the "givens" and the "boundary maintenance mechanism," should be thought of as complementary rather than a simple either/or dichotomy. By utilizing these concepts we can visualize collective identity as a sphere filled with interrelated cultural traits we may call "markers" circumscribed by a defensive ring of the boundary maintenance mechanism. The boundary itself is delineated by certain cultural traits we may call "binders," which clearly separate members of the given community from outsiders. The prohibition on eating pork among Jews and Muslims and the prescribed beard and turban among the Sikhs function as binders. Markers and binders demonstrate a great diversity, for virtually any cultural trait can become a marker or a binder.

Anthropologists seldom distinguish between markers and binders. Both are subsumed under the generic term of "cultural traits." But I believe that the division of collective identity into the core and the boundary implies a similar division of cultural traits. Let us then reserve the term "marker" for the core traits; those on the boundary can be called, following the usage of George De Vos and Lola Romanucci-Ross, "binders."

What is their relationship, one may ask? The difference lies in their significance for the collective identity. Let's say that both Ukrainians and Jews eat borscht. But Jews may see it merely as a dish, just another trait (marker) in their culinary repertoire, while to Ukrainians borscht may be an important ethnic symbol of Ukrainianness. They may even elaborate the consumption of borscht, as for example "a true Ukrainian always eats borscht with bacon and garlic." In this case, the borscht, consumed with bacon and garlic, will be a "binder," part of the boundary maintenance mechanism separating them from Jews.

Such complex cultural markers, which may be found in the core and on the periphery of different collective identities, should be distinguished from simple binders, which merely mark the borderline between two ethnies and are significant only in their juxtapositive value. Such is the prohibition on eating pork for religious Jews, which separates them from pork-loving Ukrainians. Paradoxically, the most salient boundary values may also serve as the core values of a given collective identity if they express the collectivity's essence, in its own eyes or in the eyes of its neighbors.

Cultural traits and their significance for a given cultural entity are not static but are in constant flux. Core values may migrate to the periphery and turn into binders; conversely, binders may lose their juxtapositive significance and be pushed inside into the core area.

The cultural boundary is itself a complex construct. It faces outward to the outside world and inside to members of the ethny. The dichotomy is largely that of ascription and self-ascription: how the group sees itself and how it is seen by others. Quite often the two views do not coincide. As mentioned earlier, assimilated converted Jews (or any other assimilated minority, for that matter) may think of themselves as non-Jewish while outsiders, by using different criteria, may still classify them as Jews.

***

Let us now elaborate on some collective identities in more detail. Our goal is to elucidate the difference between positive identities (those that are entity-forming), and neutral identities (those that are entity-nonforming). This distinction is very important in terms of the political problems encountered by multiethnic states and the solutions to some ethnic conflicts that can be offered. (A reminder: collectivities with positive identities lend themselves to tribalization and, potentially, statehood. Neutral ones do not.)

We will start with religious identity because in Europe and in the Middle East this was the prevalent form of collective identity. It is also an identity on which subsequent identities have been patterned. We will then continue with ethnic and racial identities, and on to those based on class, gender, and age.

RELIGIOUS IDENTITY

Religion easily serves as a bonding agent that can create ethnic and political entities. A religious community is "complete" in the sense that it allows social and biological reproduction, a division of labor, and a boundary maintenance mechanism. Even more important, it gives meaning and structure to the universe, life, and everyday existence.

To us religion is of interest only as an important ingredient in ethnic conflict and nationalism. It lends itself to power struggles as easily as do race and language but often with more vehemence. For some groups, religious beliefs provide the most important definition of who they are. In such cases, the imposition of an alien religion after a conquest may either completely dissolve a group or strengthen its determination to fight.

Today's ethnic conflicts cannot be understood properly without the religious matrix of the medieval civilization. In Europe, the modalities of contemporary nationalism grew from religious antecedents. The complex interrelationship between religion and nationalism is best understood in the context of their historical development.

We have already mentioned that during the Middle Ages religion provided the basic collective identity for Europeans. One could be a full-fledged member of society only if one was a Christian. Religion determined one's membership. This is still largely true of many, if not most, Muslim societies today. But in Europe nationalism has supplanted religion as the prime focus of collective identity.

The transition was not very smooth. Although in many cases religion was incorporated into ethnic identity, it often clashed with nationalism because world religions such as Christianity or Islam, with their message of inclusion of all the faithful, are antithetical to nationalist particularism on ideological grounds. Ultimately, religion cannot incorporate nationalism. But nationalism can and does appropriate religion and religious symbolism, which is why nationalism has almost invariably proved stronger than religion. Also, universalism, whether religious or ideological, is abstract and metaphysical. Nationalism, with its emphasis on mother- or fatherland, the people-as-family, is "warm" and affective.

The purest example of religious identity should be sought among peoples who possess a "tribal" religion (or a denomination) all their own. Among these are Armenians, Jews, Georgians, and in Asia, before the advent of Christianity, the Japanese and Koreans (and in earlier epochs the Copts and the Chinese, if we count Confucianism and Taoism as exclusively Chinese). But even ethnies that do not possess a unique religion may turn the most universal religion into a particularistic cultural marker and binder. Such was the case in Ireland, where Catholicism became the badge in the struggle against the English, or in Poland, where it helped Poles in their fight against Protestant Prussia and Orthodox Russia.

In contemporary Europe there are two areas where ethnicity has a strong religious component (that is, where religion has been "ethnicized"): Bosnia and Ulster (in the latter case it would be more appropriate to speak of denomination). Elsewhere, there are Muslims battling Christians in Karabakh, Lebanon, and the Philippines; animists in Sudan; Jews in Israel; and Hindus in Bangladesh, India, and Pakistan; and Buddhists fighting Hindus in Sri Lanka; and so on.

No area shows the creative and disruptive potential of religious identity better than the former Yugoslavia. Here people of the same ethnic stock, speaking dialects of the same language, developed into three separate ethnies— Orthodox Serbs, Catholic Croats, and Muslim Bosniaks—due mainly to differences in religion and cultural orientation.

The role of religion as a boundary maintenance mechanism is very old: as early as the fourth and fifth centuries, Egyptians (Copts), Syrians, and Armenians opted for national churches in part to escape or weaken outside control. Ecclesiastical independence strengthened their political independence and, with the spread of ethnic nationalism, was reinterpreted in nationalistic terms. But it would be wrong to deny the nationalistic element in these early religious struggles altogether. The split between the Greek and the Roman churches, traditionally dated from 1054, was not based on unbridgeable dogmatic disagreements. Theological, liturgical, and ritual issues were secondary. Rather, they became issues in a power struggle between two communities and ecclesiastical power structures based on different languages and cultural traditions.[8] Likewise, the wars between Normans and Byzantines in Sicily, the sack of Constantinople by the Crusaders in 1204, and the rejection of the union with Rome by the Greek clergy in 1439 all were episodes in a "communal" struggle that was in its time perceived as religious and, as a matter of doctrine, irreconcilable. And yet, Richard Coeur-de-Lion called the wooden castle he had constructed near Messina "Mategrifon": "kill-the-Greeklings" not "kill-the-Schismatics."[9]

Another illustration of the secondary nature of religious identity in our time is the fact that differences in religion do not impede national unity, as in Germany, Hungary, and Ukraine, to name but three countries (although Germany did experience destructive religious wars, and Uniate Ukrainians differ markedly from their Orthodox conationals in the strength of their nationalism).

Even when secondary, religion usually plays an important role in strengthening or weakening the ethnic bond. For example, if an ethnic group splits in two, religion may seal what began as a purely political separation by helping to develop two distinct ethnic groups, as happened to the Protestant Dutch and Catholic Flemings in the Low Countries and to the Muslim Bosniaks and Catholic Croats in the Balkans. With Jews, however, religion was indispensable in creating and maintaining a continuity that withstood two thousand years of exile, assimilation, and persecution.

The role of the religious component may undergo startling transformations. In early Ireland, for example, the church rite substantially differed from Roman practice in ritual and liturgy during the first five or six hundred years of its existence; the Roman rite was imposed by the English, and the reception was at first hostile. But when the conquerors chose Reform, the Irish became more Catholic than the pope and have stubbornly adhered to the Roman dogma ever since.

In the last hundred years religion has been increasingly supplanted by ideology, especially by totalitarian ideologies that provided, among many other things, an alternative "blueprint for living."[10] In a sense, ideology became a modern form of religion; many philosophers, such as Nicolas Berdyaev, saw it as a secular religion.[11]

The growth of fundamentalism in the Muslim world and elsewhere suggests that, with the demise of secular ideologies, religion may revive. Many observers have found the growth of fundamentalism baffling. We may look for answers in the withering of ideologies, which preceded the spectacular collapse of communism by at least 20 years, precisely the time frame of the appearance of fundamentalism. The fortunes of religion and ideology seem to be inverted: when one goes up the other one goes down.

In any case, the struggle between the old religion and the new—Paganism and Christianity two thousand years ago, Religion and Nationalism two hundred years ago—ended with the victory of the new religion. But in both instances the new religion incorporated much of the old ideological baggage. (The communist doctrine has often been compared to Christianity. If so, the collapse of communism was the victory of a renascent Paganism over Christianity which had exhausted itself in 70 years. Julian the Apostate won, the second time.)

After World War II, in the satellites of a new Soviet/Russian Empire, diverse sociocultural traditions of individual nations permeated their respective communist establishments and produced varieties of national communism, akin to incipient national churches.[12] But the process did not stop there. By the 1980s nationalism had dissolved the inner ideological content of the communist societies, leaving only a fragile Marxist shell. Perestroika merely cracked the empty shell.

So far we have traced the interpenetration of nationalism and religion. But religion and ideology can also serve as a means of abandoning one's ethnic identity by adopting a transcendental worldview, such as Marxism. This was the route chosen by many assimilated Jews in Eastern Europe and Russia who sought an honorable exit from a pariah status.

Those atheistic Jews may have been pioneers: in Europe, at least, the end of ideology may ultimately signal the end of religion. If ideology is a later form of religion, an old maid approaching senility, then we are witnessing the end of a very long road. (It is extremely doubtful that science can provide a secular substitute.) Very low rates of church attendance in many European countries ("three times in a lifetime: at christening, wedding, and wake") seem to point in that direction. Religion may still linger in form but not in substance. As a vital social force it may soon be gone, if it is not gone already. If so, the upsurge in fundamentalism may also signify the death throes of this major form of collective identity.

ETHNIC, NATIONAL, AND REGIONAL IDENTITIES

If religious identity implies universalism, then ethnic, national, and regional identities are particularistic. With very few exceptions, these are *territorial* constructs, even where the common territory belongs to a distant past, as in the case of diaspora minorities such as the Gypsies, the Parsis, and, until 1948, the Jews.

As a rule, each ethny is characterized by its own peculiar culture that sets it apart from all other ethnies, tribes, and peoples. Essentially, culture is a way of organizing human existence or, in Raoul Naroll's felicitous phrase, a "blueprint for living." In principle, any group that has a specific blueprint may qualify as an ethny, although such a broad definition may be too loose since castes, sects, or professional groups (and even Freemasons) that have a specific way of life would qualify. What separates ethnic, national, and regional groups from all others is the idea of peoplehood or, in its broadest term, tribe. Any group that can become a tribe is potentially an ethny.

Although many groups are susceptible to tribalization, no collectivity in the contemporary world is more prone to it than the ethny. Naroll lists six criteria that distinguish a "culture bearing unit," that is, a tribe, from all others: (cultural) trait distribution, territorial contiguity, political organization, language, ecological adjustment (fitness), and local community structure.[13] These criteria apply to ethnic groups as well.

Although Naroll's criteria may seem self-evident, in reality they often fail the empirical test: cultures influence one another so that traits are widely diffused; traits "wander" and "return" to the original culture area in a modified form; people migrate and intermingle so that territorial contiguity is destroyed; people switch to another language while retaining their old self-ascription; they gain, lose, and modify political organization; and so on. The problem of delimiting ethnies remains and, by the very nature of the ethnic phenomenon, is likely to remain.

A subjective approach is one way of dealing with this problem. Michael Moerman, for example, chooses a purely volitional definition: "someone is a Lue by virtue of believing and calling himself Lue and of acting in ways that validate his Lueness."[14] This approach shifts the entire emphasis to self-ascription, but what happens if the other Lue refuse to validate one's Lueness or if one passes for a Lue only in some specific situations?

As mentioned earlier, there are several areas in the world where ethnicity is situational, at least for people of mixed parentage who feel perfectly at ease in either culture and can pass for a member of either one. In these areas "the same cultural features can be used contextually, sometimes to express differences, sometimes to express commonality of membership."[15] Judith Nagata gives several examples of situational ethnicity in Malaysia that may seem very unusual to someone used to rigid either/ or notions prevalent in the West.

Based on her work in southeast Asia, Nagata characterized the ethny as a variety of a "reference group which defines and structures social interactions, rather than a fixed anchorage to which an individual is unambiguously bound." Seen from this angle, "ethnicity is a web of loosely defined social relationships and interactions which allow an individual great flexibility and a multiplicity of social roles."

The use of ethnicity as a "vector" is not limited to southeast Asia (see, for example, Katherine Verdery's book on Romanian villagers in Transylvania, who also used the idiom of ethnicity to understand and explain a complex social reality [much like many left-leaning intellectuals used the language of Marxism]).[16]

Where ethnicity allows for situational flexibility some individuals can oscillate between two or more ethnic groups. Cultural diacritica can be manipulated for various purposes (economic gain, status, or some other advantages). Occasionally, such flexibility de-emphasizes ethnicity so that in some circumstances ethnic bonds may be subordinated to other crosscutting binders such as religion if religious affiliation (Muslim in Malaysia, let's say) brings more advantages than ethnic origin (Hindustani, say). (This is the "functionalist" approach to ethnicity.) Finally, where flexibility rules, there may be no correspondence between various aspects of ethnicity such as customs, language, and religion. Ethnicity then becomes disorganized and unstructured.

But most areas of the world do not allow such flexibility. One's ethnic affiliation is fixed at birth and is confirmed by subsequent upbringing. In order to join another group one has to cross boundaries: learn another language, another culture, adapt to another blueprint, perhaps undergo a ceremonial conversion. For these other areas, Barth's definition is more appropriate: "an ethnic group is a population which is (a) biologically self-perpetuating, (b) shares fundamental cultural values realized in overt unity of cultural forms, (c) makes up a field of communication and interaction [in the Deutschian sense], and (d) has a membership which identifies itself and is identified by others, as constituting a category distinguishable from other categories of the same order."[17]

Ethnicity is never static. Ethnies coalesce through long gestation, develop and, occasionally, die. Their survival often depends on their ability to organize politically and to retain and develop their culture.

Ethnicity can be visualized, as Paul Brass suggested, in a continuum. At one end we find people who are differentiated by certain cultural markers but do not attach any significance to this difference. Brass calls them "ethnic categories."[18] What distinguishes them from groups based on class, gender, or age is reproduction, the division of labor, and a boundary maintenance mechanism, in other words a capacity for self-perpetuation as a group and the potential for what I call tribalization.

When ethnic categories become aware of their distinctiveness and demand corporate recognition from a central authority they become "ethnic communities," in a transition reminiscent of the transformation from the "in itself" to the "for itself" stage in the proletarian class consciousness. Or, in my terminology, they become a tribe. (But they are a tribe even if they do not demand corporate recognition. The threshold of tribalization is reached whenever people belonging to an ethnic community acquire a sense of commonality and begin to think of themselves as a distinct group.)

***

When ethnic communities demand group rights such as self-government or control over education, they are engaged in the politics of *nationalism*.[19] At this point they turn into a nationality. (Confusion may arise as to the distinction between Brass's terminology—"ethnic category," "ethnic community," and "nationality"—and mine—group mobilization, tribalization, and subsequent political entity/state formation. Please keep in mind that Brass deals exclusively with ethnic processes while my terminology refers to wider transformations in the collective identity of a group or social stratum including, but not limited to, ethnies. Figure 2 will help elucidate the difference.)

Thus, politically, a nationality is an ethny that aspires to or has attained some administrative status, or at least recognition, within a larger political entity. But the process does not stop there. In a world of nation-states, only a sovereign state, the highest mark of ethnic organization, confers the ultimate equality and legitimacy on an ethnic group. Nationalism demands a nation-state while the nation-state strengthens nationalism in a process of a continuous interaction and mutual reinforcement.

At first glance, nation and state are easily distinguishable. "A state is a legal and political organization . . . [while] a nation is a community of people," wrote Seton-Watson.[20] However, there are many states that are not nations and many nations that do not have states (they should be called "nationalities," following the Central and East European usage).

Most social scientists distinguish between political and ethnic nations, although their terminology varies, of course. Thus, Lafont divided nations

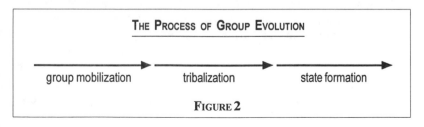

THE PROCESS OF GROUP EVOLUTION

group mobilization   tribalization   state formation

FIGURE 2

into "nations ethniques" or "biologiques" and "nations politiques" or "nations des citoyens."[21] Emmerich Francis called them "ethnic" and "demotic nations."[22] And so on.

Basically, each type derives from a different mode of state formation. One is, in Grillo's words, through the "politicization of ethnicity" (the transformation of an ethny into a nation-state typical of Central and Eastern Europe); the other is through the "ethnicization of the polity," when a state molds its population into a nation through public education and a drawn-out process of assimilation.[23] This pattern was prevalent in Western Europe, although it was not unknown in Eastern Europe, for example in Hungary in 1848-1918.

This dichotomy allows Anthony Smith to distinguish between the nation as a natural (that is, ethnic) unit and a political construct. He argues that the ethnic nation is an "ancient historical and cultural entity," but nation "as the sole basis for politics and government" is an entirely modern phenomenon.[24]

Both processes, the politicization and the state-imposed ethnicization, have been the most powerful agents of political and social change in the last two hundred years. They have, by means of nationalist ideology, completely transformed the political map of the world.

But what is nationalism? "Nationalism," wrote Gellner, "is primarily a political principle which holds that the political and the national unit should be congruent."[25] (By "national" he means "ethnic.")

Political nations then—and this is highly paradoxical—appear only in the age of nationalism, not the other way around. Before, there existed numerous ethnic categories, ethnic communities, and ethnoreligious groups, but no nations as such. It was nationalism that brought forth nations as political constructs. This does not mean, however, that ethnonationalist *sentiments* were lacking in earlier epochs. What was lacking was the ideology of nationalism.

Why did the transformation occur? Its roots in Western Europe, where it had originated, go back to the establishment and consolidation of the highly centralized absolutist states. These states needed a language fully comprehensible to all. Only standardized education—which also implied a streamlined central bureaucracy and administration—could assure the spreading of such a language. As printing gained and Latin lost, the previously unified European cultural continuum (only of the elite, of course) was segmented or, as Benedict Anderson put it, the "unified fields of exchange and communications below Latin and above the spoken vernacular" split into closed fields of communication (in the Deutschian sense), circumscribed by the literary languages based on closely related groups of vernacular dialects.[26]

This happened as early as 1539 in France (the decree of Villers-Cotteret ensuring the use of French for administrative purposes) and then slowly spread east- and southward (in Austria, for example, German as the language of government administration was introduced by Joseph II in 1784).[27]

The spread of vernacular languages, facilitated by printing, was further enhanced by the hardening of the frontiers. Earlier, they were porous and permeable, but the centralized state turned them into the linear barriers we know today.[28]

Finally, the concept of time changed as well. In medieval Europe, wrote Barbara Tuchman, "time, calendar, and history were reckoned by the Christian scheme.... Current events were recorded in relation to religious holidays and saints' days.... Hours of the day were named for the hours of prayer."[29] In other words, time was "repetitive, circular and suffused with Christian symbolism." With the Reformation this concept of time changed; it lost its circular character and acquired a linear progression. A person, according to Benedict Anderson, turned into a "sociological organism moving calendrically through homogeneous time."[30] The "script language, monarchy, temporality in which cosmology and history were indistinguishable,"[31] all changed.

Anderson sees the origins of national consciousness in the interplay of decreasing linguistic diversity, technological development (book printing), and capitalism that created monoglot mass readership. The result was an ethnocultural segmentation. As Gellner has pointed out, "when social conditions make for standardized, homogeneous, centrally sustained high cultures pervading entire populations, a situation arises in which well-defined educationally sanctioned and unified cultures constitute very nearly the only kind of unit with which men willingly and often ardently identify. The cultures now seem to be the natural repositories of political legitimacy. Only then does it come to appear that any defiance of their boundaries by political units constitutes a scandal."[32]

Of all social entities, except the family, ethnies seem the most encompassing and enduring because ethnicity works on two levels, communal and personal. On the communal level, it creates, as Cynthia Enloe pointed out, bonds of shared culture, fundamental beliefs, and values that differentiate right from wrong, define rules of conduct, and set goals and expectations. And on the personal level ethnicity gives an individual a sense of belonging; it positions him in society and the universe. When "social relations become complex and impersonal, ethnic identity may be grasped tenaciously. It is a familiar and reassuring anchor in a time of turbulence and uncertainty."[33] This is the secret of its success. It is certainly not enough that ethnic groups are biologically self-perpetuating or that they have a division of labor—many groups do. What matters is that they "share clusters of beliefs and values . . . interwoven with a community's historic past."[34] That is why, says Enloe, Catholics in Ulster are an ethnic (or ethnoreligious) community while those in the United States are not. In other words, Catholics in Northern Ireland are a tribe; those in America are not.

The fact that members of an ethnic community share clusters of beliefs and values means that ethnicity is a collection of codes, often incomprehensible to the outsiders. These codes turn ethnicity into "closed fields of communication" (a phrase coined by Karl Deutsch). In his opinion, the shared code and values permit an ethnic group to interpret its history in terms of a shared fate. This process involves "storage, recall, transmission, recombination and reapplication of a relatively wide ranges of information, [such as] memories, symbols, habits, and operating preferences," wrote Deutsch. "A larger group of persons linked by such complementary habits and facilities of communication we may call a people."[35] That is why ethnic groups sharing the same space—such as Bosniaks, Croats, and Serbs in Bosnia— see things from a radically different perspective. The same event evokes totally different memories. What counts is not the "presence or absence of any single factor, but merely the presence of sufficient communication facilities with enough complementarity to produce the overall result."[36]

However, complementarity and communication typify relations in virtually all stable social groups. "Ethnic complementarity, the complementarity that makes a people, can be readily distinguished by its relatively wide range from the narrow vocational complementarity which exists among members of the same profession . . . or vocational group . . . in their childhood memories, in courtship, marriage, and parenthood, in their standards of beauty, their habits of food and drink, in games and recreations (engineers or stamp collectors) are far closer to mutual communication and understanding with their countrymen than with their fellow specialists in other countries."[37]

***

Regionalism is very similar to ethnicity and nationhood and is frequently confused with them. Even specialists often find it difficult to distinguish between the two. This is because the inhabitants of a given region may have all the characteristics of an ethnic group—unique origin, group history, a sense of destiny, cultural individuality, solidarity—and yet fail to consider themselves an ethnic group.

This does not mean that regionalism cannot generate a passionate attachment much like ethnicity. Basically, a "region" refers to a category while an ethnic group "is a type of community."[38] A region is a more or less compact area with a distinct culture, economy, and ecology that mark it off from other parts of the country. Perhaps, the clue lies in aspirations.

Regionalist tendencies appear when the region's inhabitants want to achieve political autonomy; that is, when they want a "change in the political, economic and cultural relations between their region and central powers *within the framework of the existing state.*"[39] Regionalism does not demand independence. When it does, it becomes nationalism. That was the transition attempted by the American South in 1860.

Regionalism is usually exacerbated by an unequal structural relationship between the center and the region, especially in the presence of clear cultural differences and an economic disparity between the center and the periphery. Such disparity inevitably fuels resentment whether the disparity is favorable or unfavorable to the region. Underdeveloped regions may feel exploited by the center while more developed ones may feel that they are thwarted by the center, that their wealth is being siphoned off for the benefit of underdeveloped regions, as was the case in Croatia, Slovenia, Estonia, Latvia, and to some extent Catalonia. In other words, any difference in economic development may generate tensions.

Often, nationalist and regionalist demands coexist, overlap, or are superimposed on each other, as is the case with the Northern League in Italy.

***

If we correlate the distinction between region and ethny with Paul Brass's sequence, then the region corresponds to the ethnic category while an ethny implies ethnic community.

Regional identity is either "narrower" or "wider" than ethnic or national identity. In some countries (Germany, Italy, Spain) many regions are culturally distinct and have a strong sense of regional individuality. Often, they were independent polities in the past and continue to retain memories of their ethnopolitical distinctiveness. Normans and Gascons in France cannot be confused with Bretons; or Venetians with German-speaking Tyroleans; or Andalusians with Catalans.

Wider regions such as Scandinavia, Iberia, or the Balkans may also develop a common identity which does not, however, preclude intraregional fighting, as the tragedies in Bosnia and Karabakh prove all too clearly.

Regional identity seldom conflicts with national identity because it operates either above (supra-regional) or below it (within the state). Only when a regional group comes to perceive itself as a nationality or retains vivid memories of an independent existence in the past may a contradiction develop.

But the trend may go in the opposite direction as well, toward a passionate identification with the larger nation of which the region is a part.

R. Lepsius showed how a sociological group can shift to extreme nationalism under pressure of the "macrosocial system upon the group's micropolitical culture and social forms."[40] Much the same goes for regional groups, particularly when the pressure affects a group that determines the region's life patterns and sets the tone, like farmers in interwar Schleswig-Holstein. Using research by R. Haeberle, Lepsius showed how the destruction of farmer-dominated regionalism plunged the region into extremes of German nationalism.

But most regionalists are not extremists. They are against the rigid centralization and stifling bureaucracy endemic in a nation-state. Like many ethnic minorities they simply want more regional power.

Petrella lists several ingredients necessary to the development of regionalism: the presence of a cultural identity or a set of markers perceived and experienced as nationhood (he means "peoplehood"); a distinct dialect; the deficiency of the regional politico-institutional status; the difference in the level of economic development with the core area, whether positive or negative; and the autonomous or dependent nature of the economic development.[41]

One way to understand regionalism is within the context of nested identity. It is a step on a ladder that leads from ethnic category to ethnic community (and on to nationhood, if the ladder is followed to the last step). One can also see it in terms of the point of reference: while members of an ethny see it in reference to other ethnies, members of a regional group see it as part of a larger whole, usually a nation-state.

RACIAL IDENTITY

Race would seem to be a prime candidate for collective identity formation. Yet, there is no agreement among anthropologists and sociologists as to what constitutes a race.

I have already mentioned Ashley Montagu, who denied the existence of race altogether.[42] He preferred to see racial differences in terms of cline clusters (a cline is a "graded series of morphological or physiological differences exhibited by a group of related organisms"[43]), or, to put it simply, a grab bag of physiological traits. He reasoned that it is often impossible to indicate with any degree of precision where one race ends and another one begins because various traits—and genes—are encountered over large, often discontinuous, areas. It is the degree of gene concentration that changes, he argued, not the presence or absence of a specific gene.[44]

Not everyone agrees with Montagu. For those anthropologists who do not deny its existence, race is a means of distinguishing between phenotypically diverse populations.

Whatever the scientific verdict of the day, there is little doubt in the popular mind that race exists. Clusters of clines are reified into a "real thing" and, as a social construct, play a number of crucial social roles. And what is perceived as real becomes socially real, if only in the perceptions of the members of multiracial societies.

In some respects race is similar to ethnicity, but it is a less exclusive category. In the Old World, races consist of many ethnies, while very few ethnies include members of more than one race. (This may be changing as recent African and Asian immigrants are integrated into the host European societies, and their children assimilate into the indigenous ethnies.)

In the New World the situation is reversed. Most (political) nations in the Americas have a wide range of racial types but few primary ethnies, except for various Native American tribes. These tribes, which can be placed at various points on the Brass continuum, are often intermixed with other races in all possible combinations.

We can see the difference between racial prejudice and ethnoreligious intolerance if we compare prejudice against Jews and Blacks. "The dominant group is intolerant of those whom it can define as anti-social, while it holds race prejudice against those whom it can define as sub-social," wrote Oliver Cox. "Thus we are ordinarily intolerant of Jews but prejudiced against Negroes. In other words, the dominant group or ruling class does not like the Jew at all, but it likes the Negro in his place. To put it in still another way, the condition of its liking the Jew is that he cease being a Jew and voluntarily become like the generality of society, while the condition of its liking the Negro is that he cease trying to become like the generality of society and remain contentedly a Negro. . . . A Jewish pogrom is not exactly similar to a Negro lynching. In a pogrom the fundamental motive is the extermination of the Jew; in a lynching, however, the motive is that of giving the Negro a lesson in good behavior."[45] Although Cox unjustifiably narrows prejudice to the ruling class—it can be found in all social strata—in principle this distinction applies to any interethnic and/or religious intolerance and racial prejudice.

As a rule, race is not an independent social variable. It is usually combined with caste and ethnicity (with "ethclass" in mind, should we introduce the concept of "racecaste" or "raceclass"?). It often plays a major role, especially if phenotypical differences hinder integration. From this angle, racism is but "a special case of ethnic sentiment using phenotype as an ethnic marker."[46] In fact, some social scientists, Cynthia Enloe, for example, do regard race as a subspecies of ethnicity.[47]

In stratified multiracial societies, particularly those in the New World, where race is a major determinant of the caste hierarchy, each racial caste is defined as a social group with unique hereditary characteristics. However, as a primary marker, race is unreliable. Unless racial stratification is unusually rigid, miscegenation creates an ever increasing number of mixed-race off-spring within a few generations, and differences begin to fade. That is why an apartheid society such as old South Africa had to set up a complex system of racial denomination and identification, which eventually collapsed under its own weight.[48]

Like ethnic nationalism, racism functions as a defensive mechanism of the in-group. Both emphasize the unique origins of the collectivity, its culture, and its cohesiveness. But the unit of attachment is completely different: nationalism operates within a system of states while racism operates within a hierarchy of castes within the same multiracial society. (In that sense, Nazism was bilevel: it operated as both extreme nationalism and racism.)

Anthony Smith noted the proliferation of nationalisms and the paucity of racisms.[49] It seems that it simply reflects the great number of ethnies capable of generating (ethno)nationalism and the relatively small number of phenotypes that lend themselves to racial categorization. But as a motor for extremist movements both can be deadly.

Another distinction noted by Smith is that nationalism politicized the cultural exclusivity of ethnocentrism. In doing so it modernized ethnic prejudice by giving it an ideological foundation and an organizational structure. Racism, on the contrary, disregarded cultural markers, except as secondary binders to keep various strata separate, and elevated instead ethnocentrism's physical prejudices.[50] In the process, it tried to give them a theoretical basis.

A movement that combines both strands, racial and cultural exclusivity, is also possible. Such is the "négritude," a Black racial nationalism, that originated in the former French colonies. In a sense, it resembles the "Pan" movements of yesterday, the Pan-Germanism, Pan-Slavism and Pan-Touranianism, but here the binder is race, not language (actually, all "Pan" movements had a racial component, but their racialism was based on a misconception since all members of the Germanic and Slav—but not Touranian!—ethnies belonged to the same race).

Similar racial nationalisms arose in various countries of Latin America (*indianismo* in Peru and *serranismo* in Brazil, for example), often as a reaction to the integrative statist political nationalisms imposed by the creole elites. Such movements split Latin American nationalisms in two, creating complex bilevel nationalisms.

Africa even has trilevel ones: tribal, statal, and continental, many with a strong racial component. The last serves as the ideological foundation for a Pan-African collective identity based on race. But it differs from négritude in that Pan-Africanism includes only African Blacks, while négritude accepts all Blacks wherever they live.

Finally, in Black separatists in the United States we have a nationalistic movement based on race. In terms of ideological contents it fits within the mold of a typical nationalist movement and is a mirror image of the White supremacists.

To sum up our discussion of racial identity, in multiracial societies, race serves basically the same functions as ethnicity. It preserves group identity, unites and delimits the group, and serves to mobilize its members. The last is particularly potent: in the current ideological climate race easily turns into a vehicle of group mobilization. We know of many political movements based on race.

Race can also facilitate a group's transformation into a tribe because it can function as an entity-forming binder, one that creates a unit characterized by self-reproduction, the division of labor, and a boundary maintenance mechanism. The binder can function even if it used to be imposed from the outside (in the case of discriminated-against racial minorities).

Racial tribes can, in principle, form viable states. This happened in fact in Haiti, where the Black and Mulatto population exterminated the Whites and established an all-Black republic. And in South Africa, local Whites may eventually succeed in carving out a White homeland. However, since race is a more inclusive category than ethnicity, states based on (multiethnic) races are likely to disintegrate into their ethnic components, unless these components are completely intermixed, as Black slaves and their descendants had been in Haiti. Thus, a White homeland in South Africa, if it is established, is likely to subdivide into an Anglo and Boer subunits (although strategic and safety considerations may prevent their separation), while a Black entity may fissure into Zulu, Xhosa, and Tswana statelets. In short, race as a foundation for state creation is inherently unstable, unless the racial group also happens to be monoethnic.

CLASS AND CASTE

With class we enter the realm of constructed, man-made identities. These, and not the nations, are the true "imagined communities."

When we talk about "class," we should make a distinction between the "social class," defined economically and socially, and what Oliver Cox calls "political class," which is an entity based on social class that is fully conscious of itself and is "preoccupied with devices for controlling the state."[51] (Cox calls it "political class," but I would rather call it an "ideological," "mobilized," or "politicized" class because in contemporary American usage "political class" may be equivalent to the "ruling class" or the "politically active elite.")

By definition, says Cox, "the political [ideological] class may become 'class-conscious'; social classes, on the other hand, cannot be."[52] This distinction is close to the Marxist distinction between the class "in itself" and "for itself." This may become rather confusing, so I propose the following division: (1) a *social class* is merely a social stratum distinguished from others by income and status; (2) a *self-aware class* is a class conscious of its collective identity; and (3) an *ideological* class is a self-aware class with a will to power. When compared to Brass's ethnic continuum, social class would be equivalent to the ethnic category, self-aware class would be similar to ethnic community or tribe, and ideological class would correspond to an ethny engaged in the politics of nationalism. Marxism, then, is class nationalism (a point made by many scholars and observers, from Reston to Paul Johnson).

Perhaps the simplest (as if anything in this exploration could be simple) way to distinguish class from other social groups is by treating it as a purely economic category. From this point of view, class is reduced to a function of its economic interests and relations.

Even here at least two basic approaches are possible. According to Marx, class is determined by its relationship to the means of production. "The owners merely of labor-power, owners of capital, and land-owners . . . in other words, wage-laborers, capitalists and landowners, constitute then three big classes of modern society based upon the capitalist mode of production."[53]

Or, if we follow Max Weber and introduce status into the equation, we can define class as a social stratum whose members share status and economic interests vis-a-vis other classes of a given society. In Weber's view, "the development of status is essentially a question of stratification resting upon usurpation . . . which is the normal origin of almost all status honor."[54]

This definitional shift in emphasis to status and stratification has been marked in Western sociology, including American. Lloyd Warner, for example, reduced class to "two or more orders of people who are believed to be, and are accordingly ranked by the members of the community, in socially superior and inferior positions."[55] Whatever definition of class we adopt, in the last 150 years educated Westerners have displayed a tendency to explain almost any social conflict, including ethnic, through the paradigm of class. Robert Dahl wrote that "a preoccupation with class conflict and often an articulated assumption even among sophisticated social theorists that classes are somehow the 'real' basis of differences in an industrial society to which all others are 'ultimately' reducible, has tended to deflect attention from other differences that give rise to durable subcultures into which individuals are socialized: these are differences in religion, language, race, or ethnic group, and region."[56] The reason, according to Nagata, is that "ethnic differences are somehow considered to be more 'primitive,' more basic and even more 'irrational' than those of class." Conversely, "class divisions . . . [are deemed to] represent more 'advanced' stages of social development"[57] and are, therefore, implicitly preferable.

Marxism is (or should we say "was"?) particularly prone to this ailment. It has a tendency to reduce ethnic and racial conflicts to a symptom of the underlying economic relationships and contradictions of which class is the real expression. But orthodox Marxism was not alone in this economism. Max Weber, Ralf Dahrendorf, and many others also stressed class at the expense of all other collectivities. They postulated that since classes form part of a hierarchical stratified whole, the perception of similar interests by members of a class creates self-awareness. And similar values and life styles reinforce class cohesiveness, enabling class to play a distinct role in society and social conflict.

Even in Marxist circles, however, the relentless emphasis on the economic aspects of class, at the expense of all other parameters, did not escape criticism. Harold Wolpe, for example, argued that Marxism should dispense with the economistic conceptions of class, which is like suggesting that the Catholic doctrine dispense with immaculate conception. He believed that "race, under determinant conditions, becomes interiorised in the class struggle,"[58] and that workers may be "mobilized around interests defined in gender, religious or racial terms." In other words, groups characterized by racial, ethnic, and certain other parameters could be transformed, under certain conditions, into strata resembling and functioning like class. (This brings to mind Milton Gordon's "ethclass." Gurr calls it "ethnoclass,"[59] which is probably more euphonious.) But, while he rejected economic determinism, Wolpe still regarded the mode of production as fundamental and in that sense did not stray too far from classical Marxism.

Others, such as John Rex, concede that "the attempt to conceptualize [a multiracial social system] in classical Marxist terms is hopelessly inadequate."[60] His solution is to sever ethnic and racial conflict from class defined in the strictly Marxist sense. Perhaps, all one can say is that, to borrow from Immanuel Wallerstein, in the context of the world economic system race may become congruent with class or class may be ethnicized.[61] (And the same goes for race and religion.) Of course, one does not have to be a Marxist to agree with that.

When applied to race and ethnicity, Marxist analysis asserts that racism and ethnic prejudice provide the ideological basis for exploitation but that the prejudice itself is based on class. In other words, there are no ethnic or racial problems as such, only structural deformities built into the capitalist society. Implicit in this argument is an assumption that solving class problems will cure all other social ills, including ethnic, racial, and religious conflict.

Perhaps, this preoccupation with class may be explained by the fact that capitalism originated in societies that were either monoethnic, such as Holland, or in which ethnic minorities were politically, culturally, and economically so insignificant that they were not "part of the picture," as was the case in other Western countries. (On second thought, the Irish question in Britain and the explosive nature of racial relations in the United States should have justified a closer look at ethnicity and race in these societies. Why had they not?) In these bourgeois societies class assumed the kind of importance unknown in multiethnic, feudal societies elsewhere. Geoffrey Gorer argues that in England class is more important than ethnicity precisely for this reason, i.e., that peoples of the Celtic fringe are not part of the English community, of the English "we," and thus have little place in the English mental landscape.[62]

Although class and ethny are independent in origin and analytically distinct, in practice they often merge or coexist in a dynamic interrelationship, with one or the other predominating. Social actors may have all kinds of options to emphasize and choose either one depending on the situation. In the contemporary American context, for example, minority students may stress their low-income status when applying for student loans but their race when applying for jobs in equal opportunity companies. (Here we succumb to the functionalist approach.)

I have already mentioned Katherine Verdery's book on Transylvanian villagers who "used the language of ethnic conflict to comprehend and elucidate a complex social reality." Likewise, some (Western) intellectuals, on a different epistemological level, use the language of class conflict for the same purpose. It is not surprising. When we attempt to understand complex social reality we tend to grasp at a convenient paradigm that explains everything. The more it seems to be able to explain, the better. Unfortunately, such all-encompassing paradigms inevitably simplify the issue(s) and make us disregard or devalue other important parameters.

***

The concept of "status" is helpful in understanding the notion of "caste." In Western Europe, once early medieval society had stabilized, status was translated into a legal privilege reinforced by the economic power. And when status distinctions are guaranteed not only by laws and conventions but also by ritual, a caste results.[63]

There is no agreement about the term itself, however. On the one hand, many Indianists prefer to reserve its use only to castes in the Indian subcontinent. Most other anthropologists and social scientists, starting with Kroeber, Warner, and Myrdal, were willing to see caste as a widespread phenomenon or at least to apply the term to other societies as well. Indian caste is characterized by three features: heredity, endogamy, and restrictions on commensality.[64] The traditional caste system "consisted of a number of relatively closed status groups arranged in a hierarchical order, each group being associated with a specific set of privileges and disabilities. The status groups, i.e., castes, were kept in their respective positions by religious and moral sanctions, division of labor, distinct kinship affiliations, and political authority."[65] We may add that "caste membership is immutable . . . [with] no sanctioned method of mobility."[66]

The picture is further complicated by the fact that the Indian caste comprises two concepts: *varna* and *jati*. The four *varnas* (Brahman, Kshatriya, Vaishya, and Sudra) are categories that correspond to the Westerner's idea of caste. (Incidentally, the Sanskrit term *varna* means "color," an indicator that Indian caste is probably racial in origin. In fact, higher castes do tend to be lighter in skin color and more "European" in some other features such as the width of the nose. However, *varna* also means "appearance, exterior, color, kind, species, caste."[67])

The *jati* (the word means "birth" and implies "birth, position, rank, family, descent, kind, species"[68]) are subcastes distinguished by "a particular style of life . . . subject to certain duties and disabilities."[69] Rules of commensality and endogamy that keep castes separate are practiced on the more intimate level of *jati* although they are also enforced on the *varna* level. In the American context, not only would a caste system prevent Blacks and Whites from eating and fornicating with each other, it would also prevent White computer programmers from dating and eating with White stockbrokers. In practice it would mean that Irish baseball players would be able to socialize exclusively with other Irish baseball players. What's more, no one else would be allowed to play baseball professionally.

If we reject the strict India-only application of the caste terminology we may, along with Kroeber and Myrdal, give it a wider interpretation, regarding caste as any rigid social group. In this looser interpretation, a caste is characterized by "endogamy, ascriptive membership by birth and for life [i.e., hereditary status], and a ranking in a hierarchy . . . of other such groups."[70]

The estate system of European preindustrial society was somewhat similar to caste, although much simpler. According to Cox, six status groups could be discerned among the Merovingians. And in later medieval society only three estates—clergy, nobility, and peasantry—were generally recognized.[71] The system of estates roughly corresponds to the *varna* divisions in the traditional Indian system, although it is much simplified.

An estate is basically a group of people with the same status recognized by law and custom. Each group has its rights, duties, privileges, and obligations, publicly recognized and enforced by public authority, often by law. However, the estate system, at least as it was practiced in feudal Europe, was usually much less stringent than caste. "... although the nobility guarded its rights and privileges with considerable jealousy, it never attained the solidarity of a caste."[72] Even at its most rigid, the system allowed some mobility, an infiltration of talented or lucky individuals into the higher strata, especially the clergy.

Caste does not allow such laxity. The only advancement possible in a caste system is the change in the status of the entire (sub)caste, usually within the wider range of each of the four major subdivisions. Such advancement is made possible only by strict observance of all the rules imposed by religion and society. (Although an advancement of a *jati*, through financial success and manufacture of fictitious genealogy, has not been unknown.) Thus, advancement in a caste system, based on the entire profession, serves to reinforce the system, while advancement in the estate system, predicated upon the individual, was bound to destroy it. That is why the caste system in India survived into the twentieth century while the estate system in Europe had disintegrated several centuries ago.

If we compared class and caste we would find that class is more inclusive than *jati* but narrower than *varna*. But even within the *jati* great disparities of wealth are possible and sometimes common, depending on one's professional success. Until very recently, however, the emergence of class solidarity in societies of Hindu culture was impeded by caste strictures. Caste leads to extreme "cantonization" of society.

Ethnicity and race, where present, add yet another dimension. Like class and ethnicity, caste and ethnicity can fuse. But where class is often ethnicized, in India at least ethnicity has been "casteized." By origin, Indian castes can be divided into two major groups: one based on occupation (Blunt calls them "functional castes"), the other on ethnic origin ("tribal castes").[73] Tribal castes are former ethnic groups (tribes) turned into castes. It is a rare instance where the nonethnic element proved to be stronger. (The case seems exceptional, but it is possible that this process was operational only in premodern society. In modern India caste seems to be giving in to ethnicity.)

In societies in which caste was the usual pattern of stratification diverse communities could live in close proximity without ever mixing with each other, a very good example of a boundary maintenance mechanism. That is one of the main reasons, according to Senart, that "Hindu society has given rise to no state which is comparable even with the narrow government of the cities of antiquity, still less with our modern state."[74] And Risley observed that "there is consequently no national type and no nation or even nationality in the ordinary sense of the words."[75] (By "ordinary" he clearly means "Western.")

Status segregation of castes differs from purely ethnic segregation in that the caste structure transforms the vertical separation of ethnically segregated groups into a lateral system of super- and subordination. A caste differs from a tribe. A tribe usually has a territory, a true caste does not. (Although in India many castes, especially those that are tribal in origin, are indeed territorialized. They also have a different geographical distribution.) A tribe is socially complete, for it comprises people of every social rank; a caste is not but is often subdivided into numerous subcastes of different status. A tribe is normally a political entity; a caste, unless politicized (like the "untouchables"), is seldom so.[76]

Caste has two peculiar aspects. First, it imposes strict control on social interaction with members of other castes by limiting intercaste contact and subjecting whatever contact is allowed to strict rules, regulating even the extent of physical proximity. Second, its emphasis on occupation is peculiarly modern and can, under certain condition, be integrated into modern society. However, "the rigidity and ossified status of a traditional caste leave little room for other forms of stratification or social ranking where caste is predominant."[77]

Any of the above social categories—class, caste, or estate—can be ethnicized, especially through conquest and a subsequent imposition of the alien group as a new upper class, caste, or even estate. But this may happen even without a conquest, as had indeed happened in Flanders in the first half-century of Belgian independence.

In a contest of ethny and class, ethny usually wins. Why? Ernest Gellner offers the following (functionalist) explanation: when rapid economic and social change removes people from roles and positions they had once occupied (if they move to town, for example), they will be unable and unwilling to base their identity on what they do and their social relationships with others (because they are usually placed at the bottom of the social hierarchy without any validation accorded by tradition). In other words, they are deracinated and humiliated. Such people eagerly fasten on to new "portable" identities, such as language, religion, and skin color—in short, ethnic and racial markers.[78] If, as often happens in highly stratified societies, members of an ethnic or racial minority find themselves consigned to low-paying, low-status jobs at the bottom of the social pyramid and concentrate in the slum areas of large industrial agglomerations, they may develop into a permanent underclass with its own subculture of poverty, its own slang and "blueprint for living," and, occasionally, even its own dialect. This stratum will then fuse certain characteristics of ethnicity, class, and caste to the extent that would make it impossible to separate either aspect of its collective identity.

We saw earlier how class easily lends itself to political mobilization. The same applies to caste although, perhaps, not to the same extent. (Cox noted that "the caste is a potential interest group which may become organized for political action."[79])

Caste and, to a smaller degree, class can also serve as vehicles for tribalization, in the sense that they help to create identities and collectivities based on class and caste. But there is no direct correlation between one's ideological convictions and class consciousness. Jules Romains describes a young Parisian worker at the turn of the century who is a socialist by inclination and has no social interaction with the upper classes, except his "patron," yet in whose consciousness socialist convictions and feeling of belonging to the working-class tribe are completely divorced: "His socialist convictions make Edmond strongly believe that classes and deep class divisions do exist. . . . But it is above all an abstract notion. With Edmond, it probably does not correspond to what a commoner of yesteryear believed: that there existed two distinct races."[80]

Class—but probably not caste—can serve as a foundation for state formation. The former Soviet Union and other communist states give us an example of class-based statehood and even class-based nationalism. Here we even have a dominant class, the proletariat, akin to the dominant ethny in multiethnic societies. This class, with its avant-garde, the Communist party, at the helm, leads—paternalistically in theory, oppressively in practice—the peasantry and the toiling intelligentsia (which play the part of ethnic minorities). We even have a pseudoethnic class enemy: the bugaboo of the world bourgeoisie. (There are, of course, dissenting voices denying the existence of class in the former Soviet Union altogether. Alexander Zinoviev once said that there were only two classes in the USSR: the bosses and the masses.[81])

Conversely, can we look at bourgeois societies as multiclass societies equivalent to multiethnic ones? Probably, but here class is nonterritorial, somewhat like the secondary ethnies of the New World.

Status, expressed through caste, can also serve as an entity-forming agent. In a sense, the traditional society of India can be interpreted as a dictatorship based on caste, much like the Soviet Union was, theoretically at least, a proletarian dictatorship. Can we then speak of Brahmin "nationalism"? That is an interesting proposition although this may be stretching the analogy too far. (It will be fascinating to trace the interaction of caste with the nationalism of various ethnic groups in modern India.)

Finally, both class and caste are capable of self-reproduction, the division of labor (in the case of caste, only on the level of *varna,* not *jati),* and maintenance of boundary mechanisms. Both thus lend themselves to mobilization and tribalization.

Earlier, we have seen how computer programmers can be ethnicized. By the same token they can also be transformed into a class or caste. Already computer operators and technicians are perceived as a high-tech proletariat. All we need is a theoretician who would convince progressive intellectuals that computer operators are being exploited and that they need to take the means of production into their own hands. A few activists will then organize a liberation movement and a party that will revolutionize the toiling computer operators. Along the way there may be some rightist deviations on the part of the better paid computer technicians, but there is nothing a few comprehensive purges would not cure. So in principle there is no reason why a dictatorship of computer operators cannot be established.

Those same computer operators can be transformed into a caste. All they need is a strict enforcement of endogamy—computer operators marry only within the profession! Children born to computer operators should be assured hereditary status, that is, they will be counted as computer operators from birth. Together with programmers (the highest caste), technicians (one step lower) and data entry people (below operators, the lowest caste among computer castes) computer operators will form part of a complex stratified hierarchy that will match—well, almost—anything India has produced. With time, rules on commensality and connubium will be established, dress codes will be elaborated (the highest caste wears ties, the two highest cannot wear jeans, only the lowest caste can wear T-shirts, etc.), new customs and habits will develop, along with drinking preferences ("Internet Sauvignon") and linguistic specificities ("he abended" for "he died") and so on. . . . But let's get back to the remaining collective identities.

GENDER

Gender, historically, has been a personal, not a collective, identity. Few features are as permanent, for most people, as gender. It is assigned from conception and is retained, with very few exceptions, until death.

In most societies both genders share the same cultural values. As a result, they also share the same field of communication. For that reason, specificities of gender cannot be considered a marker or a binder, in the same sense as ethnic diacritica. Also, gender bonds are usually subordinated to other cross-cutting linkages, such as language and religion, which makes solidarity and organization based exclusively on gender extremely difficult.

In virtually all societies cultural traits are distributed across both genders although there are minor variations in speech patterns, choice of vocabulary, dress codes, and accepted modes of behavior (the last two can be quite rigid).

Modern Western societies are increasingly unisex, especially in matters of fundamental equality such as access to education and various occupations. In traditional societies gender differentiation is usually much more pronounced. Many of these societies separate and segregate genders. In a few extreme cases the separation may have been almost complete, as in some societies in the Pacific that supposedly kept men and women on separate islands and allowed them to get together only once a year for the purpose of procreation, the exact meaning of "sexual congress." (One encounters a similar story in Greek mythology: the Amazons.) There one can see certain aspects of incipient ethnicity: marked differences in language, religious practices, social organization, and customs, even territoriality. But such situations are—and were, even in the past—extremely rare.

Among contemporary societies none go farther in gender segregation than the fundamentalist Muslim societies such as Iran or Saudi Arabia. There each gender is virtually a separate caste, at least outside the home. But even there women's subset is inseparable from that of men's: both sexes live together, within the same household, rear children, manage their affairs, socialize within the same set (although the women's set is much more restricted), and so on. Under such circumstances they can hardly develop a separate collective identity.

The creation of a female collective identity had to await the emergence of feminism which, in some of its forms, can be classified as gender nationalism.

One can find isolated persons who held "feminist" views long before feminism. Christine de Pisan (1364-1430?) was probably the first "ideological feminist."[82] As a more or less coherent intellectual position, however, feminism appeared in England some time in the seventeenth century (almost contemporaneously with ethnic nationalism!). It was "a conglomeration of precepts and a series of demands by women who saw themselves as a distinct sociological group and one that was completely excluded from the tenets and principles of the new society," wrote Juliet Mitchell. "As the new bourgeois man held up the torch against absolutist tyranny and argued for freedom and equality, the new bourgeois woman wondered why she was being left out."[83] "If all Men are born free," asked Mary Astell in 1700, "how is it that all Women are born slaves?"[84]

This line of reasoning was continued by subsequent generations of feminists and men who sympathized with women's plight: Mary Wollstonecraft's "A Vindication of the Rights of Woman," written in 1792 (two years earlier she had written "A Vindication of the Rights of Men"); Margaret Fuller's "Woman in the Nineteenth Century";[85] and John Stuart Mill's "The Subjection of Women" (published in 1869 but written a decade earlier).[86]

The language of class oppression and the philosophy of liberation provided a new mode for feminist conceptualization and greatly facilitated the spread of feminism. None other than Friedrich Engels described the subjection of women in terms of class: ". . . the first class oppression coincides with that of the female sex by the male."[87] Nor is it by accident that American feminism was born out of the abolitionist struggle,[88] while in the 1960s "women's groups developed out of the radical movements of the 1960s much as they did in the 1840s and 50s when women from the abolition and peace movements came to form their own organizations because men, in those very movements against oppression, retained sex-oppressive structures and behavior."[89]

Olive Banks divides the history of the feminist movement into four periods: Early Feminism (1840-70), a social movement for equality, influenced by the evangelical and socialist traditions; the Golden Years (1870-1920), a political movement for votes, with a strong moral(izing) undercurrent; then a forty-year intermission (1920-60), once full political equality seemed to have been achieved; and finally the liberation movement (from the late 1960s), characterized by radicalism and, in its extreme forms, rejectionism.[90] In other words, gender has experienced a transformation from gender category to gender community, in a transition similar to ethnic transformation.

It was in the last stage that some feminist radicals attempted tribalization based on gender, that is, they tried to create a collective female identity based on gender. Ironically, class and class-based ideology that had initially helped the women's movement now hindered it. When the women's liberation movement started in the late 1960s, "dislodging class from its previous centrality became one of the budding feminist's first tasks," wrote Anne Phillips.[91] "Class, we argued, must be shifted from the centre of the stage, for its language has denied the experience of women."[92]

For many British feminists, many of whom were socialists, practical experience with Marxist and labor organizations proved a major disappointment. They found the labor movement "brutal in its determination to maintain male power within the institutions and organizations of the working class."[93] As new historical research explored the position and the role of women in earlier epochs and in other societies, many feminists came to the conclusion that "sex [the author clearly means 'gender'] as a form of oppression [is] independent of social class. Indeed patriarchy, the oppression of women by men, [was] seen as not only predating capitalism but continuing after capitalism itself has been superseded [though it has not been superseded]."[94]

As they tried to forge a new gender-based identity, feminists discovered that other identities could not easily be discarded. In the words of a Black woman living in Britain, ". . . if you're a Black woman, you've got to begin with racism. It's not a choice, it's a necessity."[95] But their main problem was probably the refusal of most women to be tribalized, to see themselves as an entity opposed to men. In her research, Elizabeth Roberts found "little feeling among the majority of women interviewed that they or their mothers had been particularly exploited by men, at least not by working-class men. . . . In their interviews many women indicated their awareness of the limited horizons and opportunities of their lives, but were just as likely to associate their menfolk with this lack of choice."[96] In other words, most nonfeminist women refused to erect and maintain a boundary mechanism.

This did not prevent some feminist avant-garde from forging ahead. In 1971 men were excluded from the National Women's Liberation Conference in Britain (ostensibly, because they were disruptive; actually, because they disagreed with some radical anti-male speakers?); and the central office of the London Women's Liberation Workshop was closed to men three years later.[97]

In the United States, paradoxically, the major practical achievements, the Equal Pay Act of 1963[98] and the Civil Rights Act of 1964, occurred before the latest efflorescence of the feminist movement. The Civil Rights Act of 1964 was intended to deal with racial discrimination. The word "sex" was added by a Southern congressman in a last-ditch effort to kill the bill. The bill passed, and women got their equality by chance. However, the Equal Employment Opportunities Commission refused to enforce the sexual provisions of the act and this led to the formation of the National Organization for Women (NOW) in 1966.[99] Other feminist organizations appeared at the peak of the radical phase: the Women's Equity Action League was founded in 1968; the National Women's Political Caucus was founded in 1971.[100] But new organizations could not prevent the decline of radical feminism in the 1970s.[101] Tribalization failed. Why?

There are many reasons, not least the fact that women, despite their awareness of "womanhood," refuse to set themselves against their sons, brothers, fathers, and, yes, occasionally even husbands.

Another important reason is purely biological: the impossibility of procreation within one gender. Many social groups, even when they are biologically self-perpetuating, lack the division of labor. Gender is an exception: it lends itself to the division of labor but lacks the capacity for self-perpetuation.

Also, in the industrial and postindustrial societies, gender-based division of labor and the assignment of men and women to different slots in the job market are on the way out. Even the boundary mechanism between the genders seems to disintegrate (transvestites and transsexuals are the cutting edge of disintegration because they dispense with socially constructed gender altogether.) Thus, postindustrial society is destroying the wall separating the sexes. And this makes entity-formation based exclusively on gender ever more difficult. In that sense, feminism goes against the tide of the times.

SEXUAL ORIENTATION

The success of feminism proved that gender may serve as a reference group. In fact, it is a rigid category: although certain gender-specific diacritica, such as dress, mores, and manners, lend themselves to manipulation, oscillation is precluded for the vast majority of people. Thus, gender lacks the flexibility of situational ethnicity seen, for example, in Malaysia.

This may not be true for a small number of versatile transsexuals and transvestites who can assume personae of either gender. Bisexuals and those gays who can put on a straight appearance also display a degree of gender flexibility impossible for most individuals.

At the other end of the gender spectrum, among exclusively homosexual gays and lesbians whose identity and self-ascription are based primarily on sexual orientation, gender has the kind of rigidity prevalent among exclusive heterosexuals. The extremes meet.

For those who are exclusively homosexual and have opted for the so-called gay life style, the gay community serves as an in-group and functions as a field of communications in a way described by Karl Deutsch for an ethnic community.

Gay identity is another child of modernization, along with identities based on class and gender. Although some scholars claim that continuous homosexual subcultures have existed in some European countries since as early as the twelfth century,[102] their existence does not prove the existence of a gay identity. Until the nineteenth century, according to John D'Emilio, "in Western Europe and in the portions of North America populated by European settlers, men and women engaged in what we would describe as homosexual behavior, but neither they nor the society in which they lived defined persons as essentially different in kind from the majority because of their sexual expression. The absence of rigid categories called 'homosexual' and 'heterosexual' did not imply approval of same-sex eroticism. Men and women caught in such an act were severely punished, but their behavior was interpreted as a discrete transgression, a misdeed comparable to other sins and crimes such as adultery, blasphemy, and assault."[103] (England's "buggery statute" of 1533, for example, prescribed death for sodomy. As late as 1950 two states in the United States still classified sodomy as a felony. Only murder, kidnapping, and rape called for heavier sentences.[104]) "Earlier generations," continues D'Emilio, "would . . . have been puzzled by the categorization of a group of people on the basis of their erotic behavior."[105]

To acquire a collective dimension, homosexuality had to lose its character as a personal or psychological problem. This shift in the conceptualization of homosexuality occurred some time during the nineteenth century. "The person defined by society and by self through a primary erotic interest in the same sex—is a nineteenth-century invention."[106] "The label," writes D'Emilio, "applied not merely to particular sexual acts, as 'sodomite' once had, but to an entire person whose nature—acts, feelings, personality traits, even body type—was [supposed to be] sharply distinguishable from the majority of `normal' heterosexuals."[107] Thus, some time in the nineteenth century, gays ceased to be an "ethnic category" and became an "ethnic community" conscious of their collective identity.

Like women and American Blacks, gays faced the task of liberation. Their unfreedom was the defining element of their identity. As Harry Hay, one of the pioneers of gay liberation in the United States, put it, "[gays faced] the heroic objective of liberating one of our largest minorities from . . . social persecution."[108]

The years 1864-1935, according to John Lauritsen and David Thorstad, witnessed the early phase of the homosexual rights movement.[109] It was inaugurated by Karl Ulrichs, a Hannover lawyer, who opened the debate on homosexual rights in a book published in 1864.[110]

The early movement was an entirely European phenomenon. It centered on Germany, where the struggle for gay liberation was headed by the Wissenschaftlich-Humanitares Komitee (Scientific-Humanitarian Committee) founded in Berlin on May 15, 1897, by Magnus Hirschfeld, Max Spohr, and Erich Oberg.[111] At its peak in 1928-30 the World League for Sexual Reform numbered 130,000 members.[112] But the movement was destroyed by the Nazis, who killed it in Germany and throughout German-occupied Europe. The Institute for Sex Research in Berlin was sacked on May 6, 1933; many of its collections were destroyed and its books burned.[113]

As was mentioned earlier, the pogrom against European gays coincided with persecutions of gays in the Soviet Union. Initially, in December 1917, the Bolshevik government did away with all laws against homosexual acts.[114] Ten years later reaction set in. In 1928 homosexuality was decried as a "social peril" and abortions as "evil."[115] Marcuse believed that "as the Soviet state pressed for rapid industrialization, it installed the productivist/ reproductivist ethic favored by Victorian capitalists, which similarly aimed to create an expanding labor supply and disciplined work force."[116] Whether one accepts Marcuse's assessment or not, in 1934 the gay community in the Soviet Union was decimated. In January 1934 mass arrests of gays were carried out in Moscow, Leningrad, Kharkov, and Odessa.[117] And in March 1934 a law punishing homosexual acts with up to eight years imprisonment was adopted.[118]

With the suppression of the gay movement in Europe its center moved to North America, where a gay subculture "was evolving in American cities that would help to create a collective consciousness among its participants and strengthen their sense of identification with a group."[119] In 1924 the first gay group in the United States, the Society for Human Rights, was created.[120]

A wave of conservatism that later crested in McCarthyism undercut the beginnings of the gay movement in the United States. A 1949 *Newsweek* article titled "Queer People" characterized gays as "sex murderers."[121] And when a gay man was killed in 1954 by local hoodlums Miami newspapers "demand[ed] that the homosexuals be punished for tempting 'normals' to commit such deeds."[122]

In this atmosphere gay activists had to be extremely cautious. Still, the foundation of the Mattachine Society in Los Angeles in 1951[123] and the Daughters of Bilitis society in 1955[124] marked the beginning of the second phase in the gay struggle. These groups continued the nonconfrontational, educational style of the earlier period. All gay groups were still extremely small; as late as 1960 the Mattachine Society had only 230 members while Daughters of Bilitis membership stood at 110.[125] Perhaps the only difference was that the movement had many former Communists or fellow travellers who knew their Marx. "Their definition of homosexuals as a minority 'unaware' of its existence put the founders on more familiar ground and suggested to them an initial course of action. Their formulation resembled the Marxist distinction between a class 'in itself' and a class 'for itself'. . . (in the former case, workers constituted an objective social category; in the latter, they recognized their common interests). . . . According to Marxist theory, the transformation from one to the other made the working class a cohesive force able to fight on its own behalf. Homosexuals, too, were trapped by false consciousness, by a hegemonic ideology that labeled their eroticism an individual aberration."[126] But while early Marxists could spread their gospel among factory workers, gays were too dispersed and too much underground to allow for a concerted effort. By 1958-59 the movement retreated into respectability and adopted an accommodationist stance.[127]

The Civil Rights movement deeply affected gays, much as it affected feminists. "Inspired by the example of civil rights activists, the militant wing of the movement abandoned the accommodationist approach of the 1950s."[128] But there was also a qualitative change. Like the Black nationalists, "gay and lesbian veterans of the New Left movements no longer wanted to define themselves in terms left over to them by the heterosexist opposition; rather, they sought to build a new gay culture where gay people could be free. Civil rights and integration seemed like endless begging for the charity of liberals who conveniently ignored the everyday physical and psychological violence exerted by homophobic society."[129]

From 1965 there was a noticeable shift toward militancy and an increase in membership of gay organizations.[130] The change was particularly significant in San Francisco, where "new organizations took root within the bar subculture, and the movement, breaking out of its isolation, at last found influential allies [ministers] committed to work in its behalf. . . . Gay life in San Francisco had reached a qualitatively new stage in its evolution."[131] Even more important was the fact that politicians in San Francisco started courting the gay vote.[132]

The real watershed occurred on the night of June 27, 1969, when the New York police raided the Stonewall Inn, a gay bar in Greenwich Village.[133] (The area has a high concentration of gays, one of the few areas where they approached the "critical mass.") In the next two or three nights gays in Greenwich Village rioted and resisted. A month later, on July 31, 1969, the Gay Liberation Front was founded.[134]

Stonewall marked the beginning of gay tribalization. In D'Emilio's opinion, "the post-Stonewall era witnessed a significant shift in the self-definition of gay men and women. . . . [It saw] the creation of 'community' institutions. Gay men and lesbians formed their own churches, health clinics, counseling services, social centers, professional associations, and amateur sports leagues. [They created a] . . . distinctive cultural life. The subculture of homosexual men and women became less exclusively erotic. Gayness and lesbianism began to encompass an identity that for many included a wide array of private and public activities. Stonewall thus marked a critical divide in the politics and consciousness of homosexuals and lesbians. A small, thinly spread reform effort suddenly grew into a large, grassroots movement for liberation."[135]

From the very start, however, deep fissures between gay men and lesbians appeared within the movement. Many lesbian women were torn between their womanhood and their identity as homosexuals. As it often happens, outsiders decided the issue. Many lesbians were purged from NOW by Betty Friedan in 1970, in an attempt to fight the "lavender menace."[136] (Friedan was afraid that the women's movement would be mislabeled as "homosexual.") A little later, a growing dissatisfaction with gay male leadership and a more general distaste for gay male subculture led to the split with gay males. According to Barry Adam, lesbian separatism emerged in 1972-74. Like other nationalisms, it "embarked on synthesizing a transhistorical women's mythology that reordered the universe in terms of gender opposition."[137] Thus, both communities have become cognizant of their history and have developed, at least in the United States, social rituals, ceremonies, and public events (such as the Gay Pride Parade, now spreading to other countries) that have always characterized secondary ethnicity (defined as ethnic groups composed of people who had migrated as individuals, not as members of an organized community such as the Mormons, the Pentecostals, and so on).

Gayness is now perceived as a new (secondary) ethnicity, and militant gays are now demanding corporate recognition in a move parallel to the transmutation of an ethnic community into a nationality. (With amazing prescience, Proust depicted homosexuality "not as a few isolated individuals but as a social world." Gays became "'a race accursed, persecuted like Israel,' and finally, like Israel, 'under a mass opprobrium of undeserved abhorrence,' taking on mass characteristics, the physiognomy of a nation. 'They form in every land an Oriental colony in diaspora from Sodom', which leads Proust in pursuit of his analogy to Israel to imagine [but discount] a new Sodomite nation."[138])

Indeed, those gays who live in gay ghettoes immersed in the gay subculture(s) are a diaspora ethnic community of a kind. The step from life style to a way-of-life to a blueprint-for-living is not a very long one.

But even the most class conscious, *fur sich* gays and lesbians cannot overcome their inability to perpetuate themselves as a group. That has always been a major stumbling block on their way to tribalization. Collectively, all they can hope for is the status of a diaspora minority with all the disadvantages that such a status entails.

Science and technology may change the situation dramatically in two ways. The first would be if it became possible to detect the homosexual gene(s) in a foetus. A number of parents might then decide to abort homosexual foetuses, thus effectively putting an end to the homosexual community. This, however, may not be possible if the "homosexual radical" (according to Thorkil Vanggaard)[139] is present in all humans. If so, homosexuality is ineradicable. The second change would be the ability of homosexuals to procreate in vitro, in retro, or in an artificial uterus, which is becoming increasingly feasible, and thus develop into a self-perpetuating collectivity.

However, even if gays do coalesce into a self-procreating, self-perpetuating group, the heterosexual radical may prove to be equally ineradicable. In that case, homosexual parents may produce, to their great chagrin, heterosexual offspring who will opt for traditional life styles and a traditional identity.

In any case, the longer the gay and lesbian communities continue to exist as structured communities the more likely they are to reinforce their collective identity and establish boundary maintenance mechanisms similar to those delimiting ethnic groups. Then we may see a gay nationalism of which the Act Up movement could be a harbinger. And if the larger society turns less tolerant we may yet see a movement for the establishment of a gay polity.

To summarize, neither groups based on gender nor those based on sexual orientation can naturally reproduce themselves. Yet. But they do have boundary maintenance mechanisms and the potential for the division of labor. If they acquire reproductive capacities through artificial means we may see the emergence of entirely new pseudoethnic groups.

In retrospect, it is clear that both the feminist and the gay movements used liberation ideology and Marxist class concepts to create first social movements, then new collectivities.

Their history also proves that both groups can be mobilized and politicized. In terms of their communal development, gays and lesbians (though not heterosexual women) are in the process of advanced tribalization. Potentially—but this is a very remote possibility—these tribes can build polities of their own. If this proves to be the case, this may be the wonder of the next century.

AGE AND PROFESSION

Age is even less susceptible to the process of entity formation than gender. If gender is a given, for most of us, age is ever changing.

The nearly complete absence of age cleansing would seem to indicate that no collective identity has been based on this parameter. The killing of infants ordered by Herod is one of the few clear cases of age-based cleansing. But this was an anomaly, like the murder of beggars by Vlad the Dracul.

We will find more instances of cleansing if we turn to old age. Some "primitive" societies,[140] when resources were scarce, abandoned persons who reached a certain age when they changed camps, or forced them, by custom, to retire into the wilderness to await death.[141] Among these were Tasmanian islanders and some Eskimo groups.[142] This, however, was practiced sporadically and only in lean years, so it does not amount to a systemic cleansing. Rather, it was a safety valve that allowed society to let off the excess steam of relative overpopulation in times of scarcity.

In many primitive societies we do find generation-based social groups ("age sets" or "age grades") based on age, such as young bachelors, wise old men, young maidens, and so on. These age grades have distinct social roles and elaborate initiation ceremonies often associated with maturation passage rites (such as the Chisungu among the Bemba of Zambia)[143] that define them as a group and differentiate them from other age and sex groups. In short, these age grades serve as reference groups with some sort of boundary maintenance mechanism. This does not apply to modern societies, of course. As a closed grade, that is, as a social group, age is extinct in virtually all contemporary societies.

While many traditional societies are quite rigid in terms of age-defined roles, in most contemporary societies age by itself lacks structure, political organization, language, and virtually all other forms of collective identity. Minor differences such as variations in fashion and slang developed by each successive generation do not create a community.

Occasionally, particularly in the United States, generational cohorts such as the Baby Boomer or Sixties generation do acquire self-ascriptive characteristics, a common outlook and style, that turn them into semientities. What's more, many members of the Sixties generation display a deep attachment to their generation and its values vaguely reminiscent of the attachment to an in-group, even to an ethnicity. For these people age serves as a reference group that provides them with a sense of belonging and a collective identity replete with elaborate boundary markers (clothing, beads, haircuts, and so on) and boundary maintenance mechanisms. We now have the Disco Generation, Generation X, and, eventually, many others.

There is one thing, that may infuse age with an entity-forming potential: discontent. In the last two hundred years old age cohorts have been consistently losing status while younger cohorts and "professional affiliation" have gained. This is yet another consequence of modernization and increased social mobility. (On the other hand, the stress on achievement should favor the older cohorts. Why is it that the potential of the young is more important, or rather has a higher market value, than the actual achievements of the old?)

The discontent caused by the very real loss of status and strained financial circumstances of the elderly inevitably led to efforts to organize them. This effort has a history of its own. Williamson, Evans, and Powell distinguish several periods in the struggle to organize the elderly (following Mauss) in this country.

The first one, from 1920 to 1950, was the period of incipiency when the elderly and their allies "grope(d) toward the establishment of a shared identity based on a perception of threat to their common interests."[144] (The first organization to support the elderly founded during this period was a national brotherhood, The Fraternal Order of the Eagles).[145] It was followed by coalescence (1950-65), characterized by the "formation of alliances, caucuses, and ad hoc committees, in addition to the organization of local and regional formal associations."[146] (Among the organizations founded during this period were The National Council on the Aging in 1950 and the American Association of Retired Persons in 1958.) The third period, that of institutionalization, has been from 1965 to the present. This was a time when "established political institutions officially recognize[d] a social problem or movement and began to devise a series of routine measures for dealing with it."[147] Thus, the 1971 White House Conference on Aging, among other things, "provided a national forum for coalition formation among diverse groups interested in legislation impacting the elderly."[148]

These developments allowed some specialists such as Arnold Rose to claim, already in 1965, that there was a growing subculture of the elderly.[149] Rose saw an "emerging age consciousness." In other words, the elderly were going through a transition from an "age category" to an "age community."

But, like commonalities based on gender and sexual preferences, the development of an age-based collectivity could go only so far. Campbell in 1971 and Binstock in 1974 pointed out that there is a "substantially greater heterogeneity of interests among the old than among younger groups." "The heterogeneity of the elderly will continue to inhibit the development of a strong elderly voting block and evolution of the elderly as a highly organized interest group. . . . [M]ost would agree that the crosscutting sources of identity, loyalty, and perceived self-interest such as social class, race, and ethnicity will remain and continue to affect political attitudes and behavior."[150] Indeed, "most of the elderly will have other [non-age-related] more important sources of political identification and loyalty, such as social class, occupational background, and ethnicity. Most of the elderly have had these other sources of identity much longer than they have had the identity of "elderly persons"; as a result, the influence of these other sources is stronger. Most people also feel more positive about these other sources of identity than they feel about their old age identity."[151]

Still others, such as Neal Cutler, have pointed out that "it is not necessary to assume a high degree of unanimity among the elderly in order to predict that age could be a salient political referent." Like ethnic power, "senior power, even if characterized by a wide diversity of interests, could nevertheless become highly influential politically in the form of a multifaceted, multi-issue, loose coalition of interests that converge on some issues while diverging on others. The Black and women's movements did not require such unanimity in order to be politically influential, and the same may hold true for senior power."[152] In fact, Williamson, Evans, and Powell predict that "over the next several decades we can reasonably expect mass media technology to enhance the elderly's potential for effective mobilization around political issues they perceive as important."[153] (A number of studies have found that interest and information levels with regard to political affairs are consistently higher in old age.[154])

Mauss, who studied the life cycles of social and political movements, found that most go through five stages. We have already mentioned three: incipiency, coalescence, and institutionalization. The two final stages are fragmentation and demise.[155] However, this sequence is applicable only to social movements that fail to develop a collective identity among their members. It would be applicable only if seniors remained an interest group and nothing else. Another outcome is also possible: creation of a collectivity, that is, tribalization.

To achieve that stage the elderly must satisfy three conditions: self-reproduction, a division of labor, and a boundary maintenance mechanism.

The boundary maintenance mechanism is probably the easiest requirement of the three. Many markers, including appearance, can be (and frequently are) used to delineate the boundary. (At the same time, age can be highly situational in the Nagatian sense. And age manipulation and passing in our age- and status-conscious societies are a time-honored pastime.)

Division of labor is somewhat more problematic, although any mature age cohort allows much flexibility, except in the age of physical debility. It is problematic for the simple reason that most people of retirement age don't work. There are, of course, self-contained retirement communities in Florida, Arizona, and elsewhere that can be economically independent. But can they achieve an adequate degree of self-sufficiency to exist in isolation? Probably not.

It is reproduction, however, that presents an insurmountable obstacle to the creation of an old-age collectivity. Old age, as a group, does not reproduce itself. (Technically, this is no longer true: very recently, new procedures perfected by Italian researchers have made it possible for women past the age of menopause to bear children. Even so, it is unlikely that many women at that stage of their life would want to have children.)

Ultimately, although age cohorts can achieve a certain measure of collective identity and are capable of creating self-sufficient communities, their tribal aspects are insufficient. Of all the parameters we have so far studied age is one of the least "tribalizable." And, since it fails tribalization, it cannot create a political entity.

***

In modern and modernizing societies profession is a matter of choice, although not always a completely free choice, since it is largely a function of the level of economic development of a given society and, often enough, family connections.

In most industrial and postindustrial societies profession has become the prime focus of one's identity. In the United States the first question one asks about a stranger is "What does he or she do?" What he or she does tells us what he or she is. Not surprising, members of professional entities such as trade unions often develop a keen sense of solidarity and belonging. But they, like age groups, can seldom compete with cross-cutting linkages of family ties, social custom, and religion.

Trade unions and other professional interest groups serve well as foci of mobilization because they defend group interests. If they can be mobilized, can they be tribalized? They easily allow for self-reproduction and boundary maintenance, but division of labor is another matter. A society based on one profession is impossible. So, strictly speaking, tribalization is not feasible. But a society based on any number of mono- or uniprofessional groups *(jati!)* can and did exist.

Where do we locate profession in the Brass continuum? Amazingly, here humanity seems to be going backwards. Members of the *jati* or any other hereditary occupational castes had a clear notion of belonging to a community; they were, in a sense, equivalent to ethnic communities. In the modern world, profession has retreated to the level of a category. This is a paradox since profession is increasingly important as a determinant of individual status. But it is a profession determined largely by an individual choice. Thus, while its importance to the individual has increased, its significance to the group as a (hereditary) entity has decreased. In short, there is little to no likelihood that we will see polities based on profession or individual professions attaining the complexity of even diaspora minorities (unless a diaspora minority chooses or is forced to choose a particular profession; in that case, ethnicity and profession would fuse).

SOME CONCLUSIONS

Our survey shows that collective identity can crystallize around virtually any combination of ethnic or racial markers. To these we may add religion, class, and, in the last 20 or 30 years, gender and sexual orientation. In fact, we are witnessing an unprecedented increase in the number of positive (entity-creating) binders, with new and more diverse collective identities being formed before our eyes.

Shared values, common origin, or a common enemy can unite people into in-groups with collective identity. Once the in-group acquires a permanent character it develops an internal structure, a hierarchy, rules of inclusion/

exclusion and initiation, and a sense of community. These parameters, in turn, help to reinforce the group's cohesion and ensure its continued existence. They are mutually reinforcing. A collective identity cannot be constructed from nothing. One has to start with a number of features, some of which will serve as markers and others as binders. Perhaps the most striking feature in the process of group formation is the diversity of factors that can serve as the kernel around which a collective identity is formed. Ethnic, religious, and racial diacritica lend themselves relatively easily to identity construction. They are used as building blocs in the construction of "natural" identities. With synthetic identities such as politicized class, gender, or sexual orientation the process of collective identity formation is more complicated. It helps if the binding feature—social status or sexual orientation, for example—is an instrument of discrimination or is perceived as such. In the climate of "everybody has a legitimate grievance," any grievance is a marketable commodity and can serve as a binding element in group formation (ethnic, racial, and religious discrimination are also useful, but "natural" identities can be formed even without perceived inequality and discrimination).

Modernity has streamlined the process of group formation. "The breaking up of feudal society organized around kin and hierarchy," wrote Barry Adam, "created a world with new possibilities, especially for traditionally oppressed classes: peasants and serfs, women, national minorities, and Jews."[156]

The process of group formation rests on four main "tenets": secondary education, nationalism, the ideal of liberty and liberation, and Marxism.

The spread of secondary education in the nineteenth century taught millions of people to think in terms of categories and apply these categories to humans. For example, where before one could find individuals engaged in sinful acts, the educated, scientifically trained mind of the nineteenth century lumped these individuals into a group based on sexual orientation. (In a curious recent example of this impulse, *Newsweek* devoted an entire issue to "The Overclass." What is this new mysterious entity? It is "a new elite of highly paid, high-tech strivers pulling away from the rest of America."[157] The magazine goes on to list some of its members. They include people of most disparate backgrounds and occupations united by only one quality: they are simply professionally successful people. Thus *Newsweek* has created a new category, based only on professional success, by using the notion of the "underclass." Where there is an "underclass," can an "overclass" be far behind? Thus new categories are easily formed, virtually from nothing.

Nationalism reinforced this tendency. If one could build a community from speakers of closely related dialects, why not a community based on gender? But nationalism did more than that. As a new religion of the areligious, nationalism resacralized life. It provided community life with a structure, an internal coherence, and a blueprint for living, all of which were on the wane when religion went into a decline. It also redirected the passionate attachment earlier given to religious matters to ethnicity and nation. In the process, it created and glorified strong affective ties of community-as-family. "The seduction of nationalism," writes Svetlana Boym, "is the seduction of homecoming and total acceptance: one doesn't even have to join the party; one simply belongs."[158] People who lament the excesses of nationalism fail to see that nationalism, to its adherents, spells love and brotherhood, not hatred. Hatred appears only when the Nation-as-Family—Motherland, Fatherland, ethnic brothers—is violated. As a religion of brotherhood and love, and as an organizing principle, ethnonationalism serves as a model to other nascent communities.

The spread of nationalism was made easier by the ideals of liberty and liberation proclaimed by the French Revolution. They caught the imagination of millions of people who suffered from various forms of inequality and discrimination. In the United States, for example, feminism as a political movement grew out of the struggle for Black emancipation.

The great contribution of Marxism was the reification of a social stratum into a discrete entity and the creation of a "scientific" liberationist ideology that justified and legitimated not only liberation but also a takeover of the state apparatus. The development of the concept of class and the exploitation of the proletariat became a classical example followed by other disadvantaged groups. Although Marx confined the notion to the proletariat, Marxist premises could be applied to almost any social group, and were. In the United States, for example, Marxism was instrumental in launching gay liberation.

Deprivation is a starting point in the process of a synthetic group formation. (People with physical disabilities and those with eating disorders are a good example of the human material that can be used as the basis for new entity formations.) A movement to fight discrimination and injustice galvanizes the deprived into an in-group that goes on to develop hierarchy, internal structure, and rules of inclusion/exclusion.[159] (Elise Boulding calls it "conscienticization," that is "the process of awakening, on the part of a subjugated group, to a consciousness of the facts of structural dominance." The term, however, is very awkward, so we will try to avoid using it.) Unorganized atomized individuals are mobilized into a self-conscious movement or, in the Marxist parlance, the group makes the transition from the "in itself" to the "for itself" stage. (Or, if we use Brass's continuum, it transforms from a category into a community.)

If the group acquires a permanent character, is capable of self-reproduction, can develop the division of labor, and can establish some sort of
a boundary maintenance mechanism it can be transformed ("coagulated," I
would say) into a "tribe." This is not a tribe in the usual anthropological
sense of the word. I use the word "tribe" for lack of a better term. It describes the second stage in the process of group formation, which can be
called, again for lack of a better designation, "tribalization," which is the
formation of a cohesive, self-sufficient, and self-perpetuating entity that can
develop a complex social structure and act as a (relatively) independent
social and political actor.

If the tribe has a territory or can acquire territoriality (in the sense that
"class" in early Communist Russia took over the territory of the Soviet Union)
it can build a state. Territoriality is a sine qua non of the third stage in group
formation, statehood.

Needless to say, this three-stage process is a simplified diagram (see
Figure 2). One should keep in mind that markers and binders of different
groups and on different levels are present within the same person in an overlapping
pattern of concentric nested identities and allegiances, sometimes conflicting
but sometimes pulling in the same direction.

We all have an ethnic or national identity, often with a regional subidentity,
a religion, even if we don't practice it, a race, a gender, an age, a profession,
and a sexual orientation. Some identities reinforce one another, for example
the Greek Orthodox Church and Greek ethnicity; others may work against
each other, such as Catholicism and homosexuality. Together, these simul-
taneous multiple identities create patterns of daunting intricacy and complexity that are difficult to disentangle. As Anne Phillips put it, "no one is
'just' a worker, 'just' a woman, 'just' black. The notion that our politics can
simply reflect one of our identities seems implausible in the extreme; there
is no symmetry between the different oppressions, and those who are our
allies on one front may well turn out enemies on another. We cannot always
have it both ways, and when the conflict arises we are forced to say which
matters most."[160]

A striking feature of our time is the increasing tendency to create and
establish new groups, classes, and categories based on reified collective
identities in a series of liberation movements that affect more and more
groups. This process leads to the ever increasing division of society into
collectivities, each with its own corporate identity and hierarchy and its
own blueprint for living. Minorities, especially ethnic ones, are actively
rediscovering and recreating their identities in a process of fragmentation
that is parallel to the further atomization of society into mobile individuals

unburdened by ties of kinship and rigid social stratification. In an increasingly atomized world this is inevitable, since in-groups offer affective ties earlier provided by family and the close-knit local community. The more atomized the modern world is, the more the desire to belong, to join a collectivity, manifests itself.

The general direction seems clear: the liberation of Man from the constraints of Nature, at least as far as procreation is concerned. From in vitro fertilization to the creation of an artificial uterus to the creation of humans virtually *ex nihilo.* Such deracinated (actually, never "enracinated") individuals will seek protection and comfort in almost any collectivity they can join. New groups and strata will coalesce from the process of reification through mobilization to tribalization and, for those endowed with territory, on to (possible) statehood.

It may seem that the process of fragmentation is at odds with a clearly discernible tendency to create gigantic political and economic superblocs such as the European Union. Actually, both processes are but two sides of the same coin, a dialectical relationship of thesis and antithesis leading to the still unforeseeable synthesis. While political fragmentation is gathering steam the economic and cultural unification (often mislabeled "Americanization") manifested in the creation of the global village will continue to pull the nominally independent units together. In fact, no amalgamation is possible without initial fragmentation since some dinosaurs—the former Soviet Union, for one—are too large to be successfully integrated.

As more and more groups are galvanized and new tribes appear on the scene, we are headed for more political turmoil than we might think. We can now understand why: our collective identity, our blueprint for living, is not something abstract but is rather the pattern of our day-to-day existence, which gives texture and color to our everyday life. The imposition of an alien blueprint violates the very core of our social being and existence.

Until recently, Westerners in general and Americans in particular have known immigrants mostly eager to integrate into the American mainstream; they are used to other people adapting to their way of life. That is why the turmoil brought forth by interethnic struggles elsewhere seems absurd and senseless to many. They might gain a new perspective if Spanish became the second official language in the United States or if multiculturalism introduced or even enforced alien customs such as female circumcision.

Traditional hierarchical societies could successfully combine several collectivities under one political roof because they were built on subordination, often theologically enshrined, which prevented or at least slowed down fragmentation. With the spread of the ideals of self-determination, liberation, and democracy, cohabitation of unequal social groups became increasingly difficult. It is not unlike grownup children who no longer want to live with their parents. And the process of grievance articulation, by using notions of exploitation and deprivation, facilitates entity-formation. It provides a ready-made mechanism for bringing together individuals into a collective whole. It turns proletarians into the proletariat. Thus, fragmentation and entity-formation are a natural result of the maturation of the former ethnic, racial, political, gender, and other "peripheries."

Understandably, the established political, social, and cultural elites find this process inconvenient. They forget that they, or at least their prominent representatives, glorified and propagated the ideals of freedom, equality, and representative democracy that naturally lead to fragmentation. (For example, throughout the Cold War the West dangled the carrot of freedom in front of enslaved East Europeans. The West, of course, meant individual freedoms in existing states. But East Europeans, with their strong Herderian background, reinterpreted this message in the ethnocollectivist sense. In addition to individual freedoms they also demanded group, that is, ethnic, freedom. The ultimate result was the collapse of the Soviet Union, the implosion of Yugoslavia, and the division of Czechoslovakia.)

Most (Western) elites see group rights and the fragmentation they engender as a nuisance. As well they may be, but they seem to be here to stay. Instead of averting our gaze from the excesses of various liberation movements we should think about how to manage the process, about how to incorporate it into the management of world affairs. We don't have any other choice.

PART II

Chapter 4

AREAS OF CONFLICT: WHICH ONES TO CHOOSE?

Now that we have acquainted ourselves with the history of cleansing, its typology, and its interaction with collective identity, let us closely examine some—let's say ten—conflict areas where ethnic strife has been endemic and where cleansing and/or genocide have occurred repeatedly; in short, areas where hatreds run deep and prospects for a peaceful settlement are at best tenuous. We will do this not merely from detached curiosity but in the hope of finding practical, workable solutions to conflicts that have all too often defied any solution.

Which ones shall we choose? There are a number of considerations to guide us. We have already established the first requirement: we will examine conflicts that are recurrent, that flare up periodically. Recurrent conflicts necessarily defy easy solutions. Quite often, they are conflicts that involve claims to the same territory by two or more adversaries. Here, then, is one more useful aspect: irreconcilable territorial disputes, especially those involving areas that have high historic and/or symbolic value for one or both adversaries.

Mixed populations are another common feature of recurrent and irreconcilable conflicts. Areas in which different populations live in a checkerboard pattern make settlement difficult.

Discontinuous ethnic pattern is a frequent ingredient in this kind of conflict, especially where a minority lives far enough from the border area to create an enclave problem that makes a border adjustment impractical. A degree of autonomy may satisfy the aspirations of some minorities, but areas in which autonomy is denied or where a minority finds limited autonomy unacceptable present an insurmountable problem because self-determination for such a minority inevitably leads to a Swiss cheese configuration that is rarely feasible.

There is also the issue of security. Vulnerability of one or both adversaries is one of the main causes of ethnic conflict. It often leads to constant strife and repeated assaults. In fact, long-term vulnerability was the driving force behind many cleansing campaigns. Adequate security arrangements are extremely important.

In addition, it will be worthwhile to examine conflicts where different solutions have already been tried and have been found wanting, especially those areas where international mediation has failed, where peace treaties have been disregarded, or where border rectifications have not worked.

We should also try to cast our net as widely as possible, drawing examples from various parts of the world. We should look for examples in every continent and major geocultural area, such as the Middle East.

We should also strive for typological diversity; our sample should contain examples of as many kinds of conflict as possible: ethnic, racial, religious.

Finally, we should probably leave out purely historical examples with no or little relevance for the present and concentrate instead on contemporary conflicts.

Armed with these basic requirements, we can now make our choice.

Some conflicts virtually leap out at us: Bosnia, Rwanda, Karabakh, Kosovo, Sri Lanka. These are all contemporary conflicts of long duration, characterized by periodic flareups, with a history of unsuccessful mediation and intervention. Two more troubled areas, Northern Ireland and the Palestinian problem, seem to be inching toward pacification. It is too early to tell whether this time the pacification will work, but past experience calls for skepticism. In all other respects, both areas fit our parameters very well. We can also look at two "sleepers," that is, conflicts that have been major international problems in the past, have never been definitively resolved, and, despite the fact that war at present is unlikely, threaten to explode in the future: Cyprus and the Hungarian minority in Transylvania. Finally, I would also add a very recent problem, that of the Russian minorities in the Near-Abroad. This is not a cyclical problem, nor is it a problem with a long history. On the contrary, it is of very recent provenance, so that hardly any solutions have been tried. In short, it barely fits our requirements. And yet, the problem of Russian minorities in the Near-Abroad should not be excluded because it is very similar to that of German minorities in eastern Europe after World War I, and thus potentially extremely dangerous to the preservation of world peace. It also gives us wider geographical and typological distribution.

This list by no means exhausts the list of contemporary ethnic problems that could fit our requirements: Moldova, South Africa, and Turkish minorities in Bulgaria and elsewhere could also be included. But space limitations prevent us from taking more than ten cases.

How successful were we in satisfying our requirements? We satisfied some. All our conflicts are contemporary. Except for the Russians in the Near-Abroad, all are cyclical and of long duration. As a rule, they have defied most, and often any, solutions. Kosovo, Palestinians, Transylvania, and Ulster involve historical and symbolic claims that make territorial accommodation extremely difficult. Bosnia, Kosovo, Russian minorities, Rwanda, and Ulster are areas of highly mixed populations where most border rectifications would be hopelessly inadequate. Bosnia, Karabakh, and Transylvania (and to some extent many Russian minorities, Sri Lanka, and Ulster) have large concentrations of minorities deep within their territory. Finally, virtually all sides in these conflicts, with the possible exceptions of the Russians and the Romanians of Transylvania, are vulnerable.

Our list often does not so well satisfy some other of our requirements, however. It does not provide much for geographical diversity: all our cases are found in the Old World (four in Europe, three in Asia, one in Africa, and two straddling Eurasia, the Russian minorities and Cyprus). The relatively narrow scope of the geographical distribution is explained by the fact that countries of the New World have been largely spared cleansing in this century. Or if they have not, as in Honduras and the Dominican Republic, cleansing has not been a cyclical problem.

Our list also has a narrow typological range: virtually all our examples involve ethnic or ethnoreligious conflicts (although the conflict between Russians and the indigenous peoples in the republics of Central Asia occasionally has racial overtones). Again, this is the result of the relative paucity of class-defined or racially defined conflicts among contemporary problem areas.

As we examine each conflict, we will follow the same plan. We will devote a chapter to each conflict. Each chapter will consist of three sections: (1) general information (land area, population, ethnic composition, and so on); (2) historical background (describing, in broad outline, the history of the area); and (3) present-day conflict (the latest cycle of violence, which may require looking back years or even decades if the latest outbreak has been going on for some time).

For the sake of convenience I will present the conflict areas alphabetically: Bosnia, Cyprus, Karabakh, Kosovo, the Palestinian problem, Russian minorities, Rwanda, Sri Lanka, Transylvania, and Ulster.

Chapter 5

BOSNIA

GENERAL INFORMATION

Bosnia is located in the heart of the Balkan peninsula, at the geographical center of the former Yugoslavia. Two sides of the Bosnian triangle, the north and the west, border on Croatia; to the east and south lies the rump republic of Yugoslavia. Bosnia covers 19,741 square miles (51,129 square kilometers).

By 1991, Bosnia's population reached 4.5 million people. It was one of the most ethnically and culturally diverse areas in Europe. By the time of the breakup of Yugoslavia, Bosniaks (Slav-speaking Muslims) were the largest group in Bosnia (about 40 percent of the population), followed by Orthodox Serbs (30 to 33 percent) and Catholic Croats (about 17 percent). The picture was complicated by a growing number of "Yugoslavs": people who chose a neutral Yugoslav nationality. Their numbers fluctuated from census to census, which makes exact ethnic composition difficult to ascertain, but the general trend was up. (A study by the University of Belgrade put the number of people of mixed ethnic origin in former Yugoslavia at 4 million, in a population of 24 million.[1]) The increase in the number of "Yugoslavs" had seemed to indicate the appearance and strengthening of a "Yugoslav" identity, and has been taken as a sign of a growing cohesion of Yugoslavia. Subsequent developments showed how ephemeral those hopes had been.

Not only was the composition of the population extremely complex, its distribution was no less confusing. The Muslims resided in the center and the west, Croats in the south, and Serbs in the north, the east, and in between. Many areas with Croat and Serb majorities were far removed from the titular republics and so could not be easily attached to the "mother countries." Finally, a belt of Serbian settlement in Croatia's Krajina region almost cut Croatia in half and surrounded Bosnia with a Serbian barrier. In short, it was (and still is) a demographic and geopolitical nightmare.

HISTORICAL BACKGROUND

Originally, the territory of Bosnia, Croatia, and Serbia had been inhabited by Illyrians, a group of tribes that spoke related Indo-European dialects. By A.D. 14 Illyrian lands south and west of the Danube were occupied by Rome. They remained Roman for the next 400 years, and by the time the first Slavs appeared in the Balkans in the late fourth century the autochthonous inhabitants of the area had been thoroughly Latinized.

At first the Slavs penetrated the area in small bands, but in 517 Slav hordes overran the entire peninsula and penetrated deep into Greece, as far as Thermopylae and Epirus. By the middle of the sixth century they started settling permanently, and toward the end of the eighth century most of the area of the future Yugoslavia had been settled by Slavs.

Gradually, the newcomers split into three distinct ethnic entities, which eventually developed into Serbs, Croats, and Slovenes. We will leave the Slovenes out of this account, but the Croats and Serbs deserve a closer look.

Religion and civilization divided these ethnic cousins from very early on. During the seventh to ninth centuries the ancestors of Croats (and Slovenes) were converted to Roman Catholicism, while Serbs (and Bulgarians) found themselves in the Byzantine sphere of influence and became Orthodox. Thus, while the Croats throughout their history looked West toward Rome and Germany, the Serbs looked East to Constantinople and, since the seventeenth and eighteenth centuries, to Russia.

But the religious divisions were never static for long. In the tenth century Bosnia was swept by the Bogomil heresy.[2] In Bosnia, the heresy provided a foundation for the development of a strong regional identity which in effect tore Bosnia from the body of Croatia.

It seems that after years of Catholic repression mutual revulsion between the Bogomils and the Catholics was such that when the Turks appeared on the scene the Bogomils converted en masse. In any case, the share of Muslims increased from 18.4 percent of Bosnia's population in 1489 to 46 percent by 1520-30.[3] Many, if not most, converts came from the Bogomil background. Thus, from the middle of the sixteenth century, Bosnia became an Ottoman Muslim stronghold squeezed between the Catholic and the Orthodox worlds. Muslims were favored by the Turkish authorities, and many were landowners (because quite a few aristocratic families had converted

1. Bihac (to Croatia, to be restlled by Bosnian Croats, along with Krajina)
2. Muslim area
3. to Serbia

to Islam in order to retain their wealth and status), so that religious differences between the Muslims and the non-Muslim peasantry, both Catholic and Orthodox, were reinforced by class tensions. When the Ottoman Empire disintegrated, Bosnian Muslims found themselves in the position of a former imperial minority, not unlike Germans, among hostile neighbors who regarded them as turncoats.

Let us now take a closer, if perfunctory, look at each major South Slav state in the region.

Serbia

In the early period of their history Serbs were concentrated in Kosovo, Montenegro, and Hercegovina, their heartland lying further south than it does today.

The first Serbian statelet emerged in the middle of the ninth century and, despite its Orthodox religion and Byzantine orientation, from the very start came under strong Bulgarian and Byzantine pressure, which it found hard to withstand.

Serbia revived in the eleventh century and was consolidated by the beginning of the thirteenth. The new state was anxious to shake off Byzantine interference, and established an autocephalous Church with a Serbian bishop in 1219. The kingdom reached its peak under King Dušan in the middle of the fourteenth century; the year 1346, when Dušan was crowned Tsar of the Serbs and Greeks, probably marked its zenith (note that his capitals, Skopje and Ohrid, were both in Macedonia).

Serbian efflorescence was brief, however. From 1345 onward the Serbs had to defend themselves against the Turks who won decisively at the battle of Kosovo Pole in 1389. For the next 400 years Serbia was part of the Ottoman Empire. During this time a massive outflow of Serbian population denuded southern Serbia and Kosovo of its Slav inhabitants, shifting the Serbian demographic center north, toward the Danube. Thousands of Serbs— over 200,000 in 1690 alone[4]—moved across the Danube into what was then southern Hungary and west to Croatia, creating large areas of mixed population and inadvertently sowing the seeds of future discords.

As Turkey weakened, Serbia's fortunes revived. The first major revolt in modern times occurred in 1804. It was suppressed with great brutality by the Turkish army with some help from Bosnian and Albanian Muslims, but it was only the beginning. An intermittent struggle against Turkey ensued, in which Serbia enjoyed occasional support from Russia.

By 1830 Serbia had become largely autonomous, although de jure independence was not granted until 1878, at the Congress of Berlin. Even after 1878 many Serbs remained outside of independent Serbia. Passionately nationalistic, the country embarked on a policy of aggressive territorial expansion fueled by irredentism. With the Austrian annexation of Bosnia in 1908 and the demise of European Turkey in 1912-13, Austria-Hungary became Serbia's arch enemy (with Bulgaria a close second).

Participation in World War I on the winning side allowed Serbia, with the blessing of the Allies, to cobble together a large new state, Yugoslavia, which "gathered" all the Serbs but also included Croats, Slovenes, and many other nationalities. The new state was dominated by Serbs and Serbian bureaucracy, and other ethnic groups, even fellow Slavs, chafed under Belgrade's heavy hand.

Feeble attempts at conciliation came too late. When Yugoslavia fell to the invading Germans, Italians, Hungarians, and Bulgarians in April 1941, the non-Serbian nationalities either sat on their hands or actively supported the invaders. Yugoslavia was destroyed. Rump Serbia, devastated by the war, had to accept thousands of Serbian refugees fleeing from Bosnia and Croatia, where Serbs were being massacred by Croatian fascists.

After three years of brutal German occupation and a savage guerrilla war exacerbated and complicated by a civil war, the country was liberated in winter 1944-45, and Yugoslavia was reconstituted as a Communist state. Although the new Yugoslavia was a federal state headed by Tito, a Croat, Serbs continued to exercise hegemony. Occasional explosions of local nationalisms, like the one in Croatia in 1971 or in Kosovo in 1982, merely strengthened the Serbian hold on the state apparatus and the army. After Tito's death in 1980 the country remained on an automatic pilot, but ethnic problems (especially troubles in Kosovo), economic decline, Serbian attempts to maintain their hegemony, and failures of collective leadership all contributed to the demise of Yugoslavia. Another contributing factor was the collapse of the Soviet Union and the democratic revolutions that swept through Eastern Europe. The demise of the Soviet Union eliminated a major threat to Balkan security and made Yugoslavia redundant.

At present, the war of the Yugoslav succession is still going on.

Croatia

Croatia's political history starts in 803 with the acceptance of Charlemagne's suzerainty. Thus, from its inception, the country found itself on the fringes of the Western world.

A more or less sovereign kingdom was established a century later, in 924. But early succession struggles gave Hungary an opportunity to interfere in Croatia's affairs. A settlement reached in 1102 put the Hungarian king on the Croatian throne. However, the terms of the agreement were sufficiently vague, so that Hungarians could insist (and always did) that Croatia was a part of the Hungarian kingdom, while Croats saw their country as an independent kingdom that shared a ruler with Hungary, like the Polish-Lithuanian Commonwealth of the sixteenth century or the Austro-Hungarian empire after 1867.

In the sixteenth century most of Croatia was overrun by the Turks. In 1527, after Hungary fell, the Croatian Sabor (Parliament) offered Croatia's crown to Ferdinand Habsburg of Austria, thus inaugurating 400 years of Austrian supremacy superimposed on the Hungarian one.

Between 1526 and 1699 Croatia was contested territory between the Habsburg and Ottoman empires, and suffered repeated devastation. Since conditions in the area were very unsettled, the Habsburgs established a military frontier administration as a defensive measure. Serbs fleeing from Turkish persecution were particularly welcome. Thousands of Serbian refugees settled in the area that became known as Krajina (the borderlands; same root as "Ukraine"), which virtually cut Croatian ethnic territory in half, and planted the seeds of later ethnic strife.

By 1700 Austria achieved a decisive advantage over the Turks, and Croatia found peace within the Habsburg empire. Austrian Croatia had a chance to partake of the general advance of Western civilization. Croatia remained Austrian, with a short Napoleonic interlude in 1805-15, until 1918, when it was joined to the newly formed state of Yugoslavia.

Initially, the union with Serbia had many Croat supporters. Ever since the beginning of the nineteenth century a strong ideological movement known as Illyrianism had agitated for the union of all southern Slavs. Illyrianism saw Serbs, Croats, and Slovenes as tribes of a larger South Slav nation. The idea survived into the twentieth century, despite tensions of the 1867-1914 period, when Croatia's Serbs often sided with Hungary. (Croats were usually allied with Vienna against Budapest.) The influence of that early movement caused expectations for the new Yugoslavia to run high at first, particularly among some sections of the Croatian intelligentsia.

The new state, however, proved a disappointment because the Croats were denied the leading role they had aspired to play. Nor were they prepared for Serbian hegemony and the "Oriental" (in Croat perception) style that characterized the heavy-handed central bureaucracy in Belgrade. As a result of constant tensions with Belgrade, large segments of the Croatian population became disaffected. Belated attempts at compromise, such as endowing Croatia with a limited autonomy (the so-called Sporazum [Understanding] reached in August 1939) could not cancel two decades of bitter acrimony.

When the Germans invaded in 1941 many Croat soldiers refused to fight, and large sections of the Croatian people were ready to collaborate with the invader. Even worse, the Croatian fascists, the Ustashe, in their zeal to make Croatia Croatian (Croats made up barely half the population of Greater Croatia), killed thousands of Serbs, Jews, and Gypsies in a wave of grisly massacres throughout Croatia and Bosnia.

The Croat puppet state, incorporating Bosnia, with an Italian figurehead king but ruled by a Croatian dictator Pavelic, led a precarious existence during the war and was reincorporated into Yugoslavia in 1945.

Although Croatia, along with other territorial ethnies, was granted some autonomy within a federal system, in effect the Serbian hegemony was reestablished. Initially, the fact that Tito was a Croat helped Croatia to come to terms with the new arrangement, but discontent with Communist rule and Serbian hegemony continued to simmer, flaring up from time to time. Discontent reached its peak in 1971, in a movement that was somewhat reminiscent of the Prague Spring, and that was suppressed just as quickly.

Croatia had to wait another 20 years before it could gain independence. Initially, Croatia and Slovenia proposed to transform Yugoslavia into a loose confederation. When Belgrade balked, they opted out; the separation was approved in popular referenda. Since then Croatia has been at war with Serbia, although the fighting has, at present, died down. The country has paid a heavy price for its independence: until August 1995 one-third of its territory was occupied by the Serbs, it has had to resettle thousands of refugees, and it is in dire economic straits. But it appears that this time it will retain its independence.

Bosnia

Bosnia has always been a buffer zone between Croatia and Serbia and, therefore, between Catholic and Orthodox Christianity, between East and West. In the ninth to eleventh centuries most of Bosnia belonged to Croatia while Hercegovina was part of Serbia. The first Bosnian principality arose toward the end of the twelfth century. From its inception the new entity faced a major problem: the fact that its elites were largely Bogomil. This fact prevented a peaceful incorporation into the Catholic world, and gave Rome and Hungary a repeated pretext to launch crusades against the heretical state.

Dynastic disputes in Hungary eased Hungarian pressure and allowed a revival of independent Bosnia in the early fourteenth century. By the 1370s its ruler, Tvrtko, had consolidated the country and in 1377 assumed the title of king. Independence was short-lived, however; in 1463 Bosnia succumbed to the Turks, and it remained under Turkish rule until 1878. Many of its inhabitants, particularly the Bogomil nobility, embraced Islam and thus turned into supporters of Ottoman rule. But there have always been strong Orthodox (Serbian) and Catholic (Croatian) minorities scattered throughout the country.

Bosnia's modern history dates from 1875, when a tax revolt by the predominantly Christian peasantry erupted. The disturbances spread throughout the Balkan provinces of the Ottoman Empire and were savagely suppressed by the Turks, particularly in Bulgaria, which in turn led to the Russian intervention, a Russo-Turkish war, and the Congress of Berlin in 1878. The Treaty of Berlin created modern Bosnia-Hercegovina and gave conditional occupation rights to Austria, although Turkey remained the nominal ruler of the province. In 1908 the province was annexed by the Austrian Empire, to great Serbian outrage. A Serbian nationalist and a member of the anti-Austrian underground, Gavrilo Princip assassinated the heir to the Austrian throne in Sarajevo in June 1914 and thus triggered World War I.

After the war, Bosnia was incorporated into Yugoslavia. For most of the interwar period Muslim Bosnians stayed out of the bitter Serbian-Croatian dispute, but when both sides reached the Sporazum (Understanding) of August 1939, which created an autonomous Croatian province, some of Bosnia's border areas inhabited by Croats passed to Croatia.

During World War II Bosnia was made an integral part of Croatia, with Muslims generally taking an anti-Serbian stance. Some of them even helped the Croats to kill and expel their Serbian neighbors. They in turn were persecuted by Serbian Chetniks, especially in the area along the Drina.

After 1945 Bosnia became an autonomous republic within the Yugoslav federation. It remained in Yugoslavia until March 1992, when its Muslim and Croat citizens voted in a referendum to secede and form an independent republic. The Bosnian Serbs abstained: they were in the minority and did not want to legitimize the referendum by their participation. The intractable positions taken by both sides set the stage for the present conflagration.

THE PRESENT CONFLICT

Although ethnic enmity usually has long antecedents, in the case of Croats and Serbs it is fairly recent. In the first half of the nineteenth century Illyrianism promoted unity and cooperation between the two peoples. It was the elevation of Hungary to the status of an (almost) equal partner in the Habsburg empire that gave rise to the alliances of Croats with Vienna and Croatia's Serbs with Budapest. But even in the early twentieth century large segments of Croatian society favored some form of a Pan-South Slav union.

No such feelings were manifest among the Bosnian Muslims, who were allied with Ottoman Turkey and were often regarded by their Christian neighbors as turncoats and traitors. On occasion, as in 1804, Bosnian Muslims helped Turkish troops to suppress Christian uprisings, which did not endear them to Christians. Even so, Muslim and Christian communities had for the most part found a certain modus vivendi between each other.

The creation of Yugoslavia and the imposition of centralized rule from Belgrade drastically changed the South Slav equation. Throughout the 1920s and 1930s opposition to Serbian hegemony led to the creation of a Croatian underground, which launched a terrorist campaign against Yugoslav officials and Serbs that culminated in the murder of the Yugoslav king Alexander in Marseilles in 1934.

As Yugoslavia's international situation deteriorated in the late 1930s, the Serbian elites sought an accommodation with their Croatian counterparts (the Sporazum mentioned earlier). But when Yugoslavia collapsed, a significant number of leading Croats seized the chance to create an independent state, which in reality was a German puppet regime. Like many right-wing, Nazi-influenced Europeans of the time, the Croatian dictator Pavelic and his coterie were obsessed with racial purity. Their desire for purity grew from fear and insecurity: the population of the German-sponsored Independent State of Croatia was highly mixed and there was a Serbian majority in Bosnia; altogether, Serbs amounted to about one-third of new Croatia's population of 6.3 million.[5]

From the start, the Croatian leadership took an uncompromisingly hostile position toward the Serbian minority. In April 1941 an Ustashe official, Kvaternik, said that one-third of the Serbs in Croatia would be forced to convert to Catholicism, one-third would be forced to leave, and one-third would be exterminated; this dictum was repeated by other Croat officials. At the same time, Pavelic said that Croatia's Serbs had forfeited their rights to protection and citizenship.[6]

In June 1941, racial laws prohibited Gypsies, Jews, and Serbs from state employment and forbade "interracial" marriages. By that time a campaign of extermination against the undesirable minorities was already under way. It was accompanied by the deportation and expulsion of Serbs into rump Serbia.

The approximately 750,000 Bosnian Muslims were regarded ambivalently by Croatian authorities, probably because they were regarded as racially Croat. Although the Ustashe did commit some atrocities against them, in other instances Muslim gangs were encouraged to attack Serbs and Jews. And the minister of education, Milan Budak, declared in June 1941 that Croatia would be a state of two religions, Catholicism and Islam.[7] It was a rare instance in which members of one Christian denomination found Muslims preferable to fellow Christians.

The extermination of Serbs started almost at once upon the establishment of independent Croatia, especially in the former military frontier regions of Kordun and Bjelovar with their thick Serbian populations. The mass murder was conducted with utmost cruelty. Occasionally, as in the village of Glina, the males were herded into the church and burned alive. Altogether, over 300,000 Serbs lost their lives.[8]

After World War II, as in so many other conflict areas, it seemed that the demon of ethnic enmity had been exorcised in Yugoslavia. All major indigenous nationalities were given relatively wide autonomy within the federal structure and even non-Slav Albanians and Hungarians enjoyed limited local autonomy. Although the road was sometimes bumpy, as in Croatia in 1971, Yugoslavia experienced no major outbreaks of interethnic violence comparable to those in India or the Middle East. It was long accepted that much of the credit for this went to Tito. However we assess Tito's role in preserving Yugoslavia's unity, there is no doubt that his death in May 1980 was a watershed. With Tito gone, it became increasingly clear that the country could not be held together.

The first sign of impending dissolution was the explosive situation in Kosovo. The outbreak of an Albanian intifada in Kosovo in 1981 and the mass exodus of the non-Muslim, mostly Serbian, population from the area spread anger and distrust among the Serbs throughout the country. These events caused Serbs to reconsider and reject the relatively conciliatory 1974 constitution, which was the foundation of Yugoslav unity. Whatever the price they would have to pay, they would not relinquish their hegemony without a fight. Events in Kosovo also demonstrated their vulnerability. Many Serbs yearned for a strong Serbia that would unite and protect all Serbs.

The fall of Yugoslavia displayed certain parallels with the collapse of the Soviet Union. But there was also a major difference: the USSR was to some extent destroyed by Russians themselves, because a significant proportion of the Russian population came to see the empire as a liability and a brake on Russia proper. Serbs, on the other hand, never rejected the federal state as such and fought to preserve it.

For their part, the Croats and the Slovenes felt that their wealth and resources were being siphoned off and squandered in a mismanaged effort to help the less developed republics. They decided that they would be better off on their own. As a first step, Croatia and Slovenia proposed in October 1990 a looser federation—a confederation, in effect—which the Serbs would not accept since they perceived it as the first step toward a "parcelization" of Serbia.[9] The walkout of the Slovenian delegation from the Fourteenth Extraordinary Congress of the League of Communists of Yugoslavia on January 22, 1990, marked the beginning of the end of the federation.

On June 25, 1991, Croatia and Slovenia declared their independence; within days, fighting erupted in Serbian-inhabited Krajina, which comprised 15 percent of the territory and 12 percent of the population of Croatia.[10] The war was on.

Slovenia escaped virtually unscathed, largely because it had no Serbian minority that could ally itself with Serbia. Other republics were less fortunate. Despite the destruction and bloodshed visited on secessionist Croatia, Bosnia-Hercegovina, and Macedonia soon followed suit. In October 1991, despite strenuous objections from Serbian parliamentarians, Muslim and Croat representatives voted for Bosnia's sovereignty. A popular referendum held on February 29 and March 1, 1992, showed a strong preference on the part of the Muslims and the Croats for an independent Bosnia. The Serbs, not surprisingly, were against; as noted earlier, they boycotted the referendum since they were in the minority. Soon Bosnia was engulfed in a vicious war with Serbia and Bosnian Serbs, a war accompanied by all kinds of horrors and atrocities: mass murder, ethnic cleansing, rape, pillage, detention in concentration camps, mistreatment of prisoners, and so on. So far, Macedonia has managed to stay out of the conflict altogether. Slovenia had a two-week war from which it emerged victorious, largely because it did not have a Serbian minority within and also because the Serbs concentrated their efforts on Croatia. But Croatia and Bosnia could not avoid the conflict, and there the war was particularly brutal because the Serbs felt that they were "paying back" for past massacres.

The war in the former Yugoslavia can be divided into three periods. The first featured successful Serbian assaults on Croatia—including the detachment of Krajina, the destruction of Vukovar, and the bombardment of Dubrovnik— and on Bosnia. As a result, Serbs (those of Serbia, Bosnia, and Croatia) occupied some 70 percent of Bosnian and 30 percent of Croatian territory.

The second period was largely static in terms of major gains. Fighting continued on all fronts. The siege of Sarajevo by Bosnian Serbs continued to be the main theater of operations although there was occasional action elsewhere, such as the overrunning of Goražde in April 1994 (the Serbs later withdrew),[11] or the Serb counterattack at Bihać in November 1994.[12]

If Serb-Bosniak interaction was characterized by stasis, Croat-Bosniak relations have undergone significant changes. They started at a low point, with Croats and Bosnian Muslims fighting each other in Western Hercegovina around Mostar, where a beautiful medieval bridge over the Neretva was destroyed in November 1993.[13] In these encounters Bosniaks proved effective, despite the presence of thousands of Croatian troops sent over from Croatia proper.[14] Once the Croatian government realized that Bosniaks could hold their own, they agreed to peace talks, which started in Washington on February 26, 1994.[15] The agreement, reached on March 18 (with much American prodding), envisioned the creation of a federation of Bosnian Croats and Muslims with a possibility of later joining Croatia in a loose confederation.[16] Most important, the agreement provided for the establishment of a united Croat-Bosniak army. Despite continuing tensions between the two communities, Croatia's Tudjman and Bosnia's Izetbegović continued to work on strengthening the strategic alliance.[17]

Croats also tried to re-establish links to Serbs and Serbia. There is a strong, if uncorroborated, suspicion that as far back as 1990 Milošević and Tudjman reached an agreement to carve up Bosnia. Their above-board relations started with a pact with the rump Yugoslavia, signed on January 19, 1994, to normalize relations.[18] Croatia even opened a "bureau" in Belgrade on March 18.[19] They also showed great flexibility regarding the Serbs of Krajina, first mounting an unofficial blockade of the rebel area,[20] then signing an agreement to re-establish key services to the region on December 2, 1994.[21]

Bosnian Muslims, their backs to the wall, could not play such games. Throughout the war they remained mostly on the defensive, although they did occasionally mount successful counterattacks: against Croats in November 1993,[22] against Serbs in October 1994,[23] and together with Croats against Serbs in central Bosnia, Bihać, and around Sarajevo in November 1994.[24] But the Bosnian army was seriously hampered by lack of ammunition and internal splits.

Such splits plagued all sides in the conflict. There was a secessionist move in Bihac led by a wealthy entrepreneur named Fikret Abdić in October 1993,[25] including the formation of a local political party in September 1994,[26] until the enclave was overrun by Bosnian government troops on August 21, 1994.[27] In the Serbian camp, Yugoslavia was forced to impose a blockade on Bosnian Serbs on September 14, 1994,[28] in order to have sanctions imposed by the United Nations in 1992 suspended.[29] (They were "relaxed" on September 24, 1994.[30]) And even in Croatia, which managed to maintain a higher degree of unity, Tudjman was concerned about excessive regionalist tendencies in Istria.[31]

International participation was probably the most complicated part of the conflict. It was characterized by deep divisions between NATO and the United Nations, between Western Allies and Russia, between America and England and France. In general, America was reluctant to commit ground troops, preferring air strikes and lifting of the arms embargo on Bosnian Muslims instead. Indeed, the United States announced, on November 11, 1994, that it would no longer enforce the embargo.[32] England and France, on the other hand, were afraid of retaliation against their troops (their fears were justified when Serbs kidnapped hundreds of United Nations soldiers in July 1995 and used them as hostages and bargaining chips). For its part, the United Nations lacked the mandate or the physical force to execute its decisions. From time to time the United Nations would spring into action, such as creating "safe areas" in May 1993.[33] Eventually, however, on February 6, 1994, it had to request help from NATO. A NATO ultimatum on February 9 followed.[34] Indeed, NATO planes shot down four Bosnian Serbian planes near Banja Luka on February 28, 1994,[35] with more air strikes on April 10,[36] August 5,[37] and on other occasions. The air raids provoked deep resentment and outrage in Russia. President Yeltsin declared on February 15, 1994, that Russia must be involved in solving the problems in Bosnia[38] and State Duma denounced the strikes in April.[39]

Mediation, both Western and Russian, also proved largely ineffective. After the Bosnian Serb Assembly rejected the Vance-Owen peace plan in April 1993, efforts shifted to the Union of Three Republics proposal, which envisioned the division of Bosnia into three main ethnic areas.[40] However, when it became apparent that Bosnian Croats and Serbs saw the plan as the first step toward Anschluss, the Bosnian government abandoned it. In principle, it opposed partition.[41] Later, representatives of the Croat-Bosniak federation demanded 58 percent of Bosnia's prewar territory, although they eventually agreed to a compromise of somewhere between 51 and 58 percent (Bosnian Serb leader Radovan Karadzić insisted on no less than 49 percent).[42] A so-called Contact Group consisting of France, Russia, the United Kingdom, and the United States was formed in London on April 19, 1994, "to work . . . towards a full cessation of hostilities."[43] The Contact Group came up with a plan and a map of its own on July 6, 1994,[44] but a Bosnian Serb referendum, on August 27-28, rejected the plan by 96.12 percent.[45] Jimmy Carter's visit in late December 1994 proved no more successful.[46]

Meanwhile, slaughter and cleansing continued. At least 68 people were killed and 197 more wounded when a mortar shell hit a Sarajevo market place on February 5, 1994.[47] Serbian artillery periodically bombarded Sarajevo and other besieged Bosnian cities such as Goražde and Maglaj,[48] and cleansed thousands of Bosniak civilians from Banja Luka, Prijedor,[49] Bijeljina,[50] as well as Croats, Hungarians, and Slovaks from eastern Slavonia.[51] Bosnian Muslims also alleged that they were being killed and evicted by Croats in Mostar in October 1994.[52]

At present it appears that the stasis is coming to an end. At the end of July 1995 the Bosnian Serbs captured Srebrenica and Žepa, the two easternmost Muslim enclaves in eastern Bosnia, and were barely prevented from capturing Goražde a second time.

And the Croats, in a blitzkrieg advance through Krajina during August 3-6, 1995, have recaptured most of the area, causing a massive exodus of the remaining Serb population. Serbia seems exhausted, while Croatia is rearmed and ready for action. Whether this augurs a major change in the fortunes of each contending party remains to be seen. But whatever happens in the future, it is quite clear that the unitary, multiethnic Bosnia envisaged by many Bosnians at the beginning of the conflict cannot be resurrected.

Chapter 6

CYPRUS

GENERAL INFORMATION

Cyprus is a small island in the eastern Mediterranean. It is divided by a bitter conflict between its Greek and Turkish communities. The island's Greek southern part covers 2,276 square miles (5,896 square kilometers)[1] and has a population of some 520,000. The Turkish north covers 1,295 square miles (3,355 square kilometers),[2] or 36.4 percent of the island's territory,[3] and has a population of some 193,000. The population of the Turkish area has been augmented by the influx of immigrants from Turkey, but before the partition the ratio was 78 percent Greek to 18 percent Turkish.[4]

Neither Greek nor Turkish Cypriots form separate ethnic groups. They are part of the larger Greek and Turkish ethnies, although they do speak distinct dialects and have a fairly strong regional identity.

In the last several decades the Greek community has experienced a large-scale emigration. There are now numerous colonies of Greek Cypriots living abroad, mostly in Britain and Australia.

The island's fate has often been determined by its geographical location: 40 miles from Turkey, 60-odd miles from Syria, and 650 miles from Greece. The island's proximity to the Middle East makes it a natural hub of commerce, but it also makes it vulnerable.

HISTORICAL BACKGROUND

The third largest island in the Mediterranean, Cyprus developed one of the earliest European civilizations in the sixth millennium B.C. The modern Greek population of Cyprus descends from Greek settlers who arrived in several waves in the second millennium B.C. First came the Mycenean Greeks, around 1500 B.C. They were followed by the Achaeans, in the thirteenth century B.C. While Greeks colonized the western and northern shores of the island, the east and the south retained close links with Phoenicia.

A small island like Cyprus could not withstand mighty empires. By 1500 B.C. it was dominated by Egypt. In the eighth century it was conquered by the Assyrians; then by Persia in the sixth; in 333 B.C. it passed on to Alexander the Great and, after his death, to his heirs the Ptolemies.

Throughout, Cyprus and its rulers managed to retain a large degree of self-rule. Only the incorporation into the Roman Empire in 58 B.C. imposed foreign administration. When the empire split, the island, along with the rest of the eastern Mediterranean, remained a part of Byzantium.

Arab raids in the seventh century detached the island from the Byzantine Empire. For about 300 years the islanders paid tribute to the Arabs and the Byzantines. The island was reintegrated into the Byzantine Empire after the Byzantines decisively defeated the Arabs in 965.

In the twelfth century, during the Third Crusade, the island was con-quered by Richard the Lionhearted who sold it to the Knights Templars who turned it over a French noble Guy de Lusignan in 1192. From then on Cyprus evolved into a strange hybrid, a nominally independent Byzantine kingdom ruled by a French dynasty that tried to impose Catholicism on a stubbornly Orthodox population.

In 1489 the island was acquired by Venice, which occupied the island until 1571; in that year it was conquered by the Turks who stayed for the next 300 years.

In 1878, in exchange for British assistance in a possible confrontation with Russia, Turkey ceded the administration, but not the sovereignty, of the island to Britain. Britain formally annexed the island in 1914 and occupied it until August 16, 1960, when Cyprus finally became an independent re-public. But independence did not end the island's troubles.

THE PRESENT CONFLICT

When the Turkish army disembarked on the island in 1570 it encountered stiff resistance; 20,000 died in the sack of Nicosia.[5] Soon, however, Greeks were reconciled to the change of authority. Indeed, they felt no allegiance to the relatively oppressive Venetian rule, which had not even recognized the "Schismatic" Greek church. In contrast, the Turkish authorities restored the Orthodox archbishopric and abolished the feudal system.[6]

Relations between the two communities began to sour during the War of Greek Independence in the 1820s, when a number of Greek Cypriots fought against the Turks on the mainland. Afraid of "contagion," the Turkish

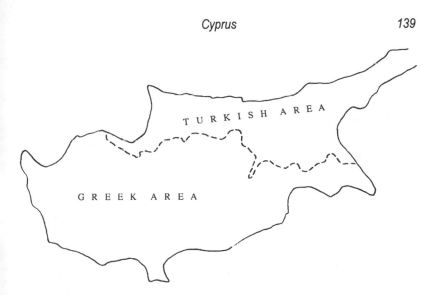

Cyprus

authorities hanged the archbishop and several bishops accused of supporting the revolt.

The question of *enosis* (union with Greece) was raised soon after Greece won independence, but was then merely a dream. The political realities of the time were against it. When the British occupation began, the Greek Cypriots initially reacted favorably to it. There was a widespread expectation that the British would hand the island over to Greece, as they had done with the Ionian Islands. On the contrary, the Turkish Cypriots, who had overnight turned into an unprivileged minority, did not greet the British with open arms: they would have preferred to remain a part of Turkey.

By 1900 calls for *enosis* grew louder, and in 1903 Greek representatives in the Legislative Council voted for a union with Greece. But Britain did not want to give up control of an island that was so close to its vital route, via the Suez Canal, to India. (In 1915 Britain offered Cyprus to Greece in exchange for Greek entry into the war on the Allied side. Greece refused.)

Mounting frustrations among Greek Cypriots and the worsening economic situation in 1929-30 led to riots in 1931 and a rather severe repression.[7] The British abolished the Cypriot constitution, banned political parties and public display of Greek and Turkish flags, and even discontinued teaching Greek and Turkish history in schools. Britain was determined to hang on.

The situation changed drastically after World War II. Weakened by the war, Britain offered self-rule. However, the Greek side repeatedly rejected the offers (in 1948, in 1956, and later) because they were afraid that self-rule would prevent *enosis.* (In a plebiscite of January 1950, 96 percent of Greek Cypriots voted for the union.)[8] The Turkish side accepted the concept for the same reason and sided with the British, a development that the British administration used to its advantage. Thus, by the 1950s, there had occurred a complete reversal in both sides' sympathies: the Greeks were anti-British while the Turks supported continued British rule as the lesser of two evils.

The civil war in Greece slowed the struggle for independence in Cyprus, but by the early 1950s some Greek Cypriots were ready for a showdown, or thought they were. When Greek remonstrances for *enosis* at the United Nations in 1954 brought no results, EOKA (National Organization for the Cypriot Struggle) launched a terrorist campaign in April and March 1955,[9] targeting military bases, radio stations, government officials, and, increasingly, civilians. By 1959 more than 500 people had died, half of them civilians. Most of these were Greek; only 60 were of Turkish extraction.

That most victims were Greeks shows that the campaign had aspects of a civil war within the Greek Cypriot community, but it affected the Turkish community as well. For example, Turkish houses in more than 30 villages were destroyed, creating numerous Turkish refugees (6,000 according to some accounts).[10] In self-defense, Cypriot Turks created their own underground forces that targeted the Greeks and called for a partition of the island. The plight of Turkish Cypriots found a lively response in Turkey, where anti-Greek riots broke out on September 6-7, 1955.

By 1959 all sides in the conflict were tired and wanted a settlement. Representatives of Britain and both communities met in Zurich and London and finally came up with the following solution: Cyprus was to be an independent republic, with each ethnic community autonomous in its internal affairs. Its president would be a Greek, its vice-president a Turk; both would have the power of veto. The share in the central government was to be set at a 7:3 ratio and in the army 6:4,[11] which was actually favorable to the Turkish side since Turks amounted to less than 20 percent of the island's population. Most important, *enosis* and partition were ruled out.

On August 16, 1960 Cyprus was proclaimed independent. But the old problems remained. The Greeks felt they had given too much, the Turks felt they had gotten too little. The main bones of contention were taxation and the creation of ethnically separate municipalities in five major cities; the

Greeks feared that the latter would lead to a de facto partition. Greek nationalists began to draw plans for a government takeover and a subsequent *enosis*, and both sides continued to arm themselves. In an effort to prevent war, Archbishop Makarios, the republic's president, proposed 13 amendments to the constitution that would have undermined many of the protections accorded to the Turkish minority. The amendments were flatly rejected by the Turkish side.

By December 1963 the conflict had degenerated into open intercommunal violence. The Greek side blamed the Turkish irregulars while the Turkish side blamed Makarios. Both communities suffered in the struggle that ensued, but the less numerous Turkish minority found itself mostly on the receiving end. Thousands of Turks fled from mixed villages to protected all-Turkish areas. Turkish Cypriots withdrew from organs of state and administration while the Greeks blockaded many of the Turkish enclaves.

There followed an ineffective UN mediation, including a landing of the Peacekeeping Force in March 1964, a new conference in London, and even a plan offered by Dean Acheson, who proposed a de facto partition of the island, with Turkey establishing two or more exclusively Turkish cantons in the north and getting a large military base, in addition to a small Greek island off the Turkish coast.[12]

All efforts at mediation failed. After a Greek attack on the Turkish village of Kophinou near Larnaka in December 1967,[13] the Turks established the Provisional Turkish Cypriot Administration, an important step toward partition. By then hostilities had engulfed the entire island: Turkish Cypriots had been evicted or fled from 103 villages and had suffered about 500 killed, 1,000 wounded, and 200 missing.[14]

While the interethnic violence continued sporadically, large sections of Greek opinion became disenchanted with Makarios's cautious approach. They were actively supported by the junta in Greece. When an assassination attempt on Makarios failed on March 8, 1970, the right-wing underground movement prepared for the overthrow of the Makarios government. The coup d'etat was launched on July 15, 1974. Makarios escaped and flew to London. Turkey, which had come close to invading the island in the summer of 1964, used the coup as an excuse. Its forces started landing on July 20, 1974.

Neither Cyprus nor Greece could resist the invasion. Three days later the junta in Athens fell, but it was too late for Cyprus. By mid-August Turkey had occupied almost 40 percent of the island's territory (with about 70 percent of its economic potential) sending a wave of 200,000 Greek refugees fleeing south;[15] in the process, some 1,619 Greek Cypriots were unaccounted for, most of them presumed dead.[16]

The Turkish invasion divided the island. To strengthen the Turkish element in the northern part of the island, 65,000 settlers from mainland Turkey were brought in.[17] This sealed the partition and brought the situation to an impasse. As of this writing there is no end in sight.

Chapter 7

KARABAKH

GENERAL INFORMATION

K arabakh is a predominantly Armenian enclave within Azerbaijan. But the conflict that pits Armenians against Azeris in Karabakh should be seen within a larger regional framework that includes Armenia and Azerbaijan. The republic of Armenia covers 11,506 square miles (29,800 square kilometers), or about 10 percent of historical Armenia. Its population of 3.5 million is extremely homogeneous: at least 93 percent is Armenian (the percentage is probably even higher now after the expulsion of about 150,000 Azeris). Since 1920, Armenians within the borders of the former Soviet Union have experienced explosive population growth, from 1,568,000 in 1926[1] to over 4.6 million today. Until 1988 about one-third of Soviet Armenians lived outside the republic, mostly in adjacent Georgia and Azerbaijan (about half a million in each republic). Since 1988, however, virtually all Armenians in Azerbaijan living outside Karabakh have fled.

Outside the former Soviet Union there is a large Armenian diaspora: some 650,000 in the United States, over 300,000 in various Arab countries, 250,000 in France, 200,000 in Iran, 150,000 in Turkey, and smaller communities elsewhere; altogether from 6.5 to 7 million.

Their adversaries, the Azeris, number about 15 million. Of this number some 8 million live in Iran and 5.7 million in the former Soviet republic of Azerbaijan. Another 1.5 million are scattered throughout the former Soviet republics of Georgia, Kazakhstan, Uzbekistan, and Russia (mostly in Daghestan). Virtually all Azeris from Armenia had been expelled.

HISTORICAL BACKGROUND

Armenia descended from Urartu, an ancient state established by an Indo-European speaking people in the ninth century B.C. in eastern Anatolia. The country was later subjugated by Assyria and Persia, and it is a Persian inscription of 522 B.C. that first mentions "Armina" among other satrapies of the Persian Empire. Like the rest of the empire, Armenia was conquered by Alexander the Great and after his death in 323 B.C. passed on to the Seleucids.

Throughout its history Armenia suffered from disunity imposed by its mountainous terrain. As the country passed from empire to empire, usually with some degree of local autonomy, it was subdivided into small statelets whose rulers constantly quarreled with each other. Occasionally, one of them achieved preeminence and established a strong dynasty, but for the most part Armenia remained decentralized through most of its history.

In the beginning of the first century B.C. the Armenian king Tigran II took advantage of a temporary weakness that then afflicted all the surrounding empires—Roman, Parthian, and Seleucid—and united all Armenian territories under his rule. He then embarked on a policy of conquest. By 70 B.C. his empire encompassed Syria, Phoenicia, Cilicia, and Mesopotamia.

The new empire posed a threat to Rome. In 69 B.C. a Roman army under Lucullus invaded Armenia; the three year war that ensued was somewhat inconclusive, but Tigran was forced to surrender his throne. From then on Armenia became a semiautonomous state, a buffer zone between two powerful empires, Rome and Parthia. This was a role Armenia was destined to play often in its long and turbulent history.

The tug of war between the two empires led to a massive Roman invasion of Parthia under Trajan in A.D. 113. Parthia lost; its defeat led to Parthia's decline. By 226 the tottering Parthia was replaced by the Sassanid empire, which proved to be a more determined foe. The Sassanians wanted to restore the Achaemenid empire at its peak and enforce the Zoroastrian religion. From 226 until 387 the Sassanids battled Rome, mostly in Armenian territory. Since neither empire was strong enough to defeat the other decisively, they eventually partitioned the country, the larger share going to Persia.

It was during this turbulent time that Armenia's conversion to Christianity, traditionally dated from 301, occurred. The monophysite Armenian Church created a powerful national binder for the Armenian people. A hundred years later, in 404, the invention of the Armenian alphabet further reinforced Armenian identity.

Constant strife between the leading families of Persian Armenia led the nobility, in a rare act of political suicide, to petition the Persian shah to

1. Karabakh
2. Nakhichevan

abolish the Armenian monarchy. The shah was only too happy to oblige. In 428 eastern Armenia became a province of the Sassanid empire.

In the sixth and seventh centuries the titanic struggle between Byzantium—the heir to Rome—and Persia continued. Utterly exhausted, the two empires could not withstand the onslaught of the Arabs when they swept through the Middle East in the seventh and eighth centuries. Persia was defeated and converted to Islam; Byzantium survived but lost all its African and most of its Asian provinces, except Asia Minor.

Arabs appeared in Armenia in 640 and in 642 they captured the capital, Dvin. Armenia was caught between Byzantium and the Caliphate, once again a buffer zone between two empires. Christian Armenia, interestingly, sided for the most part with the more flexible Caliphate, which did not interfere as much in its internal affairs as long as the taxes were paid. Perhaps in recognition of this leaning, Armenia was granted the status of an autonomous tributary state in 653-54.

Once the balance of power between the Arabs and the Byzantines had stabilized, Armenia could again revive. From the middle of the ninth until the beginning of the eleventh century the country experienced a period of economic and cultural efflorescence. By the middle of the eleventh century Byzantium managed to incorporate some of the most important Armenian principalities, mostly through skillful diplomacy. Anxious to preserve its hold, Byzantium tried to destroy and neutralize the Armenian nobility and prevent the creation of local defenses. Leaderless and disarmed, Armenia could not withstand the Seljuk Turks, who swept across the country in 1064, destroying its capital, Ani. The destruction of Armenia opened the way into Byzantium, which was defeated in 1071 at Manzikert. Fatally weakened, Byzantium succumbed to the Crusaders in 1204. In Armenia, the Seljuks were followed by the Mongols, who in 1236 completely devastated the area. The now sparsely populated country offered ample land for the nomads. Still more ferocious was the slaughter perpetrated by Tamerlane in 1368-69. The new conqueror swept the land like a hurricane, but did not stay. Instead the country was divided between two rival Turkoman dynasties, the Black and the White Rams, who bickered with each other in sporadic warfare. Eventually the White Rams won, only to be defeated by the re-emergent, this time Safavid, Persia in 1502.

While the country was being torn asunder by this series of invasions and wars, many Armenians fled south into Cilicia. The first group was settled by the Byzantines in the tenth century. They wanted to secure the recently reconquered area by settling it with a Christian population. As the Turks, Mongols, and other nomads rammed their way across Armenia, other Armenians followed earlier settlers. By 1080 the Armenians in Cilicia felt confident enough to declare their independence. Thus, in a rare historical occurrence, a sovereign Armenian state was reconstituted some 600 miles south of the original core area. The new state, known as Lesser Armenia, lasted almost 300 years, until 1375, and finally succumbed to the Mameluks, largely as a result of the same internal strife that had previously plagued Larger Armenia.

During the sixteenth and the beginning of the seventeenth century Safavid Persia battled Ottoman Turkey, and Armenia yet again became a buffer zone between two empires. By the middle of the seventeenth century the border stabilized; it ran through Armenia, dividing the country between the rival empires.

The balance of power between Turkey and Persia began to crumble with the Russian advance into the Caucasus region, which started in the eighteenth century and gained momentum after 1795. The advance reached

Armenia only in 1813, when Russia, after a successful campaign against Persia, obtained the Persian province of Karabakh by the treaty of Gulistan.

An unsuccessful Persian invasion of 1826 was rebuffed the following year, and by the treaty of Turkmenchai of February 1828 Russia gained all of Persian Armenia, including Yerevan and Nakhichevan. Once again, Armenia was divided between two empires. But now Armenia's strategic position was reversed, with Muslim Turkey in the west and Christian Russia in the east and north.

Russia's war with Persia was followed by a war with Turkey in 1828-29, in which occurred the first Armenian massacre by the Turks in modern times, at Akhaltsikhe on March 5, 1829. Although Russia was again victorious, it relinquished most of its conquests. But between 60,000 and 90,000 Armenians followed the retreating Russian army to Russian-held territory. These emigres greatly increased the Armenian population in the area and created the nucleus of Russian Armenia.

The geographical distribution of Armenians within the Russian empire was unusual: the mass of the peasantry lived in historical Armenia; the intelligentsia was concentrated in Tbilisi, Georgia; and the bourgeoisie preferred the oil-rich Baku in Azerbaijan. This distribution created a split within the Armenian community and retarded the development of the Armenian heartland, which was greatly expanded by the acquisition of Kars and Ardahan in the Russo-Turkish war of 1877-78.

The position of Russian Armenians changed drastically after the assassination of Alexander II in 1881. The new tsar, Alexander III, was bent on Russification, and a small Orthodox people seemed a prime candidate for that. Another cause for imperial concern was that the spread of socialist ideas in Russia influenced the Armenian intelligentsia; in 1885 the first Armenian political party appeared. By 1895 the Russian government was sufficiently worried about what it mislabeled "Armenian nihilists" to stop interceding on Armenia's behalf in Turkey. Relations hit a new low in June 1903 when a government decree put the management of Armenian Church property in Russian hands.

The degree of mutual estrangement became apparent during the first Russian revolution. When Azeri-Armenian clashes flared up in February 1905 the authorities either did nothing or even sided with the Azeris. In the first round in Baku about 1,500 people were killed, some 900 Armenians and 600 Azeris. The outbreak in Baku was followed by anti-Armenian pogroms in Nakhichevan in May, Yerevan in June, and Shusha in September, the last of which ignited another conflagration in Baku. This time the Azeris set fire to the oil fields causing enormous damages. But the Armenian community was better prepared than it had been in February, and of the 600 victims only one-quarter were Armenian.

The estrangement between Armenians and the Russian government proved temporary. By 1912 there was revived interest among Russian ruling circles in acquiring Turkish Armenia, and Russian official attitudes reverted to a pro-Armenian stance.

***

In the Ottoman Empire, the fate of the Armenians was much worse.

The total number of Armenians in the empire seems to have declined from about 2.5 million in the middle of the nineteenth century (precise data is lacking) to just over 2 million by 1912. Much of the decline was due to emigration, although some was probably due to assimilation.

About 60 percent of Ottoman Armenians lived in the east, in the six provinces comprising historical Armenia. The rest lived in Constantinople or were scattered throughout the empire. In Armenia proper, Armenians constituted 38.9 percent of the population, Turks 25.5 percent, and Kurds 16.3 percent (the rest were Assyrians, Greeks, and others).[2] Thus, some time before 1900 Armenians had lost their numerical majority even in historical Armenia.

The sociological distribution of Russian Armenia was replicated in Turkey: while a significant number of Armenians in the capital were merchants who enjoyed wealth and privilege, those in Armenia proper were mostly poor peasants oppressed by Turkish officials and Kurdish landholders. Armenian peasants had little hope of improving their situation and, when pressed, were prone to revolt. The first rumblings of discontent occurred in 1862-63 in Zeitun, Van, and Marash, but these early riots and insurrections ended in a stalemate.

Russian victories in the Russo-Turkish war of 1877-78 gave encouragement to Armenian nationalists. The Armenian National Assembly requested local self-government and protection for Armenians. Turkey, supported by Britain (which was anti-Russian), refused. An Armenian delegation was sent to European capitals to apprise European governments of the situation in Armenia; it also tried to obtain guarantees at the Congress of Berlin. But it failed in the face of Britain's opposition and the indifference of other powers. It received only empty promises and meaningless guarantees: the Cyprus Convention and Article 61 of the Berlin Treaty, which called upon "the Sublime Porte to carry out improvements and reforms demanded by local requirements in the provinces inhabited by Armenians, and to guarantee their security against Circassians and Kurds."[3]

Abandoned by the powers, Armenians began to organize on their own. The first Armenian political party, Armenakan, was founded in the fall of

1885. Others, the Hnchaks and Young Armenia, soon followed. By 1890 they were active in Turkish Armenia, dispensing vengeance (or justice, depending on one's point of view) to Kurds and, occasionally, establishment Armenians who were against the struggle. There were riots in Erzerum in June 1890 (provoked by the authorities) and later a challenge to the Armenian establishment in Constantinople. In response, the Turkish government created Hamidiye cavalry regiments consisting mostly of Kurds. This move killed two birds with one stone: it gave rebellious Kurds something to do and created units to suppress the Armenians.

In August 1894 the first large-scale Kurdish attack destroyed three Armenian villages (Semal, Shenik, and Gelieguzan) south of Moush; between 900 and 3,000 inhabitants perished.[4] The affair destroyed whatever good will toward the Ottoman government had still existed among the Armenians. On September 30, 1895, the Armenians organized a large protest demonstration in Constantinople; it was brutally suppressed, with 20 killed and 100 wounded. In the aftermath, the authorities incited Turkish mobs to a pogrom, with riots lasting until October 10.

Then a wave of massacres hit the provinces. At least 920 Armenians were killed in Trebizond on October 8, at least 630 at Bitlis on the twenty-fifth, 350 in Erzerum on the thirtieth; about 1,000 in Diyarbekir on November 1-3, 1,200 in Sivas on the twelfth, 1,500 families in Gurun, and so on.[5] These are the major massacres, with hundreds of victims, but there were dozens more, in smaller towns and villages, in which the number of victims was "only" in the dozens. The assaults reached their peak with a vicious massacre at Urfa in December and then began to die down. Altogether, by modest estimates, between 50,000 and 100,000 Armenians had died.[6] The Turks did not achieve their goals everywhere; Zeitun and Van successfully defended themselves. But in general the disarmed, poorly organized Armenians were an easy target for Turkish soldiers and Kurdish irregulars.

Embittered by the slaughter, 25 Armenian revolutionaries captured the Ottoman Bank in Constantinople on August 26, 1896, and threatened to blow it up unless their demands were met. The affair was quickly resolved, but another massacre, this time in Constantinople, followed. By conservative estimates, between 5,000 and 6,000 Armenians perished and 75,000 fled from the capital.[7]

The revolution of 1908 brought about an unheard of fraternization among Muslims and Christians, even between Armenians and Turks. Several thousand Armenians and Turks gathered together at the graves of the victims of the massacres of 1895-96 to offer prayers. For a short while it seemed as though the old enmities had been buried for good, but this proved to be an illusion. On April 13-16, 1909, a major massacre broke out in Adana. As a result, some 2,000 Armenians were killed in the town and between 15,000 and 25,000 in the surrounding villages; 15,000 fled their homes. The massacre was repeated on the twenty-fifth. Similar massacres took place all across Cilicia and around the Gulf of Alexandretta. This time the new revolutionary government decided to act and prosecuted 34 Turks and 6 Armenians for their part in the communal strife.[8] The events in Adana made Armenians more careful. As the Young Turks grew more nationalistic, Armenian disillusionment increased.

World War I presented the Turkish government with an excellent opportunity to rid Turkey of its minorities. The actual decision—the Turkish equivalent of the Nazi Wannsee conference—seems to have been taken in mid-February of 1915 by the Central Committee of the Committee of Union and Progress. In the last ten days of February, Armenian officials and government employees were dismissed, Armenian soldiers were taken from combat units and placed in labor battalions, and Armenian officers were imprisoned. Then the government demanded that Armenians surrender all arms. It also arrested large numbers of men and held them as hostages.

Once Armenians had been disarmed, deportations began. They usually followed the same pattern: first, a proclamation would announce that the Armenian population was to be evacuated, would give the reason (usually, military security), and would assure the population of the government's benevolence. It would also invite all men to come to the government building. From there they would be taken to prison, held for a day or two, then marched to an isolated place and killed. Several days later, the rest of the population— women, children, and old people—would be sent off marching along endless roads, mostly without food, water, or shelter, until they dropped dead. On the way, they would be mercilessly robbed and raped. In their place some 750,000 Turkish refugees, mostly from western Thrace, were resettled. Only a few places, such as Van, managed to organize a spirited defense and hold out against overwhelming odds. But Van was once again an exception, not the rule.

In Constantinople, the "final solution" started on the night of April 23-24, 1915, when the government arrested 235 leading Armenians, then 600, then 5,000. The arrested were first incarcerated, then sent to the interior and butchered. Massacres and deportations were then unleashed on the whole community: 15,000 died in Bitlis, about 60,000 in and around Moush (where many victims were driven into wooden sheds and burned alive), 20,000 in Erzerum and 45,000 in the surrounding plain, 17,000 in Trebizond, 150,000 in the province of Sivas, and an astounding 570,000 killed in Diyarbekir (a

Kurdish town upon which many refugees and deportees from other areas had converged). Along with Armenians, the Turks also attacked and exterminated Assyrians, Jacobites, and Nestorian Christians. Only at Musa Dagh could Armenians escape by being evacuated on French and British ships. Talaat Pasha, one of the Young Turk leaders, even ordered the killing of Armenian orphans from Turkish orphanages and Armenian children adopted by Turkish families.[9]

Altogether, approximately a million Armenians were killed in the extermination campaign, about a quarter of a million escaped to Russia, 200,000 were forcibly converted to Islam, and only some 400,000 (20 percent of the original Armenian population) lived through the atrocities. In addition, between 50,000 and 100,000 Armenians died during the Turkish invasion of Transcaucasia in May-September 1918 and another 250,000 died in 1918-22 during the struggle for independence.[10]

***

In World War I the Russian armies at first scored impressive victories against Turkey. By the summer of 1916 they had occupied large chunks of Turkey's Armenian territories: Erzerum, Trebizond, all of the Lake Van district. However, by the time the Russians came, most of Turkish Armenia had been cleansed of its Armenian inhabitants.

The Russian revolutions of 1917 stopped the Russian advance. Tired of the war, the Russian armies began to disintegrate, which allowed the Turks to recapture some of their lost territories, such as Moush and Bitlis. But they waited until February 1918, when it became clear that Russia no longer had a viable fighting force, to launch a major assault. In the face of a determined Turkish onslaught Russian resistance crumbled, and in the Treaty of Brest-Litovsk, imposed by Germany in March 1918, Russia surrendered Kars, Ardahan, and Batum, all taken from Turkey in 1878. For Armenia, this was a major disaster.

Encouraged, the Turkish armies continued to advance into helpless Transcaucasia, despite several useless peace conferences, until ragtag Armenian units stopped them in a desperate battle at Sardarabad on May 24, 1918. While the battle was going on Georgia declared its independence (under German protection). With Georgia's departure the Transcaucasian federation, established after the March revolution, collapsed. Armenia had no choice but go it alone, proclaiming its independence on May 30.

At this point the country was at Turkey's mercy. The Treaty of Batum, signed on June 4, stripped Armenia of most remaining territories, leaving it only 11,000 square kilometers. This landlocked entity had only 300,000

Armenians and 300,000 Armenian refugees (plus 100,000 Azeris).[11] There were more Armenians in the Georgian capital Tiflis than in all of the Republic of Armenia. So weak was the new country that it was obliged to let through Turkish armies heading toward Baku (which they captured on September 14), where they massacred another 20,000 Armenians.[12]

The Paris Peace Conference of 1919 (and Woodrow Wilson in particular) promised much but delivered very little. None of the Allies was prepared to fight for Armenian interests. Armenia was left alone and isolated, surrounded by hostile neighbors greedy for Armenian territory. There was a short war with Georgia in December 1918 and Azeri uprisings in Karabakh and Nakhichevan. The results were inconclusive, but strategically Armenia lost again: while the western powers were noncommittal, in the east Soviet Russia found a useful ally in Kemalist Turkey. And the best way to win over and retain its friendship was at Armenia's expense.

Abandoned by the Allies, looking for protection against Turkey, the Armenian government felt it had to reach an understanding with Russia on any terms. At the time, Armeno-Soviet relations were complicated by the suppression of a pro-Bolshevik uprising in Armenia in May. While an Armenian delegation negotiated in Moscow and the Eleventh Red Army squeezed Karabakh and Zangezur, the Russians stalled and delayed. In these desperate circumstances Armenia was constrained to sign an agreement with Soviet Russia on August 10, 1920, which allowed a temporary occupation of some Armenian territory. By coincidence, on that same day the Allies and Turkey signed the Sevres peace treaty by which Turkey recognized Armenia's independence and renounced its claims to much of eastern Armenia. Unfortunately for Armenia, the treaty's clauses concerning Armenia were unenforceable and were never implemented. Almost immediately the Turks broke the treaty: they attacked Armenia in September 1920 and advanced to within 40 miles of Yerevan. By November 17 Armenia, badly mauled in the fighting, had no choice but to accept Turkish diktat.

In these circumstances the only alternative left was Bolshevik Russia, so when Soviet forces entered Armenia on the twenty-ninth, the government decided not to resist. The Revolutionary Committee composed of Communist Armenians from Baku entered the country on December 5; the next day Cheka (the secret police) was set up. Thus, by the end of 1920, Armenia lost its independence. That was not all. Soviet Russia satisfied virtually all Turkish demands and awarded Karabakh and Nakhichevan to Azerbaijan; only Zangezur was left to Armenia. Soviet forces also suppressed Armenian nationalistic uprisings in February 1921. But at least the rump Armenia, although devastated and stripped of many territories, was saved.

(It is a little-known fact that deportations of the remnant Armenian population continued even in Kemalist Turkey. Estimates of those deported in 1929-30 reach some 30,000 people.[13])

THE PRESENT CONFLICT

After 1920 Armenia enjoyed 70 years of peace. But the seeds of the present-day troubles sown in the cataclysmic events of 1915-20 were only waiting to germinate.

When the topic of Armeno-Azeri conflict comes up in the contemporary media only Nagorno-Karabakh is usually mentioned. Actually, Karabakh is only one of three territories, the other two being Nakhichevan and Zangezur, where a highly mixed population has lived in an uneasy proximity for centuries.

Each community has its own version of events. The Armenians argue that these territories are historically Armenian, and that they had temporarily lost their Armenian majority due to flight from nomadic depredations, wars between Persia and Turkey, and large-scale deportations, such as the removal of 60,000 Armenian families from Old Julfa in 1604.[14]

The Azeris claim that the Armenian majority in these territories is a recent phenomenon resulting from the mass in-migration of Armenians from Persia and Turkey in the nineteenth century. Whatever their origin, by the second decade of this century Armenians were in the majority in most of these areas. In Shusha, the administrative center of Karabakh, they comprised 85 percent of the population.[15]

Initially, it was the British, ensconced in Baku and still pro-Turkish despite four years of bloody war, who tipped the balance in the Azeri and Turkish favor. In November 1918 they compelled the Armenian forces under Andranik to stop their advance at the gate of Shusha. Their support for the local Azeri notable Sultanov enabled him to impose provisional Azeri control over Karabakh. And, as often happens in such cases, the provisional later became permanent.

The Azeris were less successful in Zangezur and Nakhichevan, where local Armenians refused to accede to their demands. Nakhichevan was lost later, when Soviet Russia bowed to Turkish pressure in 1921.[16] By 1990 its previously numerous Armenian population had dwindled to barely 2,000. Ultimately, only Zangezur remained, a narrow proboscis reaching out toward Iran.

Although the decline in the Armenian population of Karabakh was less precipitous than in Nakhichevan, it was considerable enough—from 94 percent in 1921 to 74 percent in 1987[17]—to cause concern. It made Armenians realize that if present trends continued (caused by slower population growth and higher emigration) they would eventually lose their majority even there.

Until perestroika protest was impossible. Only with the opening up of Soviet society could Karabakh Armenians hope to change the status of their region. First, they collected signatures for a petition requesting the unification of Karabakh with Armenia and sent it to Moscow, where the Karabakh delegation was received by the Central Committee on December 1, 1987. The petition was backed by numerous rallies throughout the republic in January-February 1988.[18]

As the conflict escalated, Azeri and Armenian authorities, as well as people on both sides, were inevitably drawn in. The Azeri government in Baku applied pressure in an attempt to make Karabakh Armenians back down. In the atmosphere of increasing nationalism and ethnic hatred open clashes were only a matter of time.

The first Azeri attacks on Armenians throughout Azerbaijan started on February 21, 1988. Probably the most violent was the assault of several thousand Azeris from Agdam on the Armenian town of Askeran, in which several dozen Armenians were wounded and two Azeris were shot.[19] The next day anti-Armenian violence erupted in Sumgait, a dismal industrial city north of Baku, where, in a veritable pogrom, 27 Armenians were killed, 17 women raped, and 276 soldiers injured (according to official figures).[20] The attack had been well prepared: for example, sharp iron rods used in the assault had been manufactured at one of the city plants, a fact that implicates local Azeri authorities and, possibly, party leaders.

As thousands of Armenian refugees streamed into Armenia, local paramilitary groups (the "bearded ones") started expelling Azeris living in the republic. Most of the Azeri expellees from Armenia ended up in Baku, where they proved to be an explosive mix used by local nationalists to incite further anti-Armenian violence against the 200,000 Armenians then still living in the city (not that they needed much encouragement).

The rest is well known: the ferocious anti-Armenian pogrom in Baku on January 13-15, 1990, in which up to 60 people, mostly Armenians, were killed; the assault of the Soviet army on Baku on January 19-20 as Moscow tried to reimpose control (according to the official data, 83 people died in the storming of the Azeri capital); the blockade of Armenia by Azerbaijan; guerrilla warfare between Armenians and Azeris in Karabakh and along the border between the two republics; and finally, after the collapse of the Soviet Union, open warfare over Nagorno-Karabakh.[21]

For the first time in centuries Armenians have scored impressive victories. Large sections of western Azerbaijan have been overrun by Armenian militias; up to a million Azeri refugees have fled east. As of this writing an uneasy truce has put the war on hold, and the presidents both countries are reported to be negotiating by fax. The conflict has disappeared from the front pages of the leading western newspapers. But the blockade continues. The people of both countries are still suffering, with Armenians without fuel and food and thousands of Azeri refugees still homeless in refugee camps. Even worse, the war may flare up at any moment; without a comprehensive settlement it is only a matter of time.

Chapter 8

Kosovo

General Information

K osovo is a small autonomous province in the southwest of Serbia. Within the rump Yugoslavia it borders on Serbia and Montenegro; externally, on Albania and Macedonia.

Ethnically, Kosovo is about 90 percent Albanian. According to 1991 census figures published by the Yugoslav Federal Board for Statistics, there were 1,727,000 Albanians in rump Yugoslavia, of whom 1,687,000 lived in Serbia (that is, in Kosovo plus Sanjak).[1] Since the number of Albanians in Serbia outside Kosovo reaches only 100,000, Kosovo has about 1.5 million Albanians. These are official figures; unofficial estimates put the total number of Albanians in the rump Yugoslavia at 2 million, which means that their numbers in Kosovo may reach 1.8 million.

Kosovo Albanians are part of a larger Albanian ethnic continuum that includes over 3 million Albanians in Albania proper, some 500,000 in Macedonia (as high as 700,000 according to Albanian claims), about 100,000 in Serbia outside Kosovo and some 50,000 in Montenegro. There are smaller Albanian pockets in Bosnia and Greece, for a total of about 6 million in the Balkans. (Some estimates go as high as 7 million, but this seems unwarranted.)

There is also a small Albanian diaspora in the West: 120,000 in southern Italy; and over 100,000 in the United States. The total probably does not exceed 300,000.

Historical Background

Albanians are descendants of Illyrian tribes who arrived in the Balkans some time around 1000 B.C. and settled south of the Sava and Drava rivers and along the eastern coast of the Adriatic Sea. Basically, the western half of the Balkan peninsula, roughly corresponding to the territories of former Yugoslavia and contemporary Albania, was Illyrian.

Two factors have been of paramount importance throughout Albanian history: chronic disunity that made long-term resistance to invasion difficult (until very recently, Albanians have been divided into often-warring clans), and a pervasive Greek influence emanating from Greece proper to the south and from a few Greek colonies on the coast.

Only once, in the third century B.C., did one of the Illyrian tribes, the Ardaei, succeed in establishing a more or less independent political entity. Soon, however, sea piracy by Illyrians led to a conflict with Rome. Between 229 and 167 B.C. the Romans subjugated virtually the entire Illyrian territory. A major revolt in A.D. 6-9 was mercilessly crushed, and from then on the tribes were subject to vigorous Romanization. Romanization succeeded in much of Illyrian territory, but in the south, in present-day Albania, it was hampered by the proximity of Greece. Via Egnatia, the dividing line between Latin and Greek spheres of influence, cut Albania's territory in half, and the pulls of two strong cultural influences may have created a neutral zone that helped preserve Illyrian dialects in the region. When the Roman empire split in two the now much reduced Illyria passed to Byzantium.

The barbarian invasions that started in the third century A.D. devastated the Balkans. The original inhabitants were either killed or fled into the mountains or farther south. By the time of the great Slav migration in the sixth and seventh centuries much of the peninsula had been cleared of Romanized Illyrians. Those who remained were quickly overpowered by Slavs and were soon assimilated.

Mountainous Albania, farther south, was less vulnerable to northern invaders, and its population was probably reinforced by a flood of refugees from the north. Most likely, the concentration of Illyrians in a relatively small area around the important port of Durres allowed them to withstand assault and assimilation. Another contributing factor was Byzantine rule, which lasted for about 800 years and provided some continuity with the past. At the same time, its instability helped Albanians to preserve their ethnicity. Expansion by Bulgaria and Serbia and interludes of Norman and Venetian rule put some Albanian tribes and, occasionally, the whole country, outside the Byzantine sphere of influence.

After the capture of Constantinople by the Crusaders in 1204, Charles I of Naples tried to set up a Kingdom of Albania centered around Durres, but this creation did not last either.

Throughout all the turbulence, the rhythms of Albanian life remained largely unchanged. Distant governments were mostly interested in taxes and left Albanian clans to themselves. Always in search of better pastures,

1. to Albania
2. to Serbia

Albanians spread far and wide: south into Greece (where they settled en masse in Attica and Peloponnesus), east into Macedonia, and north into Serbia and Hercegovina.

The Turks entered the Balkans in 1352, and victories over Bulgaria in 1371 and over Serbia in 1389 at Kosovo Pole inaugurated 500 years of Turkish (mis)rule in the area. At first, disunited Albania offered relatively little resistance and seems to have been subdued without major battles. Later, however, under the leadership of Skanderbeg, Albanian resistance stiffened. Between 1430 and 1478 they waged a war of stubborn resistance against Turkey. The last stronghold, Durres, did not fall until 1501.

Unexpectedly, in light of their earlier resistance to Turkish encroachments, Albanians proved to be highly adaptable in the Turkish empire. To those who accepted Islam, the sky was the limit. Good soldiers that they were, many Albanians made brilliant careers in the Turkish service. Some of the highest military commanders in Turkey were of Albanian origin. One of these, Mehmet Ali, was the founder of the last Egyptian dynasty.

The concerted Ottoman policy of Islamization did not start until the seventeenth century, but in the eighteenth and especially the nineteenth centuries about two-thirds of Albanians converted to Islam. About 20 percent remained Orthodox and 10 percent were Catholic. Ironically, Albanians accepted Islam when Turkey's fortunes were on the wane. This had a disastrous effect on Albania's later struggle for independence and territorial integrity.

Under Turkish rule Albanians continued to spread north and south. In this they were supported by the Turkish governments, which found it useful to have Muslim allies in non-Muslim areas. In the north, their movement was helped by the reflux of Serbian population from the old Serbian heartland in southern Serbia. The great Serbian migration of 1690 sent up to 300,000 Serbs (estimates vary) into Vojevodina in what was then southern Hungary (and is now northern Serbia). While the Serbs retreated north, Albanians followed. By the nineteenth century they reached Serbia's old capital of Nis. (In a sense, the Albanians were resettling their ancestral Illyrian lands.) And in the south there were large Albanian settlements in Greece, including Attica and the Peloponnesus.

Turkish defeat in the Russo-Turkish war of 1878 brought forth the first major nationalist movement in Albania, the Prizren League, exactly 400 years after the fall of Kruje (a stronghold that had been the center of resistance to the Turkish invasion). But Albania did not have a powerful protector, as Slav Bulgaria and Serbia had in Russia. As a result, some ethnic Albanian territory was ceded to Greece, Montenegro, and Serbia. Serbia tried to cleanse the newly acquired territories of southern Serbia, pushing thousands of Albanians south into Kosovo. And, once peace was re-established, the Turkish government suppressed the Prizren League in 1881.

The Turkicization policy of the Young Turks in 1908 provoked deep resentments among all minorities, including Albanians. An Albanian revolt broke out in 1909. It was not until August 1910 that the Turkish army took the last stronghold, Shkoder. Smaller uprisings continued through 1911 and flared up again in 1912; 30,000 Albanian rebels operated in Kosovo alone.[2]

The First Balkan war (October-December 1912) and the support of Italy and Austria-Hungary (each hoped to expand its sphere in the Balkans) allowed the Pan-Albanian congress at Vlore to proclaim Albanian independence on November 28, 1912. However, the borders of the new state drawn at the Ambassadors' Conference in London did not include many Albanian-majority areas in Kosovo, Greece, Macedonia, and Montenegro. At the same time a large Greek-speaking minority was left in southern Albania (claimed as northern Epirus by Greece). Albanians in Kosovo, angered by the separation from Albania, rebelled, but proved no match for the regular Serbian army.

The new state was extremely unstable; the first king, Prince Wilhelm of Wied, was forced to leave the country after only eight months on the throne. By the time World War I broke out, Albania had no effective central government. Northern Albanians allied themselves with Austria-Hungary, in an effort to stave off Serbian and Montenegrin encroachments, while southern Albanians chose the Entente in the hope of preventing a Greek takeover. These hopes were in vain: the war brought Serbian and Montenegrin occupation in the north and Greek occupation of the south. Then Austrian troops marched in from the north while Italian and French troops occupied the south. Toward the end of the war, Italy sought to establish some form of control over the entire country, but by August 20, 1920, under pressure from the great powers, it had to recognize Albanian territorial integrity and independence. The Versailles Peace Conference of 1919 confirmed the pre-war borders, which meant that Kosovo remained under Serbian control. Once again the 440,000 Albanians of Kosovo did not accept the partition of their ethnic territory. They waged a guerrilla war against Yugoslavia until 1924, but once again the uprising was suppressed.

From the start, Yugoslav rule in Kosovo was less than benign. In the interwar years the use of the Albanian language was prohibited.[3] The Yugoslav authorities, like other governments in Eastern Europe, used agrarian reform to change the ethnic composition of the area by bringing in about 40,000 Slav settlers.[4] Albanians' relations with Belgrade were so bad that when Yugoslavia was dismembered in April 1941 and Kosovo, along with

Albanian-inhabited areas in western Macedonia, was attached to Italian-occupied Albania (which had been seized by Fascist Italy two years earlier), many Albanians in Kosovo greeted the Italians as liberators. They hoped that after the war Kosovo would remain Albanian.

But this was not to be. After Italy's capitulation in September 1943 the Germans took over and held the country until November 1944. When they left, Albanians in Kosovo tried to stave off the Yugoslav takeover but, as in 1912-13 and 1918-24, failed. By the spring of 1945 their resistance was crushed and thousands of Albanians were arrested and incarcerated. Albanian sources estimate that between 1945 and 1948 some 36,000 Kosovo Albanians were murdered, while Albanian emigre sources put the numbers even higher, at 60,000.[5]

Initially, Tito hoped to solve the Albanian problem by incorporating all of Albania into Yugoslavia. However, these plans fell through when Albania allied itself with the Soviet Union after Tito's break with Stalin. Fearful of the constant discontent, the Yugoslav government encouraged Albanians to emigrate, mostly to Turkey. By 1966 about 230,000 Kosovo Albanians, often posing as ethnic Turks, had left Yugoslavia.[6]

Despite the substantial emigration, Albanian population in Yugoslavia continued to increase rapidly. In Kosovo, 42.5 percent of the current Albanian population is aged 14 and under; an average Albanian family has 3.6 children, compared to an average Serbian family with 2.1; and in 1971 an average Yugoslav household contained 3.8 members, while ethnic Albanian households in Yugoslavia had 6.6 members; as a result, Yugoslav Albanian population grew at a 3.05 percent annual rate compared to the Yugoslav average of 1.14 percent.[7] Due to this high natural increase, the Albanian population in former Yugoslavia has grown more than four-fold in the last 70 years, and in Kosovo, where in 1971 Albanians accounted for 73.6 percent,[8] their share has now increased to 90 percent.

Given their rapidly increasing share of the population and the inadequacies of the political system, it was only a matter of time before the Albanians of Kosovo demanded more autonomy. The province was a time bomb.

THE PRESENT CONFLICT

As early as November-December 1968 there were large demonstrations in Kosovo and Albanian-populated areas of Macedonia demanding an Albanian republic within Yugoslavia. The Central Committee of the League of Communists of Yugoslavia rejected these demands at a session presided over by Tito on February 4, 1969.[9] However, Tito met Albanian demands halfway: Kosovo was granted broad autonomy, which was further expanded in 1971 and 1974.

While flexible Tito was alive, he managed to keep the lid on. When he died, all minorities grew restless. Even the far-reaching concessions of 1969, 1971, and 1974 failed to quell Albanian demands. A student demonstration at the Pristina University on March 11, 1981, escalated into widespread disturbances by early April. Although the riots were contained and eventually died down, ethnic tensions continued to rise. From then on the Serbs and Montenegrins of Kosovo found themselves increasingly on the defensive. Serbian cemeteries were vandalized, Serbs were harassed, Serbian women occasionally raped. As a result, an increasing number—20,000 between 1982 and 1986 in a Serbian population of only 230,000—left the province.[10] But the Serbs would not give in either. After 1986 the Serbian counterattack gathered steam. To stop Serbian out-migration the sale of real estate involving Albanians and Serbs was prohibited.[11] There were far-reaching purges among the local Albanian elites. With the accession to power of Slobodan Milošević the anti-Albanian campaign intensified. There were trials against prominent Albanian Kosovars in October 1989.[12]

The situation worsened with the collapse of Yugoslavia and the emergence of a strong nationalistic Serbia. In 1990 the provincial parliament was dissolved.[13] A new program of instruction limiting the use of Albanian was introduced in the schools of Kosovo and at the Pristina University. Some 73,000 professionals and civil servants were dismissed, a considerable number in a province of only 2 million.[14] The daily newspaper *Rilindja* was closed down in August 1990. The Serbian-dominated police force of 60,000 was beefed up.

In response, members of the former provincial assembly met at Kacanik on September 7, 1990, and created a shadow government, which proclaimed Kosovo a constituent republic within Yugoslavia. The measure was approved by a clandestine referendum held on September 26-30, 1991. On October 19, 1991, the legislature went further and proclaimed Kosovo a sovereign and independent state.[15] The declaration confirmed Serbs' worst fears. It is understood by both Serbs and Albanians that Kosovo will eventually seek unification with Albania.

In the parliamentary and presidential elections held on May 24, 1992, 511 candidates from 22 parties contested 143 seats.[16] However, the democratic character of the elections is open to debate: the sole presidential candidate, Ibrahim Rugova, received 99.7 percent of the vote. Also, Kosovo's 36,000 Gypsies were not included in the proportional representation system.[17] And, like their cousins in Bosnia, Kosovo Serbs boycotted the elections.

By now a stalemate seems to have been reached between the Albanians of Kosovo and the government in Belgrade. On the one hand, Albanian leaders rejected repeated invitations from Belgrade in May and June 1992 to discuss issues of mutual interest. On the other hand, the Serbian police and the security forces seem to have managed to contain Albanian discontent within tolerable bounds. At the very least, there has been no open uprising or large-scale guerrilla war in Kosovo. No doubt, the tragic examples of Bosnia and Croatia, and the realization that Serbs will not stop at massive retaliation, have played their part. It is quite likely, however, that once the war in Bosnia and Croatia is somehow resolved, the Serbs' attention will turn to Kosovo. And since Kosovo is sacred ground for the Serbs, for historical reasons, their fury may dwarf anything seen so far in Bosnia and Croatia.

Chapter 9

THE PALESTINIAN PROBLEM

GENERAL INFORMATION

The conflict between Arabs and Jews has been played out not only in Israel within its present borders but also in the adjacent territories: the so-called West Bank, the Gaza Strip, Jordan, the Sinai peninsula, the Golan Heights, and much of southern Lebanon. It also has a wider dimension since it has often involved the entire Arab and Muslim world, as well as the world community and the major powers, which have often tried to intervene in local conflicts. Rivalry between major powers has been an important element in the Middle East, as elsewhere.

Israel is a very small country. Its territory within the 1967 borders is only 8,019 square miles. The West Bank and the Gaza Strip together cover an additional 2,947 square miles; by comparison Jordan spreads over 35,635 square miles, Syria over 71,498, and Egypt over 386,662 square miles. Among the neighboring states only Lebanon is of comparable size at 4,015 square miles.[1]

The Jewish population of the area now stands at 4.5 million. The number of Arabs under Israeli control in 1992 was 2.6 million; of these some 870,000 were Israeli citizens.[2] In the surrounding areas some 4 million Arabs live in Jordan, about 200,000 in southern Lebanon, and the Sinai peninsula is very sparsely populated.[3] Altogether, Israel, the territories it controls, and the adjacent area are home to some 7 million Arabs and 4.5 million Jews. These numbers do not include the total population of Egypt (60 million), Lebanon (3 million) and Syria (close to 15 million).

Outside Israel, there are some 9 to 10 million Jews (the largest community, 6 million, reside in the United States) and 160 to 170 million Arabs,
mostly in Africa (100 to 110 million) and Asia (approaching 60 million).[4]
(The total population of the Arab countries is much larger, but it includes
numerous non-Arab groups such as the Berbers in Maghreb and the Ne-
groid peoples of Sudan.)

HISTORICAL BACKGROUND

The lands of the Fertile Crescent and Mesopotamia have always attracted
migrants from the desert. Several waves of nomads converged from the south,
east, and north to find new homes in the area. Among these migrants were
the nomadic or seminomadic ancestors of the Jews, who migrated into what
today is Israel sometime in the nineteenth century B.C.

This early phase of Jewish history left few records, but we do know
that groups of Hebrews (and other Asians) periodically reached Egypt
and settled there before 1720 B.C. (the time of the Hyksos invasion)
while others remained in Canaan (present-day Palestine). After Egypt
had shaken off the Hyksos rule in about 1580-1567 B.C. non-Egyptians
were regarded with suspicion; the liberation inaugurated an era of antiminority
persecution, and the Hebrews of Egypt suffered accordingly. Some of
them, perhaps even the majority, escaped in the twelfth century B.C. and
joined their brethren in Canaan. By 1000 B.C., after a prolonged struggle
with the Philistines, they succeeded in establishing the first Jewish state.

It did not last long. In 926 B.C. internal differences split it into Israel in the
north and Judah (Judea) in the south. Israel was conquered by the Assyrians in
722 B.C. and many among its elites were deported to Assyria, where they gradually assimilated into the surrounding population. Judah held on until 597-587
B.C., when it succumbed to the Neo-Babylonian empire. Again, many of the
Judean elites were deported to Babylon and other areas in Mesopotamia, but
after 537 B.C., under the more benevolent Persian rule, many exiles returned and
re-established the Jewish administration in Judea.

The Neo-Babylonian empire was followed by Persia. As part of the
Persian empire the country was conquered by Alexander the Great in 332
B.C. and then passed on, after his death in 323 B.C., to Ptolemaic Egypt,
which eventually lost it to the Seleucids.

Faced with extreme diversity, the Seleucid emperors tried to weld their
multiethnic empire into a more coherent whole. To that end they introduced a
number of measures aimed at assimilating the non-Greek populations, including the Jews. These measures, inaugurated after 175 B.C., included
emperor worship, which seemed blasphemous to the Jews. They rose in

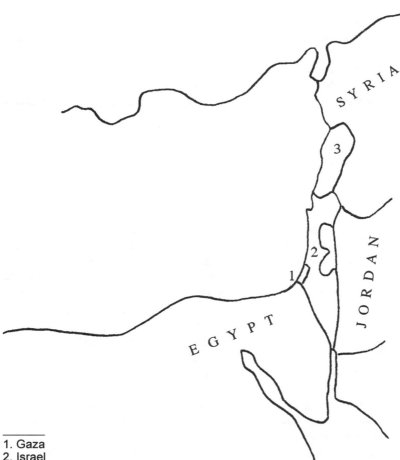

1. Gaza
2. Israel
3. Lebanon

revolt and, after a prolonged guerrilla war, in 167-142 B.C., freed the country. An independent Judea was re-established in 142 B.C.

The second state was also short lived. In 63 B.C. Judea was coerced into becoming a Roman client state and from A.D. 44, after 80 years of slow encroachment, it was reorganized as a Roman province. A massive Jewish revolt in 66-73, numerous uprisings in Jewish colonies throughout the Mediterranean in 115-117, and then another major uprising led by Bar Kohba, in 132-135, failed to dislodge the Romans. In the suppression of these revolts much, if not most, of the Jewish population of the country fled, was annihilated, or sold into slavery. For example, after the first uprising, Jerusalem was completely destroyed and depopulated, its people either killed or enslaved. And in the second revolt, during 132-135, 985 towns and villages were destroyed and 580,000 Jews died in the fighting, not counting thousands more who died of starvation and epidemics.[5] The whole land was laid waste.

But some Jews remained even after the catastrophes. There was yet another revolt in 351; and in 614, when the Persians captured Jerusalem, they returned it to the Jews. This last Jewish interlude lasted until 629, when the Byzantines recaptured the city and massacred, yet again, its Jewish inhabitants. Seven years later, in 636, the Byzantines were decisively beaten by the invading Arabs in the battle of Yarmuk, and by 640 all of Judea was occupied by the invaders.

The varying and multifaceted Jewish experience in diaspora is well beyond the narrow bounds of this chapter. From the earliest beginnings in the eighth century B.C. Jewish diaspora communities in virtually all countries experienced periods of relative acceptance and fluctuating tolerance, interspersed with outbursts of expulsion and massacre. Perhaps, the best known episodes of persecution are the Crusader pogroms in 1096-99, the expulsion from Spain in 1492, the Khmelnytsky massacres in Ukraine in 1648-54 and, of course, the worst mass murder in human history, the Holocaust, which killed some six million people.

After the Arab conquest, the Jewish population of Judea gradually dwindled while the majority of the non-Jewish inhabitants embraced Islam. However, the Jewish community, although greatly diminished, never entirely disappeared. In other words, the continuity of settlement was always maintained. As in other parts of the Arab world, Jews and Arabs lived in an uneasy coexistence somewhat similar to that in the Christian countries. Occasionally, there were periods of efflorescence, as in Muslim Spain, but on the whole Jews suffered discrimination and sporadic persecution visited upon all non-Muslim populations.

By the time the Crusaders arrived in 1099 most of the inhabitants were Muslim although there were numerous Christian and Jewish communities as well. The Crusader interlude lasted until 1187. It was followed by another period of Arab rule until 1250, when the country was occupied by the Mameluks. It was then conquered by the Ottoman Turks in 1517, who stayed, with brief interruptions (by Napoleon in 1799 and the Egyptians in 1834-42), until 1917, when the invading British pushed them out. The modern history of Israel starts from that point.

THE PRESENT CONFLICT

The present conflict between Jews and Arabs in Palestine started toward the end of the nineteenth century, when thousands of east European Jews, driven by European anti-Semitism, returned to the land of their ancestors to rebuild a "national home," a place where Jews from all over the world could find refuge. Palestinian Arabs resisted, hence the conflict.

We may note, in passing, that this was not the first Jewish return to the Holy Land. Occasionally, for example after the expulsion from Spain, a large number of Jewish refugees settled in Palestine, but forced resettlement by the Ottoman authorities (for example, in 1571, from Safed to Cyprus) and subsequent emigration sapped the vitality of the Jewish population.

In the nineteenth century the trickle of Jews into Palestine significantly increased. By 1860 there was a Jewish majority in Jerusalem. But this increased immigration still followed the traditional pattern: individual endeavors of deeply religious men and women who believed they were fulfilling God's Commandments.

The Russian and Ukrainian pogroms of 1881 served as a major catalyst for the development of Zionism and the Jewish migration from eastern Europe. The very next year saw the publication of Leo Pinsker's *Auto-Emancipation,* a cornerstone of the ideology of return, and the first wave of Zionist emigration to Palestine.

In the West the Jewish awakening came a decade later, with the first Dreyfus trial of 1894 and the publication of Herzl's *Judenstaat* in 1896. Thus, by 1900, major segments of world Jewry, east and west, turned their eyes toward the land of their ancestors. They were pushed out of their countries of residence by a strong and rising wave of anti-Semitism, especially in France, and the continued persecution in Russia, such as the Kishinev pogrom of 1903 and the turmoil that followed the revolution of 1905, when pogroms erupted all over Russia.

The turning point in Jewish fortunes came in the middle of World War I. On November 2, 1917, Britain issued the so-called Balfour Declaration, which committed Britain to establishing a Jewish National Home in Palestine. It was done partly from calculation and out of self-interest, but there was also a strong desire on the part of some British statesmen to right a historical wrong, the dispossession and the persecution of the Jewish people. A month later, after 400 years of Turkish rule, the British forces under General Allenby entered Jerusalem and then proceeded to dislodge the Turks from the rest of the country.

At first, Arab-Jewish relations in Palestine looked promising: representatives of both communities reached an accord in 1919 to demand from the Versailles Peace Conference the establishment of a Jewish state in Palestine and an east Arab state stretching from Iraq to Yemen. In effect, the accord divided the entire area between Arabs and Jews. But Britain and France had another division in mind: they wanted to divide the area between themselves (the Sykes-Picot agreement).

After some haggling, the San Remo conference in 1920 granted Britain the mandate over Palestine (France got Syria and Lebanon) with the understanding that it would facilitate the establishment of a Jewish National Home. The mandate was confirmed by the League of Nations in 1922.

Almost at once (actually, the decision was made by Churchill in March 1921)[6] Britain divided the country. The area to the east of the Jordan river, known as Transjordan (later, simply Jordan), was reorganized as an entirely new entity, with an Arab princeling soon installed on the throne. The area to the west was allocated to the Jewish National Home. This First Partition cost Palestine 76 percent of its original territory. It was the result of British interest in oil and Arab markets, British desires to build alliances with Arab elites and appease the Arab masses and, to some extent, widespread anti-Semitism among British decision makers.

But the appeasement failed. The vast majority of the Arabs rejected the reestablishment of the Jewish presence in what they regarded as Arab land. Led by the mufti of Jerusalem, they repeatedly rioted, trying to tilt British policy in their favor. Increasingly violent Arab riots shook the country in 1920, 1921, 1929, and 1936-39. Hundreds of Jews were killed. Particularly gruesome were the massacre in Hebron in 1929 and the first intifada of 1936-39, in which hundreds of Jews and several thousand Arab moderates were killed; thousands of moderate Arabs were forced to flee the country.

Increasing Arab hostility led to a tightening of British policy on Jewish immigration precisely at the time when European Jews needed an escape as never before. As the Nazi persecution of Jews in Europe mounted and more Jews sought refuge in the Jewish National Home, the British increasingly gave in to Arab pressure to block Jewish immigration and even undermine the Jewish National Home. In 1937 the Peel Commission recommended a second partition of the Jewish National Home into a tiny Jewish enclave and an Arab state, which was to be merged with Transjordan.

Two years later the Chamberlain White Paper put an end to the Jewish National Home altogether and promised to stop Jewish immigration within five years. The British also blockaded Palestine in order to prevent illegal Jewish immigration. While the Germans and their allies killed Jews in Europe, the British held the major escape door shut; thus, they also bear major responsibility for the six million dead. (Appeasement failed in the Middle East just as it had in Czechoslovakia. The leader of Palestinian Arabs, the mufti of Jerusalem, went to Berlin in 1941 where he urged Hitler(!) to destroy the Jews. Subsidized by the Germans, he did what he could to promote German victory. Among his endeavors was a trip to German-occupied Sarajevo, where he urged local Muslims to mount a pogrom against the

Jews. He also helped to organize Muslim SS units that killed Gypsies, Jews, and Serbs.)[7]

After the war Britain continued the blockade. Holocaust survivors trying to reach Palestine were sent to detention camps in Cyprus or even back to Germany. Meanwhile, the Jewish underground launched a series of attacks to dislodge the British. By 1947 Britain had had enough. Weakened by the war, its empire crumbling, it surrendered its mandate to the United Nations.

The United Nations came up with yet another partition scheme (Resolution 181 on November 29, 1947),[8] which allocated 10 percent of Western Palestine to the Jews (or 2 to 3 percent of the original territory), the rest to the Arabs. The Jews, having no alternative, had to accept it, but the Arab side did not.

It is ironic, in light of the subsequent developments, that neither the American State Department nor the British Foreign Office wanted the creation of Israel. It was the massive vote of the Soviet bloc that decided the issue. (Needless to say, it was not altruism or commiseration that prompted Stalin's pro-Israel stance. Stalin believed that a socialist Israel would be a thorn in the imperialist side. It is thus also ironic that socialist Israel became an American client state and that America has consistently shown preference for the socialist Labor Party over the non-Socialist Likud.)

In May 1948, immediately after the proclamation of Israel's independence, six Arab armies invaded the country. In the war that followed (the Israeli War of Independence), Jordan's Arab Legion (officered by the British) occupied sizeable chunks of Western Palestine, including the Old City of Jerusalem, destroying all Jewish settlements in its path; Egypt tore away Gaza. The rest fell to Israel in what was in effect the Second Partition.

From then on the struggle between Arabs and Jews continued on two levels. On the level of state relations several wars have been fought, all of them initiated or provoked by the Arab side: (1) with Egypt in 1956 (the Sinai Campaign), after Egypt blockaded the Israeli port of Eilat; (2) with Egypt, Jordan, and Syria in 1967 (the Six Day War), after Nasser promised to destroy Israel, closed off the Strait of Tiran, removed the UN forces that were supposed to keep both sides apart, and moved 100,000 soldiers and armor to the Israeli border; (3) with Egypt and Syria in 1973 (the Yom Kippur War), when both countries attacked Israel on the Day of Atonement; (4) the Israeli entry into Lebanon in 1982 in response to incessant PLO attacks on northern Israel; and, finally, (5) the bombardment of Israel by Iraq during the Persian Gulf War in 1991.

But there is another level on which the conflict is played out. In addition to wars, there have been incessant terrorist attacks on the Israelis. The best known are the murder of Israeli athletes in Munich in 1972; the killing of 26 people, mostly children, in Ma'alot in 1974; the massacre of 35 people on board an intercity bus in 1978; and thousands of other incidents involving fewer people but just as savage.[9] Chronologically, these attacks were carried out mostly from Egypt in 1952-56, Jordan in 1968-1970, and Lebanon after 1971.

At present, terrorism continues, despite peace treaties with Egypt and Jordan and the so-called Peace Process. On October 19, 1994, for example, a suicide bomber exploded a bomb on a crowded Tel Aviv bus killing 22 and wounding 50 people. Similar acts have been perpetrated in Jerusalem and elsewhere. Concessions that have so far been offered by and extracted from Israel have failed to satisfy the other side. But then, appeasement did not work fifty years ago, and it is unlikely to work now.

Chapter 10

THE RUSSIAN MINORITIES IN THE FORMER SOVIET REPUBLICS

GENERAL INFORMATION

The new Russia, formerly known as the RSFSR (the Russian Soviet Federative Socialist Republic, the main constituent republic of the former Soviet Union), is still the largest country in the world. Its territory is 6,592,849 square miles (17,075,400 square kilometers).[1]

Its population has now reached 150 million, 82.6 percent of which are ethnic Russian. Like its predecessor, Russia is a multiethnic country, but the overall share of the minorities has been drastically reduced. The largest, the Tatars and Ukrainians, number only 4 and 3 percent respectively.[2]

However, after the collapse of the Soviet Union, about 25 million Russians, or about 16 percent of the entire ethny, found themselves outside their homeland, in the former Soviet republics known in the contemporary Russian terminology as the Near-Abroad. Of these, the largest number, roughly 10 million, live in Ukraine. Other former Soviet republics also have large Russian minorities.[3] See Table 10.1.

Thus, in Kazakhstan, Latvia, and Estonia the Russian share of the total population surpasses 30 percent, while in Ukraine and Kyrgyzstan it is over 20 percent. Only in Transcaucasia, Lithuania, Uzbekistan, Turkmenistan, and Tajikistan is the percentage of ethnic Russians below 10 percent.

TABLE 10.1
PERCENTAGE OF ETHNIC
RUSSIANS IN FORMER SOVIET REPUBLICS

Republic	1959(%)	1989(%)
Slav Republics and Moldova		
Belarus	8.19	13.21
Ukraine	16.94	22.04
Moldova	10.16	12.94
Baltics		
Estonia	20.07	30.33
Latvia	26.58	3.96
Lithuania	8.52	I 9.35
Transcaucasia		
Armenia	3.20	1.56
Azerbaijan	13.56	5.59
Georgia	10.09	6.28
Central Asia and Kazakhstan		
Kazakhstan	42.73	37.82
Kyrgyzstan	30.18	21.53
Tajikistan	13.26	7.60I
Turkmenistan	17.32	9.52
Uzbekistan	13.46	8.34

Source: Hajda/Beissinger, Tables IC on p. 182 (Ukraine, Belorussia and Moldavia), p. 216 (The Baltic republics), p. 237 (Trans-caucasia), and p. 263 (Central Asia)

Despite the fact that the share of non-Russians in the new state (17.4 percent) is much lower than in the former Soviet Union (approximately 48 percent), the importance of non-Russian areas within the new Russian state should not be disregarded. Among these, only Daghestan, with 11.6 percent Russians, does not have a substantial Russian minority. In six areas the titular nationality is in the minority, with Russians ranging from 50.4 percent to 72 percent (Buriatia, Karelia, Komi, Mordva, Udmurt, and Soha [Yakutia]). And nine areas have substantial Russian minorities, between 26.0 percent and 47.5 percent (Bashkirtostan, Kabardino-Balkaria, Kalmykia, Mari, North Ossetia, Tatarstan, Tuva, Chechnya and Ingushetia, and Chuvashia).[4] In short, the Russian hold on most of the minority areas is now much more secure.

THE HISTORICAL BACKGROUND

Russian history can be divided into five distinct periods. The first Russian state centered on the upper Dnieper valley, with the capital at Kiev and a

1. Former Soviet Republics in Europe
2. Transcaucasia

major center in Novgorod. It was created in the middle of the ninth century by the Varangians (the Vikings) from Rodslagen (modern Sweden) seeking trade routes to Byzantium and the Orient. Kievan Russia reached a brief efflorescence in the eleventh century but was conquered by the Tatar-Mongols in 1236-41. The Tatar yoke comprised the second period. It lasted until 1480.

The third Russia was ruled from Moscow, a new center that rose under the Tartar domination, first as a Tatar ally, then as a challenger to the Tatar power. It was a closed-off and largely self-sufficient country ruled by despots who claimed to be the heirs of Rome and the protectors of the Orthodox peoples everywhere.

Shortly after 1700, Peter the Great opened Russia to the West and transferred its capital to a new city he had built on the Neva, St. Petersburg (founded in 1703, made the capital in 1712). For next 200 years the Russian Empire remained a relatively backward country with a Europeanized elite and a mass of conservative peasantry estranged from the aristocracy and its foreign ways. This fourth incarnation of Russia collapsed in 1914-21 under the strain of World War I, two revolutions, and a bloody civil war.

The new, Communist Russia moved its capital back to Moscow, cut itself off from the outside world, and, in the following 70 years, attempted to build communism. It failed. The communist empire collapsed in 1991, and now we are witnessing the emergence of a sixth, yet unknown, Russia, which is still in its infancy. It seems plausible, judging by its first steps, that the new Russia has finally rejoined the world.

Throughout its entire history, despite all its vagaries, Russian society has known quite a few constants. Migration east is one of them. The present distribution of the Russian population reflects this relentless drive eastward. The Russian migration east that started in the fifteenth century was a continuation of earlier population movements. It was preceded by the East Slav migration to the northeast, in the direction of Moscow, in the twelfth and thirteenth centuries and by an earlier Slav migration up the Dnieper valley in the seventh through ninth centuries. It is interesting to note that the East Slav migration, under the pressure from the nomads, was organized by the Kievan princes, that is by the state, and probably contributed to the authoritarian nature of the future Russian polity.[5]

The Tatar invasion and the Golden Horde blocked further expansion of the Russian ethny, but once the Tatar yoke was shaken off and the citadels of Kazan' and Astrakhan' conquered (in 1552 and 1556, respectively), the movement east resumed. In 1581 the *pervoprokhodtsy* (pioneers) crossed the Urals, and by 1639 they had conquered Siberia. This new migration was assisted and encouraged by the government. Already in 1571 a line of fortifications from the Donets to the Irtysh rivers was constructed to protect Russian settlers from nomad incursions.[6] The movement was largely propelled by demographics: relative overpopulation in the Russian core areas, fast Russian population growth starting in the eighteenth century, and concomitant decline of the ratio of agricultural land per person and resulting poverty.

During the seventeenth and eighteenth centuries more than 2 million migrants went south to Ukraine and into the steppe of southern Russia and Kazakhstan, and 400,000 went to Siberia.[7] The number of migrants who moved south in 1800-1914 is estimated at 12 to 13 million, while an additional 4.5 million moved to Siberia and Central Asia.

The migration was interrupted by World War I, the revolutions, and the civil war, but resumed in the mid-1920s. In 1926-39 more than 4 million people moved east, particularly to Kazakhstan. And the mass evacuation of 1941, in the early months of the German invasion, further reinforced the prevailing pattern.

After 1945 the movement continued, but at a slower pace. By then the Slav population was more urbanized, and its rate of population increase of 9.4 to 14.4 percent in 1959-70 could not compete with the explosive Muslim birth rates of 46.3 to 52.9 percent.[8] Inevitably, the percentage of Russians in the total Soviet population fell from 54.65 percent in 1959 to 50.78

percent in 1989.[9] Even in the other Slav areas, Belarus and Ukraine, the migratory balance turned largely negative from the mid-1970s. Only in the Baltic republics did the Russians maintain their position, due mostly to Balts' demographic weakness. The changes in the Russian demographic presence in the last thirty years can be seen in Table 10.1.[10]

Thus, the centuries old pattern was reversed: most Russian migrants went west to the Baltic and the Slav republics, while the percentage of Russian population in Transcaucasia and Central Asia plunged.

But the Russian influence was actually stronger than the numbers suggest since most of the nonindigenous population in the republics were *russkoiazychnyie* (russophones) and thus added to the Russian segment. For example, in Estonia the ethnic Russian population of 400,000 was reinforced by an additional 200,000 mostly Russian-speakers who nominally belonged to other nationalities but were fearful of anti-immigrant backlash and so were often anti-Estonian and pro-Russian. The total, 600,000 strong, was a formidable minority for a country of only 1.5 million people.

THE PRESENT CONFLICT

When the Soviet Union collapsed in August 1991 Russians living in the union republics suddenly found themselves under foreign jurisdiction, among populations that were vehemently nationalistic and anti-Russian after 70 years of Soviet—and often centuries of Tsarist—misrule.

Their position is strongly reminiscent of German minorities in Central Europe after the collapse of the German and Austrian empires in 1918. Suddenly, the tables were turned, and Russians, formerly the elder brother, the guiding light, the first among unequals, in effect the imperial masters, found themselves a barely tolerated minority.

Their present situation differs greatly from country to country. But even in the more civilized environment of the Baltic states Russians have to learn local languages and satisfy other requirements to obtain local citizenship. In other republics individual Russians are often assaulted and even killed. And everywhere they are objects of popular hatred and victims of unofficial or semiofficial discrimination.

It is not surprising, therefore, that many Russians are moving back to Russia. In this, they are no different from other imperial minorities such as the Germans and the Magyars who flocked by the thousands into their historic homelands after 1918.

Large scale migration into Russia, especially from Central Asia, started even before the collapse of the Soviet Union. But until the 1970s more people settled in outlying ethnic regions than came back. In 1961-65, for example, the Russian republic had an outflow of 861,000 people. In 1966-70 the outflow jumped to 1,567,000 people.[11]

The return *(obratnichestvo)* started in Kyrgyzstan around 1970 and spread to the rest of Central Asia by the mid-1970s. In 1971-77 199,000 more people left Central Asia and Kazakhstan than arrived. Out-migration was particularly widespread in rural areas where the pressure of the indigenous population was especially intense. For example, half the Russian population in the Tashkent rural hinterland left in 1970-79; and *all* Russian settlers in the villages of Karakalpakia in northern Uzbekistan departed.[12] More than 400,000 "Europeans," most of them ethnic Russians but also other Slavs, left Kazakh villages in the early 1980s.

In the 1980s the outflow of Europeans from the east continued; only the Baltic republics continued to attract nonindigenous settlers, although at a slower rate. In this period the RSFSR gained a whopping 1,768,000 migrants, Ukraine gained 153,000, and the three Baltic states combined gained 246,000.[13] All other republics lost people, especially Kazakhstan (784,000)

TABLE 10.2
DECREASE IN RUSSIAN POPULATION IN
TRANSCAUCASIA AND CENTRAL ASIA, 1979-89

Armenia	0.74%
Azerbaijan	2.31%
Georgia	1.12%
Kazakhstan	2.98%
Kyrgyzstan	4.37%
Tajikistan	2.28%
Turkmenistan	3.08%
Uzbekistan	2.46%

Sources: Hajda/Beissinger and Lydolph:148

and Uzbekistan (507,000). As a result, the share of Russians in Transcaucasia and Central Asia decreased in 1979-89 by:[14]

When one compares figures for 1959, the high point of Russian penetration of the east, and 1989, the difference is even more remarkable. While in the west, Russian share of the population had inexorably moved up, causing deep anxieties, especially in the Baltics, the Russian decline in the East clearly gained momentum. See Table 10.3.

As fewer Russians are left in the former Soviet republics and pressure on the remainder increases, their appeals for help get louder. But they are far from helpless. They are organized locally in the so-called interfronts or intermovements (which, in a curious example of doublespeak, stand for internationalism but in effect promote Russian interests) and find generous support in Russia proper from conservative, ultrapatriotic organizations such

TABLE 10.3
CHANGES IN SIZE OF RUSSIAN POPULATION, 1959-89

Belarus	+5.02%
Ukraine	+5.01%
Moldova	+2.78%
Estonia	+10.26%
Latvia	+7.38%
Lithuania	+0.83%
Armenia	-1.64%
Azerbaijan	-7.97%
Georgia	-3.81%
Kazakhstan	-4.91%
Kyrgyzstan	-8.65%
Tajikistan	-5.66%
Turkmenistan	-7.8%
Uzbekistan	-5.12%

Based on Hajda/Beissinger, Tables IC on p. 182 (Ukraine, Belorussia and Moldavia), p. 216 (The Baltic republics), p. 237 (Trans-caucasia), and p. 263 (Central Asia)

as the United Front or the Bloc of Russian Patriotic-Public Movements. Their plight is skillfully used by politicians across the entire political spectrum (except some liberals), from Zhirinovsky to Yeltsin. And like Germans in Central Europe in the 1930s, Russians in the Near-Abroad offer Russia a perfect pretext for intervention, in the guise of helping their oppressed brothers. Thus, Russians in the former Soviet republics present a grave danger not only to the new countries of the Near-Abroad but also to European and world peace.

Chapter 11

RWANDA AND BURUNDI

GENERAL INFORMATION

R wanda and Burundi are small countries in the heart of Africa. Rwanda's territory is 10,169 square miles (26,338 square kilometers) and Burundi's is 10,745 square miles (27,830 square kilometers).[1]

Before the latest massacres, Rwanda's population reached 8 million; Burundi's was almost 6 million.

The people of both countries are divided into three main ethnic groups. Before the massacres, the Hutu accounted for 89 percent of Rwanda's population and 85 percent of Burundi's. The minority Tutsi reached 10 and 14 percent respectively. And the Twa amounted to only 1 percent in each. (If the estimates of the massacre victims in Rwanda—some 500,000—are not exaggerated and about 80 percent of the victims—400,000—were Tutsi, then the Tutsi population of Rwanda has been reduced by half and its share in the total population has declined correspondingly, to about 5 percent.) Both groups speak closely related Bantu languages, Kinyarwanda in Rwanda and Kirundi in Burundi.

Political upheavals and lack of economic opportunities in Rwanda led to massive emigration. Outside the country about 3 million Rwandans live in Zaire, 900,000 in Uganda, 120,000 in Burundi and 40,000 in Tanzania; many are refugees or children of refugees from earlier massacres. Quite a few Tutsi emigres have now returned, after the Tutsi-dominated Patriotic Front government took over.[2] Of the Rundi ("people of Burundi"), 1.1 million live in Zaire, 530,000 in Tanzania, 480,000 in Uganda, and 280,000 in Rwanda.[3]

The divisions among Rwanda's and Burundi's populations are not purely ethnic. Rather, they are ethnosocial, since class has been historically congruent with ethnicity.

The pygmy Twa, the original inhabitants of the region, have traditionally been mostly hunters and gatherers. They have also worked as laborers for the Hutu and servants for the Tutsi. The agriculturalist Hutu arrived from the north in the seventh through tenth centuries A.D.; they comprise the peasant majority in both countries. Finally, the Hamitic Tutsi, originating somewhere in the Nile Valley, arrived in two waves in the thirteenth and the fifteenth to sixteenth centuries. They were nomads who subjugated the Hutu and established feudal statelets in which they formed the upper crust. Traditionally, they have been warriors and pastoralists.

One important factor affecting both countries is that they have the highest population densities in Africa, approaching 300 per square kilometer in Rwanda and not far behind that in Burundi. And in some areas, such as Butare in southern Rwanda, it reached 767 per square kilometer as early as 1972.

The vast majority of the local people—some 96 percent—live in rural areas. The slow pace of industrialization has caused most villagers to stay where they are. That is why the population density in utilizable agricultural areas increased from 104 per square kilometer in 1948 (77 per square kilometer average) to 200 per square kilometer in 1970, to 378 per square kilometer in 1988, and is projected to reach 534 per square kilometers in 2000.[4] This creates a relentless and increasingly heavy pressure at all levels of society and greatly contributes to social and ethnic tensions.

HISTORICAL BACKGROUND

Due to the lack of written records and scant archeological remains we don't know much about the Hutu political entities of the tenth through thirteenth centuries or the Tutsi ones of the thirteenth through fifteenth centuries. We cannot even place the Hutu or Tutsi migrations with any degree of certainty. We do know that there were two major Tutsi population movements, the first one in the thirteenth through fifteenth centuries and the second one in the fifteenth through seventeenth centuries.

The first European to set foot in the territory of Rwanda-Burundi was the British explorer Livingstone, in 1858. He was followed by Christian missionaries some 20 years later, in January 1879.[5]

At the Berlin Congress of 1884-85 the area was assigned to Germany. It became part of the German East Africa and was then known as Rwanda-Urundi.

During World War I the colony was occupied by the Allies and, as a mandate of the League of Nations, was turned over to Belgium in 1923.

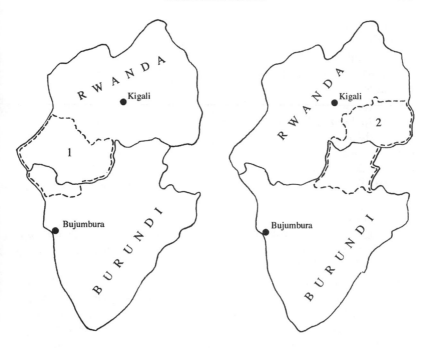

1. Option 1 (Zaire)
2. Option 2 (Tanzania)

Belgian rule lasted for almost 40 years, until July 1962, when both countries became independent.

Despite high expectations, independence brought chronic instability, not unlike that in many other former colonies. Rwanda had a coup d'etat in 1973; Burundi had three: in 1966 (which eliminated the monarchy; Rwanda's had collapsed earlier, in 1959), in 1976, and in 1987. The political instability has been greatly exacerbated by constant ethnic tensions between the numerically dominant Hutu and their former masters, the Tutsi. That and the competition for meager resources in an economy that was unable to keep up with explosive population growth made both countries susceptible to violence and fratricide, and helped turn ethnic conflict into a chronic phenomenon.

THE PRESENT CONFLICT

Independence and the introduction of democracy spelled the end of Tutsi domination. It was only a matter of time before power passed to the Hutu majority. Many Tutsi refused to accept the legitimacy of the transition, and this refusal ultimately led to the current genocidal conflict. After the Tutsi lost power, many of them fled to the neighboring countries and started guerrilla movements that periodically invaded Rwanda. Inevitably, guerrilla activities generated Hutu backlashes that led to anti-Tutsi pogroms and massacres.

There are several little-known facts that may help to explain the bitterness of the conflict. First, under Belgian rule, everyone's ethnic identity was inscribed on his or her identity card. It was thus easy to determine a person's ethnicity. We know from Soviet experience that rigid ethnic nomenclature regulated by state bureaucracy reinforces and entrenches ethnicity as a major social divide. Unfortunately, this feature of colonial administration was carried over to independent Rwanda (it was recently discontinued), exacerbating already existing tensions.

Also, both German and Belgian authorities relied on the Tutsi in the administration of the colonies. In this they were not alone: the British also preferred to deal with the indigenous aristocracy. Such preferences on the part of the colonial powers further embittered the Hutu majority, since it reinforced the "superior Tutsi/inferior Hutu" dichotomy. Indeed, in many ways the Tutsi were in the privileged position. For example, just before independence, 60.8 percent of pupils in secondary schools were Tutsi although the Tutsi ethny was in the minority.[6] Thus, both communities developed into ethclasses. And when the anticolonial struggle began in earnest many Hutu came to perceive the Tutsi as collaborators with the colonial masters.

The period of decolonization in Rwanda (July 1959-July 1962) coincided with a social and antimonarchical revolution that inevitably turned anti-Tutsi. It was spearheaded by Hutu militias, the notorious *Interhamwe* in Rwanda and the *Intagohekas* in Burundi.[7] Even without the militias the Hutu had a decisive numerical advantage. In the referendum of September 25, 1961, 80 percent of all Rwandans voted against the monarchy.[8] The Hutu-based parties received 81.2 percent of the vote; in other words, the Hutu voted against the Tutsi and the monarchy. The explosion of anti-Tutsi, anticolonial, anti-White, and antiestablishment hatreds generated tremendous violence and, not surprisingly, a flow of Tutsi refugees fleeing in all directions. The exact numbers are very hard to determine since many Rwandans subsequently left for purely economic reasons. The number of Rwandans living abroad is variously estimated in a wide range of 2 million[9] to 4 million.[10] Most of them are economic emigres, however. The High Commission for Refugees estimated the number of political refugees (including both Tutsi and Hutu) at 161,000 in 1970 and 175,000 in 1989.[11]

The Tutsi did not give in. They organized a guerrilla movement based in the surrounding countries, most notably Uganda, from where they launched raids into Rwanda. The earliest large-scale raids occurred in December 1963, the latest, before the massacres of 1994, occurred in October 1990. For 35 years, from 1959 till 1994, Rwanda lived under a constant threat from the outside, and every political upheaval, such as the coup d'etat of 1973, turned anti-Tutsi, sending new waves of Tutsi refugees fleeing for their lives and providing new recruits for the guerrilla movement.

Developments in Burundi followed a parallel track, except that the abolition of the monarchy was delayed by about five years (it was overthrown in 1966). The Tutsi never lost their predominance or their control of the army. Still, Burundi had its share of coups d'etat (in 1976 and 1987) and ethnic conflict: in 1969, 1972, 1988, 1993, and 1995. The bloodletting in August 1988 led to a power-sharing arrangement between the Hutu and Tutsi factions. It seemed for a time that the adversaries had finally found a certain modus vivendi. But the precarious balance of power between the major contenders was shattered by a failed coup in October 1993. The new political upheaval led to renewed massacres, in which about 50,000 Tutsi lost their lives. Ethnic skirmishes have become endemic, especially in the capital, Bujumbura.

Over time the Tutsi in both countries were steadily losing ground, particularly in Rwanda. According to Rwandan government sources, the Tutsi share of the population declined from 16.59 percent in 1956 to 14 percent in 1972 to 10.34 percent in 1980-81.[12] Their decline in the distribution of educational benefits was even more precipitous: in secondary education during the same period their share went from 60.9 percent to 19.7 percent. On the other hand, the power sharing alleviated their situation somewhat, increasing the percentage of Tutsi pupils to 24.9 percent. A similar trend was noticeable in the ministries, where the Tutsi share increased from a low of 10.9 percent to 19.4 percent in 1989.[13]

Similar trends were replicated in the economic sector. The percentage of unemployed Tutsi in 1989 was 19.3; among the employed they accounted for 14.3 percent.[14] In state enterprises the Tutsi percentage ranged from 2.7 to 28.4, depending on the industry, the average being 13.7.[15] In banking the average percentage was 11 (ranging from 9.8 to 24.4).[16] In the private sector as a whole the Tutsi averaged 9.7 percent in a wide range from 7 percent to 28 percent.[17] In short, after independence the Tutsi have consistently lost ground but still retained a larger portion of the economic and governmental pie than their demographic share warranted. Thus, the Hutu still perceived the Tutsi as a privileged elite while the Tutsi felt they were losing out. This disequilibrium in benefit and power distribution and perceptions between the two communities goes a long way toward explaining the constant turmoil and sporadic bloodletting experienced in both countries.

In Rwanda alone anti-Tutsi pogroms generated four major refugee out-flows: in 1959 (the beginning of the decolonization process and the abolition of the monarchy), in 1963 (post-independence), in 1966 (as a consequence of events in neighboring Burundi), and 1973 (the coup d'etat). The upheavals, according to some sources, cost about 600,000 lives.[18] According to other sources, 105,000 died in 1956-65, 150,000 died in 1972, and anywhere from 100,000 to 1 million in 1993-94.[19] The exact numbers will never be known.

The latest bout of ethnic bloodletting added thousands of new victims. It started when Rwandan President Juvenal Habyarimana and Burundi President Cyprien Ntaryamira (both Hutu) were killed in a plane crash for which the emigre Tutsi Rwandan Patriotic Front (the RPF) was blamed. (There is strong evidence that the presidents were victims of a plot by Hutu extremist factions.) The Hutu, incited by the extremist propaganda, lashed out at the Tutsi and anyone suspected of opposing Habyarimana, killing thousands of people. An RPF-led invasion followed, which dislodged the Hutu extremists from power. Two million mostly Hutu refugees fled to the surrounding countries. At present, the situation is slowly returning to normal, under the guidance of the RPF government allied with Hutu moderates; thousands of refugees have returned, but thousands more still languish in refugee camps, most of them in neighboring Zaire. As was to be expected, the Zairian welcome is wearing thin. There were several attempts by the Zairian authorities to force refugees back into Rwanda in August 1995. Even more troublesome are the signs that the Hutu government-in-exile, in a direct imitation of its Tutsi predecessors, is preparing to launch a guerrilla campaign from its bases in Zaire.

Meanwhile, in neighboring Burundi, ethnic tensions continue to boil. Tutsi-led army units periodically attack Hutu neighborhoods in Bujumbura, the capital, in a futile attempt to contain and forestall the inevitable Hutu backlash.

Very little in the present situation in either Rwanda or Burundi promises a reconciliation.

Chapter 12

SRI LANKA

GENERAL INFORMATION

Sri Lanka, formerly known as Ceylon, is an island at the southern tip of the Indian subcontinent. Its territory covers 24,962 square miles (64,652 square kilometers).[1] Its population is approaching 18 million. It consists of the Sinhalese, who number over 12.5 million; 2.8 million Tamils (including a million "estate" Tamils whose ancestors were brought over in the nineteenth century from India to work on the tea plantations); 1.3 million Moors; about 50,000 of the so-called Burghers, descendants of the Dutch, with some non-European admixture; and 1,000 Veddas, who are the remnant of the indigenous population of the island.[2]

To a large extent, religious and ethnic divisions in Sri Lanka coincide. In that sense, Sri Lankan society resembles Bosnia and Northern Ireland. The vast majority of the Sinhalese, about 93 percent,[3] are Buddhists, almost 90 percent of the Tamils are Hindu,[4] the Moors are Muslim, and the Burghers are Christian.

Throughout most of its history the country has been torn apart by a savage ethnoreligious conflict that pits the Buddhist Sinhalese who live in the center, south, and west of the island against the Hindu Tamils in the north and east.

Although the Sinhalese form a clear majority on the island, the presence of more than 55 million Tamils in India, just across the Palk Straight, makes them feel insecure. That insecurity, reinforced by tragic historical memories of Tamil invasions, make the Sinhalese less than generous in their treatment of the Tamil minority.

HISTORICAL BACKGROUND

Among the conflicts surveyed in this book none is older than the strife between the Sinhalese and the Tamils.

Although they came from far afield, from somewhere in northwestern India and, possibly, Bengal (there may have been several waves of migrants), the ancestors of the Sinhalese seem to have arrived on the island sometime in the fifth century B.C. They overwhelmed the autochthonous people, ancestors of the Veddas, and gradually spread throughout the island.

The first Tamils crossed the Palk Straight a bit later, sometime in the third century B.C., and settled in the north. From then on the history of the island has been the history of incessant warfare between the two communities, complicated by alliances and, occasionally, invasions from southern India. On top of that, chronic instability plagued the Sinhalese kingdoms because they had failed to establish rules of orderly succession.

The confrontation was exacerbated by the religious divide, the Sinhalese being Buddhist since the third century B.C. while the Tamils chose to remain Hindu. Thus, the conflict had acquired an ethnoreligious and civilizational dimension from very early on.

Despite Tamil interference as early as 177 B.C., the early Sinhalese succeeded in establishing a powerful kingdom with its capital at Anuradhapura in the second century B.C. And in spite of the devastating internal wars that often erupted when succession was in question, the kingdom survived until the tenth century A.D., when it fell to a south Indian invasion from Chola.

The interaction between the Sinhalese polities on the island and the Tamils of India and Sri Lanka followed an established pattern. When Dravidian societies in southern India turned militantly Hindu and, therefore, anti-Buddhist, they influenced the Tamils of Sri Lanka. This sharpened Tamil ethnoreligious self-awareness and turned them, occasionally, into allies of various south Indian (that is, Hindu) powers. Those living in the Sinhalese kingdoms became a veritable fifth column. Thus some Tamils allied themselves with the Pandyan invasion in the ninth century. The invaders sacked the capital but eventually were forced to withdraw.

The Chola invasion of 973 led to a protracted struggle that lasted for decades. The Sinhalese king was captured in 1017. The invaders occupied the entire island and moved the capital farther south, to Polonnaruva. By 1070, after a long war of resistance and liberation, the Sinhalese managed to expel the Chola invaders.

But invasions from India continued, and after 1255 the capital was moved once again. Meanwhile, the Tamils spread south as far as Anuradhapura, creating marches between the Sinhalese and the Tamil

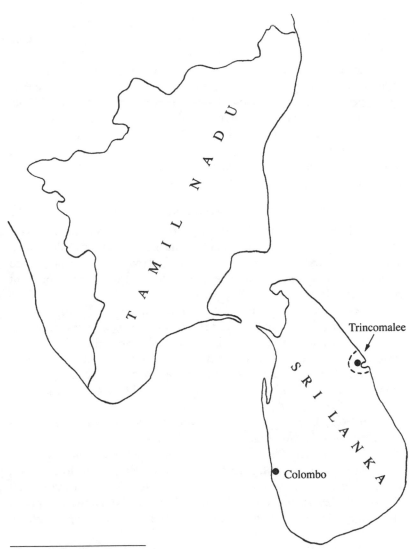

The autonomous Enclave

parts of the country. By the thirteenth century a Tamil kingdom was established in the north.

By the fourteenth century Sinhalese fortunes fell to a low point. Old irrigated areas were abandoned, and huge water tanks that had been used in irrigation helped to spread malaria and other diseases borne by mosquitos.

As the Sinhalese weakened, there were more Tamil invasions, as in 1353, and even an incursion by the Chinese in 1414. These incessant assaults split the Sinhalese community into several statelets.

Toward the end of the fifteenth century a new Sinhalese power emerged farther south, in the mountains: the Kandyan kingdom. It survived the Portuguese penetration of the island in 1505-1658 (which remained incomplete; the Portuguese never succeeded in establishing their hegemony over the entire island) and the Dutch in 1640-1796. But ultimately the kingdom succumbed to the British who ousted the Dutch in 1802. With the fall of the Kandyan kingdom in 1815 the entire island became a British colony. The British stayed until 1947. Since then the country has been independent.

THE PRESENT CONFLICT

The Sinhalese opposition to the British started from approximately 1840. Initially, it was a defensive movement for the preservation of Buddhism in the face of Christian missionary activity. The struggle gained momentum toward the end of the nineteenth century and was closely linked with a nascent nationalist movement.

Interestingly, the resurgence of Hinduism among the Tamils started an entire generation earlier, before the first stirrings of the Buddhist revival among the Sinhalese,[5] and developed in close interaction with their coreligionists in India. At first, however, the Tamils were not perceived as the main enemy. Under colonial rule Christians seemed to be the more dangerous, and the first intercommunal riots in 1883 pitted Buddhists against Catholics. The next major riots, in 1915 and 1918, were directed against the Muslims.

Until 1922, the Sinhalese and the Tamils still saw themselves as two indigenous majority communities of the island, both chafing under British rule. It was only after 1922 that the Tamils began to "slide" into the status of a minority. Until then, ethnicity proper was not a decisive factor; religion and caste were much more important. But since ethnicity was suffused with religion, the development of nationalism brought about a fusion of both into the kind of ethnoreligious nationalism that usually proves particularly dangerous.

Inadvertently, the British had helped to transform a religious conflict into an ethnic one. In their desire to avoid unrest, they tried to accommodate each segment of the population. Like most Europeans of their time, the British saw communal divisions in terms of "race" or, in contemporary terminology, ethnicity. Each ethnic group had its own laws and representation on advisory councils. And this arrangement taught the people of Ceylon to think in ethnic terms.

Unlike so many other colonies, in Ceylon the transition to independence was long (1931-47) and peaceful. When Great Britain granted Ceylon its independence on February 4, 1948, a fairly bright future seemed assured. But from early on there were clouds on the horizon: mainly, the intercommunal tensions centered around the language question. Despite a compromise reached in 1944, the Sinhalese demanded the imposition of Sinhalese as the state language. The Tamils, understandably, feared and resisted that. With the British gone, the two communities became protagonists in a drawn-out battle. The Sinhalese fought for supremacy while the Tamils tried to hold on to the status quo.

Estate Tamils were the first affected. Laws passed in 1948 and 1949 declared most of them non-citizens. (At present only about 25 percent have citizenship.)[6]

For other minorities, the year 1956 was a watershed. That year Buddhists around the world celebrated the 2,500th anniversary of Buddha's death. In the atmosphere of growing Sinhalese Buddhist nationalism, the head of the Sri Lankan Freedom Party, Bandaranaike, fulfilled his election promise to make Sinhala the only official language of the island. Since then, intercommunal antagonism has rapidly escalated.

In an effort to reduce the numbers of the Tamil minority, the Sri Lankan government reached an agreement with India in October 1964 regarding the nearly 1 million estate Tamils. Of these, 525,000 were to be repatriated to India during a 15-year period; 300,000 were to be granted Sri Lankan citizenship; and 150,000 would be subject to later negotiations.[7] However, the agreement was not implemented, and neither was another compromise, reached in 1974, to integrate 500,000 Tamils into the Sri Lankan polity.

The first major anti-Tamil riots occurred in 1958. Some 159 people were killed, several hundred injured, and about 12,000 Tamils fled for their lives.[8] Riots erupted again in 1971. And in 1977. And 1981. (This was not an exclusively Sinhalese-on-Tamil violence, as the Sinhalese-Muslim riots of 1974-75 show.) Gradually, many Tamils became convinced that only a Tamil state in the north could protect them and satisfy their aspirations. They began to organize armed bands. The best-known, the Tamil New Tigers (now the Liberation Tigers of Tamil Eelam), was formed in 1972.

By the late 1970s Sinhalese-Tamil relations reached a dead end. In 1983 Tamil militants started ambushing and killing Sinhalese soldiers. The government, fearful of losing control, declared a state of emergency in May 1983, but it was too late. In an ever-increasing spiral of intercommunal violence, the Sinhalese responded to Tamil guerrilla atrocities by anti-Tamil pogroms, especially in the solidly Sinhalese south. Hundreds, then thousands of Tamils were killed, and many Tamil houses and businesses went up in flames. Meanwhile, in the north, Sinhalese soldiers went on a rampage in Tamil villages. The Sinhalese attacks further embittered the Tamils. Their attacks on soldiers increased; eventually, they also started attacking Sinhalese villages in the north and east, inflicting horrible atrocities on the Sinhalese peasants. The situation was rendered even more chaotic by the proliferation of splinter groups—more than two dozen in the late 1970s—who fought each other as well as the government.

The assault on the Sri Lankan Tamils caused indignation and outrage among the Tamils of India. Soon after, the Sri Lankan government found itself increasingly under pressure from India. In an effort to neutralize India and to undercut Indian Tamils' pressures, Sri Lanka agreed, in July 1987, to accept Indian troops, ostensibly as peacekeepers, and resettle at least 130,000 refugees who had fled to India, and so on.[9] Other concessions followed, such as making Tamil the other official language and the April-June 1988 decision to unite the Northern and Eastern provinces in an autonomous Tamil area.

The concessions provoked the ire of the nationalistic Sinhalese, who felt they threatened Sri Lankan independence and unity. They also opened a wedge between the government and the Sinhalese nationalists, splitting the Sinhalese community. Soon Janatha Vimukhti Peramuna (JVP; People's Liberation Front), an anti-Tamil, anti-Indian, and antigovernment ultranationalist Sinhalese party led by Rohana Wijeweera, started a terrorist campaign against moderate government officials, pro-Tamil sympathizers (actually, any moderate Sinhalese), and even vendors selling Indian goods. The government responded by sponsoring death squads recruited from among members of the security forces that killed thousands of Sinhalese men and boys suspected of JVP sympathies, including the JVP leader Wijeweera.

Meanwhile, on the Tamil side the government's concessions were deemed grossly inadequate. The Tigers' relations with the Indians also quickly deteriorated, and in October 1987 they battled each other in the city of Jaffna.

By 1990 the situation reached an impasse, and the Indian troops were recalled in March 1990. (The recall was seen as a betrayal by some Tamils; in May 1991 India's prime minister, Rajiv Gandhi, was assassinated by Tamil extremists.) Since the summer of 1990 a war has been going on between the Sinhalese and the Tamils. It is superimposed on an intra-Sinhalese conflict that pits the Sinhalese ultranationalists against the government and the moderates. Both sides have committed grisly atrocities: in May 1995 the Tamil Tigers hacked 42 Sinhalese villagers to death in a small fishing village near Trincomalee. In July 1995 government forces dropped leaflets in the Tamil areas advising civilians to seek shelter in churches during an impending assault, then dropped bombs on a Catholic church killing 62 people. In January 1996 Tamil suicide bombers drove a truck loaded with explosives into the Central Bank building in Colombo killing 73 and injuring 1,400 people.[10] The total number of victims is estimated at some 40,000.[11]

In July and October 1995 the government launched two successful assaults the Jaffna peninsula, which culminated in the capture of the strategically important old Dutch fort in Jaffna in December 1995. At the same time, the new government under President Kumaratunga has offered far-reaching concessions to the Tamils and is willing to initiate yet another round of talks with militant Tamils. But most observers will be pleasantly surprised if any long-lasting agreement is reached. The Tamil desire for independence and sovereignty and the equally ardent Sinhalese insistence on preserving the unity of the country create an intractable problem.

Chapter 13

TRANSYLVANIA

GENERAL INFORMATION

The territory that is now called Transylvania is much larger than the historic principality of that name. Today's Transylvania also includes Crişana and parts of Banat. After World War I these areas, which had been part of historic Hungary for almost a thousand years, were incorporated into Romania and since then have been referred to simply as Transylvania. The territory of the expanded Transylvania is 104,000 square kilometers.[1] Its population is approaching 8 million. Of these, no fewer than 1.3 million are Hungarians, about 100,000 are Germans (fast decreasing due to mass emigration), an indeterminate number are Gypsies, and the rest are mostly ethnic Romanians.

Population statistics in many countries, including Romania, are notoriously unreliable due to political demands. Demography means power. In Romania's case, this is well illustrated by the example of the Roma (the Gypsies). In 1988, the number of Gypsies in Romania was officially estimated at 230,000,[2] virtually unchanged since the 1930s. Four years later, the results of the official Romanian census of 1992 put the number of the Roma at 409,000.[3] Their numbers had almost doubled in four years! But unofficial estimates put their numbers even higher, some as high as 2 million.

Hungarians are also undercounted. Officially, they numbered 1.6 million in 1992 (the estimate of 1.3 million in Transylvania was based on official figures), but unofficially their number is estimated at somewhere between 2 and 2.5 million.[4]

Hungarians of Romania can be found in four distinct areas: (1) approximately one-third live along the border with Hungary; (2) approximately one-third, the Szeklers, live in eastern Transylvania in the geographical center of Romania (in its present borders); they are concentrated in two counties, Harghiţa and Covasna; (3) approximately one-third live in an arc that connects the Szekler area with northeastern Hungary; and (4) the rest live in Bucharest. There are also a few pockets of Hungarians scattered throughout Moldova, the so-called Czangos.

Historical Background

Transylvania is one of those areas where who came first is virtually impossible to establish. The argument between Hungarians and Romanians has never been resolved, nor is it likely to be, except of course by the ardent nationalists on either side.

In the Romanian version, Romanians are descendants of the indigenous Dacians, whose territory included much of present-day Transylvania. In A.D. 106 the Dacians were conquered by Trajan. But the Romans did not stay long: Aurelian was forced to evacuate the province in 271 under increasing pressure from the Goths, who henceforth occupied the area. Despite the relative brevity of the Roman rule—"only" 165 years—the Dacians had been thoroughly Romanized, and present-day Romanians are their descendants. Thus, Romanians claim direct descent from the autochthonous population of the area, and this, in addition to their numerical majority, justifies their claim to Transylvania.

Hungarians, however, point to the fact that the Romanian name for Transylvania, Ardeal, is taken from the Hungarian name Erdel. They claim that most Dacians evacuated the province when the Romans left and those who did not later fled south, away from incessant barbarian invasions. Indeed, the presence of scattered Vlach population in virtually all Balkan countries, a population speaking dialects very similar to Romanian, seems to confirm this theory. On the other hand, much of Illyria and Moesia (present-day Bulgaria) had been Romanized, and modern Vlachs may very well descend from local Latin-speaking populations.

In any case, it was only in 1209 that Vlach settlements in Transylvania were mentioned for the first time. This seems to confirm the Hungarian assertion that Romanians are later immigrants, not unlike the Saxons who were invited by Geza II in 1143 or the Serbs who moved to southern Hungary en masse in 1690.

According to the Hungarian version, when Hungarians extended their rule into Transylvania around 1003 they found a desert. The only permanent

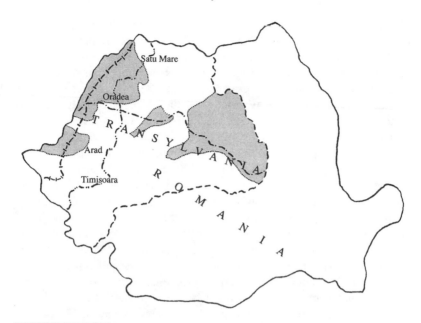

-- Transylvania
-.- Vienna award
-..- proposed border rectification (maximum)
-ı- proposed border rectification (minimum)
▨ area of Hungarian concentration

inhabitants were the ancestors of today's Szeklers who, according to Hungarian medieval chronicles, fled there in 797 when Charlemagne defeated the Avars (to whose confederation the Szeklers' ancestors had belonged).[5]

No matter who was first, from 1003 until 1918 Transylvania was part of Hungary. During this time, the Szeklers were completely Magyarized and became a part of the Hungarian ethny. Along with the rest of the country they suffered from the Tartar onslaught in 1241-42 and the Ottoman invasion of 1526.

The establishment of Transylvania as a separate principality in 1571 was a result of the Ottoman invasions, which split Hungary into three parts: the Austrian north and west (largely confined to present-day Slovakia), the center, under direct Ottoman occupation (mostly present-day Hungary), and the east, Transylvania, which was nominally a vassal of both empires but was in effect largely autonomous.

In 1686-87 Transylvania was conquered by the Habsburgs and formally annexed in 1690. The new rulers found a region devastated by 150 years of war and Turkish depredations. To repopulate the country the Austrians invited Swabian settlers and also allowed the settlement of Serbs and Vlachs fleeing from Turkish-held areas. Altogether, some 400,000 immigrants were settled in Hungary.[6] At the same time, Hungarians were distrusted because of their recurrent revolts (failed attempts to regain lost independence). That is why, since 1718, they were specifically excluded from settlement in many areas, such as the Banat of Temes.

Incessant wars had a negative impact on Hungarian population. In 1490 approximately 80 percent of the country's 4 million inhabitants were Hungarian in language and culture.[7] But by 1700 the total population was reduced to less than half that, of which only 45 percent were of Hungarian ethnic stock. Although the total population later rebounded, an influx of immigrants kept the Hungarian proportion at more or less the same level: by 1850 only 44.5 percent of Hungary's population was of Magyar stock, although the proportion slowly rose to 51.4 percent by 1900 and 54.5 percent by 1910.[8] (This increase was largely due to strong assimilationist pressure on minorities exerted by Hungarian governments after 1867 and, to some extent, to higher emigration rates among some minorities.) In Transylvania proper the Hungarian share (together with the Szeklers) stood at 25.9 percent in 1880 and rose to 31.6 percent by 1910.[9]

The defeat in World War I and the extremely harsh terms of the Peace of Trianon, signed on June 4, 1920, forced Hungary to surrender some 104,000 square kilometers to Romania along with 1.5 to 1.7 million ethnic Hungarians, 700,000 Germans, and over 2 million Romanians living there (in addition to other areas lost to Czechoslovakia, Yugoslavia, and Austria). Since then, except for a brief interlude in 1940-44, Transylvania has been a part of Romania. (In 1940 German and Italion arbitration divided Transylvania in half [the so-called Vienna Awards]: southern Transylvania remained in Romanian hands while the north went to Hungary. The area reverted to Romania after World War II.)

Under Romanian rule, the ethnic Hungarian share of Transylvania's population has been steadily decreasing, from 31.6 percent in 1910 to approximately 20-22 percent now. The reasons for this include slower population growth among ethnic Hungarians, emigration, and incentives for Romanians to settle in Transylvania. Particularly harmful to Hungarian demographic strength were periodic exodi after each historical upheaval. After World War I, some 197,000 Hungarians left for Hungary; another 169,000 emigrated between 1924 and 1940; and then the partition and the subsequent loss of Transylvania in 1940-44 sent two more waves of Hungarian refugees (160,000 to 190,000 in 1940 and 125,000 in 1944) out of the province.[10]

Since World War II this trend has accelerated, mostly due to the government-assisted influx of ethnic Romanians into urban areas. In Cluj the percentage of Hungarians fell from 47.3 percent in 1956 to 22.7 percent in 1992, in Tîrgu-Mureş from 73.8 percent to 51.1 percent, in Arad from 30 percent to 15.7 percent, and so on.[11] Ever since 1920, when they lost political control over Transylvania, the Hungarians have been losing out demographically, economically, and culturally.

THE PRESENT CONFLICT

The enmity between Hungarians and Romanians is of long duration. One cannot properly understand it without some insight into its past.

Romanians' grievances go back to medieval Transylvania, where, unlike other ethnic groups such as the Hungarians, the Szeklers, and the Saxons, they had no representation in the government. This was because Romanians had no aristocracy. The mass of the Romanian people were serfs, and those few who rose socially, such as the Hunyadi family, were absorbed into the upper strata of other ethnic groups, usually the Hungarian. Such upward assimilation was extremely difficult, however, since it meant the abandonment of Orthodox faith at a time when religion was the main component of identity. After the Union of the Three Nations in 1437 the position of Romanians became even more difficult, for one could not even gain civil rights unless one belonged to one of the politically empowered ethnic groups *(nacio)*.

Thus Romanians were politically and socially disenfranchised and subject to ethnic and religious discrimination. When they rebelled—as they did as early as 1429-38—they did so as peasants and also as Orthodox Christians. This was a recurrent pattern throughout the next 300 years. For example, during the Horea revolt of 1784 Romanian peasants attacked mostly Hungarians and the non-Orthodox. A similar pattern reappeared during the revolution of 1848, when Romanian forces under Avram Iancu helped Vienna against revolutionary Hungary.

With the Compromise of 1867 and the growth of Hungarian nationalism in the second half of the nineteenth century, minority dissatisfaction progressively increased. Although the Nationalities Law of 1868 guaranteed minorities extensive rights, it was never fully implemented. Hungary was desperately trying to achieve numerical preponderance and applied all its efforts toward assimilation of troublesome minorities, not unlike France did a hundred years earlier. Thus, the law of 1883 made the Hungarian language a compulsory subject in minority schools. Hungarian authorities also tried to suppress Romanian nationalism by putting Romanian activists on trial, notably in 1894. But the government was too clever to apply only the stick; there was also a substantial carrot: if a minority member assimilated and became Hungarian in speech and habit, he could advance as far as his abilities would take him without encountering discrimination. Thousands of Slovaks and Romanians, and especially Jews and Germans, followed this path.

World War I brought defeat to Hungary. With the annexation of Transylvania by Romania the position of the two nationalities flipped overnight. Now Romanians could pay back for all the injustices they had suffered, and then some. On January 19, 1919, a Hungarian meeting was fired upon by Romanian troops and more than a hundred people were killed.[12] In March 1920 all Hungarian street signs were replaced by Romanian ones. In 1924 Hungarian shopkeepers were compelled to pay extra taxes if they advertized in Hungarian. In 1925 many minority parochial schools were closed. In their zeal the Romanian authorities threatened to exceed prewar Hungarian administrations in repression and discrimination.

The growth of fascism in the 1930s brought about an unprecedented growth of antiminority sentiment among Romanians. In 1936 the Iron Guard attacked Jews and Hungarians in Braşov, Cluj, and elsewhere. The partition of Transylvania in August 1940 was particularly traumatic for both sides as Hungarian refugees from southern Transylvania streamed north while Romanians from northern Transylvania fled south. The Hungarian exodus was repeated at the end of the war when northern Transylvania was reabsorbed into Romania, although the first postwar governments in Romania were more conciliatory toward minorities.

The period of conciliation was very brief, however. In 1949 the communist government started persecuting non-Orthodox (minority) denominations. The Hungarian revolution of 1956, and the unrest in Transylvania that accompanied it, scared Romanian authorities, who responded with numerous arrests and deportations. In March 1959 the Hungarian Bolyai University in Cluj was merged with the Romanian Babeş University, the first a step toward Romanianization of higher education. In 1960, an administrative reorganization (actually, gerrymandering) of the Hungarian Autonomous region (established in 1952) diluted the ethnic Hungarian majority in the area. Autonomy was completely eliminated in 1968 under Ceauşescu, who set the tone for an increasingly nationalistic policy.

From there the position of Hungarians in Romania went from bad to worse. For example, Law 278 of 1973 required a minimum of 25 students for a minority language class, effectively undercutting minority education in smaller settlements; Act 63 and Law 207 of 1974 provided legal grounds for confiscation of historical documents and memorabilia; Law 372 of 1976 prohibited accommodation of non-Romanian citizens in private homes in order to prevent contacts between Transylvanian Hungarians and their ethnic cousins from abroad. All these measures resulted in persecution and day-to-day harassment of the Hungarian minority.

As the Ceauşescu regime gradually entrenched itself, the position of the Hungarian minority became more and more precarious. Toward the late 1980s Ceauşescu reached a decision to solve the Hungarian problem through massive relocation and, it was hoped, resulting assimilation. The plan, euphemistically called systematization, was announced in the party organ *Scînteia* on April 5, 1988. It was designed to reduce the number of villages almost by half, ostensibly to reclaim arable land. The population from the abandoned villages was to be resettled in agro-industrial centers, where people from minority villages were to be housed in large apartment blocs together with Romanians. To be fair, the plan was not directed exclusively at the minorities. Ceauşescu wanted to deracinate the Romanian peasantry as well, to recast it in a socialist mold. But, according to the Hungarian news agency MTI (May 8, 1988), the plan would have affected about half of Romania's Hungarians. In the process, many Hungarian churches and cemeteries were to be destroyed and turned into plowland, obliterating important cultural markers and symbols of minority heritage. In short, the plan amounted to a systematic deracination of the Hungarian minority. At the same time non-Romanian personal names and place names were banned.

Ceauşescu's hostility toward minorities contributed to his ultimate downfall, which was triggered by Hungarian unrest in Timişoara. Even after Ceauşescu's downfall, however, the position of the Hungarian minority remained extremely difficult. Initially, the new government tried to accommodate the minorities. Thus, in December 1989, while fighting was still raging, the National Salvation Front reached an agreement with the Hungarian government to restore all minority rights. Among other things, the NSF promised to create a Ministry of Nationalities and pass a law guaranteeing education in minority languages. So far, few promises have been implemented.

Antiminority feelings run high in Romania. One of the worst incidents was a veritable pogrom in Tîrgu-Mureş in March 1990, in which Romanian mobs, including peasants from the surrounding villages, attacked a Hungarian rally. Three people were killed and more than 300 injured, including the famous poet Andras Sütő.[13]

In less dramatic fashion, old practices have been revived: Gheorghe Funar, the mayor of Cluj, had Hungarian street signs removed in April 1992 and even denounced the Hungarian minority at official functions.[14]

Antiminority hostility and rhetoric are popular among large segments of Romanian population and the government knows it. So far, it has tried to walk a tightrope between the increasingly popular nationalists and the irksome, from its point of view, minorities. Thus, while it made some concessions in July 1993 at Neptune, it also agreed to a parliamentary alliance with two extremist parties, an alliance that makes any meaningful accommodation of minority demands impossible.[15]

Hungarians remain chronically underrepresented at all levels of government. In Transylvania only 13.6 percent of county-level officials and only 13.9 percent of city employees were of Hungarian ethnic stock despite the fact that the Hungarian share of Transylvania's population is officially 22 percent.[16] Hungarians are similarly underrepresented among directors of state-owned enterprises.[17] Discrimination is also evidenced by restrictions on minority education and minority media, incarceration and persecution of ethnic activists, and a complete failure to rein in Romanian extremists.[18] Now that most other minorities are gone, the Romanian government, with the full support of a significant segment of the Romanian people, is doing all it can to absorb the last remaining minority. (There are, of course, the Gypsies, but it is doubtful that Romanian nationalists want to absorb them.)

Chances of solving the problem appear slim.

Chapter 14

ULSTER

GENERAL INFORMATION

The British province of Northern Ireland (also known as Ulster) is part of the historic Irish province of Ulster, which was settled by non-Irish immigrants in the seventeenth century and remained British when the rest of Ireland won independence.

British Ulster consists of six counties, out of the original nine, the other three having been allotted to the Irish Republic (Eire). Its territory is 5,452 square miles.[1]

Its population exceeds 1.6 million, of which about 1 million are Protestant, mostly of Scottish and English origin, and some 600,000 are Catholic, mostly descendants of the indigenous Celtic inhabitants of the island. The Catholic population is growing at a faster rate than the Protestant one but has a higher emigration rate. Despite the constant drain, it is possible that by the second or third decade of the next century the Catholics may overtake the Protestants, upsetting the present political (im)balance in the province. Although rarely mentioned in public, this fact is an important background factor in the Irish crisis. The Protestants feel insecure; the Catholics feel put upon; hence the impasse.

THE HISTORICAL BACKGROUND

There are several constants in Irish history. First, the island was repeatedly overrun by invaders: the Celts, then the Vikings, then the English. Second, it never formed a coherent political whole (neither did Ulster). Its territory was divided among numerous chiefdoms that were as often at war with each other as with outsiders. Third, neither the Viking nor the early English invasions, the latter starting in 1170, significantly changed the picture; they merely added new ethnic elements to the Irish political and cultural mosaic.

The English ultimately succeeded in subjugating the whole island, but until the beginning of the seventeenth century they were no more successful in establishing and maintaining a firm grip on Ireland than other invaders had been. In 1609-11 the English evicted a large number of indigenous Ulstermen and settled Scots and Englishmen on the land. This was the beginning of the Ulster Plantation. Eviction and dispossession of the autochthonous Irish population then spread to other parts of Ireland, eventually affecting the entire island. By 1703, only 14 percent of Irish land (5 percent in Ulster) remained in Catholic (that is, Irish) hands,[2] the rest having passed to non-native Protestant ownership.

Religion made the Anglo-Irish conflict intractable. Before the Reformation both sides were Catholic, and the struggle between the Irish and the English had not acquired the civilizational dimension it did later. After the English and the Scots turned Protestant, each side came to see the conflict in apocalyptic terms, the Irish defending the Faith against the Heathen, the English trying to civilize the uncouth Irish Barbarian.

Although the English were better armed and organized (a state against a motley collection of clans), the Irish Catholics did not give up. Again and again—in 1641, 1690, 1798—they rose against England, and always lost. War and famine in 1641 were particularly devastating: about one-third of Catholic Irishmen were killed and most of the rest were reduced to the status of indigent peasants;[3] in the north thousands were evicted and their land was resettled by Protestants (the so-called Cromwellian Settlement).

The Protestant ascendancy was confirmed by the victory on the Boyne in 1690, which sealed the English hold on the island. After the suppression of yet another revolt in 1798 Ireland was fully incorporated into the United Kingdom of Britain and Ireland in 1801, in an attempt to make it an integral part of Great Britain.

Early Irish nationalism actually had many Protestants among its members, and for a time at the end of the eighteenth and the beginning of the nineteenth centuries, it seemed that the Irish struggle might lose its denominational character. This tendency, however, failed to take hold.

The struggle against Britain continued. But after the incorporation of the island into Great Britain it was carried on by other means, through parliamentary alliances and political campaigns. The so-called Second Revival of 1830-48, which aimed at the disestablishment of the Church of Ireland (the Anglican Church in Ireland), was probably the point at which the

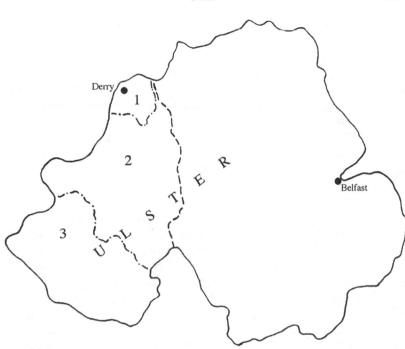

1. Derry
2. (– –) proposed border rectification (maximum)
3. Fermanagh

last chance to build an interdenominational Irish identity failed. Efforts to win Home Rule gained momentum in the 1880s but ultimately failed. Even the great famine of 1845-48—which killed up to a million people, sent several millions more across the ocean, and came close to destroying the Irish demographic base—failed to beat Ireland into submission.

The anti-British struggle intensified at the beginning of the twentieth century. After the unsuccessful Easter Rebellion of 1916, Ireland won dominion status in 1921 (at the price of losing two-thirds of Ulster and a bitter civil war in the South) and then, in 1949, full independence. But the ethnoreligious conflict in British Ulster remains unresolved to this day.

THE PRESENT CONFLICT

With the never-ending strife in Northern Ireland it is all the more remarkable that the Irish Republic has been virtually free of intercommunal conflict since it gained independence. This is due partly to the small and ever diminishing Protestant share of the population (3 percent of Eire's population belong to the Church of Ireland plus 2 percent to other Protestant denominations), and partly to the tactful attitude of successive Irish governments toward religious minorities. The safety valve of emigration, especially to Britain, where Irishmen from Eire retain the right to British citizenship, probably has also helped to maintain peace. Nor should we disregard the fact that both countries now belong to the European Union.

Until 1969 an outside observer might have thought that Northern Ireland had found a mode of relatively peaceful ethnoreligious coexistence. As in Sri Lanka and Yugoslavia, there was a long period of relative quiescence that made the prospect of gradual accommodation seem irreversible. This was all the more remarkable since religious enmity in the province has a long history. The first large-scale intercommunal riots in Belfast occurred on July 12, 1834. They shocked the city. A contemporary English witness noted that "in Belfast, where everyone is too much engaged in his own business, and where neither religion nor politics have interfered to disturb the harmony of society, it could not fail to create a great and uneasy sensation."[4]

The enmity between Catholic and Protestant derived from several factors. First, the legacy of several brutal conquests provided Catholics with a strong desire to make history right. Second, the Reformation had irreversibly split both communities, giving each the sense of a holy mission. Third, there was a class dimension to the conflict between the Protestant landlord and the Catholic peasant, since the native aristocracy had been swept away and supplanted by the English conquerors. Fourth, there was a growing siege mentality among Protestants. Fifth, industrialization took off in Ulster much earlier than in the rest of Ireland, creating strong ties with Britain and alienating the province from the rest of the island, which remained largely agrarian.

On the other hand, the conflict should not be oversimplified as a confrontation between Britain and Ireland, Catholic and Protestant. In the eighteenth century many prominent Presbyterians supported the Irish cause and among Catholics there has always been a significant number who favored union, presumably for economic motives. And distrust toward London has never been far from the surface among the Unionists. And no wonder; having no serious interest in the province, British governments after 1925 were increasingly willing to reach an agreement with Irish nationalists. Protestant Ulster came to be perceived, in some English circles, as a liability. In 1940 Churchill even dangled unification before de Valera in the hope of enticing Eire to enter the war on the Allied side (de Valera, confident of German victory, refused). These behind-the-scene maneuvers greatly increased the Loyalists' sense of insecurity and desire to hold on to the status quo.

The current conflict in Ireland can be dated from 1912 (although other starting points are also readily available). Alarmed by the prospect of the Home Rule, 500,000 Protestants signed the Ulster Covenant against it. At the same time both sides made preparations for future conflict, clandestinely amassing weapons and various military supplies.

The failed Easter uprising in Dublin in 1916 marked the turning point in the struggle for Irish independence. Despite the failure, it ignited the nationalist fire. The war of independence (1919-21) pushed Britain toward a compromise. The Government of Ireland Act of 1920 partitioned the country. The South, consisting of 26 counties, was granted dominion status, while the North, comprising the other 6, remained British.

The division of Ireland also spelled the division of Ulster: in the nine counties of historic Ulster, Protestants outnumbered Catholics by only 900,000 to 700,000. In the six counties that came to constitute British Ulster, the proportion was 820,000 to 430,000.[5] Thus, by throwing 80,000 coreligionists to the Catholic wolf, the Protestants of Ulster bought what they thought would be unchallenged hegemony in a small but relatively homogeneous stronghold. As we now know, they were mistaken.

From this point the history of the two Irelands diverged. The South exhausted itself in a bitter civil war (1922-23) between the moderates who accepted the compromise and partition and the nationalists who did not. (The moderates won.) In 1949 the South declared itself a republic, finally achieving full de jure independence.

Meanwhile, the North had an early version of the Troubles in 1921-22, in which more than a thousand people were killed and wounded (232 killed and 1,000 wounded in 1922 alone).[6] The Troubles, in effect a low intensity civil war, resulted from the Protestant desire to fight off the nationalist challenge and remain within the framework of the British state.

The province that emerged from the war and partition had three levels of authority: Westminster (United Kingdom government), Stormont (provincial parliament of Northern Ireland), and local. It is significant that the unbridgeable demands of the Protestant majority and Catholic minority remained unsolved at all levels. Intermittent violence that returned in 1932-35, during World War II, when the IRA launched yet another terrorist campaign against the British, and in 1956-62.

None of these campaigns succeeded in breaking the Protestant determination to remain British. On the other hand, a stubborn minority of Irish Catholics remained committed to the anti-British struggle and an eventual unification with Eire.

The struggle entered a new phase in 1964 with the Campaign for Social Justice, which caused disturbances in Belfast. In response, the Protestant

Ulster Volunteer Force started its own campaign in 1966. It was ostensibly
a retaliatory campaign against the IRA, but many innocent people were inevitably
caught in it.

The campaign and countercampaign further polarized the ethnoreligious
communities in the province. In 1967 the Catholics formed an umbrella organization,
the Northern Ireland Civil Rights Association, which coordinated their struggle
for full civil rights. Its first march, on August 24, 1968, announced that it
was taking a more active stance in the intercommunal struggle. Another march,
organized by People's Democracy, on January 4, 1969, was attacked by
Protestant loyalists at Burntollet near Londonderry. This was the real beginning of the latest round of Troubles, with its succession of riots, negotiations,
and terrorist acts.

The growing ferocity of the intercommunal strife forced the British government to intervene. On August 15, 1969, British troops entered mixed
neighborhoods and established what later developed into a so-called peace
line between Catholics and Protestants in Belfast. But even the peace line
failed to re-establish real peace. Despite the imposition of curfew in Lower
Falls on July 4, 1970, riots continued in Belfast and Derry throughout July
and August. On August 9, 1971, the government tried internment. Three
hundred people were arrested; in the disturbances that followed, 11 people
died and 240 houses were burned down.

The nadir was probably reached in 1972. During the so-called Bloody
Sunday in Derry on January 30, 1972, 13 men were killed by the army.
Bloody Sunday was followed by four days of rioting in Belfast, Derry, and
Dublin. The government, desperate for pacification, introduced direct rule
on March 24, 1972, but that also failed. The IRA resorted to new bombing
campaigns. There were 22 explosions in Belfast on July 21 (Bloody Friday)
in which 9 people were killed and 130 injured. And in the spring of 1973
the campaign was expanded into England proper: on March 8, 1973, 1 person was killed and 180 were injured when a bomb exploded in London. In
1972 alone there were more than 10,000 shootings, 1,400 explosions, 468
deaths, and 3,813 civilian injuries in Northern Ireland.[7]

During the next 20-odd years the bloody if inconclusive struggle waxed
and waned. Among the more important developments of the last decade
was the Anglo-Irish Agreement reached in 1985. It gave Eire a limited say
in certain internal matters of Northern Ireland, as a protector and guarantor
of the Catholic minority. But it did not change the status of the province nor
did it lead to a true pacification.

As of this writing, there are some new and interesting peace initiatives
both by the IRA and the British government. A truce has been in effect

since the summer of 1994, and is still holding. Both sides are conducting negotiations; the main stumbling block is the British demand that the IRA decommission its arms before the negotiations get going and the IRA refusal to do so before some tangible progress has been made. Although it is still too early to tell, it is not implausible that London will eventually seek some form of disengagement from Ulster. But the million or so Ulster Protestants are still there, and as long as they stay the conflict is likely to remain as intractable as ever.

PART III

Chapter 15

SOLVING IRRECONCILABLE ETHNIC CONFLICTS

Now that we have acquainted ourselves with several irreconcilable ethnic conflicts, let us reiterate what they have in common.

All, except Russian minorities in the Near-Abroad, have a long history of recurrent cyclical pattern.

All, except Rwanda and some Russian minorities, have a strong territorial component. Some Russian minority problems may develop into territorial disputes. For example, the ethnic Russian majority in some areas of northern Kazakhstan, eastern Ukraine, and northeastern Estonia may add a territorial component to formerly nonterritorial issues. In Estonia, at this point, Estonian-Russian interaction centers around minority rights; it lacks a territorial component. However, a local Russian majority in northeastern Estonia may transform the conflict into a territorial issue, as happened in Ireland when Ulster was detached from the rest of the island. On the one hand, this could make an agreement easier because it could then be settled through intergovernmental negotiations and/or by a plebiscite. On the other hand, it could create strong irredenta, both Russian and Estonian, and ultimately lead to an explosion of nationalism, which is always hard to stop.

All cases involve ethnic "cousins" across the border. This fact alone makes them extremely dangerous because of the potential widening of the conflict, with all kinds of international ramifications.

More than one area shows irreconcilable claims based on historical rights on the one side versus demographic preponderance on the other (Cyprus, Karabakh, Ulster, and the West Bank; Kosovo and Transylvania to some extent).

Several areas, of major historical importance to one claimant, are inhabited by an ethnically alien and hostile population (Kosovo, Transylvania, and the West Bank).

In many areas border rectifications are impossible due either to the lack of clear ethnic demarcation lines (Bosnia and Rwanda) or to the fact that minority areas lie far away from the border (Transylvania).

Finally, often enough, even where power sharing or border rectifications are possible, they may threaten the very existence of one of the adversaries (Bosnia, Cyprus, and Israel) or, at the very least, their existence as a sovereign and independent state (Sri Lanka). Or a change in the status quo may entail an eventual annexation to another state, as in Ulster; or even a threat to long-term survival, physical (the Tutsi in Rwanda and Burundi) or cultural (Hungarians in Transylvania). The parameters enumerated above involve general strategic considerations within the realm of international relations. They represent the macro dimension of the problem.

The micro dimension is purely internal and concerns the triangular relationship between the majority, the minority, and the government of the state where it resides. In virtually all of the areas, minorities (often on both sides, such as Romanians under Hungarian rule and Hungarians under Romanian rule) proved to be subversive, irredentist, and downright dangerous, from the point of view of the state. More than once, members of the minority disobeyed the law, rioted, rebelled, and sided with the enemy. Most important, minority leadership—and often the entire minority community—refused repeated attempts at reconciliation. (Table 15.1 shows the macro and micro dimensions of an irreconcilable ethnic conflict.)

In virtually all of these areas traditional solutions proved inadequate. They have also proved to be inherently dangerous because they have failed to prevent genocide in Rwanda, massacres in Armenia, and cleansing in the Balkans. Even in cases in which ethnic animosity does not descend into savagery, years of low-intensity strife like the current situation in Northern Ireland inflict untold suffering on millions of people and billions of dollars in damages. They are all the more dangerous because they tend to explode in cyclical violence that is difficult to stop.

Fortunately, most conflicts can be settled by traditional methods: local autonomy, respect for individual and minority group rights, interstate agreements, and the like. When all else fails, the creation of a new state may be advisable.

TABLE 15.1

The Macro Dimension:

1. The conflict is a constant threat to regional and/or world peace; it invites meddling by great powers and threatens to engulf a much wider area;
2. The stability and integrity of a state are threatened by an irredentist minority, especially if it acts as a cat's paw for a neighboring, usually co-ethnic, state;
3. Minority survival, physical or cultural, is in question;
4. Self-determination and/or border rectifications are impossible;
5. Historical claims are made to the same piece of land by more than one party;
6. Great symbolic and/or historical importance is placed on the conflict area by one or both parties;
7. Irreconcilable claims of historic rights on one side clash with demographic preponderance on the other.

The Micro Dimension. A Minority:
1. is subversive and irredentist;
2. takes part in riots and open revolt;
3. interferes with lawful administration and/or creates parliamentary roadblocks;
4. refuses civic duty; and
5. rejects all attempts at reconciliation.

However, there are numerous situations in which the populations are so mixed or where historical memories are so important that simple partition, border rectification, or self-determination are not possible. Here, some form of autonomy or minority rights may lead to pacification.

But what is to be done if a government grants a minority a significant amount of self-rule and full civil rights, but the minority refuses all offers of conciliation, threatens the very existence of the state, and presents an international danger, and if self-determination or border rectifications are, for some reason, impossible?

That is what happened in Czechoslovakia some fifty years ago. The Czech newspaper *Lidova Demokracie,* in an article published on October 29, 1945 ("We Cannot Live under the Same Roof with Germans"), wrote that

we tried even before 1938, and particularly in 1938, to reach an understanding [with minorities] in a truly liberal, humane spirit. All our attempts utterly failed. It is now clear that from 1934 on, in cahoots with Hitler and with full approval of the great majority of our Germans, the destruction of our state was being prepared. It was not a question of attaching our Germans to the Reich: 80 to 90 percent of our Germans have completely given themselves to serving barbarous Nazism, [helping it] to destroy our state and breaking all moral and cultural values of our people. And when, under Hitler's leadership and together with Reich Germans, they succeeded, they persecuted us and our country in a most barbaric and inhumane manner. Their conduct destroyed all bridges between us. We cannot live together [any more]. They must leave, for there is no other way to ensure peace in Europe.

There is a widespread opinion, especially in the United States, that multiethnic societies "work." Indeed, many do. But many don't. Or at the very least they don't work the way they are supposed to. Even a superficial examination of interethnic and interracial relations in the United States will show that the multiethnicity and multiculturalism that are part of the contemporary American credo are "what should be," not "what really is." Although the multiplicity of cultural traditions adds richness and vitality to the nation's cultural life, along with a certain number of virtually insurmountable problems, we should keep in mind that American society is generally familiar only with nonterritorial ethnicity of secondary (immigrant) ethnic groups. The intractable problems of territorially entrenched indigenous minorities prevalent in the Old World are not part of the American experience. It is no coincidence that the only intractable minority problem that threatens the breakup of a state in North America is the problem of the French minority in Canada: the Quebecois minority is fully territorial.

The example of Czechoslovakia, which may be regarded as a paradigmatic case, shows that in certain situations there can be only two alternatives: Munich (that is, the dismemberment of the state) or resettlement. This is particularly true of situations in which a minority works in tandem with an outside force inimical to the existence of the state. In his speech of June 16, 1945, at Tabor, Czechoslovakia's president Eduard Beneš said: "Germans are a fifth column. . . . I called upon them, in my speech of May 21, 1938, for tolerance, forgiveness, and mutual understanding; I emphasized that politics in a democracy is not a dictate by some against others but [involves] understanding and compromise. . . . And I simultaneously made far-reaching concessions to the Germans. . . . The whole world knows how Germans answered that: betrayal, violence, concentration camps for the Czech people, Nazi madness, attempts to destroy our democracy, instill racism and [install] a totalitarian regime. Can anyone in the world be surprised that we want to get rid of these Germans forever?"[1]

This does not mean that resettlement is a punishment for past transgressions. Rather, it is a preventive measure designed to save lives. Joseph Schechtman, a noted historian and a leading specialist on population transfers, wrote that "one can have deepest respect for the indomitable spirit of a minority group which refuses to live under the state authority of another people and strives for unification with a neighboring co-national state. There is nothing morally reprehensible in such irredentist tendencies. But when they become a manifest danger, which cannot be eliminated in any other way, the ethically neutral preventive measure of transfer offers the last resort."[2] As Sumner Welles, a former U.S. assistant secretary of state and a leading American liberal of the time, stated in regards to Transylvania (where the problem has not been solved and has been allowed to fester until today), "any solution less drastic than this [i.e., a solution not involving a transfer] would merely perpetuate a danger spot which the United Nations are now at length given the chance to eradicate."[3] Leopold Klausner, the former director of the Pan-European Union, put it even more succinctly: "To cut the cancer from a sick body is not cruel, it is necessary."[4]

Fortunately, few ethnic problems need a scalpel. But some most emphatically do, particularly those that lead to war (Bosnia, Rwanda, and Karabakh are only the latest reminders). As Viscount Cranborne stated during parliamentary debates in the House of Lords, ". . . the suffering caused by a week's war would be more than the suffering caused by the efficient resettlement of these populations whose present situation is liable to endanger future peace. . . . The saving of peace is the crucial point."[5]

The suggestion of population transfer as a viable solution to some ethnic conflicts will probably come as a shock to many readers since in the last few years the notion has been mistakenly equated with cleansing and dispossession. Especially after the brutal cleansings in Bosnia the word conjures up images of murder, rape, robbery, and expulsion. These brutalities are rightfully decried and condemned, but we should not confuse cleansing and expulsion with population exchange and transfer.

The important thing is to look at the root of the problem: an occasional incompatibility of two (or more) ethnies living in one state, under the same political roof.

In a society built upon commerce, liberalism, and democracy, the consensus is that compromise is always possible. Democracy, after all, is based on compromise, and commerce is based on negotiation, exchange, quid pro quo. These notions are particularly widespread in the United States (despite past experience with Japan, Germany, Vietnam, and Iran).

But there are many societies where "compromise" is a dirty word because it implies a betrayal or a lack of sacred principles. Even democracies built on compromise may encounter problems that defy trade-offs. As *Lidova Demokracie* wrote on July 28, 1945, "there are things, however, where compromise is not possible. These are things of principle and vital importance. To give in here and follow the path of compromise is to cut the branch one is sitting on."

Within the context of minority problems, the uncompromising attitude is reinforced by the ideals of liberty and self-determination. Even in the West, ideally, one does not compromise on liberty and equality. "You cannot be a little dead or a little pregnant," was a slogan popular among West German Greens and antinuclear activists. It might also be said: "One cannot be a little free or a little equal." The degree of freedom and equality varies from state to state and from society to society, but as a high ideal freedom is one and indivisible. The ideal is "Live free or die." It is these underlying notions of full freedom and equality that turn some minority—and ideological—problems into intractable conflicts.

Now, relatively few ethnic conflicts are truly irreconcilable. More often than not, some form of power sharing, federalization, or border rectification can solve, or go a long way toward solving, an ethnic problem. This is the ideal we should strive for. But occasionally a compromise is simply not possible.

Group coexistence is not unlike marriage: great when it works, miserable when it doesn't. Some may object that marriage is a matter of individual choice usually contracted by willing parties while "ethnic marriage" is not. But this is not always the case. Marriage between individuals may be contracted for all kinds of reasons, while "ethnic marriage" can be entered into willingly, as was the case with Czechs and Slovaks or South Slavs after World War I. Czechoslovakia's example in particular shows very clearly that, not unlike marriage between man and wife, even with good will on both sides an "ethnic marriage" may fail. We can, of course, like the Catholic Church, insist on the sanctity of marriage, but even the Vatican annuls sacred unions for good cause shown. And when the union is dissolved, one of the parties moves out.

Even the most strident moralist would not deny to the divorced couple the right to separate and disassociate. Yet, this is precisely what the world community does to ethnies that cannot peacefully coexist. They are either denounced and criticized in no uncertain terms or subjected to a barrage of unworkable proposals, such as, to pick one among many, the Vance-Owen peace plan for Bosnia. Their leaders are cajoled or pressured, often under threat of force, to accept solutions that satisfy no one. There is even a perverse belief that if no one is satisfied the solution must be fair, as if compromise is by necessity a bitter pill that both parties must swallow.

Persistent attempts on the part of the world community, led by the United Nations and the United States, to impose unworkable solutions—a "nanny syndrome"—often lead to disasters. When the historical record proves that two communities cannot live peacefully together, for whatever reason; when they display, historically, a pattern of recurrent cyclical violence; and when separation through self-determination or autonomy is not possible, for whatever reason; then population transfer may be the only instrument of pacification. It is the only solution that offers a reasonable chance for a permanent settlement of some irreconcilable ethnic problems. Fierlinger, Czechoslovakia's prime minister, said in an interview on December 1, 1945, "The Allies have fully acknowledged the justice of our request, which is not vengeance but a reasonable act of political wisdom and far-sightedness. Coexistence with Germans is for us unthinkable. There is no place in our republic for Germans. . . . The constitution and the laws [of prewar Czechoslovakia] guaranteed full rights for the German minority. Nevertheless, they were not satisfied and, with the help of the neighboring Reich, demanded more. Almost all Germans turned into proponents of Nazi Germany, of Henlein and Frank; despite major concessions given them by Dr. Beneš they rejected the proffered hand and responded with treachery and became the avant-garde of the Nazi campaign against Czechoslovakia."[6]

The same theme comes through in Jan Masaryk's (then Czechoslovakia's minister of foreign affairs) speech at the Paris Peace Conference in August 1946: "After World War I. . . our republic accepted the minority [protection] agreement. It did not limit itself to the modest stipulations of the Agreement but, of its own accord, gave the minorities everything it could in an effort not to exacerbate their discontent linked to the loss of their dominant position and old privileges and to ensure the peaceful development that our newly established state badly needed. It gave its minorities, both German and Hungarian, full democratic freedom accorded to [all] citizens, just like Czechs and Slovaks, and in the cultural realm it offered Germans and Magyars everything they already had when they were the ruling peoples. . . . For everything that we allowed and accorded to our minorities we expected nothing more than loyalty to our state, which. . . conducted an exemplary minority policy. We expected a loyalty without political concessions, without 'self-determination' that was one step away from Anschluss. . . . And what did we get? Munich and Vienna. Our minorities from the very start enjoyed minority rights. [But that was not enough.] From there they went on to demand self-determination and indulged in anti-state activities to the full. . . . [Now] we have only one answer: in the light of our Munich and Vienna experience, minority rights are out of the question! . . . The world must support our position. If the world wants peace, a lasting peace, it must support us and reject [German and] Magyar irredentism and imperialism. The year 1938 must not be repeated!"[7]

Thus, the question, ultimately, boils down to this: what to do with recalcitrant minorities when every solution, every compromise has been tried and failed? In such cases, the only workable solution is population transfer and resettlement. It goes without saying that the transfer has to be conducted in a humane, well-organized manner, like the transfer of Germans from Czechoslovakia by the Allies in 1945-47.

Although painful to the evicted populations, historically such forced migrations have played a positive role: they have helped to separate the combatants, stabilize the situation, prevent future outbreaks of violence, and promote regional peace. For example, the wars of religion that tore apart Germany and France in the sixteenth and seventeenth centuries seemed intractable. Only physical separation, often involving involuntary transfer and expulsion, provided a lasting solution. Separation eventually helped to soften religious hatreds and make tolerance possible. By the time industrialization in Germany mixed diverse religious populations once again (a large-scale mixing came only after 1945 as a result of German expulsions from Eastern Europe), religious affiliation had lost its cutting edge.

Again, we may turn to Joseph Schechtman: "[when] the very existence of such a minority within the affected state represents a permanent source of jeopardy, only the elimination of this source in its totality, i.e., the removal of the entire ethnic group, is likely radically to dispose of this menace. Suppression or deportation of even a very great number of persons directly guilty of extreme nationalistic anti-state activities cannot serve the purpose, because it does not eliminate the very roots of the problem—the presence of an ethnic entity whose mentality and objectives have proved to be incompatible with the survival or security of the state to which the members reluctantly belong. Unless the territory on which such a minority lives is detached from the state in question, there seems to be no other alternative but wholesale transfer of the disloyal population to the co-racial [i.e., "co-ethnic"] state to which it professes allegiance."[8]

Where all offers of reconciliation have been rejected, a population transfer may be the only instrument of pacification. _Transfers solve problems where everything else has failed._

HISTORICAL RECORD

Population transfer as a political solution was first advanced by Georges Montandon, a Swiss professor of ethnology at the Paris School of Anthropology. In a memo written for the Conference of Nationalities held in Lausanne on June 27-29, 1918, Professor Montandon suggested that delimitation of state frontiers according to ethnic criteria was the most durable solution for many international conflicts and border disputes. If such delimitation was impossible, then he argued that the transfer of certain ethnic minority groups within these frontiers was imperative in order to secure stability.[9]

At a time when four major empires had just come crashing down, leaving in their wake a myriad of ethnic and territorial disputes, the idea of population transfer found many adherents. Early supporters included Norwegian explorer and statesman Fridtjof Nansen (who later suggested a population exchange to Greece and Turkey), Eleutherios Venizelos, the Greek Premier at the time of the Greco-Turkish exchange, Bernard Lavergne, a professor of law at Lille University, and the well-known writer Israel Zangwill.[10]

By the time Professor Montandon made his proposal, at least one transfer had already been tried: practice had preceded theory. The first agreement regulating an interstate population transfer (properly speaking, a population exchange) in modern history was signed between Bulgaria and Turkey in November 1913 (the Convention of Adrianople) as a sequel to the Peace Treaty of Constantinople, which ended the Second Balkan War. It was designed to "facilitate the voluntary exchange of Bulgarians and Muslims as well as of their property within a 15-kilometer zone maximum along the entire common frontier."[11]

The first exchange was thus distinguished by two features: it was voluntary and it was largely strategic in its objectives, since it applied only to a 15-kilometer security zone along the common frontier. The goal was mainly to deny local support to guerrilla bands operating across the border (the *komitaji)*. Such bands had been common along many Balkan frontiers, such as the one between Bulgaria and Serbia, and often led to heightened international tensions with a concomitant threat of war. Thus, from the very start, the aim of transfer was also preventive. (The actual transfer exchanged 44,764 Bulgarians for 47,570 predominantly Turkish Muslims.[12])

The second exchange, between Bulgaria and Greece, occurred after World War I. A convention was signed by both countries at Neuilly-sur-Seine on November 27, 1920, as part of the postwar peace settlement. According to the agreement, resettlement remained voluntary. However, the convention covered all Bulgarian citizens of Greek origin and all Greek citizens of Bulgarian extraction independent of their place of domicile. Thus, it had lost the purely strategic/military context of the Bulgaro-Turkish treaty of 1913 and acquired the "total" character typical of most later population removals and transfers. By the end of 1926, 75 percent of Bulgaria's Greeks had left the country, compared to only 40 percent of Bulgarians residing in Greece.[13] In this case, as in most ethnic conflicts affecting two parties, one was more reluctant to leave than the other.

Three years later, in the aftermath of the Greek defeat in Asia Minor, the Convention of Lausanne between Greece and Turkey, signed on January 30, 1923, provided for a *compulsory* transfer of some 190,000 Greeks left in Turkey in exchange for some 356,000 Turks then living in Epirus and Macedonia.[14] (The agreement excluded Greeks of Constantinople and several islands in the Aegean; also, more than a million Greeks had already fled Turkey after the collapse of the Greek invasion in September 1922; thousands more had been slaughtered.)

Thus, within ten years, from 1913 to 1923, population exchanges had progressed (regressed is probably a better term) from voluntary, limited, and strategic to the involuntary, total transfers that we know today. Virtually all subsequent exchanges and transfers were total and compulsory (with the partial exception of the Bulgarian-Romanian exchange carried out on the basis of the Craiova Agreement of September 7, 1940; the post–World War II Czechoslovak-Soviet and Polish-Soviet exchanges; and the Czechoslovak-Hungarian exchange, which was sabotaged by Hungary). The involuntary nature of most post–World War II transfers is clearly seen in the expulsions of Germans from Czechoslovakia, Hungary, Poland, Romania, and Yugoslavia in 1945-47.

The shift in the modalities of population transfers from 1919 to 1945 reflects a shift from protecting minority rights to protecting individual rights. Despite all attempts by statesmen and professional diplomats to solve ethnic problems after World War I on the basis of minority rights, the problems stubbornly persisted. The persistence of minority problems in Europe can be explained, to a large extent, by the failures of the Versailles system.

The Versailles settlement of 1919 envisioned an elaborate system of international protection of ethnic minorities under the control of the League of Nations and the Permanent Court of International Justice. The new states that emerged after World War I were obliged, often against rigorous objections (as in the case of Poland and Romania), to sign minority protection treaties. Even those states that were not bound by minority treaties (Italy, France, Belgium, and Denmark) were also requested, although more diplomatically, to observe the stipulations of minority treaties. The Assembly of the League of Nations adopted a *voeu* to that effect on September 21, 1922.[15] Its goal was twofold: to protect individual rights of minority members by guarantees of full equality de facto and de jure and to protect their group rights, that is, the right to exist as cultural, religious, and linguistic entities.

These stipulations were directed mainly against attempts at forced assimilation exemplified by the policies of prewar Hungary.

The *voeu* was reiterated by the League Assembly in 1933 but failed to prevent minority persecutions in Fascist Italy and Nazi Germany or to stop more insidious forms of discrimination all over Eastern Europe and elsewhere. While the boundaries drawn in Versailles proved surprisingly durable—most held for 70 years—minority problems stubbornly persisted. And the reason was that in the age of nationalism self-determination becomes everyone's goal. In 1920-38, some 500 complaints were presented to the League of Nations by eighteen minorities, 131 of these coming from German groups.[16] Another reason was that statesmen tried to move borders to fit ethnic geographical distributions in an area where various nationalities and ethnic groups were hopelessly intermingled so that no workable territorial division along purely ethnic lines could be found.

The experiences of World War II, the persistence of ethnic problems throughout Europe, and the reluctance of the major powers to redraw borders led to a fundamental reassessment of the minority problem. After 1945 any resurgence of minority nationalism was regarded with deep suspicion. With the horrors of World War II still fresh in everyone's mind, the very word "nationalism" became anathema to many Western leaders and the wider public. John C. Campbell, secretary of the U.S. delegation at the Paris Peace Conference, wrote that "the study of the Transylvanian problem in Washington during the war led to the conclusion that it was insoluble so long as extreme nationalism guided the conduct of governments and national minorities in the Danubian area."[17]

In effect, the major powers made a complete turnaround; instead of protecting minorities against forced assimilation, they now regarded assimilation as a long-term solution to the minority problem. American and British delegates in Paris in 1946 now said that the peace treaties should seek assimilation rather than perpetuation of ethnic minorities. The change of opinion was facilitated by a natural American inclination (natural in light of America's historical experience of mass immigration) to regard ethnic minorities as "material" for assimilation. "It is difficult for a citizen of the United States to understand the desire to perpetuate racial [ethnic] minorities rather than absorb them," said American delegate Lieutenant General W. Bedell Smith.[18] (What would he have said about absorbing the non-White minorities? At the time, the struggle for civil rights was still some 20 years ahead.) He was seconded by Britain's Lord Hood: "I agree that our aim should be to assimilate racial [ethnic] minorities in the countries where they live rather than to perpetuate them."[19]

While the principle of protecting collective rights had been discredited, protection of individual human rights seemed more and more attractive. It was also more congruent with Western liberal notions of individual rights and responsibilities, equality before the law, and territorially defined citizenship *(jus soli)*. Unlike their Versailles predecessors, the Paris Peace treaties now stressed individual, as opposed to group, rights. They sought "to guarantee that individuals who differed from the majority in race [ethnicity], language, or religion should enjoy equal right with their fellow citizens belonging to the majority population."[20] Governments were required to secure "without distinction as to race, sex, language or religion, the enjoyment of human rights and of fundamental freedoms including freedom of expression, of press and publication, of religious worship, of political opinion and of public meeting."[21]

The switch in emphasis from group to individual rights indicated a growing conviction that universal assurance of the rights of the individual would assuage minority problems. It was also hoped that the new approach would "remove the causes of irritation on the part of the states bound by the minorities treaties."[22] In effect, the consensus of that time sought a universal bill of rights that would protect the rights and freedoms of the individual and preserve democracy against extremists of the Right and the Left. However, Western statesmen failed to understand that a disregard for group rights also had its price.

The emphasis on individual rights became the cornerstone of a new American policy that in its universalism and sweeping vision amounted to a new Wilsonianism. Article 6 of the Atlantic Charter, the United Nations declarations of January 1, 1942 (in regards to Italy), and other public pronouncements all emphasized the "universalization of equal rights and liberty of persons, in marked contrast to the specific provisions for ethnic minority groups prevalent during the interwar era."[23]

We now know, from the experience of the last 50 years, that individual rights, admirable in themselves, fail when they are decoupled from group rights. For we are not only individuals, we are also members of various groups and collectivities, whether ethnic, religious, or racial (as well as gender, sexual preference, age, and profession). Failure to protect our group rights inevitably denies our individual rights. But this was far from evident to the leaders of the Western world in 1945.

During the war it became increasingly clear that only extensive homogenization of existing political units could definitively solve intractable ethnic problems. As early as 1939 French sociologist Bernard Lavergne proposed creating linguistically and nationally homogeneous states by extensive transfers of population.[24] In effect, he was restating the position earlier taken by Georges Montandon. The proposal was a desperate attempt to prevent another world war. Unfortunately, it was rejected and ignored because, as Eduard Beneš put it, "it ran counter to the idealistic tendencies governing the 1919 plans for the new Europe."[25] Other, probably more significant reasons, included inertia, lack of creative thinking, and the difficulties of enforcement. It was also too late.

The world, and especially Europe, paid a terrible price. But, at the very least, after the war, there was an ardent desire to solve ethnic problems. That is why population transfers after World War II were carried out on an unprecedented scope. According to Schechtman, they affected over 18 million people in Europe alone.[26]

In almost all of these cases, compulsory exchange or transfer succeeded in permanently solving difficult border problems. At the very least, they ensured that there would be no irredentist minorities that could be used to destroy a sovereign state, as in Czechoslovakia in 1938 or Bosnia in 1992.

Among the exceptions were the transfer of German speakers from South Tyrol and the expulsion of Bulgarians from Greek Thrace. The transfer of Tyroleans failed because it was incomplete, and those transferees who had left were allowed to return after the war (many did). As a result, Italy was saddled with a minority problem. Terrorism originating in Alto-Adige continued to plague the country 30 and 40 years after the war. (The conflict may have finally fizzled out within the context of the European Union, but it is impossible to tell whether it will reappear in the future under less propitious circumstances. We should also note that the transfer in Tyrol was not the only incomplete transfer. Population exchanges between Czechoslovakia and Hungary, Poland and the Soviet Union were also incomplete. No Polish or Hungarian terrorism developed in western Ukraine or southern Slovakia because of the tight reins imposed by the communist regime. Now that the communists are gone the specter of irredentism is once again haunting many countries in eastern Europe, not least Slovakia. The case in Ukraine or Belarus—but not Lithuania—is different because Polish minorities in these countries are scattered and live at some distance from the border.)

Bulgaria's bid in 1941-44 to cleanse Thrace of its Greek inhabitants and resettle it with Bulgarians (many of them the original inhabitants who had left or been forced to leave in the 1920s) provides a much more serious challenge to our thesis. However, we should keep in mind that even here the renewed hostilities were the result of the general circumstances of World

War II and the unexpected opportunities presented by Italy's and Germany's invasion of Yugoslavia and Greece. Without this unexpected opportunity it is most unlikely that Bulgaria would have started a war. In other words, the renewed hostilities had not been initiated by one of the participants in the population exchange. In any case, in the absence of co-ethnic population, reattachment is much more difficult, and the Bulgarian experience in Thrace does not contradict that.

The list of partial—and thus unsuccessful—transfers may be expanded if we add unorganized removals and expulsions resulting from a change in power and/or redrawn frontiers. Among these we can name such diverse localities as Transylvania, India, Palestine, and many others. There, ethnic tensions persist and may even result in serial or periodic expulsions, such as the repeated expulsions of Turks from Bulgaria after World War I, after World War II, and in 1989.

On the other hand, virtually all complete population transfers brought about a definitive settlement of ethnic—and political—problems. The conclusion is that, as a rule, population transfers and exchanges, as a political instrument of achieving lasting peace, work.

Past Debates about Population Transfers

At the end of World War II and its immediate aftermath there were extensive discussions in the United States and Europe concerning large-scale population transfers. The idea was in the air, and many prominent scholars, politicians, and diplomats had come to the conclusion that transfers may be indispensable in solving some international problems.

Among the supporters were Herbert Hoover, former Secretary of the Treasury Henry Morgenthau,[27] former Ambassador Hugh Gibson, and many others. Gibson wrote that "in most cases the problem of mixed border people may have to be solved by the heroic remedy of transfer of populations. The hardship of moving is great, but it is less than the constant suffering of minorities and the constant recurrence of war."[28]

Sumner Welles stated that "[some] minority problems cannot be solved through frontier and territorial adjustment alone. . . . If history, and especially European history, has taught us anything, it must have taught us that the minority questions of Europe have been an eternal menace to friendly relations between peoples, a constant stimulant of fanatical nationalism, and a frequent incentive to war. Isn't it better, considering the appalling tragedy in Europe which we now confront, to get through with all the heartaches in this generation, when they may be an immediate consequence of planning for a peaceful and happier world, and thus prevent new heartaches in the generations to come?"[29]

Warren Thompson, a leading American demographer of the time, wrote that "I have gradually come to feel that the resettlement of considerable populations in Europe is indispensable to the establishment of a peace which will have a chance to last for more than a few years."[30] Stephen B. Jones was an associate professor of geography at the University of Hawaii who wrote a handbook on boundary making for the Carnegie Endowment for International Peace. He stated that "where nationalities are so dovetailed that no acceptable boundary can be drawn, the drastic remedy of population transfer may be the only solution. . . the trouble and cost are, however, vastly less than the trouble and cost of war."[31] Supporters also included Harold Butler, director of the International Labor Office in Geneva,[32] and De Azcarate, formerly the director of the Minorities Questions Section of the League of Nations, who suggested that population transfers "may be a practical means of readjustment between nationalities" although he refused to consider them "as an expedient applicable to all minorities."[33] We could also mention Bernard Newman, who believed that "whether we like the idea or not, the system of transference of population has become a matter for European politics."[34] He advocated the Polish-Soviet and Finnish-Soviet exchanges and a transfer of Germans from Poland; he also suggested transfer as a solution to the problems of Sudetenland, Istria, and Transylvania. (All, except the last one, have been carried out.)

Even politicians and scholars from nations that had experienced massive population transfers or could be involved in large-scale resettlement acknowledged their utility and validity. For example, Nicolas Politis, a Greek ambassador to France and an authority on international law, urged the widest application of the principle of transfers.[35] Other advocates included Imre Ferenczi, a well-known Hungarian population expert at the International Labor Office,[36] and Louis Dollot, a French migrations specialist.[37]

Nor was the idea confined to diplomats and population experts. The National Executive Committee of the British Labor Party declared its support at the Party Conference in May 1944: "The organized transfer of population in the immediate postwar period may, indeed, be one of the foundations of better international relations in a later phase."[38]

But resettlement never lacked opponents either. Oscar I. Janowsky, a noted interwar specialist in ethnic relations, wrote ironically that "if history and geography have created a Babel of tongues and peoples in east-central Europe, man is to step in and set things aright by sorting out and redistributing many millions of people according to national-cultural symptoms and labels."[39]

To this Schechtman objected that "there is nothing sacrosanct and eternal in conjunctures created by history and geography. Man has more than once stepped in to radically change long-established patterns which had for centuries been deemed immutable."[40] He offered an ingenious argument first enunciated by Henry Morgenthau, Jr.: "It is no longer necessary to be bound by the old feudal conception that the people go with the land. Men are no longer *glebae adscripti;* they have ceased to be a mere function of territory. . . . The old-fashioned practice of handing over large groups of people to a government they do not like and a foreign one at that should be avoided."[41]

The problem, of course, is that people do come with the territory, at least in the sense that an ethny usually inhabits a certain territory. Ideally, one should be able to trace state boundaries in such a way that they coincide with ethnic divisions. In practice, however, this is seldom possible. What's more, even the most generous protection of minority rights does not always guarantee acceptance of the status quo or even quiescence on the part of the minority. This is why, in Schechtman's words, "the idea of organized transfer of ethnic groups as a means of solving entangled and explosive territorial and national problems has, therefore, survived the end of the war and has proved its viability by having been invoked at every occasion where deeply rooted and intricate cases of this nature have come under discussion."[42]

Another opponent was Professor Erich Hula of the New School for Social Research. He rejected the idea from the moral standpoint, mainly because he refused to accord the "recognition of collective rights as against individual rights."[43] This was a recurrent theme among those who objected to transfers. Fritz Epstein, for example, lamented the transfer's "utter disregard for human rights."[44] Stellio Seferiades called it "criminal."[45] And Stephen P. Ladas believed that "wise statesmanship and great foresight could have avoided the surgical operation" of the Greek-Turkish exchange.[46] Of course, such could be said about virtually any conflict; the problem is that wise statesmanship and great foresight have often been in short supply. Even were they not, it is extremely difficult, if not impossible, to reconcile groups that had massacred each other within living memory and threaten to do so again. Fear is more potent than foresight.

Even the staunchest opponents of transfers, such as Sir John Hope Simpson, vice president of the League of Nations' Refugee Settlement Committee in Athens in 1926-30, who had called transfers "inhumane" and "cruel," was forced to admit that (occasionally) only a compulsory population exchange offers an adequate solution for hopelessly complicated minority problems.[47] Eugene M. Kulischer, another leading expert on migrations, denounced transfers as "a flagrant degradation of human beings, making them a tool for political and ethnic goals."[48] And Jean de la Robrie, a French specialist on population problems, rejected compulsory transfers from moral and political viewpoints.[49] In the same vein, David Thomson opposed Eduard Beneš's call, in an article in the *Spectator*,[50] for wholesale minority transfers on the grounds that "large-scale transfers of population involve enormous personal hardship and injustice."[51] He also believed that the creation of monoethnic states could promote and intensify exclusive nationalism. But this development has not been corroborated by historical record.

Finally, there were the moderates such as Norman Hill, who believed that transfers may be effective in small areas of highly mixed, 50-50 populations, such as Fiume or the Polish Corridor,[52] and Oscar Janowsky mentioned above, who was originally a staunch opponent of any transfers but eventually switched to a more moderate position. In a later work he acknowledged that "the exchange of minorities may be possible in special areas and on a small scale"[53] although he was still against wholesale transfers as a complete solution. Joseph Schechtman can also be listed among the moderates. "On the whole the author is in favor of the transfer of ethnic groups as a solution to those nationality problems which have proved to be insoluble in any other way," he wrote.[54]

Perhaps the most balanced approach was taken in a study of transfers done by the National Institute of Statistical and Economic Studies at the French Ministry of National Economy immediately after World War II. The study could not find moral or legal justification for transfers but acknowledged that "the transfer of population offers a constructive contribution to securing a durable peace."[55]

In conclusion, population transfers are no panacea and should be used with extreme caution. It is undeniable that they are a traumatic and painful experience for some, if not most, transferees: resettlers have to leave places where they grew up and relocate to a new community where they don't know anyone, unless the whole community is resettled in one place. It is also a disruptive process for both the country of departure and the country of resettlement, although the verdict on this point is less clear-cut than it might originally seem. Both sides may encounter significant short-term adjustment difficulties, but in the long run they benefit, especially the receiving countries. Greece and Germany profited greatly from the influx of thousands of transferees after World War I and World War II respectively. Greece, for example, aside from political (loss of a troublesome Turkish minority) and demographic (increase in the Greek population) advantages, reaped substantial economic benefits.

Barren lands were reclaimed, abandoned settlements were repopulated, and modernization and industrialization were promoted. "From 1924 to 1928, the increase in wheat production was more than threefold, thanks to the labor of the transferees. . . . The establishment of cooperative marketing and credit schemes, the influx of new capital, and a large supply of cheap labor facilitated industrialization."[56] Of course, seldom do both sides profit equally. In the Greco-Turkish exchange most economic benefits accrued to Greece, while in the Czech-German exchange Czechoslovakia won in terms of internal and external security while Germany enjoyed economic benefits.

In short, we should not overlook or underestimate the sufferings and inconvenience concomitant with a population transfer. But, as war becomes more and more destructive, preventing wars through the elimination of the underlying causes of ethnic conflict becomes ever more imperative. And whether we like it or not, population transfers do provide a permanent solution, particularly in situations where everything else has failed and "the grim necessity of a population transfer," in Beneš's words, is the only remaining option.

Based on the historical experience of the last 80-odd years, Schechtman made a balanced evaluation of the population transfer process. He acknowledged that it is an immensely difficult and complicated undertaking, which requires careful planning and preparation in many spheres. Some of these are international in scope, such as the political repercussions of the transfer, the economic consequences for the states involved, the flare-up of nationalist passions in the short run, and so on. Others are purely practical, such as transportation, hygiene, and housing problems. In principle, he believed that exchange is better than unilateral expulsion because it creates a system of mutual obligations and requires former adversaries to cooperate in finding suitable solutions. Yet, he also believed that "experience has proved that it is possible to carry out wholesale transfers of entire minority groups on the basis of interstate agreements, and that such operations can be effected without direct administrative pressure."[57]

Ultimately, we should be guided by the balance of pros and cons, just like in any other debate. Where ethnic, religious, or racial problems repeatedly defy solution, is it better to have periodic flare-ups of ethnic conflict with thousands of victims, millions of refugees, and the ever-present threat of war? Or is it more advisable to separate the combatants and give them and their children a chance to build a decent future? Even if the present generation must make some sacrifices for the benefit of their children and grandchildren? The answer seems clear.

THE MORALITY OF TRANSFER

So far we have concentrated on the practical side of the problem to the detriment of its moral aspect. Even if something works, it is not necessarily moral. The questions we should ask are: is the transfer moral? Is it moral to expel people, sometimes even against their will? And how is the moral validity of a transfer to be measured?

It should be reiterated that the concept of population transfers should be completely divorced from both the notion of collective guilt and that of collective punishment. Here again we can quote Schechtman: "the notion of guilt, as well as its corollary—retribution—cannot be applied to collectives. It constitutes a fundamentally individual category, which must in each specific case be established with regard to every single person involved. Even if the overwhelming majority of people belonging to an ethnic group are found guilty of a specific offense, the group in its totality may not be held morally or legally accountable, and be punished, for the offense committed by its members."⁵⁸

Yet individual actions cannot be divorced from group actions. It is true that if an extremist, a Bosnian Serb irregular or a Tamil Tiger, say, kills innocent civilians he is committing an individual act, even if his act is committed in the name of the community. However, if the majority or a significant portion of his community support him, and especially if the leaders of the community fail to condemn the outrage, the act inevitably acquires a communal dimension.

The principle is not limited to murder and mayhem. An ethnic group voting as a bloc makes a collective statement of its collective will, the "will of the people." When the Hungarians of Transylvania, to take one example, vote in a vast majority for the Hungarian Democratic Union in Romania (the "HDUR"), they make a collective statement. Any action taken by the HDUR inevitably acquires a communal dimension because HDUR represents the Hungarian community. This is particularly true if the action is undertaken by community leadership. If a minority, through the actions of the leaders it has elected, destroys or facilitates the destruction of the state where it lives, as did the Sudeten Germans who had voted overwhelmingly (98 percent) for Henlein, this is a collective action, which makes the minority collectively responsible. We cannot exculpate the Sudeten Germans for their part in the destruction of Czechoslovakia. But this, of course, applies to majorities as well as minorities. Was White America, as a community, responsible for the destruction of the Indian and the enslavement of the Black? Is Germany responsible for the Holocaust? The answers are clear; the communal dimension cannot be excluded.

In the last 30 or 40 years the onus has been almost exclusively on governments. Minorities, presumably, can do no wrong, especially "minorities at risk." Historically, however, that is not the case. There are many examples of restive minorities, particularly those supported from a historical homeland, who refuse every offer of accommodation coming from the government, who work toward the destruction and dissolution of the polity they regard as illegitimate.

But this line of argument misses an important point: resettlement is not a punishment. It bears repeating that

> [A transfer] is not a chastening of an ethnic group for the misdemeanor of all or part of its members, while another ethnic group is rewarded for good behavior of its members by being permitted to remain in their homes. Compulsory population transfer is in its essence a preventive measure, not a retaliatory one. If large sections of an ethnic minority within a state consistently negate their very allegiance to this state; repeatedly create friction and conflicts; neglect their elementary civic duties; look for guidance, and display allegiance to their co-national state abroad, nourish irredentist tendencies and thus jeopardize the integrity of the state; and if all attempts at reconciling this minority and integrating it into the framework of common statehood fail—then, and only then, recourse may be taken to [what Beneš called] the 'grim necessity of population transfer.'[59]

Another aspect that elicits much criticism is the compulsory nature of the transfer, its undemocratic character. Yet even in a democracy many things are compulsory: taxation, primary education, quarantine, permits for gun ownership, to name a few. When we have to choose between individual rights and the welfare of an entire community, the welfare of the community takes precedence. Protecting the community will also safeguard interests of its members. This principle of the common good cannot be excluded from solving ethnic problems. Ultimately, the problem boils down to this: to whose rights do we give precedence? Despite the fact that individual and group rights are inextricably linked and mutually dependent, we sometimes have to choose between individual rights as against group rights and state rights. Many multiethnic states concede individual rights but refuse minority group rights. In other words, a Breton may have the full individual rights of a French citizen but few or no rights as a member of the Breton community. Some Bretons are undoubtedly satisfied by this situation, but many are not, especially those who see themselves as members of the Breton community first and foremost.

But whatever rights are more fashionable at the moment—and we have seen that even in the West the emphasis shifted from group rights to individual rights after 1945—we should not forget that an individual is a member of the group. One's individual rights inevitably suffer when one's group rights are denied, and vice versa. They cannot be divorced from each other. In the context of the latest developments—the collapse of communism and the emergence of two dozen successor states—it is increasingly clear that the emphasis on individual, at the expense of group, rights is untenable.

Whatever the zeitgeist, the ultimate goal of a population exchange is preventing war and saving human lives. That is the decisive point that determines whether a particular resettlement is moral or not. *A transfer is moral when it serves the purpose of saving lives and assures the rights, individual and group, of future victims.*

SOME ORGANIZATIONAL MATTERS OF TRANSFER

Population transfers are extremely complicated procedures that pose numerous problems for the receiving and the expelling countries. Practical and organizational matters require a separate treatment that is beyond the scope of this book, but we can highlight a few important points.

First, not all transferees would necessarily choose to move to their historical homeland. On the contrary, quite a few may choose to start a new life in a third country, perhaps somewhere overseas. That may not be feasible in a world of closed borders and strict immigration quotas but, for the sake of their successful adjustment, it is highly advisable to allow them to choose their own destination, inasmuch as it is at all possible.

Second, the transfer trauma may be sufficiently alleviated if the transferees retain citizenship and property rights in the country of origin, either indefinitely or for a specified period of time (the second is preferable). A prolonged and gradual separation may ease the pain and the financial burden of the departing transferees. It may facilitate their access to legal advice and legal redress in cases of financial or family complications such as divorce from someone who is staying behind or various problems related to child custody rights. A gradual separation may also allow more time to dispose of the property.

Some members of the transferred ethny may be allowed to stay but only as individuals without minority group rights. Basically, they and their children will have to assimilate. Judging from past experience, many of them may later decide to leave. Thus, most of Czechoslovakia's Germans who had been originally exempted from expulsion chose to leave anyway, because of feelings of "ethnic loneliness" (and the communization of Czechoslovakia).

Questions relating to the disposal of personal and communal property in the country of departure are always of utmost importance. Unfortunately, they are also among the thorniest. As a rule, it is not advisable to leave the disposal of private property, especially real estate, to the transferees. The sale of so many properties within a short period of time will inevitably create a glut on the market and depress prices. Also, transferees may be subject to pressures from corrupt local authorities for bribes and kickbacks. It is far better to create trust companies on both sides. Such companies would buy out the property of the transferees and would then settle financial matters on a state-to-state basis. Such an arrangement is much more equitable and leaves far less personal bitterness, which is important in solving any group conflict. Schechtman, incidentally, noted that attempts to compensate each evacuee through mixed commissions had invariably failed.[60] The best solution, in his opinion, is an advance wholesale evaluation of the property left behind by the transferees at pretransfer prices, to be followed by the establishment of a payment schedule on a country-to-country basis, in cash or in goods.[61]

Pensions are another item that are better settled on a government-to-government basis. Here, the country of origin may continue to pay pensions to all transferees who had reached retirement age at the time of transfer; or, as usually happens, the pensions become the responsibility of the country of destination; or both sides may agree to share the burden, with the country of origin paying pensions to some categories of transferees, such as former military personnel, while the country of destination may agree to pay retirement benefits to civilians.

In addition, there is the important task of ensuring adequate medical care for thousands of people during and immediately after the transfer, with particular focus on the prevention of epidemics. Here, again, close cooperation between the country of origin and the country of destination, most likely involving active participation by international organizations, is highly desirable.

Finally, speed is essential for a successful transfer operation. Only those transfers that were carried out within a few weeks, or a couple of months at most, were fully realized. Those that were spread over longer periods, such as the Greco-Bulgarian exchange of 1919-30 and the German transfer from South Tyrol, were invariably incomplete.[62] Subsequent developments showed that they had failed to solve their respective conflicts. They had failed because they were incomplete.

Chapter 16

THE RESETTLEMENT INDEX

We have established that population transfers—including population exchange and resettlement—can be a valuable instrument in solving irreconcilable ethnic conflicts. However, we lack any quantifiable indicators that could help us in determining which adversary should be relocated (to paraphrase a popular song, "who should stay and who should go"). Let us, therefore, construct a resettlement or transfer index that will serve as a vector pointing in the right direction.

We choose an index rather than some other form of quantification because it combines several parameters in a single score. It is also economical because it can reflect a range of variation within each variable. In short, indices and scales are efficient analytical tools because they can compress much data within a single indicator.

An index is an "ordinal measure of variables"[1] that ranks units of analysis in terms of discrete variables. According to Earl Babbie, "an index is constructed through the simple accumulation of scores assigned to individual attributes."[2] A scale is more complex because it is constructed "through the assignment of scores to patterns of attributes. Thus, a scale takes advantage of any intensity structure that may exist among attributes."

In Babbie's opinion, scales are generally superior to indices because "scale scores convey more information than index scores do." However, not every set of data lends itself to scale construction: some variables do not vary in intensity. And those that do may have incompatible ranges of intensity that make meaningful comparison difficult, if not impossible. That is why the use of scales requires some prior record that would indicate the limitations of a particular parameter in this or that scale. Finally, some phenomena may be scaleable along one variable but not along another. For that reason, indices are easier to construct and, because they are more straightforward, they are more widely used than scales.

Before we decide whether we want to construct an index or a scale we should briefly examine how each one is built.

The first step is to select variables that are valid, that is, that possess logical or face validity. For example, if we are measuring nationalism, membership in nationalistic organizations would be a logical choice.

Another requirement is that variables be unidimensional. If we continue with our hypothetical example of measuring nationalism, we should refrain from including parameters indicating political conservatism even though both variables are often empirically interrelated.

The degree of variance is another important consideration. If a variable classifies everybody—or nobody—as a nationalist, then the variable is useless.

Finally, we should not forget the range of nuances within each parameter. A political nationalist may be culturally liberal or a cultural nationalist interested in preserving local language and customs with little interest in nationalist politics of self-determination.

Once the variables have been selected, the second step is to examine bivariate relationships between them. The variable must relate empirically. If several parameters reflect nationalism, then persons who appear nationalistic in terms of one variable should appear nationalistic in terms of another. However, one of two variables that display perfect correlation may be safely eliminated because it does not add anything to the index. Of course, such bivariate correlations are hardly ever perfect. Earl Babbie advises that an item "that is not related to several other items probably should be dropped from consideration."[3]

The third step involves an examination of the multivariate relationship among several variables. Once again, the goal here is to determine whether the parameters we have chosen are appropriate for the particular index under construction. For example, the more nationalistically inclined may be more conservative and more interested in preserving historical monuments but less concerned with ecology. So, a variable indicating attitudes to problems of ecology, even in the guise of "saving our nature," may be of little help in measuring nationalism.

The next step is index scoring or range delimitation. Here one must decide on the range for each variable, since extremes will usually have fewer cases and at some point the number of cases will be so insignificant as to be unrepresentative. The trade-off is between the desire to provide the widest range without slipping into unrepresentative extremes. Another important decision is whether to give equal weight to each variable. Babbie advises that "equal weighting should be the norm," unless there are "compelling reasons for differential weighting."[4]

Once the index has been built, it should be validated. The validation procedure is based on the predictive value of the index; an index, to be a valuable tool, must predict its constituent values. Several methods of validation can be used. The most popular one is the so-called item analysis, in which tables are created in which the index serves as the independent variable while one of the component variables serves as a dependent variable. If the index is good, each individual variable should correlate with the total index scores. Conversely, the index itself should predict or relate to the constituent variables.

Another method of validation is external validation. If we use our previous example, political nationalists should show nationalistic inclinations with respect to a whole range of beliefs and activities, although it would be possible to be a nationalist politically but a cosmopolitan in regards to arts and literature. In other words, persons who prove to be more nationalistic in terms of the index should also prove to be nationalistic in other spheres. Conversely, those who are less nationalistic according to the index should display a similar pattern in other aspects of ideology.

Before we plunge into constructing the resettlement index, let me say a few words about scales and why I chose not to use them. As an analytical tool, scales are more sophisticated than indices because they reflect variations in "logical or empirical intensity structures that exist among the different indicators of a variable."[5] That means that each variable may vary in intensity and that each variable may have a different impact on the index. In other words, not all variables are created equal; some are more important than others. And that is why the scales are not well suited to population transfer: some variables do not vary in intensity, but are of a binary, either/or nature.

In addition, the three scales that find the widest application in the social sciences—those of Bogardus, Thurstone, and Guttman—are better suited to research conducted with live respondents to surveys measuring beliefs, choices, and personal opinions on topics such as religiosity, nationalism, and social distance than they are to research conducted with the demographic, historic parameters of a population transfer. (There are other considerations as well. The Thurstone scale, for example, requires a panel of judges, which makes it more cumbersome.)

Finally, our index is designed to be a contributing, not a determining, factor in a decision to transfer because we are in a realm—the fate of human beings—in which mathematical equations should be used carefully and sparingly. If we take it as a guideline, an index may be helpful.

***

A resettlement index is an entirely new venture, so it will be advisable to use a previous transfer as a model. The transfer of Germans from Czechoslovakia after World War II satisfies all our requirements: it was orderly, humane, fairly well organized, especially in the later stages, and it achieved a resounding success in solving a seemingly insolvable ethnic conflict. Its success was measured by the fact that no more problems between Czechs and Germans or between Czechoslovakia and Germany have recurred since the transfer was completed. (The division of Europe into two blocs was also conducive to pacification because it "froze" the Czech/German issue. However, even after the collapse of the Soviet Empire in Eastern Europe, of which Czechoslovakia had been an integral part, no territorial or ethnic issues between Germany and the Czech republic reappeared. That it could have been otherwise is clearly demonstrated by the unfortunate examples of Hungary and Slovakia or Hungary and Romania. The reason for the difference is clearly the successful transfer of the German minorities from Bohemia and Moravia and the failed transfer of Hungarians from Slovakia and elsewhere.)

We need not look to de-Germanization in other East European countries because it seldom met the requirements of a humane population transfer. The expulsions from Poland, for example, were often cruel and chaotic; many Germans from Romania and Yugoslavia fled with the retreating German armies; and those from the Baltic region, Bukovina, and Bessarabia had been recalled. Even more important, the transfer from Czechoslovakia was organized with the full consent and participation of the Western democracies. Western journalists had full access to the transferees during the operation, which cannot be said of most other resettlement campaigns.

We should also leave out all instances of population exchange because an exchange establishes a more equitable relationship between the adversaries and results from a somewhat different set of conditions. For that reason, we should leave out the Bulgarian-Greek, Bulgarian-Romanian, Greek-Turkish, Czechoslovak-Polish and the Polish-Soviet population exchanges.

To construct the index, the first thing to do is to delimit the political and/or geographical unit from which the population is to be transferred. Logically, the unit should coincide with the area of conflict. These areas, however, can seldom be taken separately because virtually all interethnic conflicts involve the entire ethny.

In the case of Czechoslovakia it is clear that the unit was the historical Czech crown lands of Bohemia and Moravia, not the Sudetenland proper, which formed a rim around the Czech ethnic territory. (Incidentally, there were large ethnic German enclaves deep inside ethnic Czech territory, especially in larger cities such as Prague, Brno, and Iglava. A substantial proportion of these Germans took part in the struggle against the Czech state. When the Allies decided upon resettlement, these Germans were included among the transferees.)

Many commentators on the transfer of the Sudeten Germans focus on two aspects of the transfer: the legitimacy of the transfer and its feasibility. Upon closer examination, we can discern that the issue of legitimacy revolves around questions of historical precedence, the extent of victimization of the Czechs by the Germans, and Hitler's use of the Sudeten Germans for his long-term goals. The issue of the feasibility of the transfer is more circumscribed: basically, it involves the issue of how many people had to be transferred and resettled and also the place of resettlement (in the case of Sudeten Germans, the question of the number of transferees each zone of occupation within Germany would accept).

We now can provide definitions for the index and its components.

The *resettlement index* (we may also call it the "transfer index") is an index that measures the justice and the feasibility of transferring one of the ethnic groups involved in an irreconcilable ethnic conflict.

The justice of the transfer and, conversely, the right to stay, is measured by three parameters: historical precedence, past victimization, and the existence of an external threat from an adversary's powerful ethnic ally across the border.

Historical precedence refers to which ethny was first to settle in the area in question.

Victimization refers to which ethny found itself, historically, at the receiving end in the conflict; that is, which ethny was the victim of discrimination, massacre, and/or genocide.

External threat refers to the danger of intervention, on behalf of one of the contestants, by ethnic cousins in the immediate vicinity of the conflict area. It measures the vulnerability of ethny's position.

The parameters involved in the feasibility aspect of the transfer include the numerical superiority or inferiority, and the availability of a destination point for the group which is to be transferred.

Numerical superiority refers to a situation where one ethny comprises more than 50 percent of the total population. Conversely, *numerical inferiority* describes a situation where one ethny amounts to less than 50 percent of the total population. And *plurality* is defined as a numerical superiority of one group over another where the larger group accounts for less than 50 percent of the total population.

The availability of a destination point will help to determine whether the transfer will be external (outside the country) or internal (within). However, it should not be part of the index. First, it would permit negative values in the context of the index (for example, Czechs would have a "minus," Germans a "plus"), while all other variables would require positive values; this would impair the validity of the index. Second, this factor would be of the highest practical importance, so we would be forced to assign it the highest weighted value, and that would skew the whole index. Thus, we will leave it out of the index and revisit it in the next chapter.

***

Now let us assign numbers to the index.

Where quantification is impossible, we will have to make do with the binary method. Thus, we will assign a value of "+1.0" to the ethny that has historical precedence and numerical superiority; conversely, ethnies that were latecomers and are in the minority will get a value of "-1.0."

The category of external threat is more complicated. Theoretically, an ethny that is under an external threat from the adversary's ethnic cousins will get a value of "+1.0," while the one that is not under threat will get a value of "-1.0." However, we may find some situations where both contestants are under threat (Greek and Turkish Cypriots, for example) although the threat may not be equal; or where neither adversary is under external threat (e.g., the Hutu and the Tutsi). Here, we'll have to resort to approximations.

Victimization is the most complicated variable. Here, we will assign a value of "+1.0" to the victim and a value of "-1.0" to the "culprit." The problem is that in the course of history victims sometimes become butchers (like the Serbs of Bosnia) and vice versa. Let us, therefore, establish the following guidelines:

1. Genocide on the scale of the Nazi crimes will be assigned a value of "-1.0";
2. A brutal removal of an entire ethny by a totalitarian regime, such as Stalinism, accompanied by cultural ethnocide will get a value of "-0.8";
3. "Unorganized" massacres will get "-0.6";
4. Persecution, such as mass arrests and detentions, will get "+0.4"; and
5. Discrimination will get "-0.2."

Conversely, victims in these cases will be assigned "+1.0," "+0.8," "+0.6," "+0.4," and "+0.2." An ethny's victimization variable will depend on whether or not it has been victimized and also whether or not it has mistreated its ethnic adversaries.

If we add up all four parameters (historical precedence, victimization, external threat, and numerical strength) we will get our resettlement index. Evidently, the positive maximum is "+4.0," the negative maximum, "-4.0." A score of "+4.0" would provide the maximum justification for an ethny to remain in place, while a score of "-4.0" would provide the maximum justification for an ethny to be transferred.

Now let us assign the above variables as they applied to the Czechs and Germans in Bohemia and Moravia (Table 16.1).

TABLE 16.1
PARAMETERS OF A POPULATION TRANSFER
(THE CZECHS AND GERMANS OF BOHEMIA AND MORAVIA)

	Area	Hist. Prec.	Victim- ization	External Threat	Numerical Majority	Index
Czechs	Bohemia	+0.7	+0.8	+1.0	+1.0	+3.5
Germans	& Mor.	+0.3	-0.8	-1.0	-1.0	-2.5

(1) Historical precedence. Germanic (and Celtic) tribes had been present in the territory of Bohemia more than 2,000 years ago, before the arrival of the Slavs. These earlier inhabitants had either migrated elsewhere or were swamped by the massive Slav migration in the fifth century. Since the early Middle Ages Bohemia has been continuously inhabited by Slavs. The ancestors of the Sudeten Germans were later immigrants who arrived in the tenth or eleventh centuries at the earliest. There was no continuity between the ancient Germanic tribe of the Markomanni and the later German settlers. Nevertheless, we should not completely discard the earlier German presence in Bohemia. Let us, therefore, assign "+0.7" to the Czechs and "+0.3" to the Germans.

(2) Victimization. In many long-term ethnic relationships, much like in personal ones, one party is usually at the receiving end. In the case of the Germans and Czechs, the latter have clearly been an aggrieved party. This does not mean that Germans never suffered from Czech hands; they did so in 1419, in 1618, and in 1945. Historically, however, the Germans had the upper hand. In any case, the enormity of the Nazi crimes overshadows all others. But it is mitigated by the fact that the Nazis did not pursue a policy

of genocide vis-a-vis the Czechs. It is also mitigated by the discrimination against and, rarely, persecution of the German element during outbursts of Czech nationalism. So, let us assign a value of "+0.2" to the German suffering at Czech hands (up to the point when the decision to expel the Sudeten Germans was taken) and subtract it from the value of "-1.0" that the Germans would otherwise get. We'll repeat the same procedure with the Czechs, subtracting the value of "-0.2" from the Czech victimization variable of "+1.0." Thus, the Czechs end up with "+0.8" on the victimization variable while the Germans get "-0.8."

(3) External threat. An ethnic minority with ties across the border is inherently dangerous, especially if the neighboring state(s) is large, strong, and aggressive. In the case of Czechs and Germans, both parties enjoyed support from the outside. The Allies supported the Czechs in 1918-20 and again in 1945-47, while Germany supported Sudeten Germans in 1938-39. The symmetry, however, is less than perfect. The Sudeten Germans could always count on German support, even before the Nazis came to power. The Allied support for Czechoslovakia, on the other hand, was predicated on Allied interests. When the Allies (mis)perceived their interests as inimical to those of Czechoslovakia they either acted against it, as in 1938, or sat on their hands and did nothing, as in 1968. The conclusion is that the support of ethnic cousins is more often than not unconditional (the Russian, Serbian, and Hungarian stance vis-a-vis their respective minorities supports this) while the support of political allies is conditional on their interests. That is why, in the last 300 years, Czechs have been perennial victims—they deserve "+1.0"— while the Sudeten Germans, with Prussia, Austria, or the Reich looming across the border, get a value of "-1.0."

(4) Numerical strength. The numerical preponderance of an ethny is usually accepted as a reasonable justification of land "ownership." Thus, the wishes of 8 million Czechs of Bohemia and Moravia in 1945 had more legitimacy in the eyes of contemporaries—including, most importantly, the victorious Allies—than those of the 3 million Sudeten Germans. And in practical terms it is much easier, of course, to remove 3 million people than 8. In short, once again, Czechs get "+1.0" while Germans get "-1.0." (Here we can see the value of the proper geographical delimitation: the choice of Ulster or Ireland, for example, will determine the numerical strength of each contestant.)

If we now add the assigned values for each community, we get a value of "+3.5" for Czechs against "-2.5" for the Sudeten Germans. This then will be our resettlement index, with the Czechs' right to stay justified by a six-point advantage vis-a-vis the Germans.

***

Now we will apply the techniques developed above to evaluating potential population transfers in the ten areas we have discussed in previous chapters. Let us first delimit the geographical areas. Although most of the areas may seem to be well circumscribed, the situation on the ground is actually more complicated than meets the eye. Any successful solution to the Bosnian problem, for instance, has to take into account not only Serbia and Croatia but also the Serbs of Krajina who encircle Bosnia from the west (this is no longer true after the reoccupation of the region by Croatia in August 1995; however, the question of compensation may come up at the peace talks that may follow). Cyprus, Karabakh, Kosovo, Sri Lanka, Transylvania, and Ulster involve, in addition to the local adversaries, two larger contending communities in the immediate vicinity. The problem of Russian minorities in the former Soviet republics is particularly cumbersome since it involves 15 participants of varying size and distribution; and the Arab-Israeli conflict involves more than 20 Arab states, in addition to many more non-Arab Muslim states like Iran or even Malaysia. Only Rwanda, with its sister republic of Burundi, does not have a wider regional dimension, although this may no longer be true, with some 2 million refugees stranded across the border in neighboring countries.

However, extending the area of conflict to the entire Balkan peninsula or the Arab/Muslim world will immensely extend the spacial limits and will completely delocalize them. Hence, let us stay within more narrow geographical limits in each area: Bosnia, the island of Cyprus, Nagorno-Karabakh, Kosovo, western Palestine (Israel plus the West Bank and Gaza), Rwanda/Burundi, the island of Sri Lanka, Transylvania, and Ulster.

The Russian minorities in the Near-Abroad are a special case. In principle, we do not have to worry, at this point, about the former Soviet republics with an insignificant percentage of Russian minorities (the Transcaucasian republics) or those that do not border on new Russia, such as the republics of Central Asia. This does not mean that Russia will not interfere in these locations—Georgia and Moldova prove otherwise—but Russian interference there is defined more by imperial power politics than by ethnic conflicts involving local Russians.

Let us now examine specific variables for each of the ten areas (Table 16.2).

In terms of historical precedence, the cases in Cyprus, Kosovo, Israel, the successor republics of the former USSR, Rwanda, and Sri Lanka are fairly clear: in all these areas the majority ethny was there first. In Bosnia and Ulster, on the other hand, the ethnic majorities or pluralities are relative newcomers, although in Bosnia it can be argued that most of the Muslim

TABLE 16.2
PARAMETERS OF A POPULATION TRANSFER

Majorities

	Area	Hist. Prec.	Victim- ization	External Threat	Numerical Majority	Index
Muslims	Bosnia	-1.0	+0.5	+0.8	+0.4	+0.7
Greeks	Cyprus	+1.0	+0.3	+0.7	+1.0	+3.0
Armen.	Karab.	+0.7	+0.6	+1.0	+1.0	+3.3
Alban.	Kosovo	+1.0	+0.2	+1.0	+1.0	+3.2
Jews	Israel	+1.0	+0.5	+1.0	+1.0	+3.5
Non-Russ	Near-A.	+1.0	+0.8	+1.0	+1.0	+3.8
Hutus	Rwanda	+1.0	-0.4	0.0	+1.0	+1.6
Sinhal.	Sri L.	+1.0	-0.3	+1.0	+1.0	+2.7
Roman.	Trans.	+0.5	0.0	+0.3	+1.0	+1.8
Protest.	Ulster	-1.0	-0.2	-1.0	+1.0	-1.2

Minorities

	Area	Hist. Prec.	Victim- ization	External Threat	Numerical Majority	Index
Serbs	Bosnia	+0.5	0.0	-1.0	+0.3	-0.2
Croats	Bosnia	+1.0	-0.5	-0.5	+0.2	+0.2
Turks	Cyprus	-1.0	-0.4	+0.3	-1.0	-2.1
Azeris	Karab.	+0.3	-0.5	-1.0	-1.0	-2.2
Serbs	Kosovo	-1.0	-0.3	-1.0	-1.0	-3.3
Palest.	Israel	-1.0	-0.4	-1.0	-1.0	-3.4
Russians	Near-A.	-1.0	-0.8	-1.0	-1.0	-3.8
Tutsis	Rwanda	-1.0	+0.5	0.0	-1.0	-1.5
Tamils	Sri L.	-1.0	+0.3	-1.0	-1.0	-2.7
Hungar.	Trans.	+0.5	0.0	+0.3	-1.0	-0.2
Cathol.	Ulster	+1.0	+0.2	+0.3	-1.0	+0.5

population derives from the earlier Bogomil inhabitants. In any case, as an ethnoreligious community, Muslims appeared on the scene only after the Turkish conquest. The case is less clear in Karabakh and Transylvania, where no definitive proof of precedence can be found in support of either claim. However, historical monuments scattered throughout Karabakh point to a very old Armenian presence, so we may assign the value of "+0.7" to the Armenians, compared to the Azeris' "+0.3." (Nomads were an important component in the Azeri ethnic makeup. Many Azeris did not settle down until the 1930s. It may be argued that nomads do not leave as many traces as do settled civilizations, so that we are biased in favor of the farmer as compared to the nomad. In any case, the "+0.7" is not an absolute value, it reflects greater claims of an older Armenian polity.)

Finally, the Romanians and Hungarians of Transylvania each get "+0.5," since precedence of either one is impossible to establish with any degree of certainty.

Among minorities, the Croats get "+1.0" because they have been living in Bosnia since their arrival in the Balkans 1,500 years ago, while the Serbs of Bosnia get "+0.5" because they have been settled in parts of southern Bosnia since the time of their arrival, although Bosnia, as an entity, was historically, with few exceptions, outside their sphere of influence. These values are again, relative.

***

Victimization, as we have said, is the most difficult variable because it is hard to quantify. However, if we follow the guidelines set forth earlier in this chapter we will arrive at a reasonably good distribution as showed in column 2 of Table 16.2. A brief explanation is probably in order. The Muslims of Bosnia are assigned "+0.5" because, although they have been massacred and otherwise brutalized in the ongoing war (and thus "deserve" "+0.6"), they were the mainstay of the 500-year Turkish yoke and took part in suppressing numerous anti-Turkish uprisings. The Serbs of Bosnia get "0.0" because their brutality in the ongoing war has roughly cancelled out their suffering in 1941. And the Croats of Bosnia end up with "-0.5" because they massacred Serbs in 1941 but were oppressed in Serb-dominated Yugoslavia and suffered extensively in the current war (although probably not as much as the Muslims). (This example shows once again that values assigned to each ethny are relative rather than absolute.)

Among ethnies with a positive victimization variable, the non-Russians in the former Soviet republics get the highest score, "+0.8," because many of them suffered mass deportations bordering on genocide. Conversely, the Russians get "-0.8" since they were the perpetrators, usually without extenuating circumstances such as persecutions at the hands of indigenous populations.

The Armenians, as perennial victims of massacres, deserve "+0.6." The Tutsi get "+0.5," to reflect their long-term oppression of the Hutu, despite the genocidal massacres of the recent past. Jews of Israel also get a value of "+0.5": they had suffered pogroms and massacres before and during the creation of Israel and had to endure years of non-stop terrorism. The value of "+0.5," rather than "+0.6," reflects the moral costs of the occupation, although this assertion is debatable, since the West Bank and Gaza were occupied in the course of a defensive war. Also, the Arab states had long refused to enter into peace negotiations, making the occupation inevitable.

The Greek Cypriots merit "+0.3" because in the last two centuries their suffering was closer to persecution than outright massacre. Their massacres are not very recent (the exodus of 1974 from northern Cyprus was not accompanied by large-scale massacres). They lose "+0.1" for their mistreatment of the Cypriot Turks. So do the Tamils, who had suffered from pogroms and persecution but inflicted enough damage on the Sinhalese to justify the reduction; they also get a "+0.3." The Albanians of Kosovo and the Catholics of Ulster, both of whom suffered "only" discrimination (the persecution of Catholics belongs to the less recent past), get a value of "+0.2."

Two ethnies—the Hungarians and the Romanians—get "0.0" because the damage they had inflicted on each other mutually cancels out (rampant discrimination and rare pogroms, but on a relatively small scale).

Among the ethnies with negative victimization indices the Protestants of Northern Ireland are guilty of discrimination. The mistreatment visited by the Serbs of Kosovo and the Sinhalese on their adversaries is probably closer to persecution; we can assign the value of "-0.3" to both. Massacres perpetrated by the Azeris earn them "-0.5," but the Palestinians, the Hutu and the Cypriot Turks who should get a similar evaluation get off lightly, with only "-0.4" each, due to the suffering inflicted by their opponents: Palestinians, because of the hardships of the occupation, despite the anti-Jewish pogroms and massacres in mandate Palestine and decades of vicious terrorism; the Hutu, because they have suffered centuries-old oppression; and the Cypriot Turks because they have been recently (historically speaking) mistreated by their Greek adversaries.

***

The variable of external threat is somewhat easier to determine. It is based on the presence of an ethny's adversary's ethnic cousins or allies in the immediate vicinity of the conflict area and or their historical record of actively helping, especially militarily, the adversary.

Thus, for the Armenians of Karabakh, Azerbaijan is the enemy's ally. (Technically, Azerbaijan is not an outside power. But we have limited the area of conflict to Karabakh only, so from that perspective Azerbaijan is an outsider power. And there is also Turkey, which has threatened to intervene in Nakhichevan.) Serbia plays the same role for the Albanians of Kosovo, Arab states for the Jews of Israel, Russia for the indigenous populations of the former Soviet republics, India for the Sinhalese, and so on. In most of these cases, the odds for or against one of the adversaries are overwhelming, so we can assign a value of "+1.0" to the threatened ethny and "-1.0" to the ethny with an ethnic ally.

Occasionally, we find a certain reciprocity. In only one case, that of Transylvania, are the adversaries evenly matched. Within the present-day context, Romanians in the area potentially face a greater *external* threat. (Technically, of course, Romania, like Azerbaijan in Karabakh or the United Kingdom in Ulster, is not an outside power.) But a greater threat from Hungary is cancelled by Romania's greater ability to interfere in Transylvania. And since the likelihood of a military intervention in the near future is remote, we can assign a relatively low value of "+0.3" to both.

Such reciprocity is rarely of equal proportion, however: Turkey is more powerful than Greece, and Great Britain is much more powerful than the Irish Republic. Since the threat from Turkey to Greek Cypriots is proportionately larger and potentially more dangerous, the values of "+0.7" for Greek Cypriots and "+0.3" for Turkish Cypriots are not out of place. Likewise, Great Britain, the ally of Ulster's Protestants, is so much stronger than Eire that one almost hesitates to speak of a threat to the Protestants. Thus, the values of "-1.0" for Protestants and "+0.3" for Catholics do not seem unreasonable.

Bosnia, as usual, is a more difficult case to evaluate. Until very recently, Bosnia's Serbs have had the backing of the largest and most aggressive power in the Balkans. (Their recent reversals do not change that fact.) Thus, they should still get a value of "-1.0." Bosnian Croats, supported by Croatia (with roughly half of Serbia's punch), may contend with a lower value of "-0.5." And Muslims, without any regional allies in the immediate vicinity, deserve a "+0.8" ("1.0" - "0.2," where "+0.2" represents the remote possibility of Turkish interference in the conflict on the Muslim side).

The only exception among the ten cases are the Hutu and the Tutsi who do not have ethnic relatives outside the area of conflict.

***

The numerical majority parameter is even less controversial, as long as we believe official statistics. Even where the official statistics are unreliable they usually don't reverse the majority/minority ratio. At most, a gross undercounting may skew the ratio but does not relegate a majority to a minority status and vice versa. For example, according to official Romanian statistics, there are only 1.6 million ethnic Hungarians in Romania. According to unofficial estimates, the number of Hungarians may be as high as 2.5 million. But in any case, whether 1.6 or 2.5 million, Hungarians form a minority among Transylvania's 8 million inhabitants.

What values should be assigned to each majority and minority? At first glance, it may seem reasonable to try to reflect the real numerical correlations in our variable. However, the dubious reliability of some of the statistical data makes it impossible. Therefore, let us limit ourselves to a binary solution, that is, let us assign a value of "+1.0" to the majority ethnic groups and a value of "-1.0" to the minority. This way, there will be no arguments as to who gets a "plus" and who gets a "minus."

Indeed, all our conflict areas have a clear majority, except Bosnia. Here, there is no majority, only a plurality of Muslims, so a binary solution is not possible. Here, since the ratio of the three major ethnoreligious groups is well known, we can follow the ethnic distribution and assign to each group its percentage of the total population. Thus, Muslims, with some 40 percent of the population before the war, get a "+0.4," Serbs get a "+0.3," and Croats get a "+0.2" (which is rounded up from their actual prewar share of 17 to 18 percent).

***

We can now add the four variables.

The resettlement index shows a wide fluctuation within the "+4.0/-4.0" range, from the high of "+3.8" for the autochthonous populations in the former Soviet republics to a low of "-3.8" for the Russian minorities in the same area. Most of the items are self-explanatory, one adversary usually getting a positive index, the other one a negative one. Only Bosnia, once again, is a case apart because it has three contestants. Here, Muslims and Croats end up with "+0.7" and "+0.2" respectively, while Serbs get a negative value of "-0.2."

As we look at the index, we notice that all majorities, except the Protestants of Northern Ireland, show positive values while all minorities, except the Croats and the Ulster Catholics, do not. Is there a bias against minorities? Could it be that numerical superiority skews the results?

Since that variable is represented by either "+1.0" or "-1.0," it stands to reason that it could either increase or decrease the index by "+1.0" or "-1.0" (except in Bosnia). Still, let us construct a "test" index based on the first three variables: historical precedence, victimization, and external threat (see Table 16.3). Indeed, as we have expected, both indices differ by "1.0," whether "plus" or "minus," except in two cases: Bosnia and Transylvania.

Bosnia should not surprise us, since numerical strength for each ethny was represented proportionately. The ratio, however, holds, with the Muslim test index at "+0.3," the Croatian index at "0.0," and the Serbs once again coming in third with "-0.5."

The real surprise awaits us in Transylvania, where test indices for both ethnies converge at "+0.8," despite very different resettlement indices of "+1.8" for the Romanians and "-0.2" for the Hungarians. Their other parameters being equal, only the Romanians' larger numbers make transferring them less feasible.

TABLE 16.3
COMPARISON OF THE TEST AND RESETTLEMENT INDEXES

Majorities			
	Area	**Test Index**	**Reset. Index**
Muslims	Bosnia	+0.3	+0.7
Greeks	Cyprus	+2.0	+3.0
Armen.	Karab.	+2.3	+3.3
Alban.	Kosovo	+2.2	+3.2
Jews	Israel	+2.5	+3.5
Non-Russ	Near-A.	+2.8	+3.8
Hutus	Rwanda	+0.6	+1.6
Sinhal.	Sri L.	+1.7	+2.7
Roman.	Trans.	+0.8	+1.8
Protest.	Ulster	-2.2	-1.2

Minorities			
	Area	**Test Index**	**Reset. Index**
Serbs	Bosnia	-0.5	-0.2
Croats	Bosnia	0.0	+0.2
Turks	Cyprus	-1.1	-2.1
Azeris	Karab.	-1.2	-2.2
Serbs	Kosovo	-2.3	-3.3
Palest.	Israel	-2.4	-3.4
Russians	Near-A.	-2.8	-3.8
Tutsis	Rwanda	-0.5	-1.5
Tamils	Sri L.	-1.7	-2.7
Hungar.	Trans.	+0.8	-0.2
Cathol.	Ulster	+1.5	+0.5

As we examine the variables, we are forced to conclude that the numerical strength variable does indeed cause the resettlement index to favor majorities. We should keep that in mind when we make our final deliberations.

Let us now validate the index. Since our variables do not measure the intensity of the same phenomenon, like nationalism or conservatism, an item analysis will be more helpful in this case than external validation.

To validate the resettlement index by means of item analysis we should construct a table in which the index is an independent variable placed sequentially, from the highest to the lowest (see Table 16.4). We will then be in a position to compare it with the constituent variables in order to check whether the index has any predictive value.

TABLE 16.4
INDEX VALIDATION

	Reset. Index	Hist. Prec.	Victim- ization	External Threat	Numerical Majority
Non-Russ	+3.8	+1.0	+0.8	+1.0	+1.0
Jews	+3.5	+1.0	+0.5	+1.0	+1.0
Armen.	+3.3	+0.7	+0.6	+1.0	+1.0
Alban.	+3.2	+1.0	+0.2	+1.0	+1.0
Greeks	+3.0	+1.0	+0.3	+0.7	+1.0
Sinhal.	+2.7	+1.0	-0.3	+1.0	+1.0
Roman.	+1.8	+0.5	0.0	+0.3	+1.0
Hutus	+1.6	+1.0	-0.4	0.0	+1.0
Muslims	+0.7	-1.0	+0.5	+0.8	+0.4
Cathol.	+0.5	+1.0	+0.2	+0.3	-1.0
Croats	+0.2	+1.0	-0.5	-0.5	+0.2
Hungar.	-0.2	+0.5	0.0	+0.3	-1.0
Serbs/B[a]	-0.2	+0.5	0.0	-1.0	+0.3
Protest.	-1.2	-1.0	-0.2	-1.0	+1.0
Tutsi	-1.5	-1.0	+0.5	0.0	-1.0
Turks	-2.1	-1.0	-0.4	+0.3	-1.0
Azeris	-2.2	+0.3	-0.5	-1.0	-1.0
Tamils	-2.7	-1.0	+0.3	-1.0	-1.0
Serbs/K[b]	-3.3	-1.0	-0.3	-1.0	-1.0
Palest.	-3.4	-1.0	-0.4	-1.0	-1.0
Russians	-3.8	-1.0	-0.8	-1.0	-1.0

[a] Serbs of Bosnia
[b] Serbs of Kosovo

Indeed, a look at Table 16.4 shows that each parameter correlates with the index, although the correlation is not perfect and the degree of correlation differs from variable to variable. Actually, all parameters show a remarkably close correlation. The difference is somewhat more pronounced in the victimization variable, but this should not surprise us since patterns of interethnic struggle over long periods of time have been very complex and have often reversed the positions of the victim and the perpetrator.

To clarify the picture even further, we may want to distinguish an intermediate gray area from the extremes. In the index, let us designate the values higher than "+1.0" as the positive area "P" and the values below "-1.0" as the negative area "N." The gray area "i" will be the area between them, or (+P < i < -N). Thus, in the index, the line between "+1.6" and "+0.7" will separate area "+P" from area "i"; and the line between "-0.2" and "-1.2" will separate area "i" from area "-N." "P" and "N" in Table 16.4 are in bold.

Where the "+1.0" and the "-1.0" values are present (for all variables save victimization), we may designate the point where "+1.0" meets a "-1.0" as the borderline separating "i" from "P" or "N." The intermediate area will then include all items contained between the highest "-1.0" and the lowest "+1.0." (We actually have two kinds of "i": one where "+P" and "-N" overlap, as in the historical precedence and numerical strength variables, and the other kind where "+P" and "-N" do not reach each other, as in the external threat variable. Technically, only the second type is a true intermediate area; the other type, where "+P" and "-N" intermingle, should be more appropriately designated as an area of overlap. For our purposes, we need not distinguish between the two types.) In the victimization variable, where we do not have integers, we may designate the area between the highest negative value and the lowest positive value as the intermediate area.

Why is the distinction between the positive, the intermediate, and the negative values important? Because a positive resettlement index indicates the right to stay, the negative one implies the right to be resettled, and the intermediate one leaves the question open, to be determined by other inputs.

We are now in a position to calculate averages for the positives (candidates to stay) and the negatives (candidates for resettlement). Since the borderlines separating "+P" and "-N" from "i" are different in each variable, we will take only the highest (which are positive across all variables) and the lowest (which are negative across all variables) items, which turn out to coincide with the borderlines in the victimization variable. This means that we will take the top five and the bottom three. Table 16.5 shows the averages for each variable for both sets of ethnies. The difference between the two sets is evident and self-explanatory.

Before we evaluate each conflict in the light of the index (we'll do that in the next chapter) we should ask if there is a common thread linking all of them together, not just the collection of features we have enumerated above but a paradigm that may help to explain the incompatibility of these ethnies.

Let's look at the ethnic Russians in the Near-Abroad. They are a very recent minority who, until 1991, were a majority in a mighty empire. They had, and still do have, a strong imperial ethos *(velikoderzhavnaia psikhologiia),* a culture they are proud of, and a sense of innate superiority vis-a-vis the "younger" brothers of their former empire. Suddenly they find themselves in the unenviable position of a disliked minority with few real rights and virtually none of the advantages they are so used to. They even have to learn the languages of their former subjects, a "gobbledegook" unknown and totally useless beyond the borders of the new countries. They find themselves living in states to which they feel no allegiance, among people for whom they feel no affinity (and often a good deal of contempt), in societies that openly

TABLE 16.5
AVERAGES FOR CANDIDATES TO STAY AND CANDIDATES FOR TRANSFER

	Hist. Prec.	Victim- ization	External Threat	Numerical Majority	Index
Candidates to stay (top five)	+0.94	+0.48	+0.94	+1.00	+3.36
Candidates for transfer (bottom three)	-1.00	-0.50	-1.00	-1.00	-3.50

discriminate against them. Their drastically reduced status and memories of a glorious past—and a very recent past at that—make them susceptible to chronic discontent, extreme nationalism, and desire for the restoration of an imperial Russia in some new incarnation.

Where have we seen this complex before? Why, among the Sudeten (and sometimes the Reich) Germans and their ethnic German cousins all across Eastern Europe in 1918-38. Many Russians, in Russia and the Near-Abroad, clearly suffer from the Sudeten complex.

Anybody else?

We can argue that the Turks of Cyprus and the Azeris have the Turkish imperial complex. The fact that the Azeris have never been part of the Ottoman Turkish Empire is less significant than it seems: there were many ethnic German groups who had never been part of the German empire and yet eagerly supported Hitler and Nazi Germany. In fact, most of their communal organizations did.

Loyalist British Protestants in Ireland fall in the same category, even if they are fighting for the preservation, rather than regaining, of superior status. So do the Hungarians of Transylvania and the Serbs of Bosnia and Kosovo: they represent the ruling ethnies of the Hungarian and Yugoslav mini-empires. The same applies to the Arabs in general and the Palestinians in particular, especially those nationalists who espouse the Pan-Arab element in the Arab ideology, which sees the Arab world as a mighty Arab nation destined for glory and greatness: an unfulfilled empire waiting to be reconstituted. The political aspect of Islamic fundamentalism is similar to Pan-Arabism, only the point of reference is different: the Islamic universe (which is even more inclusive) rather than an Arab caliphate.

Ultimately, we have only two cases left, Rwanda and Sri Lanka. They don't seem to fit the Sudeten mold. Or do they? In Sri Lanka the nominal majority, the Sinhalese, live in the shadow of a huge neighbor, India, which supports the restive Tamil minority: a Sudeten situation, although without an imperial component.

And in Rwanda we have the formerly predominant Tutsi, who have lost their former political, social, and economic clout, a new minority bitterly resentful of its new, greatly diminished, status. Hence, once again, we have a similar pattern: drastic loss of status and a status reversal, albeit without a clearly identifiable imperial component. In any case, the Tutsi complex conforms, with some limitations, to the Sudeten paradigm.

We can now distill the wellsprings of at least one type of irreconcilable ethnic conflict: a sudden reversal of status, loss of social, economic, and political advantages, a transformation from a ruling majority to a vulnerable minority, and the presence of ethnic cousins/allies across the new borders (regarded as illegitimate). These conditions combine to produce hatreds that do not easily die down, enmities sustained by an ardent hope that a future effort may reverse the situation and return things "back to normal." It is this paradigm, in many incarnations, that leads to irreconcilable ethnic conflicts.

Chapter 17

POSSIBLE SOLUTIONS

W hen multiethnic empires fell apart in 1918 it was hoped that a judicious application of self-determination would greatly reduce the number of minorities. But when the dust settled, the new states of Eastern Europe—notably Czechoslovakia, Poland, Romania, and Yugoslavia—were also multiethnic. For a while, it was hoped that border rectifications and the protection of minority rights would appease ethnic enmity. Unfortunately, this was not to be.

World War II and the massive relocation of German and other ethnic populations simplified the ethnic configuration in the region (and elsewhere, such as in India and Palestine), but ultimately failed to cure nationalist tensions.

In Eastern Europe, the fall of communism and the subsequent collapse of the Soviet Union and Yugoslavia and the peaceful dissolution of Czechoslovakia increased the number of states from 9 to 19 (not counting the countries of Transcaucasia and Central Asia, which are not part of Europe). And yet, even now, 30 minorities account for 35 percent of the region's population.[1] If we add Transcaucasia and Central Asia, 20 of the 27 successor states have serious or potential ethnic problems or are involved in bitter ethnic disputes with neighboring states (Albania, Armenia, Azerbaijan, Bosnia, Bulgaria, Croatia, Estonia, Georgia, Hungary, Kazakhstan, Kyrgyzstan, Latvia, Lithuania, Macedonia, Moldova, Romania, Russia, Slovakia, Tajikistan, Ukraine).

In short, the likelihood that the centrifugal tendencies will continue unabated is very high. What's more, many of the ethnic problems cannot be resolved through self-determination and border rectifications, because an ethny is located in the heart of another state, because the territory where it resides has sacred monuments of another ethnic group, or for a combination of reasons. In many instances only a well-organized population exchange or transfer can solve irreconcilable conflicts, diffuse hatreds, and prevent wars and massacres.

We have already discussed, in the preceding chapters, conflicts that can be resolved only through transfer. We have also constructed a resettlement index, which can indicate potential candidates for resettlement. As was stated in the previous chapter, the index is meant to be only a guideline.

There is one more aspect of population transfer that we have not yet discussed: the availability of a destination area where the transferees can be resettled. This is a very important point. In virtually all transfers and exchanges the destination point is usually the ancestral homeland. Naturally, an ethny with a place to go has a decisive advantage over one that does not. For example, the Tamils of Sri Lanka have, at least theoretically, a place of refuge in Tamil Nadu while their Sinhalese enemies literally have no place to go to. In any population transfer this should be a major consideration.

Table 17.1 compares the availability of destination points for various ethnic groups. Here, once again, we used the binary method, assigning a "plus" sign to those ethnies that have a destination point and a "minus" sign to those without one. We end up with four groups:

1. Mixed ("-/+"): Czechs/Germans, indigens/Russians, Jews/Palestinians, and Sinhalese/Tamils;
2. Both positive ("+/+"): Greeks/Turks, Armenians/Azeris, Albanians/ Serbs, Romanians/Hungarians, and Protestants/Catholics;
3. Both negative ("-/-"): Hutu/Tutsi;
4. Special case Bosnia: where one of the contestants has a destination point that is not its ancestral land ("-/+/+").

In our paradigmatic case, that of the Czechs and the Sudeten Germans, only the Germans had a historic homeland where they could resettle. The Czechs had literally no place else to go to. The indigenous population of the former Soviet republics, the Israeli Jews, and the Sinhalese are in a similar position.

Some adversaries are fortunate in the sense that each one has a place to go: Greeks and Turks in Cyprus, Armenians and Azeris in Karabakh, Albanians and Serbs in Kosovo, Hungarians and Romanians in Transylvania and Catholics and Protestants in Ulster. The last case is unique in that the local majority, the Protestants, has a lower resettlement index than the minority. Their index would be even lower, probably as low as "-2.2," within the context of a united Ireland, where they would be a minority. If Ulster

TABLE 17.1
A PLACE TO GO

Czechs	-	+	Germans
Albanians	+	+	Serbs
Armenians	+	+	Azeris
Autochthons	-	+	Russians
Greeks	+	+	Turks
Hutus	-	-	Tutsis
Jews	-	+	Palestinians
Muslims	-	+	Serbs/Croats
Protestants	+	+	Catholics
Romanians	+	+	Hungarians
Sinhalese	-	+	Tamils

were to be attached to Eire, the resulting united Ireland would be saddled with a million-strong Protestant minority creating, most likely, another irreconcilable conflict or, rather, changing and expanding the dimensions of the old one. All the more reason to utilize a population transfer.

The least lucky—if one can speak of luck in these situations—are the Hutu and the Tutsi: neither one has a homeland outside Rwanda (and Burundi).

In Bosnia, at first glance, we find the same old pattern: Croats and Serbs have a place to relocate to, Muslims don't. But in fact Muslims also have a place to go although it is not an obvious destination (we will discuss it in detail later).

Of the four categories enumerated above, the first two can be further subdivided. In the first one, the Russians, like their Sudeten German predecessors, can be resettled in Russia (in fact, that process has already started). But the resettlement of the Palestinians and the Tamils, for various reasons, is much more problematical. Here, we'll have to seek a "parallel" solution.

In the second group, we have Cyprus and Ulster, where resettlement of either party can be effected without territorial adjustments. But we also have Kosovo and Transylvania, where some territorial adjustment is unavoidable; and Karabakh, which offers a rare opportunity for a territorial exchange.

The third and fourth categories—Rwanda/Burundi and Bosnia—are truly unique.

In the rest of this chapter we will examine each of these categories and subcategories in terms of type and interstate territorial adjustments. "Type" refers to the availability of a resettlement destination. It can be (a) mixed (one of the contestants has a place to go to, the other one does not; no interstate territorial adjustments are called for); (b) positive (both adversaries have a place to go to); (c) negative (neither one does); or (d) special cases (Bosnia).

1A. TYPE: MIXED; RESETTLEMENT DESTINA TION: AVAILABLE; TERRITORIAL ADJUSTMENTS : NONE.

Russian Minorities

After the Soviet Union's collapse, history frozen by fifty or seventy years of Soviet rule and ideology resumed in each of the fifteen successor states. Since the fall of the empire each republic has made a conscientious effort to resurrect national traditions. In the atmosphere of resurgent ethnocentrism, ethnic nationalism in virtually each of the successor republics came back with a vengeance.

Resurgent nationalism is a common denominator of minority experience in the post-Soviet Near-Abroad. However, because cultural traditions in the former Soviet empire differ widely—Muslim in Central Asia, Catholic in Lithuania, Orthodox Christian in Belorussia and Ukraine, and so on—minorities face different situations in each republic. And each situation requires a different set of adjustments.

All minorities have had to adjust to the new situation and Russians are no exception. But they suffer more because they are not used to being a minority. They suffer from an acute Sudeten complex. Even if most will ultimately choose the path of adaptation and cooperation, as seems to be the case in the Baltic republics, a significant proportion of them will always be susceptible to the extremes of Russian nationalism and delusions of imperial grandeur. And Mother Russia has already conclusively shown that it will not remain indifferent to the fate of ethnic Russians in the former republics. This has been stated many times by various Russian leaders and officials across the political spectrum, from those who are reputed to be liberal at one end to Zhirinovsky at the other. The ever-present threat of Russian intervention raises the specter of at least half a dozen Sudetenlands.

It is impossible to make sweeping generalizations about Russian historical presence in various republics because each one has had a history of its own. And Russian penetration in each area differed in timing and intensity. It would be fair to say, however, that at least in eastern Ukraine, northern Kazakhstan, and a few other areas Russians have deep roots. Elsewhere, they mostly represent later migrants.

Demographically, the picture is somewhat less confusing for they are everywhere in the minority, even in Kazakhstan (where until recently they had been a plurality) and Latvia (where non-Latvians came close to being the majority of the total population). However, there are numerous pockets, some of them quite extensive, of predominantly ethnic Russian settlement: northeastern Estonia, Daugavpils in eastern Latvia, the Crimea, eastern Ukraine, and northern Kazakhstan, to name a few.

At present, all powers in the region agree on the inviolability of existing borders. That is probably a wise decision, since any border rectification may resurrect dozens of other claims. Since the existing borders are here to stay (we hope) and Russian minorities represent a clear danger to European and world peace the only possible solution is to assist their relocation back to their ancestral homeland. Otherwise, Russia will always have an excellent pretext for intervention.

This diagnosis is further corroborated by the fact that the Russian minorities have a place to go to and a resettlement index score of "-3.8," compared to the indigenous non-Russian index of "+3.8." This clearly suggests the transfer of the Russian minorities.

The sheer task of resettling 25 million people would certainly be an undertaking of staggering proportions. However, let us point out several important facts.

First, we may disregard Russian minorities in the republics *not* bordering on Russia. These include Armenia, Kyrgyzstan, Moldova, Tajikistan, and Uzbekistan. (Moldova is a special case because of the conflict in Transdnistria. But a detailed discussion of this country will take us too far afield.) This would decrease the number of potential transferees by some 3 million, down to 22 million.

Second, experience shows that Russians are reluctant to stay in Muslim republics (see chapter 10). It is more than likely that the vast majority of ethnic Russians in Azerbaijan and Kazakhstan may want to leave as well. They would need only financial help and organizational assistance to find suitable places in Russia. This would further reduce the number of reluctant transferees by about 8 million, down to 14 million.

Third, most Russians would be glad to leave war-torn Georgia, where the situation will remain unsettled for a long time to come.

Ultimately, we are left with "only" Baltic states, Belarus, and Ukraine: approximately 13.5 million Russians, a number similar to the number of Germans transferred from various parts of Eastern Europe in 1945-47. This number does not include the *russkoiazychnyie* (russophone) members of other nationalities who are linguistically and culturally Russian and who often side with the Russians. These people (in Estonia, for example, in 1994, they accounted for between one-sixth and one-third of the non-Estonian population) should have the option of going to Russia, since they are culturally Russian, or to the country of their origin. Many may be allowed to stay, depending on the geographic and demographic situation in the republic and their willingness to be loyal citizens by refraining from supporting Russian nationalism. For example, russophone Ukrainians in Latvia may be allowed to stay (at Latvia's discretion, of course, which can be decided by a plebiscite) since Ukraine is no threat to Latvia, as long as they have not supported pro-Russian organizations such as the Interfront. Both Russians and non-Russian russophones should also have the option of going to third countries such as Canada or Australia. Among the 13.5 million ethnic Russians many would be happy to relocate. Between 1989 and 1994 the ethnic Russian population of Estonia, for example, has gone down from 475,000 to 436,000,[2] a decrease of 39,000, or 8.2 percent. This number corresponds to the number of russophone residents of Estonia who said in an April 1992 survey that they were "doing everything they [could] to leave in the coming months."[3] The actual number of russophones willing to leave Estonia may be much higher since each respondent in the survey probably corresponds to a family of two or three people. In addition, 42 percent said they had discussed the possibility of leaving with friends and neighbors in Estonia and 31 percent had sought advice about leaving from relatives and friends back in their hometowns outside Estonia.[4] In fact, several private remigration firms and semiofficial organizations have already come into existence and have been inundated by requests for assistance. On the other hand, some 54 percent of Estonia's Russians have opted for Estonian citizenship, which indicates a desire to stay.[5] In Latvia, 637,000 non-Latvians (about one-half of the minority population) have declared their desire to acquire Latvian citizenship.[6] In short, approximately half of the Russian and russophone population in the Baltic republics would like to stay. The figure is probably higher in Belorussia and Ukraine, but even there, if, say, three-quarters of ethnic Russians would like to stay the number of reluctant transferees would be reduced to some 10 million or less.

This is still a formidable number, but there is plenty of space in Russia. Much of it, granted, is in the underdeveloped, hard-to-access areas of the Far North or the Far East, but for all practical purposes the availability of land in Russia is virtually unlimited.

Given the enormity of the task, the whole process will have to be spread over many years. In general, it is not recommended that a transfer be spread over long periods, but in this case the dimensions of the project do not allow a quick resettlement.

Finally, the transfer of ethnic Russians and russophones should not be used as an instrument of Russification in non-Russian areas, such as Bashkirtostan, Tatarstan, or Soha (Yakutia). Such settlement would simply replicate the old pattern of settler/autochthone antagonism in the former Soviet republics and would exacerbate the tense situation in the non-Russian areas of the new Russia. This may create an explosive situation in many ethnic areas, leading to more Chechnyas.

Countries bordering on Russia and Germany will always be at risk. This is particularly true of small countries such as Latvia and Estonia. The presence of a large Russian minority makes these countries extremely vulnerable. The share of non-Estonian population increased from 3 percent in 1945 to 38.5 percent by 1989.[7] If the Russian minority remains and if Estonia is occupied once again—neither possibility is science fiction—within a few years Estonians may find themselves a minority in their own land. The margin of safety for Latvians is even smaller. If they become a minority, the likelihood of their ever regaining independence will be very small indeed. The resettlement of the Russian minorities is designed to prevent that. The objective is to diffuse the potentially dangerous situation in the Near-Abroad and to prevent Russia from recreating the empire in any guise or form.

1B. TYPE: MIXED; RESETTLEMENT DESTINATION: UNAVAILABLE, TERRITORIAL ADJUSTMENTS: NONE.

Here we have two cases in which self-determination for one adversary spells ruin, subjugation, and destruction for the other. Can we square the circle?

Sri Lanka

Sri Lanka presents a very difficult problem. If the Tamils achieve self-determination in almost any form, a vulnerable Tamil entity will be forced to forge a close alliance with India or even, quite possibly, seek a union with Tamil Nadu. This will make the Sinhalese part of the island indefensible and turn the Sinhalese state into a de facto protectorate. The ever present external threat, along with other factors, pushes the Sinhalese index to "+2.7," compared to the Tamil index of "-2.7." And, since the Tamils have a place to go to, everything points to the resettlement of the Tamil minority in Tamil Nadu.

The reality is quite different. Due to various political and economic difficulties involved, the transfer of the Tamils to India is unlikely. Earlier agreements have not been implemented, so there is little reason to believe that new ones will be.

And yet, only a transfer can definitively solve this cyclical conflict, which is, at more than 2,000 years, perhaps the longest-running conflict in the world, and which feeds upon irreconcilable differences between the two ethnoreligious communities. Even if we exclude the estate Tamils from the transfer, because they have kept aloof from the Sinhalese-Tamil confrontation, the rest of the Tamil community present a formidable problem of integration.

In many aspects, the confrontation in Sri Lanka is a classical Sudeten conflict. The Sinhalese enjoy historical precedence and a comfortable numerical majority. But the Tamil minority enjoys the support of more than fifty million ethnic cousins across the Palk Straight. Because of the Indian dimension and bitter historical memories, any solution based on Tamil autonomy or federalization would be unacceptable to most Sinhalese, who would fear a possible annexation of Tamil-inhabited areas by India. At the very least, proximity invites India's interference.

If resettlement outside Sri Lanka is impossible, there is another possibility: concentrate the Tamils deep inside the country, far from India, where they will not present a security problem, and create an autonomous enclave on the Hong Kong model.

Trincomalee offers the best opportunity. The town, with its excellent harbor and a convenient location, could become a great trading and commercial center of some 2 or 3 million people, similar to Hong Kong or Singapore. Another great advantage is that the port and the surrounding area already have a large Tamil population that would not have to be resettled. (Nor would estate Tamils. It is highly ironic that previous attempts at the Tamil transfers from Sri Lanka involved precisely this subgroup.) Thus, relocation would involve only the population of the Northern Province and those areas of the Eastern Province which would fall outside the enclave. The total number of transferees would probably remain under 2 million, perhaps between 1.5 and 2 million. While this is a substantial number for a poor country of 18 million, resettlement would ultimately prove much cheaper and much more humane than endless guerrilla warfare, massacres, and the ever present danger of Indian involvement. With appropriate planning and international assistance, the resettlement should not be impossible.

There are other advantages as well. Such a solution would satisfy most of the Tamil aspirations for autonomy and a decent standard of living. It would minimize the chance of future involvement by India and would greatly improve relations between the two countries. It would also go a long way toward allaying Sinhalese fears of invasion and partition. Finally, the creation of a flourishing international trade center in the area would speed up economic development throughout the island and in southern India and might eventually lay to rest the ghost of ethnic hatred between the Sinhalese and the Tamils. It is a solution worth looking at.

West Bank and Gaza

A similar situation prevails in the West Bank and Gaza. The irreconcilable claims of the two ethnoreligious communities, Jewish and Arab, have shaped and determined the entire course of the Arab-Israeli conflict.

Here, size is very important, more so than in most other conflicts. Any Palestinian entity in the occupied territories, even a state comprising all of Gaza and the West Bank, would be too small to accommodate the rapidly growing Palestinian population, even if Palestinians in the diaspora did not return. And Israel within the Green Line, aside from the mounting pressure from a rapidly increasing population, would be much too small and vulnerable to provide reasonable security to its people. In the age of missiles, territory is essential. A surrender or even partial relinquishing of control over the West Bank would leave Israel extremely vulnerable militarily, not unlike Croatia was yesterday or Czechoslovakia was after Munich. Israel's defense requirements demand the retention of the West Bank.

Water is another factor. The aquifers located under the West Bank provide most of the area's water supply. The power that controls water controls the whole area. There is little doubt that if the aquifers pass into Arab hands water will be used to blackmail Israel.

And then there is Islamic fundamentalism, which spurns the very idea of a compromise and reconciliation. Even the most generous concessions on Israel's part would not stop the tide. Recent terrorist attacks in Israel, especially in Tel Aviv, clearly demonstrate that the fundamentalists want Israel's destruction, nothing less. Appeasement does not work: in Egypt fundamentalism blossomed *after* the peace treaty had been signed. Throughout the world, Iranian and Algerian fundamentalists target Jewish institutions even though neither country has actually been at war with Israel. In short, terrorism will continue even if all Arab countries sign peace treaties. The idea that peace agreements will somehow bring pacification and an end to terrorism is simply wishful thinking.

Nor will peace bring substantial trade and economic cooperation in the foreseeable future, much less regional integration. Again, Egypt provides a clue: eighteen years after the signing of the peace accords trade is negligible, tourism at a trickle, and the government of Egypt still refrains from any meaningful rapprochement.

Nor does the limited autonomy now being tried in Gaza and Jericho provide a solution. It is a dead end because it does not solve the main issue that pits the Arab against the Jew: Jerusalem. Even if Israel concedes everything else, it is most unlikely it will give up Jerusalem. And Palestinians will not agree to a settlement that excludes the city.

What's more, once the Palestinian state is established, it would be contiguous with areas within Israel, in Galilee, inhabited by Israeli Arabs. Undoubtedly, they would want to join their brethren. The right to self-determination would be on their side. Before long, Israel would be forced into a new Camp

David accord, which would further reduce its territory and turn it into a concentration camp. It would be only a matter of time before a new war broke out. In short, the so-called peace process is a disaster in the making, both for the Israelis and the Palestinians.

Aside from purely strategic considerations, the Arab-Israeli confrontation displays all the characteristics discussed above of a Sudeten conflict that can be solved only through a population transfer. Without a transfer, the confrontation in the Middle East is likely to continue indefinitely.

If we examine the claims of both parties we will see that historically, Jews preceded Arabs by about 2,000 years. Demographically, Jews also currently have the upper hand, 4.5 million versus 3 million Arabs (in western Palestine, including Israeli Arabs). These and other contributing factors, such as the danger of the Arab invasions, push the Israeli Jewish index to a high of "+3.5," compared to the Palestinian index of only "-3.4."

Palestine has already been divided twice in this century, in 1922 and 1948, with the Arab side getting three-fourths of the original territory. These previous partitions did not solve the problem.

Factors that would facilitate transfer are enormous Arab oil wealth and two dozen Arab states, whose combined territories comprise 5,414,000 square miles, where the transferees can be resettled. In principle, Palestinian Arabs could choose from among 22 Arab states, while Israeli Jews have no other place to go to.

In short, all fundamentals suggest the transfer of the Palestinian Arabs from western Palestine.

The problem is that no one "wants" the Palestinians. None of the Arab countries would accept them in sufficient numbers, if at all. Jordan did open its borders to most of the 300,000 Palestinians expelled by Kuwait, but expecting a country whose population barely exceeds 4 million to absorb 3 million is not realistic. Even if Jordan does accept some, a substantial number will remain across the river in Israel.

The only solution left is the Hong Kong model, to be achieved by resettling Palestinian Arabs in Gaza and creating an autonomous city-state there. Gaza has other advantages as well: it could be developed into a major port; its location would facilitate its transformation into a dynamic hub of international trade; and the over 800,000 Palestinians already living there would not have to be resettled, reducing the total number of transferees to just over 2 million.

Politically, it would be an autonomous, self-ruling enclave whose outside borders would be patrolled by Israel. Such an arrangement would satisfy both Israeli security requirements and Palestinian aspirations for self-rule. It is not an ideal solution by any means, but it is the only one left when the folly of the present approach becomes evident.

2A. TYPE: POSITIVE; RESETTLEMENT DESTINATION: AVAILABLE; TERRITORIAL ADJUSTMENTS: POSSIBLE BUT NOT NECESSARY.

Cyprus

For the time being, the Cyprus problem seems to have been settled, de facto if not de jure. The island has been effectively partitioned between the two communities and they are now living in a state of precarious peace. Shouldn't we leave well enough alone?

Probably not. The balance, on the island and between Greece and Turkey, is extremely fragile. It is maintained mostly by Greek weakness and the constraints imposed upon Turkey by its NATO membership and its aspirations to enter the European Union. If the overall balance tips against Turkey (if, for example, Greece concludes a military alliance with some of Turkey's neighbors), or if Turkey turns away from Europe and NATO (which may be happening right now since, with the collapse of the Soviet Union, Turkey does not need NATO quite as much), or if the widening Balkan imbroglio sucks in both countries (on opposite sides), chances for a new confrontation in Cyprus will increase dramatically. Periodic confrontations between Greece and Turkey, the most recent one in April 1996, may also involve Cyprus.

Even without direct outside involvement, the problem of Cyprus displays all the typical characteristics of a Sudeten conflict: a cyclical pattern, a former imperial minority, and the impossibility of accommodating the diametrically opposed aspirations of the two communities. These preconditions make Cyprus potentially explosive and a good candidate for a solution involving population transfer. What are the options?

With the Cypriot Greek index at "+3.0" and the Turkish index at "-2.1" it seems that the Turkish community would have a smaller justification to stay. Indeed, the Greek side has all the variables in its favor. Historically, Greek settlement on the island preceded Turkish by some 3,000 years. Demographically, even the influx of Turkish settlers did not change the island's predominantly Greek character, with more than half a million Greek Cypriots against fewer than 200,000 Turks, Cypriot and mainland. (Before the influx of Turkish settlers, the island's population was 82 percent Greek and 18 percent Turkish. Turks claim that the true ratio was 74.7 percent Greek to 24.6 percent Turk,[8] but in any case the Greek numerical preponderance is evident.) Greeks have also been mostly at the receiving end in the Greco-Turkish confrontation and have had to live under an ever present Turkish threat.

Thus, all factors support the transfer of the Turkish minority to the mainland. We can call it Option 1. It will require resettling some 200,000 Turkish Cypriots and settlers in mainland Turkey, which is a manageable task for Turkey. (In 1989 it successfully resettled a similar number of Turkish expellees from Bulgaria.) Greece might then compensate Turkey by the transfer of some Greek islands in the Aegean or, perhaps, some territory in Thrace.

However, we have so far disregarded the fact that Cyprus lies only 40 miles from Turkey but 650 miles from mainland Greece. In peacetime a Greek Cyprus would be a constant irritant to Turkey, and in any future confrontation between Greece and its powerful eastern neighbor the island would be virtually indefensible. That is why, despite all the indicators in Greek favor, the transfer of the Greek community may be a more desirable option. We can call it Option 2. (This, incidentally, will give strategic considerations, represented by the external threat variable, a disproportionate importance. And yet, this option should not be completely disregarded.)

Option 2—resettling half a million Greek Cypriots in Greece—would be a more serious problem for Greece, a relatively poor country of "only" 10 million. However, Greece may be interested in this scheme as well because of a common perception, in Greece, of "shrinking Hellenism." While Turkey's population expands, Greece is demographically stagnant. The once numerous expatriate communities in Europe and the United States are assimilating and losing their Greek character. Greece wants demographic reinforcement; its willingness to accept thousands of Pontic Greek immigrants coming from the former Soviet Union is a case in point. Nor should we forget that Greece has had extensive and, on the whole, successful experience in resettling thousands of refugees in difficult conditions. With appropriate international aid, especially from its European partners, the resettlement of Cypriot Greeks may be made manageable despite some short-term problems. An additional half million Cypriot transferees and, quite possibly, an equal number of Pontic Greeks would boost the country's population to more than 11 million. This would not tip the demographic balance in Greece's favor, but it would add vitality to the Greek community.

If Option 2 is put into effect, Greece may be compensated by a territorial acquisition from Turkey somewhere in Rumelia. Strategically, and in the interest of a definitive settlement, Option 2 may even be preferable. In any case, either option is open, especially with an adequate territorial compensation (which may, of course, generate additional resettlers), because either community can be resettled in its respective mother country.

Ulster

The truce declared by the IRA in 1994 and the prospect of success in its negotiations with the British government have revived hopes for a peaceful settlement in Northern Ireland. And yet, the aspirations of both ethnoreligious communities remain largely irreconcilable. That is why population transfer possibly with minor territorial adjustments, may ultimately offer the best solution.

As with other conflicts considered in this book we will leave out some other options involving unitary, federal/confederal, codetermination, repartition, or self-determination solutions because none of these adequately satisfies the aspirations of either ethnoreligious community in Northern Ireland. Readers interested in such solutions are referred to a detailed discussion of them in the recent collection *The Future of Northern Ireland.*[9] We will concentrate on solutions involving population transfer since only those options offer a complete and lasting solution to the intractable problems facing the province.

Here, once again, we encounter a cyclical, periodically recurrent, and relatively violent conflict (although the number of victims is smaller than in some other areas). However, in its basic variables, the situation in Northern Ireland is in many ways opposite to the situation in other conflict areas we have surveyed so far: the aggrieved minority—the Catholics—have a clear right of historical precedence. On the other hand, the demographic balance clearly tilts in the Protestants' favor, at least within the confines of Northern Ireland. The external threat, to the extent that this term may apply to an intervention in what is technically an internal British problem, looms from the United Kingdom. But if Ulster were to achieve independence, Eire would be more likely to intervene. Because victimization historically affected Catholics much more than Protestants, we have an index of "-1.2" for the Protestants and "+0.5" for the Catholics in a reversal of the usual Sudeten-type pattern of positive majority/negative minority index. In other words, most of the indicators point to the resettlement of Protestants, not Catholics.

Fortunately, both parties have a place to go to. In terms of sheer numbers it would be easier, of course, to resettle half a million Catholics (Option 1) than a million Protestants (Option 2), but either undertaking is rather modest when compared to suggested transfer schemes elsewhere.

Most Catholics could find a place in Eire. Even if all Ulster Catholics were resettled there, they would increase its population by not more than 14 percent, from about 3.5 million to some 4 million people, which is a manageable increase for a country of Eire's size (despite its high rate of unemployment; if destitute Greece and devastated Germany could successfully absorb millions of transferees without much international help, Eire, a member of the European Union and a recipient of contributions from millions of Irish emigres worldwide, could certainly do the job).

But the number of actual Catholic transferees to Eire would probably be much smaller. A significant proportion of Ulster Catholics—up to a third, by some counts—would probably like to remain in the United Kingdom.[10] They should be given a chance to rebuild their lives elsewhere in Britain, outside the province. They could be assisted in migrating and resettling on the English "mainland," where there are already up to 2.7 million Irish people and their descendants (depending on how many generations back one counts). This would leave only some 300,000 Catholics to be transferred to Eire.

With the Catholics gone, the Protestants could either integrate into the United Kingdom or declare independence. Independence might look increasingly attractive, as long as Eire remained pacific. The agreement might also include minor border rectifications, such as the transfer of the Catholic majority areas of Fermanagh and Derry to Eire, which would significantly decrease the number of Catholic transferees.

Or (Option 2), a million Protestants could be transferred to Britain, which is a difficult but manageable undertaking for a relatively prosperous country of 58 million. Scotland alone, whose population has been stagnant since 1920, could stand the infusion of several hundred thousand economically active immigrants, many of whom are of Scottish origin. It will, of course, put a strain on the British and Scottish economies in the short run, but in the long run such transfusions have a most beneficial effect, as Germany and Israel demonstrate. With the Protestants gone, the majority of Catholics in Northern Ireland will probably choose to join Eire. Even if they do not, which is unlikely, it will be an internal Irish matter that will not disrupt Britain or Europe.

The important thing is that either option offers a definitive solution to a quagmire that has evaded solution for the last 80 years—or 800, if we count from the very beginning.

2B. Type: Positive; Resettlement Destination: Available; Territorial Adjustments: Necessary.

Kosovo

Kosovo is yet another area where conflicting claims of two ethnoreligious communities and the extraordinary importance of the region for one of the claimants (the Serbs) make a lasting and equitable solution without a population transfer impossible. How do these claims stack up?

Historically, there is little doubt that Albanians are descendants of the autochthonous population that had preceded the Slavs by some 1,500 years (although the Serb presence in Kosovo goes back a respectable 1,300 years). Numerically Albanians also predominate: they account for up to 90 percent of the province's total population. They have also been victimized by successive Serbian and Yugoslav governments. All these factors, along with the overwhelming threat from Serbia, push the Albanian index to "+3.2," compared to the Serbian index of only "-3.3." Thus, Albanians "lead" in every parameter we have applied in determining ethnic rights to an area. It would seem, therefore, that they should be entitled to an undisputed possession of Kosovo.

The problem, as we already know, is that Kosovo is the heartland of historic Serbia; it is also the site of the Battle of Kosovo Pole, where Serbia lost its independence in 1389 and a place sacred to the Serbs. It is most unlikely that Serbia could ever reconcile itself to the loss of Kosovo.

On the other hand, it cannot indefinitely hold onto a territory inhabited by (soon to be) 2 million hostile Albanians. Past attempts at granting Kosovo provincial autonomy proved fruitless. Is any solution possible?

Yes, even here a compromise could be worked out. A look at the map shows that Kosovo Pole lies in the middle of the province. Thus a division of the province that would leave Kosovo Pole, along with eastern Kosovo, in Serbian hands and give the western part to Albania should be acceptable to both sides.

The settlement would be unsuccessful, however, without a population exchange: the transfer of all Serbs from western Kosovo to Serb-held territory and of all Albanians on the Serbian side to the territories allocated to Albania. Although exact statistical data on the ethnic composition of either section is unavailable (because neither area coincides with present or past administrative divisions), we can make an educated guess that the number of Serb transferees would not exceed 100,000 (half of all Serbs now living in Kosovo) while that of Albanians would be in the 650,000-800,000 range (again, half of all Albanians now living in the province).

The Albanian transferees should be spread all over the country and not just in western Kosovo. Albania, with a total population of 3.4 million and a population density of 298 persons per square mile, can accommodate these migrants, especially because the country is underurbanized. Tirana, the capital, is a city of only 240,000, or 7 percent of the country's population, a figure much lower than comparable figures in most other European countries. Thus, the city could be substantially expanded to provide homes for thousands of newcomers. Other cities and towns across Albania could accommodate thousands more. The boost in urbanization rates would ultimately prove beneficial to Albania's economy.

Although resettling 650,000 to 800,000 people would be a very heavy burden for an impoverished country of only 3.4 million people, a successful resettlement could be achieved with the help of the international community, especially the European Union.

To ease the hardships of a massive resettlement, the transfer may have to be stretched out over a period of time, like that of the Russian minorities. Although generally not recommended, that may prove to be unavoidable in this case. The partition of Kosovo between Albania and Serbia, with the subsequent population exchange, offers the best possible solution to a thorny and otherwise irreconcilable ethnopolitical problem. A lasting peace is definitely worth it.

Transylvania

This is another area where the final settlement has the best chance of success if the population transfer is accompanied by a territorial adjustment.

The pattern of ethnic relations in Transylvania clearly shows that Hungarians and Romanians do not get along. In fact, they never did. Although massacres and pogroms were infrequent, especially compared to many other conflict areas (but they did occur in 1920, 1940, and October 1944, namely, during every major upheaval),[11] Hungarians under Romanian rule—and Romanians under Hungarian—have always been subjected to discrimination, forced assimilation, and slow cultural ethnicide. Even worse, the mistreatment of minorities has always poisoned relations between the two countries. And in virtually every major European upheaval in the last 100-odd years both adversaries came to blows. One may hope that the situation will improve once Hungary and Romania join the European mainstream, but the historical record does not bode well for the future. The question, as always, remains: What can be done?

Historians on either side have so far failed to offer irrefutable evidence on who was first to settle in the area. At most, one can say that there are convincing arguments on both sides of the divide and that during the last 800 years, at least from the first mention of Wallachians in Hungarian sources, Transylvania developed as an area of highly mixed ethnoreligious cohabitation. In fact, Transylvania is a classical example of a multiethnic, multicultural area and may have successfully developed as such had its ethnic Hungarians and Romanians not been subjected to the powerful pull of Greater Hungarian and Greater Romanian nationalisms. But they were, and we must take this into account.

Thus, historically, the verdict is mixed. Demographically, however, Romanians have a comfortable majority of 70 to 78 percent. Combined with the rather inconclusive victimization and external threat variables, Romanians score a relatively high "+1.8," compared to Hungarian "-0.2," on the transfer index. In short, everything points to the transfer of the Hungarian minority to Hungary, which would require the relocation and resettlement of between 1.6 and 2.5 million people (the number could reach 2.5 million if all ethnic Hungarians decide to leave, but this is unlikely. Some, especially those who are officially Romanian, would probably want to stay. They should be allowed to do so since they are well on their way to complete assimilation and would not endanger Hungaro-Romanian relations. Two million is probably a reasonable estimate between the official low of 1.6 million and the unofficial high of 2.5 million).

The resettlement of 2 million people in a country of 10 million would be a difficult undertaking. We would do well to leave as many Hungarians and Romanians in place as possible in order to minimize the number of potential transferees.

All previous attempts at arbitration broke over the rock of Hungarian geographical distribution: the concentration of one-third of Romania's Hungarians right in the geographical center of Romania, which makes any readjustment unaccompanied by a population transfer meaningless. But while the economy, trade, communication lines, and the Hungarian population stretch along the east-west axis, any territorial adjustment would have to follow the north-south line.

There were two prior attempts at cut this Gordian knot. One, the Vienna Awards of 1940, followed the ethnic and economic distribution principle. As a result, it handed northern Transylvania to Hungary. (Romania, anxious to retain as much as possible, offered to cede 14,000 square kilometers to Hungary, but that offer, made in the summer of 1940, was regarded as too little too late by Hungary.[12]) As might have been expected, this partition left about half a million Hungarians—a third—under Romanian jurisdiction. It also led to the emigration and flight (self-transfer, really) of 200,000 Romanians and some 60,000 Hungarians who found themselves on the wrong side of the border.[13]

The other attempt, made after World War II, was more limited in scope. Initially, Hungary demanded 22,000 square kilometers inhabited by 866,000 Romanians and 495,000 Hungarians (thus leaving at least a million Hungarians in Romania).[14] The idea was not so much to create ethnically homogeneous political units as to balance the number of minority members in each country, making both governments hostage to good treatment of their respective minorities. When this proposal was rejected, Hungary made a bid for a smaller area of 11,800 square kilometers where, according to the census of 1930, there lived 442,000 Hungarians and 421,000 Romanians.[15] This proposal was also rejected, and we know the consequences: 50 years later the problem of Transylvania is still intractable and still poisoning the lives of some 8 million people living in the region (or 33 million, if we count the combined populations of Hungary and Romania), as well as relations between the two countries.

The problem, however, could be relatively easily solved if Romania were to cede a narrow belt of territory from Satu Mare in the north to Arad or Timişoara in the south, where Hungarians are (or have been, until recently) in the majority, and transfer the rest of its Hungarian minority to Hungary. Romanians who find themselves on the Hungarian side of the border would have to move to Romania. Romania would lose little territory but all its Hungarians, something it has ardently desired and tried to achieve all along. For its part, Hungary would gain some territory and between 1.5 and 2 million people who would be a welcome addition to Hungary's shrinking population. The actual transfer would involve even fewer Hungarians, since about 30 percent of Transylvania's Hungarians live along the border. We are thus talking of somewhere between 1 and 1.3 million Hungarian transferees (plus a certain number of Romanian transferees from areas annexed to Hungary).

While the numbers are considerable, the project would not be impossible. We already have a successful precedent in the area: the Bulgaro-Romanian settlement of 1940, which also involved a population transfer and territorial readjustment. That agreement has held through all the vicissitudes of the last 55 years. It is likely that an agreement along similar lines between Hungary and Romania would also have a solid future. It would give both countries a chance to establish—finally!—normal neighborly relations. There would be no more unwelcome and hostile minorities in either country. And Hungarians of Transylvania would be free from the discrimination and persecution of the last 70-odd years.

2C. TYPE: POSITIVE; RESETTLEMENT DESTINATION: AVAILABLE; TERRITORIAL ADJUSTMENTS: EXCHANGE.

Karabakh

Karabakh offers interesting possibilities. If suffering is any basis for making political decisions, Armenians deserve every possible consideration. In the

Armenian/Azeri and Armenian/Turkish conflicts they have been a perennial victim. But we cannot and should not base our recommendations on only one parameter.

Although long-term population trends work against them, Armenians still predominate in Nagorno-Karabakh. In terms of historical precedence, however, the picture is much less clear. Like certain areas along the Germanic/Slavic divide, the region changed hands, ethnically, several times. Through most of its history the area found itself within the orbit of several Armenian polities, but its original inhabitants were probably Caucasian Albanians (not to be confused with European Albanians) who served as an important component in the ethnogenesis of the Azeri people. By 1800, in any case, most of its inhabitants were Azeri. It seems to have acquired an Armenian majority only since the middle of the nineteenth century, mostly through the immigration of thousands of Armenians from Persia and Turkey.

In short, the historical antecedents are confusing, so that establishing a clear precedence is very difficult, if not impossible. One thing is not in doubt, however: the deep emotional attachment of both communities to Karabakh (where many of the Azeri writers and poets came from) and the ever present danger of Turkish intervention in Karabakh proper and Armenia in general.

The Armeno-Azeri strife clearly fits the parameters of a Sudeten conflict, the kind that can be resolved only through a population transfer of one of the contending parties. With an index of "+3.3," Armenians of Karabakh have a good lead over the Azeris, whose index is only "-2.2." If we are to choose a candidate for a transfer, it will be the Azeri people.

Fortunately, both sides have a place to go to: Armenians to Armenia, even though it is a small, overcrowded country (Option 1), and the Azeris to Azerbaijan (Option 2). Both options are open, but in this case a somewhat unorthodox solution may be implemented.

A closer look at the map provides the answer. There are two enclaves in the area: one is Nagorno-Karabakh, the other is Nakhichevan, an Azeri enclave squeezed between Armenia and Iran. It is inhabited by some 300,000 Kurds and Azeris and separated from the rest of Azerbaijan by the Armenian sliver of Zangezur. (In the past, it had a large and thriving Armenian community. But during the years of Azeri rule the Armenian population has dwindled to some 2,000 people.) Will the Azeris agree to surrender Nakhichevan to Armenia in exchange for Armenia's relinquishing all claims to Nagorno-Karabakh (Option 3)?

If they do, the settlement would involve an exchange of some 150,000 Armenians from Karabakh for the 300,000 Muslims from Nakhichevan (the number includes a large number of Kurds). These figures may seem lopsided, but they don't include some 250,000 to 300,000 Armenian refugees from Baku, Sumgait, and Ganja who had fled to Armenia (and elsewhere) after the outbreak of anti-Armenian violence and some 150,000 to 200,000 Azeri expellees from Armenia. If we add these earlier refugees and expellees, we would have an exchange of some 450,000 Armenians for about 500,000 Muslims, a roughly comparable figure.

Under the circumstances, this unusual exchange may be the most equitable solution. It will also have the best chance of success.

3. TYPE: NEGATIVE; RESETTLEMENT DESTINATION: UNAVAILABLE; TERRITORIAL ADJUSTMENTS: NECESSARY.

Rwanda/Burundi

Even a perfunctory overview of events in the twin countries of Rwanda and Burundi over the past 30 years makes it clear that without a comprehensive settlement the tragic events of the past will be repeated again, and again, and again. The conflict between the Hutu and the Tutsi in Rwanda and Burundi shows the same cyclical and cataclysmic pattern as the conflict in Bosnia and Karabakh. It is the kind of conflict that calls for a population transfer: the ethnies cannot live together.

Historically and demographically the Hutu have precedence. Their index is "+1.6" against the Tutsi "-1.5." The Tutsi, therefore, are the candidate for transfer.

The trouble is that the Tutsi have no place to go to: there is no chunk of either Burundi or Rwanda that they could call their own, where historical rights or a simple numerical majority would make a Tutsi administrative unit possible, especially after the latest round of massacres. So, self-determination is out of the question.

On the other hand, if the Tutsi remain a minority in either of these states, it is more than likely that they will continue to be massacred and persecuted, even if they control the army, as they still do in Burundi. Clearly, the Tutsi must have a homeland of their own where they will be safe from the Hutu threat.

The solution is the creation of contiguous, Tutsi-majority administrative units in both Rwanda and Burundi, and their joining together in a Tutsi mini-state, or their attachment to one of the neighboring states as a federal or an autonomous canton. The second variant may be preferable since Tutsi canton(s) would be too small and weak to withstand a determined Hutu assault.

Zaire seems to be the logical choice because most Rwandan (Tutsi?) emigres already live there. And if the Tutsi canton(s) were to be attached to Zaire, it follows that they should be carved from southwestern Rwanda and northwestern Burundi, preferably in contiguous territory (although in the case of Burundi that may be too close to the country's capital). This is Option 1.

Or, the cantons could be placed on the border with Tanzania, in southeastern Rwanda and northeastern Burundi (Option 2).

There is yet another possibility (Option 3): to make the canton(s) a codependency of Zaire (or Tanzania, depending on where they are located), Rwanda, and Burundi, not unlike Andorra used to be a codependency of France and Spain. Some form of United Nations sponsorship is also possible.

Whatever option is chosen, only a transfer will save the Tutsi from further depredations of their belligerent neighbors.

4. Type: Mixed; Resettlement Destination: Unlikely; Territorial Adjustments: Inevitable.

Bosnia

The war in Bosnia astounded the world by its sheer barbarity and revolting outrages. Beneath all the slaughter and rape, the conflict in former Yugoslavia betrays a pattern similar to other Sudeten conflicts. Although it is relatively recent—it began, at least in its latest phase, only in 1941—it shows a pattern of recurring violence typical of these conflicts. The problem is that even if these conflicts are resolved by traditional means of negotiation and (sometimes forced) compromise, there is no guarantee they will not flare up 30 or 40 years later. After all, neither 45 years of peace from 1945 to 1990, nor 4 million people of mixed ancestry, nor the growing number of census "Yugoslavs," which seemed to indicate a spirit of increasing accommodation among various nationalities, prevented the explosion of ethnoreligious hatreds. It seems that a surgical, as opposed to the usual homeopathic, solution is called for.

In looking for a way out we first turn to the historical rights and demographic ratios of each community. However, as it often happens in these situations, this exercise is not as definitive as might be expected: both Croats and Serbs have been living in the area since the fifth to seventh centuries, and the Bosniaks are mostly descendants of Islamized Slavs.

Nor are ethnic ratios much help: historically, they have been very unstable. Ethnic distribution has been shaped by the volatile history of the area. Krajina, for example, became predominantly Serbian relatively recently, in the course of the Turkish wars. And right before our eyes, in August 1995, it was cleansed of Serbs. In Bosnia, Serbs were the largest ethnoreligious group until the massacres of 1941, and even now Bosnian Muslims are only a plurality.

The region's political problems are exacerbated by the extreme geographical discontinuity of the main ethnic groups in the area. Before the latest events, the Croat majority area was subdivided into four virtually disjointed segments; Serbs were separated from the Montenegrins by a mixed population with a strong Muslim component, and Muslims were spread over a wide area where they were intermixed with other ethnic groups.

Because of its tortured ethnic configuration, Bosnia, at first glance, may appear to be a perfect candidate for the Swiss solution. Indeed, the Vance-Owen plan was based on the Swiss-inspired model of cantonization (the Swiss cheese option). The crucial difference with Switzerland, however, is that from 1291 until 1815 the Swiss polity developed as a union of German cantons only. It did not have a history of ethnic diversity and ethnic enmity (although religious strife did not bypass it). Bosnia, on the other hand, will be burdened for a long time to come by the horrible legacy of ethnic brutality.

Also, the Swiss communities did not develop strong psychological ties to their larger ethnic counterparts across the border because Switzerland emerged as a state before the era of nationalism. That is, Swiss Germans regard themselves as a breed apart and so do the Swiss French and Italians. The Croats and Serbs of Bosnia, on the other hand, developed as parts of the larger Croatian and Serbian ethnic entities and dream of joining their respective countries. Most of all, they are afraid of being minorities among brutal majorities. And we know they have every reason to be.

Nor do they have the lateral ties and divisions that characterize the Swiss. Swiss French and Germans are divided into Catholic and Protestant subcommunities that feel strong ties to their coreligionists across the linguistic and cultural divide. (This came out in the secession of the three Catholic French Jura cantons from the Protestant-majority Bern; the other French cantons, all Protestant, stayed with Bern.) These ties help to bridge the ethnic divide. In Bosnia, on the other hand, the religious divide coincides with the ethnic one, reinforcing and exacerbating it. It makes the gap between the ethnic communities unbridgeable.

What's more, Bosnia is surrounded on all sides by hostile neighbors who dismembered it. On the contrary, none of Switzerland's neighbors ever invaded Switzerland or interfered in its internal affairs the way Croatia and Serbia did in Bosnia (except Napoleon, but that was almost 200 years ago and far less brutal).

In short, the position of an independent Bosnia with its huge and irredentist Croatian and Serbian minorities, surrounded on all sides by the enemies, will be untenable.

The situation is further complicated by Croatia's predicament. If it is limited to ethnically Croatian areas, it will consist of three or four disconnected segments, with Serbian-held Krajina jutting to within 40 miles of Zagreb. (This problem may have been solved by the reoccupation of Krajina by the Croat forces and the mass exodus of the Serbs. This is another instance where ethnic "rearrangement" could have been achieved much less painfully through an organized population transfer.)

Nor are the Serbs satisfied, either in Bosnia or Croatia. The Serbian populations of both Bosnia and Krajina have repeatedly expressed a desire to join Serbia despite the fact that they are separated from the mother country by huge chunks of alien territory. Even though the map has been greatly simplified by the exodus from Krajina, the problem remains, since the Muslim and Croat populations of Bosnia are still squeezed in, from east and west, by Serbian-held lands. In short, no one is happy with the present situation, and no one will be if the territory is carved up according to the ethnic majority principle.

Clearly, traditional methods cannot solve the Bosnian conundrum. A division of the whole area between Bosnia, Croatia, and Serbia is called for. But—and here comes the most difficult part—no viable division is possible without large-scale population exchange and transfer.

No matter what the future borders of Bosnia may be, it would always be a small, vulnerable, largely indefensible entity at the mercy of Serbia and, to some extent, Croatia. Croatia would also remain extremely vulnerable, in its present configuration, especially if a hostile power occupied Bihać. And all sides in the conflict would be plagued by territorial discontinuity and pockets of hostile alien population located perilously close to vital centers. Thus, any lasting solution will have to include not only border adjustments but also population transfers.

We have already calculated the transfer indices for the three major groups in the area. At "+0.7" Muslims have the highest, Serbs with "-0.2" the lowest and Croats, at "+0.2," are in between. In other words, there is less justification, in terms of demographic, strategic, and historical considerations, to resettle Croats than Muslims and even less to resettle Serbs than Croats. The Serbs, therefore, are prime candidates for transfer. Also, we should keep in mind that Serbs and Croats have a place to go to, unlike the Muslims. This fact substantially complicates the picture. What can be done?

There are at least two major possibilities. In Option 1, (a) the Krajina Serbs, who numbered 600,000 before the war (most of whom have fled the area), could be resettled in eastern Bosnia, in areas adjacent to Serbia, for an eventual union with that country; (b) Croats from Bosnia (who number over 700,000) could then resettle in Krajina and western Bosnia, let's say in the Bihać salient (to account for about a 130,000 difference in numbers between the Bosnian Croats and the Krajina Serbs); (c) the Bosnian Muslims could then relocate to western Bosnia, the area west of the Neretva river, centered on Banja Luka (now a Serb stronghold); and (d) the Serbs could then take possession of Bosnia east of the Neretva river. This option should satisfy, at least to some extent, all combatants.

Option 1 also demands a federation between Croatia and Bosnia (already in place). Alone, the Muslim polity would be too vulnerable; also, as Turkey's experience shows, Muslim Bosnia's entrance into the European Union would likely be barred. If it were federated with Croatia, however, most objections to its entry would evaporate. A Bosnian-Croatian confederation would streamline borders, greatly reduce the risk of future conflict, and simplify the area's integration into Europe.

There is another solution, more radical and comprehensive: Option 2. It is also a more promising solution in the long run, at least in terms of complete pacification. Option 2 would extricate the Bosnian Muslims from a never-win situation in the Balkans and transfer the whole Bosniak population to Turkey.

We are talking of transferring about 2 million people. If this number sounds big, it is certainly dwarfed by the 10 to 14 million Germans who were forced out of Eastern Europe 50 years ago. At least one-third of the Bosniaks are now refugees with no place to go. They will be glad to go anywhere at all. From the Turkish side, 2 million people amount to some 3 percent of Turkey's population of 64 million, roughly equivalent to the percentage of Turks who relocated from Greece in the 1920s in relation to the Turkish population then. They were all successfully integrated. Would Turkey willingly accept these refugees? It is very likely. On May 31, 1989, at the height of the Turkish expulsions from Bulgaria, the spokesman for the Turkish Ministry of Foreign Affairs offered to take in all Bulgarian Turks, 700,000 people by official count and up to 1.5 million unofficially.[16] If Turkey was willing to take in up to 1.5 million, it probably will not refuse to take in 2 million, especially with substantial international assistance. Option 2 would not be easy, but it would achieve full pacification in Bosnia (which could then be divided between Croats and Serbs). And the future generations of Bosnian Muslims would be spared the horrors of ethnic wars that, I am afraid, are bound to recur if the problem is left unsolved.

Option 2 provides the best chance to ensure peace and prosperity of all ethnoreligious communities in the area. But whatever option serves as the foundation of a future settlement, only large-scale population transfers will ensure a lasting peace.

***

We can now draw some conclusions.

As we survey the conflicts (and this applies to virtually all intercommunal conflicts, not just those marked by ethnicity or religion), we notice that some have degenerated into open hostilities, others are tottering on the edge of open hostilities, while still others remain tense but quiescent. We can designate them "hot," "warm," and "cold," respectively, depending on the degree of intensity.

Among the conflicts we touched upon in this book, Bosnia, Karabakh, and Sri Lanka clearly belong to the first category. Rwanda has been taken off the stove for the time being, but it is still very "hot," a powder keg that may and most likely will explode within a few years as the Hutu, now exiled in Zaire, try to retake the country. But for now, at least, Rwanda can be relegated to the "warm" group, which also includes Kosovo, the Palestinians, and Northern Ireland. The reason these conflicts have not boiled over is that one party is much stronger than the other. If the balance of power is upset, as may be happening in the Middle East, the "warm" conflicts may easily heat up.

And in the third group—Cyprus, most of the Russian minorities in the former Soviet republics, and Transylvania—the conflict areas are quiet but they continue to fester. We should not underestimate their real explosive potential. If someone had told us back in 1990 that Bosnia could degenerate into the kind of appalling barbarity it since has, most of us would not have believed it. Specialists on Yugoslavia would have cited impressive figures on communal intermarriage and long traditions of mutual tolerance going back centuries, and would have dismissed the massacres of 1941 as a historical aberration. If we should learn anything at all from Bosnia, Rwanda, and other conflicts, it is how fast an intercommunal confrontation can degenerate into an all-out war. Unfortunately, there are many more Bosnias and Rwandas already happening or waiting to happen: Burundi, East Timor, Kurdistan, Moldova, Tibet, and more.

The division of conflicts into "hot," "warm," and "cold" suggests that they can be subdivided into ongoing ("hot") and potential ("warm" and "cold"), and that intervention should be fashioned accordingly: active in the case of ongoing conflicts, preventive in the case of potential ones.

The division also raises the question of which conflicts should be tackled first. At first glance, it may seem that we should be guided by the conflict intensity: the ongoing ones should be first in line, followed by the "warm"

and the "cold." However, experience shows that by the time conflicts degenerate into open hostilities it is too late. A settlement, including a humane
population transfer, can be implemented only when the guns are silent. That
is why the order of priority should be changed to "warm," "hot," and "cold,"
with the understanding that while the "warm" conflicts are being settled, "hot"
ones should be cooled by a truce to a point where the work on the final
settlement can be started. (Let us omit the question of who should manage
the process of conflict resolution. The world community has several mechanisms to do that, including the United Nations, the United States, and major
and regional powers. Each method has its advantages and disadvantages.)

In any deliberations concerning population transfers special attention should
be paid to (1) the creation and maintenance of stable, secure, and easily
recognizable borders, (2) geographical distribution of the minority (in order
to eliminate, as much as possible, any future calls for territorial adjustments),
(3) numerical strength (because in a democracy the numerically predominant ethny will usually have the last say), and (4) the rate of growth of each
ethnic element to make sure that differences in population growth rates do
not change ethnic ratios in the future. (Different rates in growth may gradually lead to a shift in the balance of power, causing a subsequent realignment
of the main antagonists, as has happened in Lebanon and is probably happening in Ulster. Everything must be done to eliminate the likelihood of future
conflicts. Just as in a war infantry decides who controls the territory, in peace
population is the ultimate guarantor.)

Regrettably, few powers would be willing to implement a resettlement
scheme in a conflict that is merely "warm," not to say "cold." Yet, when one
looks at Bosnia, one cannot help thinking that all the bloodshed could probably have been avoided by a timely population transfer. The irony, in this
particular case, is that the success of the final settlement will depend on
brutal ethnic cleansing carried out by various participants in the heat of battle.
A preventive resettlement would have been immeasurably more humane and
effective.

Conclusions

Existing historical records indicate that cleansing has been practiced for nearly 3,000 years, most likely even longer. Although it has significantly changed over time, cleansing has always been directed at groups that were considered dangerous, groups that had to be eliminated.

Modern cleansing derives from the religious intolerance of the Middle Ages. Medieval Christianity—but also Islam, Manichaeism, and Zoroastrianism—sought to establish an ideal community of true believers, a community that required absolute purity. They saw the world divided into the Realm of Light and the Realm of Darkness, their ceaseless struggle a determining factor in human affairs. In the context of the eschatological struggle, the quest for purity supreme was inevitably translated into a series of cleansings directed against the contaminants, forces representing Darkness.

As an organizing political principle, the concept was enunciated by the formula *cuius regio eius religio,* which was adopted at Augsburg in 1555. Although originally applied to Germany, the principle was successfully implemented by most early centralizing states of Western Europe that had the means to put it into effect.

Later, the same principle was expanded to include *eius nacio,* class, gender, and other parameters. Each conceptual redefinition of what was deemed unacceptable in a given polity led to new cleansing campaigns that affected new social strata based on ethnicity, race, class, and sexual preference. Even imagined communities, such as "witches," were not spared.

Tracing the evolution in the modalities of cleansing prompts a fundamental question: What was the driving force behind the shifts in the pattern of cleansing? Why did Spain in the fifteenth to seventeenth centuries cleanse religious minorities (although Spanish religious intolerance was tinged by strong racist overtones)[1] while Nazi Germany and Stalinist Russia, 500 years later, tried to eliminate "inferior" races and "parasitic" classes?

The answer lies in changes in collective identity. Cleansing serves as a litmus test for determining the focus of collective self-definition: polities that define themselves in religious terms cleanse religious minorities, those that see themselves in terms of class get rid of the class enemies, and so on. The same applies to ethnicity, race, and all other parameters that serve as the basis for identity formation. By following the shifting patterns of cleansing we can trace the shifting focus of collective identity.

The old, superseded identities are not discarded, however. Civilization accumulates identities, like rings on a tree, in ever expanding circles. A medieval Christian had few other identities; a modern man and woman are defined by their ethnicity, race, class, occasionally religion and, possibly, gender and sexual preference. Modernity, among other things, means complexity.

This is not to say that various identities cannot lose their relative importance. Their success or failure depends to a large extent on whether they are "natural" identities based on religion or ethnicity (no matter how socially [re]constructed) or whether they are synthetic "imagined communities" created by human endeavor, like mobilized class or gender.

The last 200 years witnessed the creation and proliferation of several synthetic identities. This was made possible by the intellectuals' penchant for conjuring up social categories based on specific socioeconomic or genetic traits, their propensity for category reification, their search for a "Grand Design," a theory or ideology that would explain everything, and their ability to infect the masses by means of ideological viruses. In the process, it was not only the masses that the *clercs* betrayed; they also deluded themselves.

Marxism gave intellectuals a paradigm for collective identity formation. What had been done to class was later done for other groups based on different sociological or biological criteria. The process has accelerated since 1850 and especially in the twentieth century with the creation of new identities based on gender and sexual preference. And other identities based on age, profession, and even physical disability are not far behind. If anything, the last two centuries prove how easy it is to create, reconstruct, and promote new collective identities.

The creation of gay identity exemplifies the process of identity creation. "Homosexual identity," writes Margaret Cruikshank, "is distinct from the phenomenon of same-sex behavior."[2] Earlier, there were people who engaged in homosexual acts. Those were sins, *individual* deviations, which implied no communal dimension. The shift from individual to communal was effected when both gays and nongays assigned people engaging in homosexual acts to a separate category. Its development was helped by the fact that during World War II the "condition of being homosexual itself became undesirable and a new class of persons came under surveillance."[3] Why did gay identity coalesce in the United States? There are many reasons. One of the most important is that American society was in the forefront of modernity. Among other factors one can list a "tradition of interest groups and ethnic voting blocs, weak national parties, the idea of liberal individualism, and 'above all, the very American belief that we have the power to invent ourselves from scratch.'"[4]

Like other collective identities, the gay identity went through several stages, from an equivalent of ethnic category, through mobilization, to "tribe." (It remains to be seen if the gay community engages in gay nationalism.) On the individual level, the experience of discovering and reassessing gay identity gave structure and substance to the everyday existence of thousands of people.

There are many reasons that explain the proliferation of collective identities, but three stand out: (1) a drastic decrease in family size and the weakening of family ties, which lead to atomization (all of these resulting from increased levels of urbanization and industrialization); (2) the spread of secondary education, which creates a critical mass of literate (but not necessarily civilized) individuals; and (3) the possibility of a presumably limitless upward social mobility, which makes everyone dissatisfied. As a result, modern society is swarming with isolated, frustrated individuals. Accustomed to sociological categorizing, to thinking in "class terms," these individuals eagerly join movements. Their sense of grievance makes them easily susceptible to any leader(s) with a program, leaders who can direct their dissatisfaction against a symbolic authority figure or a suitable social or ethnic/racial/religious category. That is why modern collective identities start as liberation movements.

At the lowest common denominator, many modern (that is, ideologically mobilized) collective identities are based on envy and resentment dressed up in a Bill of Rights (which also includes a Bill of Wrongs for which the Other has to pay). (This is not to say that the injustices suffered by various groups are purely imaginary. But if common sense is lacking in rectifying old injustices, new injustices will be created.)

The democratic system gives resentment a voice. However, representative democracy, the way it has evolved in the West, tilts toward individual rights at the expense of group rights. (There are many exceptions, of course.

And Western democracy does not discourage voluntary associations based on economic self-interest. It is in noneconomic matters that the emphasis on the individual hurts the group.)

When it comes to ethnicity, this system works best in monoethnic societies or in polities created through mass immigration, such as the countries of the New World. It does not work half as well in multiethnic societies of the Old World, where members of ethnic and religious minorities may still suffer discrimination as members of minority groups, even if their political rights as citizens of a given country are (theoretically) respected.

In a system in which one person equals one vote, numerical strength translates into political power. If the society is multiethnic, and especially if it is ethnically stratified, the more numerous ethny usually wins. And if minority rights are not sufficiently protected—which is quite often the case, even in the developed countries—the minorities are forced to submit to decisions unfavorable to their interests.

Even if the minority has a chance to change the ethnic balance, through higher birth rates, it is usually a long, drawn-out process. The winning ticket usually belongs to the more prolific team and, more often than not, people on a different level of socioeconomic development. Historically, the principle seems to be "procreate your way to political power."

Representative democracy would not be quite so lethal, from the ethnic point of view, without the ideal of the nation and national freedom spread by the French Revolution. The ideal appeared and developed in one of the oldest nation-states of Western Europe, established well before the onset of the age of nationalism. When Herder and his disciples redefined the nation in ethnic terms and passed the new concept to Eastern Europe, it combined with the "French" ideals of freedom and self-determination in a combustible mixture now known as (ethnic) nationalism.

Ethnonationalism makes ethnic coexistence extremely difficult. Very few countries are able to achieve some semblance of balance. (Here we will be reminded of consociationalism. But consociated democracy works best in West European countries where divisions are nonethnic, such as Austria or the Netherlands. Where ethnicity or ethnicized religion are important, as in Belgium or Lebanon, the consociated systems quickly break down.)

Change in ethnic balance or lack of concurrence between ethnic ratios and the distribution of power keep the modern world in constant turmoil. This is inherent in political systems based on representative democracy and imbued with the ideals of freedom and self-determination. As more and more groups awaken to self-awareness and demand corporate recognition, we will encounter more and more conflicts.

There are many possible solutions to ethnic problems. At one extreme is the secession of an ethnic group inhabiting a compact territory. The problem with this is that few ethnic territories are compact or easily delineated.

At the other extreme is a long-term assimilation process that may work with nonterritorial minorities, particularly the immigrant groups of the New World, and usually before the onset of the age of nationalism, but that often fails if nationalism has been awakened, especially among territorial minorities in the Old World.

Then, there are several types of federalism: (1) federation (such as the former USSR or Yugoslavia), (2) confederation, (3) devolution, and (4) consociation. All these options have their pros and cons. The most important negative aspect of the federal option is that the federal system creates and entrenches ethnic elites, which can then lead the fight to destroy the system, even in fairly benevolent states like Czechoslovakia.

Among less tried solutions are condominium, as in Andorra, which was quite successful, and a "personal," nonterritorial ethnicity attempted in Moravia in the beginning of this century.

Unfortunately, there are many conflicts that defy federal—or any other—solutions. This is especially true in those areas where ethnic hatreds acquire a cyclical repetitive pattern. Such conflicts have to be solved by different means.

When none of these solutions works and secession is impossible, as in the Sudeten situations described in previous chapters, then a divorce is called for, including, but not limited to, population exchanges and transfers.

Logically, one may deduce that the creation of homogeneous political units will complete the process of state-building, stabilize ethnic and political boundaries, fortify political units and, ultimately, deactivate nationalism as a powerful political force. In other words, to paraphrase Oscar Wilde, the easiest way to overcome nationalism is to give in. Eventually, one may hope, the satisfaction of the nationalist impulse should bring forth the long-awaited, long-prophesied but so far elusive end of nationalism. (It is unlikely it will bring us the end of history, but subsequent history will probably, one may hope, lose its savage tribal component.)

Even where transfers are effective, the range of possible outcomes and complications is quite impressive. This is particularly true of the former Soviet republics, where the situation is extremely fluid. There is a tremendous difference, however, between Latvia and Estonia, where the line separating indigenous ethnic groups from russophones is distinct, and areas such as Belarus and Ukraine, where it is not.

Ukraine, for example, is divided into two parts: the nationalistic west and center and the Russian-oriented east and south, which are home to most of Ukraine's 11 million ethnic Russians. What's more, many of local Ukrainians are russophones: 25.3 percent in the east and south, 56.2 percent in the major industrial center Donetsk.[5] Not only ethnic Russians but also many ethnic Ukrainians in the heavily Russified east and south feel more attached to Russia than Ukraine. Together, these two groups form overwhelming majorities in the urban centers of southern and eastern Ukraine, reaching some 90 percent in such places as Simferopol.[6] The conundrum facing Ukraine is truly unenviable: leaving 11 million ethnic Russians and their Ukrainian allies in place may split Ukraine in half (and subjugate the country to Russia, which will bring about the rebirth of the Russian empire in a new form). But a transfer of these gigantic proportions, even if spread across many years, would have staggering economic costs. (These costs would be lower in transfers involving smaller numbers of people, such as Sri Lanka, or in divided economies such as Cyprus, although even there the expenditures would be substantial.) Right now, Ukrainian authorities are trying a full-speed assimilation, especially by means of Ukrainianizing secondary and higher education. But it is too early to say whether they will succeed.

Thus, it bears to be repeated, population transfers and resettlement are no panacea. But to deny the great advantages of such an ethnic divorce in situations in which it has every chance of success and is the only viable solution is not unlike denying marital divorce to a couple. Bosnian refugees, for example, are often asked, "Do you think you can live together?" as if cleansing and massacre have not provided a sufficiently clear answer. No, they cannot. Even if the conflict is patched up now, the possibility of future conflicts, with concomitant death and destruction, is too high. It is the children and grandchildren of today's refugees who will pay the price. The gradual easing of religious tensions in France and Germany, achieved through the separation of religious denominations by means of population transfers, points the way to solving ethnic conflicts where all else fails. To deny this option is to condemn millions of people and their children to unnecessary suffering in the generations to come.

Appendix

Typology of Cleansing

I. The historical dimension:
- A. Antiquity (economic/political)
- B. Middle Ages and Renaissance (religious)
- C. Modern
  1. ethnoreligious (till 1750 in the West, till present elsewhere)
  2. colonial (1750-1900)
  3. ideological (1917-1960)
  4. postcolonial (1950-1980)
  5. purely ethnic (1913-present)

II. The geographical dimension:
- A. Old World
- B. New World (colonial)

III. The paradigmatic dimension:
- A. Physical
  1. Racial
  2. Invalids
- B. Cultural Markers
  1. Ethnic
  2. Religious
  3. Civilizational

IV. The ideological dimension:
- A. Class
- B. Political foes

V. The strategic dimension
- A. External
- B. Internal

VI. The economic dimension

VII. Miscellaneous:
    A. Gender and Sexual Preference
    B. Age
    C. Mental patients
    D. Social undesirables:
        1. Beggars
        2. Prostitutes
VIII. The temporal dimension:
    A. Permanent
    B. Temporary

Notes

CHAPTER 1

1. B. Oded, paper given at the Rencontre Assyriologique 1975 in Göttingen. Also, *Encyclopaedia Judaica,* vol. 6, pp. 1034ff., 1971, both in A. de Zayaz, *Nemesis at Potsdam* 1989, p. 187, 3ff; and *Encyclopaedia Britannica,* 21:925.

2. H. Hall, *The Ancient History of the Near East* (New York: Macmillan, 1935), p. 474.

3. 2 Kings 24:14-16.

4. J. Oates, *Babylon* (London: Thames and Hudson, 1979), p. 130.

5. M. L. W. Laistner, *Greek History* (Boston: D.C. Heath & Company, 1932), pp. 134-35.

6. P. Green, *Alexander of Macedon* (Berkeley and Los Angeles: University of California Press, 1991), p. 45.

7. Green:149.

8. Green:147.

9. Green:149.

10. S. L. Utchenko, ed., *Ancient Rome* (Moscow: State Pedagogic Publishing House of the Ministry of Education of the Russian Soviet Socialist Republic, 1950), pp. 89-90.

11. M. Grant, *History of Rome* (New York: Charles Scribner's Sons, 1978), p. 162.

12. Grant:143.

13. Grant:143-44.

14. Cassius Dio, *Roman History,* book 69, quoted in P. Johnson, *A History of the Jews* (New York: Harper & Row, 1987), p. 142.

15. Grant:184.

16. Charles Dickens, *A Child's History of England* (London: J.M. Dent & Sons, 1907/1978), p. 28.

17. Pierre van den Berghe, *The Ethnic Phenomenon* (New York and Oxford: Elsevier, 1981), p. 34.

18. R. Schumann, *Italy in the Last Fifteen Hundred Years* (Lanham, MD: University Press of America, 1986), p. 114.

19. B. Wilkinson, *The Later Middle Ages in England* (New York: David McKay, 1969), p. 190.

20. Wilkinson:162.

21. A. Klima, "The Czechs," in M. Teich and R. Porter, eds., *The National Question in Europe in Historical Context* (Cambridge: Cambridge University Press, 1993), p. 228-29.

22. J. Limbert, *Iran* (Boulder, CO: Westview Press, 1987), p. 61.

23. M. Gilbert, *Jewish History Atlas* (New York: Collier Books, 1969), p. 44.

24. A. Eban, *My People: The Story of the Jews* (New York: Behrman House and Random House, 1968), p. 170.

25. Howard M. Sachar, *Diaspora* (New York: Harper & Row, 1985), p. 229.

26. Johnson:226.

27. S. Payne, *A History of Spain and Portugal* (Madison: University of Wisconsin Press, 1973), p. 214.

28. Payne:288.

29. Howard M. Sachar, *Farewell España* (New York: Alfred A. Knopf, 1994), pp. 162-63.

30. Gilbert:47. According to Stanley Payne, the last execution for heresy occurred in 1826.

31. Gilbert:40.

32. C. Brinton, J. Christopher, and R. Wolff, *A History of Western Civilization* (Englewood Cliffs, N.J.: Prentice-Hall, 1955), p. 515.

33. Brinton:504.

34. S. Collinson, *Europe and International Migration* (London: Pinter Publishers, 1993), p. 31.

35. Brinton:579.

36. S. Cronin, *The Irish Nationalism: A History of its Roots and Ideology* (New York: Continuum, 1981), p. 9.

37. J. F. Shearouse, "Protestant Activities as Contributing Factors to the 1731 Expulsion of the Salzburg Lutherans: Viewed in Light of the 1648 Peace of Westphalia," (Ph. D. diss. Northwestern University, 1985).

38. J. Daigle, "L'Acadie, 1604-1763: Synthèse historique," in J. Daigle, ed., *Les acadiens des Maritimes: Etudes thématiques* (Moncton: Centre d'études acadiennes, 1980), p. 47.

39. M. K. Roy, "Peuplement et croissance démographique en Acadie," in Daigle:166.

40. Daigle:48.

41. F. Prucha, *American Indian Policy in the Formative Years* (Cambridge: Harvard University Press, 1962), p. 227.

42. Report of Senate Committee on Public Lands, Jan. 9, 1817, in *American State Papers: Indian Affairs*, 14 cong., 2 sess., pp. 123-24.

43. Prucha:231.

44. Prucha:235.

45. R. Satz, *American Indian Policy in the Jacksonian Era* (Lincoln: University of Nebraska Press, 1975), p. 66.

46. Satz:86.

47. Mary E. Young, "Indian Removal and Land Allotment," in P. Gates, ed., *The Rape of Indian Lands* (New York: Arno Press, 1979), p. 44.

48. L. Carranco, "Chinese Expulsion from Humboldt County," in R. Daniels, ed., *Anti-Chinese Violence in North America* (New York: Arno Press, 1978), pp. 329-40.

49. S. W. Kung, Chinese in American Life (Seattle: University of Washington Press, 1962), p. 87.

50. J. Shipps, *Mormonism* (Urbana: University of Illinois Press, 1985), pp. 158-59.

51. R. J. Robertson, Jr., "The Mormon Experience in Missouri, 1830-1839," *Missouri Historical Review* 68, no. 3 (1974):280-98; no. 4(1974):393-415.

52. J. Gunther, *Inside Australia* (New York: Harper & Row, 1972), p. 74.

53. P. Biskup, "Aboriginal History," in G. Osborne and W. F. Mandle, eds., *New History* (Sydney: George Allen & Unwin, 1982), p. 25.

54. J. Rickard, *Australia: A Cultural History* (London: Longman, 1988), p. 238.

55. J. Metge, *The Maoris of New Zealand* (London: Routledge and Kegan Paul, 1967), p. 41.

56. Metge:44.

57. K. S. Salibi, *The Modern History of Lebanon* (New York: Frederick A. Praeger, 1965), p. 49.

58. Salibi:106.

59. Salibi:107.

60. D. M. Lang, *The Armenians* (London: Unwin Paperbacks, 1988), p. 10.

61. V. Nadein-Raevski, "The Azerbaijani-Armenian Conflict: Possible Paths towards Resolution," in K. Rupesinghe, P. King, and O. Vorkunova, eds., *Ethnicity and Conflict in a Post-Communist World* (New York: St. Martin's Press, 1992), p. 118; quoted by Nadein-Raevski: L. A. Hushudyan, *Istina— iedinstvennyi kriteriy istoricheskoynauki* (Yerevan: Yerevan State University Publishing House, 1989), p. 10, and Y.G. Barsegov, *Pravo na samoopredeleniye—osnova demokraticheskogo resheniya mejnatsional'nykh problem: k probleme Nagornogo Karabakha* (Yerevan: Ayastan, 1989), p. 88.

62. *The Keesing's Record of World Events* (London: Longman, 1988), p. 36035.

63. Nadein-Raevski:124.

64. Lang:29.

65. R. Clogg, *A Short History of Modern Greece* (Cambridge: Cambridge University Press, 1979), p. 113.

66. Clogg:118.

67. Clogg:121.

68. Yu. Bromley, ed., *Narody Mira* (Moscow: Sovetskaia Entsyklopediia, 1988), p. 555.

69. Clogg:201.

70. Zaim M. Necatigil, *The Cyprus Question and the Turkish Position in International Law* (Oxford: Oxford University Press, 1989), p. 128.

71. UN doc. S/18880 of May 29, 1987, quoted in Necatigil:128.

72. Liah Greenfeld, *Nationalism: Five Roads to Modernity* (Cambridge: Harvard University Press, 1992), p. 191.

73. Hugh Seton-Watson, "Russian Nationalism in Historical Perspective," in Robert Conquest, ed., *The Last Empire: Nationality and the Soviet Future* (Stanford: Hoover Institution Press, 1986), p. 20.

74. Graham Stephenson, *Russia from 1812 to 1945* (New York: Praeger, 1970), pp. 63-64.

75. Brig. Peter Young, ed., *Illustrated World War II Encyclopedia* (Orbis Publishing, 1978), p. 6.

76. Robert F. Byrnes, *Pobedonostsev: His Life and Thought* (Bloomington: Indiana University Press, 1968), p. 207.

77. Nicolas Berdyaev, *The Origin of Russian Communism* (Ann Arbor, The University of Michigan Press, 1960), p. 37.

78. N. Mandelshtam, *Vospominaniia* (New York: Izdatel'stvo imeni Chekhova, 1970), p. 330.

79. Robert Conquest, *The Harvest of Sorrow* (New York/Oxford: Oxford University Press, 1986), p. 217.

80. Conquest:219.

81. Iosif V. Stalin, *Works*, v. 7, (Moscow: 1953-55), p. 71, quoted in Conquest:219.

82. Conquest:306.

83. M. B. Olcott, *The Kazakhs* (Stanford: Hoover Institution Press, 1987), p. 185.

84. A. Kirch and M. Kirch, "National Minorities in Estonia," in Rupesinghe, King, and Vorkunova:94.

85. R. J. Misiunas and R. Taagepera, *The Baltic States: Years of Dependence, 1940-1990* (Berkeley and Los Angeles: University of California Press, 1993), p. 354.

86. Misiunas and Taagepera:358.

87. E. Laasi, "Veelkord lunkadest," *Sirp ja Vasar*, 26 February, 1988, quoted by Kirch and Kirch, in Rupesinghe, King, and Vorkunova:94.

88. Yu. Mironenko, "Other National Groups," in N. K. Deker and A. Lebed, eds., *Genocide in the USSR* (New York: Scarecrow Press, 1958), p. 56.

89. G. Vvedensky, "The Volga Germans and Other German Groups," in Deker and Lebed:52.

90. Mironenko:56.

91. R. Conquest, *The Nation Killers* (London: Macmillan, 1970), p. 111.

92. D. Arbakov, "The Kalmyks," in Deker and Lebed:34.

93. R. Karcha, "The Peoples of the North Caucausus," in Deker and Lebed:47.

94. Eugene Kulischer, *The Displacement of Population in Europe* (Montreal: International Labor Office, 1943), p. 298.

95. R. Wixman, *Language Aspects of Ethnic Patterns and Processes in the North Caucasus* (University of Chicago, Dept. of Geography, Research Paper no. 191, Chicago: 1980), p. 134.

96. Conquest 1970:65.

97. E. Kirimal, "The Crimean Turks," in Deker and Lebed:23.

98. Ernst Bruckmuller, "The National Identity of the Austrians," in Teich and Porter, p. 199, table 8.1. As late as 1964, only 47 percent of Austrians polled agreed with the statement that "Austrians constitute a nation." Only in 1970 did the percentage reach 66 percent. Although polls are often unreliable we may postulate that the separation occurred some time in the late 1960s.

99. L. Dawidowicz, *The War against the Jews* (New York: Holt, Rinehart and Winston, 1975), p. 544.

100. The 219,700 figure is listed by D. Kenrick and G. Puxon in *The Destiny of Europe's Gypsies* (New York: Basic Books, 1973), p. 184; the higher estimates are presented by F. D. Mulcahy in the foreword to J. Yoors, *Crossing* (Prospect Heights, IL: Waveland Press, 1971), p. 4.

101. R. Plant, *The Pink Triangle* (New York: Henry Holt and Company, 1986), p. 212.

102. H. Heger, *The Men with the Pink Triangle* (Boston: Alyson Publications, 1980), pp. 11-14.

103. Plant:218-19.

104. Rudiger Lautmann, "The Pink Triangle," *Journal of Homosexuality* 6 (1980-81):146, quoted in Barry D. Adam, *The Rise of a Gay and Lesbian Movement* (Boston: Twayne Publishers, 1987), pp. 52-53. Richard Plant gives a somewhat higher estimate of 50-63,000 homosexuals, including 4,000 juveniles and 6 lesbians, even though sex between women was not against the law.(Plant:149)

105. Plant:214.

106. Plant:217.

107. Kulischer 1943:53.

108. Kulischer 1943:54-55.

109. Kulischer 1943:72.

110. Kulischer 1943:25.

111. J. Schechtman, *Postwar Population Transfers in Europe, 1945-1955* (Philadelphia: University of Pennsylvania Press, 1962), p. 61.

112. Schechtman 1962:75.

113. Schechtman 1962:77.

114. Schechtman 1962:90-91.

115. Schechtman 1962:92-93.

116. Schechtman 1962:190.

117. F. Golczewski, "Nationale Minderheiten in Polen und die Wende," H. Huttenbach, ed., *Nationalities Papers* 22, no. 1, (spring 1994):96.

118. Schechtman 1962:195.

119. Schechtman 1962:132.

120. Schechtman 1962:146.

121. Kulischer 1948:299.

122. J. W. Byrkit, *Forging the Copper Collar* (Tucson: University of Arizona Press, 1982), p. 204.

123. R. D. Heinl, Jr. and N. G. Heinl, *Written in Blood* (Boston: Houghton Mifflin, 1978), pp. 125-29.

124. J. Chome, *La crise congolaise* (Brussels: Editions de Remarques Congolaises, 1960), pp. 128-29.

125. *U.S. Army Area Handbook for Algeria,* Dept. of the Army, Pamphlet 550-44, (Washington: 1965), pp. 52, 82-83.

126. Ch. M. Ali, *The Emergence of Pakistan* (New York: Columbia University Press, 1967), p. 261.

127. J. B. Schechtman, *The Arab Refugee Problem* (New York: Philosophical Library, 1952), p. 18.

128. Schechtman 1952:5.

129. Schechtman 1952:11.

130. Schechtman 1952:7.

131. J. P. Augelli, "Nationalization of Dominican Borderlands," *Geographical Review* 70(1980):24.

132. I. Bell, *The Dominican Republic* (Boulder, CO: Westview Press, 1981), p. 67.

133. Heinl and Heinl:527.

134. Augelli:24.

135. Bell:68.

136. W. H. Durham, *Scarcity and Survival in Central America; Ecological Origins of the Soccer War* (Stanford, CA: Stanford University Press, 1979), p. 59.

137. Th. P. Anderson, *The War of the Dispossessed* (Lincoln: University of Nebraska Press, 1981), p. 49.

138. Anderson:75.

139. Anderson:93.

140. Anderson:99.

141. Anderson:141.

142. B. Dahm, *History of Indonesia in the Twentieth Century* (London: Praeger, 1971), p. 239.

143. Jose Ramos-Horta, *Funu: The Unfinished Saga of East Timor* (Trenton, N.J.: The Red Sea Press, 1987). Also, *East Timor Violations of Human Rights* (London: Amnesty International Publications, 1985).

144. *Keesing's* 1970:24025.

145. *Keesing's* 1970:24029.

146. *Keesing's* 1975:27469.

147. N. A. Poliakova, ed., *Strany Mira* (Moscow: Izdatel'stvo politicheskoi literatury, 1991), p. 183.

148. *Keesing's* 1978:29272.

149. D. Gwyn, *Idi Amin: Death-Light of Africa* (Boston: Little, Brown, 1977), p. 90.

150. Gwyn:112.

151. Gwyn:102.

152. Gwyn:113.

153. Konstantin Fotić, *The War We Lost: Yugoslav Tragedy and the Failure of the West* (New York: Viking Press, 1948), p. 124.

154. Fotic:119.

155. V. Žerjavić, "The Losses of Yugoslav Population in the Second World War," *Geographical Papers,* vol. 8, (Institute of Geography, University of Zagreb, Croatia: 1991, p. 96.

156. Fotić:139-40.

157. Helsinki Watch, *War Crimes in Bosnia-Hercegovina* (New York: Human Rights Watch, 1992), p. 140.

158. *Time,* August 24, 1992, p. 46.

159. *Time,* August 17, 1992, p. 23.

160. *Keesing's* 1990:37794.

161. *Keesing's,* 1991:38362.

162. *Keesing's,* 1993:39695.

163. Oliver Cromwell Cox, *Caste, Class, and Race: A Study in Social Dynamics* (Garden City, N.Y.: Doubleday, 1948), p. 399; quotation from Lord Acton's *The History of Freedom and Other Essays* (London: Macmillan, 1907), pp. 93-94.

164. Arend Lijphart, "Political Theories and the Explanation of Ethnic Conflict in the Western World: Falsified Predictions and Plausible Postdictions," in Milton J. Esman, ed., *Ethnic Conflict in the Western World* (Ithaca and London: Cornell University Press, 1977), p. 53.

165. Karl Kautsky, *Neue Zeit* (1886), 522-25, cited in H. B. Davis, *Nationalism and Socialism* (New York and London: Monthly Review Press, 1967), p. 142; ref. in Anthony Smith, Nationalism in the Twentieth Century (New York: New York University Press, 1979), p. 163.

CHAPTER 2

1. Theodore Zeldin, *France, 1848-1945* vol. 1, (Oxford: Clarendon Press, 1973), p. 744.

2. G. Jackson, *The Spanish Republic and the Civil War, 1931-1939* (Princeton, N.J.: Princeton University Press, 1965), p. 539.

3. Jackson:535.

4. Jackson:526.

5. S. Collinson, *Europe and International Migration* (London: Pinter Publishers, 1993), p. 43.

6. R. Plant, *The Pink Triangle* (New York: Henry Holt, 1986), p. 217.

7. Eugene M. Kulischer, *Europe on the Move: War and Population Changes, 1917-47* (New York: Columbia University Press, 1948), p. 31.

8. David Marshall Lang, *The Armenians* (London: Unwin Paperbacks, 1988), p. 83.

CHAPTER 3

1. P. Meyer, ed., *Romania* 21 (1892), 50-52, quoted in Christopher Allmand, *The Hundred Years War* (Cambridge: Cambridge University Press, 1988), p. 140.

2. Albion W. Small, *General Sociology* (Chicago: University of Chicago Press; London: T. Fisher Unwin, 1905), p. 495.

3. George C. Homans, *The Human Group* (New York: Harcourt, Brace & World, 1950), pp. 82-86.

4. George De Vos and Lola Romanucci-Ross, *Ethnic Identity: Cultural Continuities and Change* (Palo Alto, CA: Mayfield Publishing Company, 1975), p. 1.

5. F. K. Lehman, "Who Are the Karen, and If So, Why? Karen Ethnohistory and a Formal Theory of Ethnicity," in Charles F. Keyes, ed., *Ethnic Adaptation and Identity* (Philadelphia: Institute for the Study of Human Issues, 1979), p. 236.

6. R. D. Grillo, Introduction to R. D. Grillo, ed., *"Nation" and "State" in Europe* (London: Academic Press, 1980), p. 14.

7. Clifford Geertz, *Old Societies and New States* (London: Free Press of Glencoe, 1963), p. 109.

8. Jaroslav Krejčí and Vítězslav Velímský, *Ethnic and Political Nations in Europe* (New York: St. Martin's Press, 1981), p. 228.

9. Steven Runciman, *A History of the Crusades* vol. 3, (Cambridge: Cambridge University Press, 1951), p. 39.

10. Raoul Naroll, "On Ethnic Unit Classification," *Current Anthropology,* 5(1964):288.

11. Nicolas Berdyaev, T*he Russian Revolution* (Ann Arbor: University of Michigan Press, 1971), p. 56.

12. Krejčí and Velímský:230.

13. Naroll:283-91, 306-12.

14. Michael Moerman, "Ethnic Identification in a Complex Civilization: Who Are the Lue?" *American Anthropologist* 67(1965):1222.

15. Judith A. Nagata, "What is a Malay? Situational Selection of Ethnic Identity in a Plural Society," *American Ethnologist* 1, no. 2(1974):333. See also Charles F. Keyes, introduction to Charles F. Keyes, ed., *Ethnic Adaptation and Identity* (Philadelphia: Institute for the Study of Human Issues, 1979), p. 19.

16. Katherine Verdery, *Transylvanian Villagers* (Berkeley: University of California Press, 1983).

17. Fredrik Barth, introduction to Fredrik Barth, ed., *Ethnic Groups and Boundaries* (Bergen: Universitets Forlaget, 1969), pp. 10-11.

18. Paul Brass, "Ethnicity and Nationality Formation," *Ethnicity* 3(1976):226.

19. Brass:227.

20. Hugh Seton-Watson, *Nations and States: An Enquiry into the Origins of Nations and the Politics of Nationalism* (London: Methuen, 1977), p. 1.

21. R. Lafont, *Sur la France* (Paris: Gallimard, 1968), p. 35.

22. E. K. Francis, *Interethnic Relations* (New York: Elsevier, 1976), p. 387.

23. Grillo:7.

24. Anthony D. Smith, *Nationalism in the Twentieth Century* (New York: New York University Press, 1979), p. 168.

25. Ernest Gellner, *Nations and Nationalism* (Ithaca: Cornell University Press, 1983), p. 1.

26. Benedict Anderson, *Imagined Communities* (London: Verso, 1983), p. 47.

27. E. H. Buschbeck, *Austria* (Oxford: Geoffrey Cumberlege, Oxford University Press, 1949), p. 83.

28. Fernand Braudel, *L'identité de la France* (Paris: Arthaud-Flammarion, 1986), p. 298.

29. Barbara W. Tuchman, *A Distant Mirror* (New York: Alfred A. Knopf, 1978), p. 54.

30. Anderson:31.

31. Anderson:40.

32. Gellner:55.

33. Cynthia H. Enloe, *Ethnic Conflict and Political Development* (Boston: Little, Brown, 1973), p. 15.

34. Enloe:17.

35. Karl W. Deutsch, *Nationalism and Social Communication* (Cambridge: MIT Press, 1953), p. 96.

36. Deutsch:97.

37. Deutsch:98.

38. Anthony D. Smith, *The Ethnic Revival* (Cambridge: Cambridge University Press, 1981), p. 65.

39. Riccardo Petrella, "Nationalist and Regionalist Movements in Western Europe," in Charles R. Foster, ed., *Nations without a State,* (New York: Praeger, 1980), p. 10. (Emphasis added.)

40. M. Rainer Lepsius, *Extremer Nationalismus* (Stuttgart: 1966), quoted by Abraham Ashkenasi, *Modern German Nationalism* (New York: John Wiley & Sons, 1976), p. 17.

41. Based on Petrella:12.

42. Ashley Montagu, "The Concept of Race," *American Anthropologist* 64(1962):919-28.

43. *Webster's New Collegiate Dictionary* (Springfield, MA: G. & C. Merriam Company, 1976), p. 209.

44. One encounters a similar problem in linguistics. It is often difficult to establish where one linguistic area ends and another one begins [within one language family, of course]. There are large areas of intermediate dialects between, say, Russian and Belorussian, or between langue d'oc and langue d'oui or between High and Low German. Such areas display traits, represented by isoglosses, encountered on both sides of the ill-defined borderline. Nowadays, the imposition of literary tongues has created clear linguistic frontiers. But even before the spillover of literary tongues into everyday speech one could not confuse the French of Paris and the Italian of Florence. Even a thousand years ago these were already distinct languages. Thus, within the linguistic group, language formation was initially largely a function of distance. Something similar occurred in race. In any case, no one denies the existence of discrete languages even though a clear borderline, on the level of dialects, is sometimes hard to establish.

45. Oliver Cromwell Cox, *Caste, Class, and Race. A Study in Social Dynamics* (Garden City, N.Y.: Doubleday, 1948), p. 401.

46. Pierre van den Berghe, *The Ethnic Phenomenon* (New York and Oxford: Elsevier, 1981), p. 241.

47. Enloe:24-25.

48. T. R. Fehrenbach, *Fire and Blood: A History of Mexico* (New York: Da Capo Press, 1995), pp. 238-39. Colonial Mexico had an even more elaborate system of racial categories denoting every possible racial combination of White, Indian, and Black. It had a bewildering array of nomenclature; the South African system was simple and straightforward by comparison. There were four main divisions: White, Indian, Negro Castes, and "Corruptions," each subdivided into castes.

> The White race, for example, included seven castes:
> European father and Negra mother = Mulatto
> European father and India mother = Mestizo
> European father and Mulatta mother = Cuarteron
> European father and Mestiza mother = Criollo
> European father and China mother = Chino blanco
> European father and Cuarterona mother = Quintero
> European father and Quinterona mother = Blanco

All combinations, note, were based on a union of a European father and a non-European mother; a union of a European mother and a non-European father was evidently unthinkable.

49. Smith 1979:99.

50. Smith 1979:92.

51. Cox:155.

52. Cox:162.

53. Karl Marx, *Capital* (Moscow: Foreign Languages Publishing House, 1962), p. 862.

54. Hans Heinrich Gerth and Charles Wright Mills, eds., *From Max Weber: Essays in Sociology* (London: K. Paul, Trench, Trubner & Co., 1948), p. 188.

55. W. Lloyd Warner and P. S. Lunch, *The Social Life of a Modern Community* (New Haven: Yale University Press, 1941), quoted in Raja Jayaraman, *Caste and Class: Dynamics of Inequality in Indian Society* (Delhi: Hindustan Publishing Corporation, 1981), p. 18.

56. Robert A. Dahl, *Polyarchy: Participation and Opposition* (New Haven and London: Yale University Press, 1971), p. 106.

57. J. Nagata, "The Status of Ethnicity and the Ethnicity of Status," *International Journal of Comparative Sociology* 17, nos. 3-4:242.

58. Harold Wolpe, "Class Concepts, Class Struggle and Racism," in John Rex and David Mason, eds., *Theories of Race and Ethnic Relations* (Cambridge and New York: Cambridge University Press, 1986), p. 123.

59. Ted Robert Gurr, *Minorities at Risk* (Washington, D.C.: United States Institute of Peace Press, 1993), p. 19.

60. John Rex, "The Role of Class Analysis in the Study of Race Relations—A Weberian Perspective," in Rex and Mason:78.

61. Immanuel Wallerstein, *The Modern World System* (New York: Academic Press, 1974), quoted in Rex and Mason:77.

62. Geoffrey Gorer, "English Identity over Time and Empire," in De Vos and Romanucci-Ross:156-72.

63. Gerth and Mills:188.

64. E. A. H. Blunt, *The Caste System of Northern India* (Delhi: S. Chand & Co., 1969), pp. 1-2.

65. Jayaraman:10.

66. Jayaraman:24.

67. O. Bohtlingk and R. Roth, *Sanskrit-Worterbuch* (Petrograd: 1855-75), quoted in Cox:93.

68. Cox:93.

69. Jayaraman:9.

70. van den Berghe:159.

71. Cox:125-26.

72. Cox:130.

73. Blunt:3-4.

74. Emile Senart, *Caste in India* (London: 1930), pp. 8-9, 198, quoted in Cox:72.

75. Sir Herbert Hope Risley, *The People of India* (Calcutta: 1908), pp. 25, 272, 289, quoted in Cox:72.

76. For the distinction between caste and tribe see Gerth and Mills:398-99.

77. For a concise exposition on the differences between caste, estate, and class, see T. H. Marshall, "Social Stratification: Caste, Estate and Class," in Eric A. Nordlinger, ed., *Politics and Society* (Cambridge: Harvard University Press, 1970), pp. 44-47.

78. Gellner quoted in John Breuilly, *Nationalism and the State* (New York: St. Martin's Press, 1982), p. 31.

79. Cox:27.

80. Jules Romains, *Montée des perils* (Paris: Flammarion, 1958), pp. 252-53.

81. See Alexander Zinoviev, "Sovietskii obraz zhizni" ("Soviet Lifestyle") in *My i Zapad* (We and the West) (Lausanne: Editions l'Age d'Homme, 1981), p. 127.

82. Joan Kelly, *Women, History and Theory* (Chicago and London: University of Chicago Press, 1984), p. 65.

83. Juliet Mitchell, "Women and Equality," in Juliet Mitchell and Ann Oakley, eds., *The Rights and Wrongs of Women* (London: Penguin, 1976), p. 387, quoted in Anne Phillips, *Divided Loyalties: Dilemmas of Sex and Class* (London: Virago, 1987), p. 2.

84. Mary Astell quoted in Phillips:73.

85. Marie Mitchell Olesen Urbanski, *Margaret Fuller's "Woman in the Nineteenth Century"* (Westport, CT: Greenwood Press, 1980), p. 47.

86. Phillips:76.

87. Friedrich Engels, *The Origin of the Family, Private Property and the State* (1884), quoted in Kenneth Neill Cameron, *Marxism: The Science of Society* (South Hadley, MA: Bergin & Garvey Publishers, 1985), p. 124.

88. Phillips:10.

89. Kelly:55.

90. Olive Banks, *Faces of Feminism* (New York: St. Martin's Press, 1981).

91. Phillips:108.

92. Phillips:5.

93. Ann Pettifor, "Labour's Macho Tendency," *New Socialist* 30(Sept. 1985):39, quoted in Phillips:157.

94. Banks:228.

95. Phillips:143.

96. Elizabeth Roberts, *A Woman's Place: On Oral History of Working-Class Women, 1890-1940* (Oxford: Basil Blackwell, 1984), p. 2, quoted in Phillips:57-58.

97. Phillips:119.

98. Banks:210.

99. Banks:212.

100. Banks:213.

101. Banks:235.

102. E. William Monter, "Sodomy and Heresy in Early Modern Switzerland," *Journal of Homosexuality* 6 (winter 1981):42; Randolph Trumbach, "London Sodomites," *Journal of Social History* 11, no. 1(1977):9, quoted in Barry D. Adam, *The Rise of a Gay and Lesbian Movement* (Boston: Twayne Publishers, 1987), p. 7.

103. John D'Emilio, *Sexual Politics, Sexual Communities: The Making of a Homosexual Minority in the United States, 1940-1970* (Chicago and London: University of Chicago Press, 1983), pp. 4-5.

104. D'Emilio:14.

105. D'Emilio:9.

106. Lillian Faderman, *Surpassing the Love of Men* (New York: 1981); Kenneth Plummer, ed., *The Making of the Modern Homosexual* (London: 1981); Jeffrey Weeks, *Coming Out: Homosexual Politics in Britain from the Nineteenth Century to the Present* (London: 1977); quoted in D'Emilio:4.

107. D'Emilio:4-5.

108. Personal papers of James Kepner, "Remarks Made by Harry Hay to First Discussion Group," November 1950, Los Angeles, quoted in D'Emilio:9.

109. John Lauritsen and David Thorstad, *The Early Homosexual Rights Movement (1864-1935)* (New York: Times Change Press, 1974), p. 5.

110. Adam:14.

111. Adam:17.

112. Lauritsen and Thorstad:38.

113. Adam:50.

114. Lauritsen and Thorstad:62-63.

115. Lauritsen and Thorstad:67.

116. Herbert Marcuse, *Soviet Marxism* (New York: Vintage, 1961), quoted in Adam:48.

117. Lauritsen and Thorstad:68.

118. Lauritsen and Thorstad:69.

119. D'Emilio:13.

120. Jonathan Katz, *Gay American History* (New York: Crowell, 1976), pp. 385-89; *The Gay/Lesbian Almanac* (New York: Morrow, 1983), pp. 554-61; quoted in Adam:42. Amazingly, it was founded by an itinerant preacher and laundry, railway, and postal workers; it was incorporated in Chicago on December 10, 1924. The inspiration came from Henry Gerber, a German-American who was in Germany from 1920 to 1923 and took part in the German movement at that time.

121. Adam:58.

122. Clark Taylor, "Folk Taxonomy and Justice in Dade County, Florida, 1954," *Anthropological Research Group on Homosexuality Newsletter* 4, nos. 1-2(1982):9, quoted in Adam:59.

123. Adam:62.

124. D'Emilio:102.

125. "Minutes of Meeting of Daily Committee of Board of Directors," October 13, 1960, NYMS; Jaye Bell (DOB president), "An Official Statement," ONE, April 1961, p. 10; quoted in D'Emilio:115.

126. D'Emilio:65-66.

127. D'Emilio:125.

128. D'Emilio:150.

129. Adam:74.

130. D'Emilio:173.

131. D'Emilio:195.

132. D'Emilio:203.

133. Adam:75.

134. John Clark, "The Global Lesbian and Gay Movement: Mass Movement, Grassroots, or by Invitation Only," in Aart Hendriks, Rob Tielman, and Evert van der Veen, eds., *The Third Pink Book: A Global View of Lesbian and Gay Liberation and Oppression* (Buffalo, N.Y.: Prometheus Books, 1993), p. 56.

135. D'Emilio:238-39.

136. Rita May Brown, "Take a Lesbian to Lunch," in Karla Jay and Allen Young, eds., *Out of the Closets* (New York: Douglas/Links, 1972), quoted in Adam:90.

137. Adam:93-94.

138. Marcel Proust, "By Way of Sainte-Beuve," in Alistair Sutherland and Patrick Anderson, eds., *Eros* (New York: Citadel, 1963), p. 276; quoted in Adam:30.

139. Thorkil Vanggaard, *Phallos: A Symbol and its History in the Male World* (New York: International Universities Press, 1974), p. 16.

140. Though this is neither a currently fashionable nor truly accurate term, it is useful, so let us accept the following definition: primitive societies are those "with little or no surplus wealth available for distribution among members. To the extent that a material cushion is often a prerequisite for the development of an elaborate culture, the term *primitive societies* roughly parallels what some authors refer to as 'preliterate' or 'tribal' societies," in John B. Williamson, Linda Evans, and Lawrence A. Powell, *The Politics of Aging: Power and Policy* (Springfield, IL: Charles C. Thomas, 1982), p. 28.

141. Williamson, Evans, and Powell:19-20.

142. Williamson, Evans, and Powell:35.

143. Audrey I. Richards, *Chisungu: A Girl's Initiation Ceremony among the Bemba of Zambia* (London and New York: Tavistock Publications, 1956).

144. A. Mauss, "On being strangled by the stars and stripes: the New Left, the Old Left, and the natural history of American radical movements," *Journal of Social Issues* 27(1971):185-202, in Williamson, Evans, and Powell:81.

145. Williamson, Evans, and Powell:82-83.

146. Williamson, Evans, and Powell:89.

147. Williamson, Evans, and Powell:95.

148. Williamson, Evans, and Powell:96.

149. Williamson, Evans, and Powell:144-45.

150. A. Campbell, "Politics through the lifecycle," *Gerontologist* 11(1971):112-17; R. H. Binstock, "Interest group liberalism and the politics of aging," *Gerontologist* 12(1972)265-80, in Williamson, Evans, and Powell:256.

151. Williamson, Evans, and Powell:x.

152. Williamson, Evans, and Powell:145.

153. Williamson, Evans, and Powell:122.

154. Williamson, Evans, and Powell:10.

155. Williamson, Evans, and Powell:98.

156. Adam:45. Note that "class" is applied to women and ethnoreligious minorities. Two hundred years ago the word *nacio* was equivalent to "category." One could say "the nation of lawyers" and even "the nation of birds." In other words, "nation" was a paradigm for collectivity. Marxism endowed "class" with a paradigmatic quality. We now say "a class of lawyers," "a class of women/Jews/ethnics," perhaps even "a class of birds."

157. *Newsweek,* July 31, 1995.

158. Svetlana Boym, *Common Places: Mythologies of Everyday Life in Russia* (Cambridge: Harvard University Press, 1994), p. 287.

159. Elise Boulding, *The Underside of History: A View of Women through Time* (Boulder, CO: Westview Press, 1976), p. 37.

160. Phillips:12.

CHAPTER 5

1. *Newsweek,* October 5, 1992, p. 53.

2. The heresy derives from a perennial question: If God is good and omnipotent, why does Evil exist? Either God is good or omnipotent, He cannot be both.

The roots of the Bogomil movement go back to Manichaeism, a religion which originated in Babylonia in the middle of the 3rd century A.D. Its founder, prophet Mani (of Persian extraction), taught that there exist two opposite and mutually independent principles, God and Matter, represented by Light and Darkness. Our present world is the result of an invasion of the Realm of Light by Darkness and is, therefore, a mixture of both. The ideal is a complete restoration of the original dualism which can be achieved by a gradual liberation of Light from Darkness. In the human realm the liberation involves the liberation of human soul from the prison of the Matter/Body. See Dmitri Obolensky, *The Bogomils: A Study in Balkan Neo-Manichaeism* (Cambridge: Cambridge University Press, 1948), p. 5.

The original doctrine spread throughout the Mediterranean world in the third through seventh centuries and influenced early Christianity. The second wave, known as neo-Manichaeism, spread throughout Europe in the ninth through fourteenth centuries. Unwittingly, Byzantium played a vital role in the spread of the doctrine. In the second half of the seventh century the heresy won many converts in Armenia and Asia Minor. By this time it had been thoroughly "Christianized"—adapted to the doctrines and practice of Christianity. Its adherents were known as "Paulicians." Obolensky:8.

Byzantine emperors did not spare efforts to promote Orthodoxy and often persecuted the sect. The persecutions reached their peak in the ninth century under Theodora who ordered a wholesale massacre of the Paulicians in an attempt to extirpate the heretical sect. The ferocity of the persecution is explained not only by important doctrinal differences but also by the fact that Paulicians, a border population between Byzantium and the Caliphate, often allied themselves with the Arabs, which is not surprising in light of Byzantine hostility. When efforts to destroy Paulicians physically failed, Byzantium turned to an old policy of transplanting—cleansing—inimical populations to a far-off corner of the empire. Thrace, devastated by the Barbarian invasions from the north, was a common dumping ground for heretics. Already in 745 a large colony of Syrian Monophysite heretics was settled there. Obolensky:28-29; *Theophanes,* Chronographia de Boor, ed., (Leipzig: 1883), p. 422, in Obolensky:60.

Thus, Paulicians were just another heretical sect dumped in Byzantine "Siberia." Unexpectedly, the sect found fertile ground in Thrace/Bulgaria. The spread of Orthodox Christianity in the Balkans was closely associated with the spread of the Byzantine influence. While other countries, like Russia, were too far away to be effectively controlled by Byzantium, Bulgaria was very close. From as early as the ninth century, a strong anti-Byzantine party was formed in Bulgaria which resisted the penetration of the Byzantine influence. In this atmosphere Paulicianism seemed like a good alternative. Obolensky:64-67.

By the middle of the tenth century the teaching had been thoroughly Slavicized and, in its Slav version, became known as Bogomilism. (Bogomil = Dieu-Aimé) In its new reincarnation, the doctrine grew increasingly ascetic. Marriage, for example, was to be avoided, since procreation reproduced Matter and thus contributed to the realm of the devil. (Few adherents went to such extremes, however.) Obolensky:111; 114.

The collapse of the First Bulgarian Empire in 1018 and its occupation by Byzantium resulted in a suppression of all heterodox movements. Repression was less felt in Macedonia, the westernmost province of the Bulgarian state, far removed from Byzantium and separated from the rest of Bulgaria by mountains. That is why, already after 972 (the conquest of eastern Bulgaria by the Byzantines), Macedonia became the center of Bogomilism. It was also in Macedonia that Bogomilism attained its final doctrinal form. Obolensky:152.

During the Byzantine rule, until 1186, sectarians headed Bulgarian resistance, and here once again the Bogomils played an important role. In the Second Bulgarian Empire (1186-1393) Bogomilism experienced a great efflorescence in the thirteenth century and then a rapid decline and disappearance in the fourteenth. It is interesting that by this time Bogomilism had completely lost its earlier puritanism and had become associated with sexual indulgence. However, this was probably a reflection of a general decline which affected all classes of Bulgarian society at this time. Obolensky:169; 230; 251-52.

After the Turkish conquest in 1393 the sect quickly withered and disintegrated. But in its heyday, it had spread to Serbia (as early as the 10th century), Bosnia (where it acquired a distinct ideological coloration; its adherents were known as "Patarenes"), and further west to northern Italy and southern France, where the movement was called Albigensian, by its main center, Albi. Its adherents were known as "Cathars" or, among their Catholic opponents, as "Bulgarians" (hence "bougre," from which comes English "bugger"). Although Cathars had also developed a distinct doctrine, the Bogomil influence is clearly discernible. Obolensky:266; 285; 288.

3. Fred Singleton, *A Short History of the Yugoslav Peoples* (Cambridge: Cambridge University Press, 1985), p. 20.

4. Jill A. Irvine, *The Croat Question* (Boulder, CO: Westview Press, 1993), p. 21.

5. Singleton:175.

6. Irvine:96.

7. Singleton:177.

8. Vladimir Žerjavić, "Thee Losses of Yugoslav Population in the Second World War," *Geographical Papers,* vol. 8, Institute of Geography, University of Zagreb, (Zagreb, Croatia:1991), p. 96.

9. Irvine:277.

10. Irvine:282.

11. *Keesing's Record of World Events* (London: Longman, April 1994), p. 39966
12. *Keesing's*:40286.
13. *Keesing's*:R104.
14. *Keesing's*:39827.
15. *Keesing's*:39871.
16. *Keesing's*:39925.
17. *Keesing's*:40196.
18. *Keesing's*:39828.
19. *Keesing's*:39927.
20. *Keesing's*:40111.
21. *Keesing's*:40328.
22. *Keesing's*:R104.
23. *Keesing's*:40247.
24. *Keesing's*:40286.
25. *Keesing's*:39696.
26. *Keesing's*:40196.
27. *Keesing's*:40154.
28. *Keesing's*:40195.
29. *Keesing's*:38918.
30. *Keesing's*:40195.
31. *Keesing's*:40072.
32. *Keesing's*:40287.
33. *Keesing's*:R103.
34. *Keesing's*:39870.
35. *Keesing's*:39871.
36. *Keesing's*:40154.
37. *Keesing's*:40154.
38. *Keesing's*:39871.
39. *Keesing's*:39966.
40. *Keesing's*:R104.
41. *Keesing's*:40072.

42. *Keesing's*:40017.

43. *Keesing's*:39967.

44. *Keesing's*:40110.

45. *Keesing's*:40754.

46. *Keesing's*:40327.

47. *Keesing's*:39870.

48. *Keesing's*:39926.

49. *Keesing's*:40072.

50. *Keesing's*:40196.

51. *Vjesnik,* May 4, 1994, quoted in *Keesing's*:40018.

52. *Keesing's*:40248.

Other publications used in preparing this chapter:

Helsinki Watch, *War Crimes in Bosnia-Hercegovina* (New York: Human Rights Watch, 1992).

Peter F. Sugar, Peter Hanak, and Tibor Frank, eds., *A History of Hungary* (Bloomington and Indianapolis: Indiana University Press, 1990).

CHAPTER 6

1. *Country Atlas* (Rand McNally, 1994), p. 36.

2. *Country Atlas*:36.

3. *Strany Mira* (Moscow: Politizdat, 1991), p. 189.

4. *Strany Mira*:188.

5. Howard M. Sachar, *Farewell España* (New York: Alfred A. Knopf, 1994), p. 87.

6. Dominick J. Coyle, *Minorities in Revolt* (Rutherford, N.J.: Farleigh Dickinson University Press, 1983), p. 153.

7. Coyle:156.

8. Pierre Oberling, *The Road to Bellapais: The Turkish Cypriot Exodus to Northern Cyprus* (Boulder, CO: Social Science Monographs; New York: Colombia University Press, 1982), p. 39.

9. Coyle:161.

10. R. R. Denktash, *The Cyprus Triangle* (London: K. Rustem & Bro. and George Allen & Unwin, 1982), p. 24.

11. Oberling:65.

12. Coyle:187.

13. Denktash:35.

14. Denktash:39.

15. *The Cyprus Problem* (Nicosia: Press and Information Office of the Republic of Cyprus, 1988), p. 54.

16. *The Cyprus Problem*:55.

17. *The Cyprus Problem*:49.

Other publications used in preparing this chapter:

Crisis on Cyprus (Washington, D.C.: American Hellenic Institute, 1975).

Cyprus (Encyclopedia Britannica Year Book, 1995).

Cyprus (Nicosia: Republic of Cyprus Press and Information Office, 1990).

Richard Clogg, *A Short History of Modern Greece* (Cambridge: Cambridge University Press, 1986).

Lawrence Durrell, *Bitter Lemons* (New York: Penguin Books, 1991).

Peter W. Edbury, *The Kingdom of Cyprus and the Crusades, 1191-1374* (Cambridge: Cambridge University Press, 1991).

George Kelling, *Countdown to Rebellion* (New York: Greenwood Press, 1990).

D. George Kousoulas, *Modern Greece: A Profile of a Nation* (New York: Charles Scribner's Sons, 1974).

Nicos Kranidiotis, "The Cyprus Problem" (speech delivered at the International Symposium on Cyprus at the Panteios School of Political Science in Athens on March 10-14, 1975).

Zaim M. Necatigil, *The Cyprus Question and the Turkish Position in International Law* (Oxford: Oxford University Press, 1989).

H. D. Purcell, *Cyprus* (New York and Washington: Frederick A. Praeger, 1969).

Eric Solsten, ed., *Cyprus: A Country Study* (Washington, D.C.: Library of Congress Federal Research Division, 1991).

On The Cyprus Problem: 1964-88 (Resolutions adopted by the United Nations).

CHAPTER 7

1. *Peoples of the Soviet Union* (Moscow: Novosti Press Agency, 1989), pp. 30, 42.

2. Richard G. Hovannisian, *Armenia on the Road to Independence, 1918* (Berkeley and Los Angeles: University of California Press, 1967), p. 36, quoted in Christopher J. Walker, *Armenia: The Survival of a Nation* (London: Croom Helm, 1980), p. 96.

3. Walker:115.

4. Walker:136-142.

5. Walker:161.

6. Walker:165.

7. Walker:168.

8. Walker:187.

9. Walker:226.

10. Walker:230.

11. Walker:258.

12. Walker:261.

13. FO 371/13827.6419, quoted in Walker:348.

14. David Marshall Lang, *The Armenians: A People in Exile* (London: Unwin Paperbacks, 1981), p. 83.

15. Walker:270.

16. Walker:329.

17. Anatoly N. Yamskov, "Inter-Ethnic Conflict in the Transcaucasus: A Case Study of Nagorno-Karabakh," in Rupesinghe, King, and Vorkunova, eds., *Ethnicity and Conflict in a Post-Communist World* (New York: St. Martin's Press, 1992), p. 135.

18. V. Nadein-Raevski, "The Azerbaijani-Armenian Conflict: Possible Paths towards Resolution," in Rupesinghe, King, and Vorkunova:119.

19. Nadein-Raevski:120.

20. Nadein-Raevski:121.

21. *Keesing's Record of World Events,* News Digest for January 1990, pp. 37169-37170.

CHAPTER 8

1. Fabian Schmidt, "Kosovo: The Time Bomb That Has Not Gone Off" in RFE/RL Research Report, vol. 2, no. 39, October 1, 1993, p. 21.

2. Ramadan Marmullaku, *Albania and the Albanians* (Hamden, CT: Archon Books, 1975), p. 27.

3. Elez Biberaj, *Albania: A Socialist Maverick* (Boulder, CO: Westview Press, 1990), p. 113.

4. Biberaj:113.

5. Biberaj:114.

6. Biberaj:119.

7. Marmullaku:147.

8. Marmullaku:147.

9. Marmullaku:150.

10. Biberaj:126.

11. Biberaj:127.

12. Biberaj:129.

13. Schmidt:23.

14. Schmidt:23.

15. Schmidt:23.

16. Schmidt:23.

17. Eggert Hardten, *Die Albaner in Restjugoslawien, Expertenbericht ueber Minderheitenkonflikte* (Trento: Deutsch-Italienische Gesellschaft fuer Soziologie, University of Trento, 1993), quoted in Schmidt:23.

Other publications used in preparing this chapter:

Miranda Vickers, *The Albanians: A Modern History* (London and New York: I. B. Tauris, 1995).

CHAPTER 9

1. *World Atlas* Rand McNally & Company, 1994, pp. 3-6.

2. Benjamin Netanyahu, *A Place among the Nations* (New York: Bantam Books, 1993), p. 301.

3. *World Atlas*:3-6; Netanyahu:301.

4. Yu. Bromley, ed., *Narody Mira* (Moscow: Sovetskaia Entsyklopediia, 1988), pp. 550, 557.

5. Cassius Dio, *Roman History,* book 69, quoted by Paul Johnson, *A History of the Jews* (New York: Harper & Row, 1987), p. 142.

6. Netanyahu:62.

7. Elliott A. Green, "Arabs and Nazis—Can It Be True?" *Midstream,* October 1994, pp. 9-13.

8. Netanyahu:77.

9. Netanyahu:200.

Other publications used in preparing this chapter:

Saul B. Cohen, *The Geopolitics of Israel's Border Question,* Jaffee Center for Strategic Studies (JCSS) Study no. 7 (Boulder, CO: Westview Press, 1987).

Shmuel Sandler, *The State of Israel, the Land of Israel: The Statist and Ethnonational Dimensions of Foreign Policy* (Westport, CT: Greenwood Press, 1993).

Chapter 10

1. *World Atlas* (Rand McNally, 1994), p. 5.

2. *Country Atlas* (Rand McNally, 1994), p. 44.

3. Roman Solchanyk, "Ukraine, Belorussia, and Moldavia: Imperial Integration, Russification, and the Struggle for National Survival," in Lubomyr Hajda and Mark Beissinger, eds., *The Nationalities Factor in Soviet Politics and Society* (Boulder, CO: Westview Press, 1990), p. 182, table 1c (Ukraine, Belorussia, and Moldavia); p. 216, table 1c (The Baltic republics); p. 237, table 1c (Transcaucasia); and p. 263, table 1c (Central Asia).

4. Paul E. Lydolph, *Geography of the U.S.S.R.* (Elkhart Lake, WI: Misty Valley Publishing, 1990), p. 149.

5. Richard Pipes, *Russia under the Old Regime* (New York: Charles Scribner's Sons, 1974), p. 40.

6. Pipes:14.

7. Pipes:15.

8. Viktor I. Kozlov, *Natsional'nosti SSSR* (Moscow: Statistika, 1975), p. 5.

9. Solchanyk:182, table 1a.

10. Hajda and Beissinger:182, table 1c (Ukraine, Belorussia, and Moldavia); p. 216, table 1c (The Baltic republics); p. 237, table 1c (Transcaucasia); and p. 263, table 1c (Central Asia).

11. Michael Rywkin, *Moscow's Muslim Challenge* (Armonk, N.Y. and London: M. E. Sharpe, 1990), p. 79.

12. E. A. Pain, "Etnosotsiologicheskiie usloviia razvitiia sel'skogo rasseleniia (po materialam Uzbekskoi SSR)" (Moscow: Avtoreferat, 1983), p. 11, quoted in Rywkin:81.

13. Nadia Diuk and Adrian Karatnycky, *The Hidden Nations: The People Challenge the Soviet Union* (New York: William Morrow, 1990), p. 267.

14. Based on Hajda and Beissinger:182, table 1c (Ukraine, Belorussia, and Moldavia); p. 216, table 1c (The Baltic republics); p. 237, table 1c (Transcaucasia); p. 263, table 1c (Central Asia); and Lydolph:148.

Chapter 11

1. *Country Atlas* (Rand McNally, 1994), pp. 35, 44.

2. *Strany Mira* (Moscow: Politizdat, 1991), pp. 377-78.

3. *Strany Mira*:381.

4. Francois-Xavier Bangamwabo et al. *Les relations interethniques au Rwanda à la lumière de l'agression d'octobre 1990* (Ruhengeri: Editions Universitaires du Rwanda, 1991), p. 271.

5. Karl-Heinz Hausner and Beatrice Jezic, *Rwanda, Burundi* (Bonn: K. Schroeder, 1968), p. 59.

6. Bangamwabo et. al.:154

7. J. 'Bayo Adekanye, "Rwanda/Burundi: 'Uni-ethnic' Dominance and the Cycle of Armed Ethnic Formations," *Social Identities,* vol. 2, 1(1996):45.

8. Bangamwabo et. al.:172.

9. Bangamwabo et. al.:191.

10. Yu. Bromley, ed., *Narody Mira* (Moscow: Sovetskaia Entsyklopediia, 1988), p. 377.

11. Bangamwabo et. al.:191-92.

12. Bangamwabo et. al.:302-3; 9.77 percent according to ibid:315.

13. Bangamwabo et. al.:316.

14. Bangamwabo et. al.:317.

15. Bangamwabo et. al.:319.

16. Bangamwabo et. al.:320.

17. Bangamwabo et. al.:321.

18. Bangamwabo et. al.:67.

19. "World Military and Social Expenditures," quoted in *Newsweek,* April 18, 1994.

Other publications used in preparing this chapter:

J. F. Gotanegre, C. Prioul, and P. Sirven, *Géographie du Rwanda* (Bruxelles: Editions A. de Boeck; Kigali: Editions Rwandaises, 1974).

CHAPTER 12

1. *Country Atlas* (Rand McNally, 1994), p. 46.

2. *Strany Mira* (Moscow: Politizdat, 1991), pp. 254-56.

3. Argus John Tresidder, *Ceylon: An Introduction to the "Resplendent Land"* (Princeton, NJ: D. Van Nostrand, 1960), p. 30.

4. Tressider:34.

5. K. M. De Silva, *A History of Sri Lanka* (London: C. Hurst & Company; Berkeley and Los Angeles: University of California Press, 1981), p. 351.

6. Richard F. Nyrop et al., *Area Handbook for Ceylon*, (Washington, D.C.: The American University, 1971), pp. 275-76.

7. De Silva:529.

8. S. A. Pakeman, *Ceylon* (New York and Washington: Frederick A. Praeger, 1964), p. 187.

9. *The New Republic*, July 27, 1987, p. 14.

10. *The New York Times*, February 2, 1996, p. 4; February 4, 1996, p. 14.

11. *The New York Times*, February 2, 1996, p. 12.

Other publications used in this chapter:

Russell R. Ross and Andrea Matles-Savada, *Sri Lanka, a Country Study* (Washington: U.S. Government Printing Office, 1990).

O. H. K. Spate, *India, Pakistan and Ceylon: The Regions* (London: Methuen, 1972).

S. J. Tambiah, *Sri Lanka: Ethnic Fratricide and the Dismantling of Democracy* (Chicago and London: University of Chicago Press, 1986).

CHAPTER 13

1. John F. Cadzow, Andrew Ludanyi, and Louis J. Elteto, eds., *Transylvania: The Roots of Ethnic Conflict* (Kent, OH: Kent State University Press, 1983), p. 211.

2. Yu. Bromley, ed., *Narody Mira* (Moscow: Sovetskaia Entsyklopediia, 1988), p. 547.

3. Helsinki Watch, *Struggling for Ethnic Identity. Ethnic Hungarians in Post-Ceauşescu Romania*, (New York: Human Rights Watch, 1993), p. 6.

4. Elemer Illyes, *National Minorities in Romania: Change in Transylvania* (Boulder, CO: East European Monographs, 1982), p. 33.

5. Cadzow, Ludanyi, and Elteto:11.

6. Peter F. Sugar, Peter Hanak, and Tibor Frank, eds., *A History of Hungary* (Bloomington and Indianapolis: Indiana State University, 1990), p. 143.

7. Rudolf Joó and Andrew Ludanyi, eds., *The Hungarian Minority Situation in Ceausescu's Romania* (Boulder, CO: Social Science Monographs; Highland Lakes, N.J.: Atlantic Research and Publications, 1994), p. 110.

8. Emil Niederhauser, "The National Question in Hungary," in Mikuláš Teich and Roy Porter, eds., *The National Question in Europe in Historical Context* (Cambridge: Cambridge University Press, 1993), p. 258.

9. Illyes:56.

10. Illyes:23-24; Joó and Ludanyi:113 list a much lower figure for Hungarians who fled southern Transylvania after the Vienna Award: "only" 60,000.

11. Joó and Ludanyi:69.

12. Cadzow, Ludanyi, and Elteto:28.

13. Hungarian Human Rights Foundation ("HHRF"), "International Protection of National Minorities: An Imperative for the Hungarians of Romania," Memorandum for the Copenhagen Meeting on the Human Dimension, Conference on Security and Cooperation in Europe, June 5-29, 1990, p. 2.

14. HHRF, Letter to the Representatives at the Parliamentary Assembly in the Council of Europe, September 24, 1993, p. 17.

15. *Keesing's Record of World Events,* News Digest for January 1993, p. 39282.

16. HHRF, "Romania's Policies and Practices toward National Minorities," Summary for the Geneva Meeting of Experts on National Minorities, Conference on Security and Cooperation in Europe, July 1-19, 1991, p. 12.

17. HHRF, "An Unbroken Record of Broken Promises," October 18, 1993, p. 15.

18. HHRF, October 18, 1993, p. 15.

Other publications used in preparing this chapter:

R. W. Seton-Watson, *A History of the Roumanians* (New York: Archon Books, 1963).

CHAPTER 14

1. *World Atlas* (Rand McNally, 1994), p. 5.

2. John Darby, *Conflict in Northern Ireland: The Development of a Polarized Community* (Dublin: Gill and Macmillan; New York: Barnes & Noble Books, 1976), p. 3.

3. Dominick J. Coyle, *Minorities in Revolt* (Rutherford: Farleigh Dickinson University Press, 1983), p. 39.

4. J. Barrow, *Tour round Ireland* (John Murray, 1836), quoted in Darby:6.

5. Darby:9.

6. Darby:10.

7. Northern Ireland Office, quoted in Coyle:74.

Other publications used in preparing this chapter:

John McGarry and Brendan O'Leary, eds., *The Future of Northern Ireland* (Oxford: Clarendon Press, 1990), pp. 177, 209.

CHAPTER 15

1. "Republiku musíme odgermanisovat'," *Lidová Demokracie,* June 17, 1945.

2. Joseph Schechtman, *Postwar Population Transfers in Europe, 1945-1955* (Philadelphia: University of Pennsylvania Press, 1962), p. 365.

3. Sumner Welles, *Where Are We Heading?* (New York: 1946), pp. 12-30, in Schechtman:371.

4. Leopold C. Klausner, "Danger Zones in Europe," *World Affairs Interpreter* (summer 1944), p. 133, in Schechtman:375.

5. Viscount Cranborne, Parliamentary Debates, House of Lords, March 8, 1944, in Schechtman:375.

6. "Misto evakuace Čechů—odsun Němců," *Lidová Demokracie,* December 1, 1945.

7. "Národní menšiny nebezpečím pro mír," *Lidová Demokracie,* August 8, 1946.

8. Schechtman:365.

9. Michel Pierrac, "Les transferts des populations," *Voix de Peuples,* Geneva, October 16, 1940, in Schechtman:389.

10. Schechtman:389.

11. Stellio Seferiades, *L'échange des populations* (Académie de Droit International, Recueil de cours, 1928), vol. 4, p. 353, in Schechtman:22.

12. Stephen P. Ladas, *The Exchange of Minorities: Bulgaria, Greece, Turkey* (New York: 1932), p. 20, in Schechtman:22.

13. Schechtman:22.

14. Schechtman:23.

15. Schechtman:3.

16. Herbert von Truhart, "Schlussbilanz der Deutschen Beschwerden in der Genf," *Nation und Staat* July-August, 1938, p. 611, quoted in Schechtman:33.

17. Schechtman:4.

18. Schechtman:17.

19. Schechtman:18.

20. Schechtman:19.

21. Article 3 of the Peace Treaty with Romania, in Schechtman:19.

22. Schechtman:19.

23. Schechtman:20, see also Jacob Robinson, *From Protection of Minorities to Promotion of Human Rights* (Jerusalem, 1949), pp. 136-7; and Joseph Schechtman, "Decline of the International Protection of Human Rights," *The Western Political Quarterly* 4, no. 1 (March 1951).

24. Schechtman:22.

25. Eduard Beneš, "The Organization of Post-War Europe," *Foreign Affairs* 20, no. 2 (January 1942), p. 235.

26. Schechtman:vii.

27. Henry Morgenthau, Jr., *Germany is Our Problem* (New York: 1945), pp. 159-60, in Schechtman:369-70.

28. Herber Hoover and Hugh Gibson, *Problems of Lasting Peace* (New York: 1942), p. 238, in Schechtman:390.

29. Welles:119, 125, 127.

30. Warren Thompson, letter to Schechtman, in Schechtman:390.

31. Stephen B. Jones, *Boundary-Making: A Handbook for Statesmen, Treaty Editors, and Boundary Commissioners* (Washington, D.C.: Carnegie Endowment for International Peace, Division of International Law, 1945), in Schechtman:391.

32. Harold Butler, *The Lost Peace* (New York: 1941), p. 229, in Schechtman:391.

33. Pablo de Azcarate y Flores, *League of Nations and National Minorities, an Experiment* (Washington, D.C.: 1945), p. 130, in Schechtman:391.

34. Bernard Newman, *The New Europe* (New York: 1943), pp. 21, 131-32, 176, 228-29, 327, 416, 465, in Schechtman:391.

35. Nicolas Politis, "Les transferts de populations," *Politique Etrangère* (April 1940), in Schechtman:391.

36. Imre Ferenczi, "On Shifting Europe's Peoples," *New York Herald Tribune,* March 21, 1944, in Schechtman:391.

37. Louis Dollot, *Les grandes migrations humaines* (Paris: 1946), p. 93, in Schechtman:391.

38. Schechtman:392.

39. Oskar I. Janowsky, *Nationalities and National Minorities* (New York: 1945), p. 136, in Schechtman:369.

40. Schechtman:369.

41. Morgenthau:159-60.

42. Schechtman:370.

43. Erich Hula, "Exchange of Population," *New York Herald Tribune,* February 11, 1944, in Schechtman:392.

44. Fritz Epstein, *New Europe* July/August, 1944, in Schechtman:392.

45. Seferiades:420.

46. Ladas:724, 729-30.

47. Sir John Hope Simpson, "The Exchange of Populations," *Spectator*, December 5, 1941, in Schechtman:392.

48. Eugene M. Kulischer, "Population Transfers," *South Atlantic Quarterly*, October 1946, in Schechtman:393.

49. Jean de la Robrie, "Transferts des populations en Europe," *Le Monde français*, June 1946, in Schechtman:393.

50. Eduard Beneš, "The Europe of Tomorrow," *Spectator*, September 12, 1941, in Schechtman:393.

51. David Thompson, "Back to the Minority Problems," *Spectator*, September 19, 1941, in Schechtman:393.

52. Norman Hill, *Claims to Territory in International Law and Relations* (New York: 1945), pp. 185-86, in Schechtman:393.

53. Janowsky:139.

54. Schechtman:ix.

55. "Les transferts internationaux de populations," Institut National de la Statistique et des Etudes Economiques (Paris: 1946), pp. 36-39, in Schechtman:394.

56. Schechtman:28.

57. Schechtman:24.

58. Schechtman:364.

59. Schechtman:364-65.

60. Schechtman:26.

61. Schechtman:27.

62. Schechtman:25.

CHAPTER 16

1. Earl Babbie, *The Practice of Social Research* (Belmont, CA: Wadsworth Publishing Co., 1986), p. 361.

2. Babbie:362.

3. Babbie:365.

4. Babbie:371.

5. Babbie:383.

Other publications used in preparing this chapter:

Paul Lazarsfeld, Ann Pasanella, and Morris Rosenberg, eds., *Continuities in the Language of Social Research* (New York: Free Press, 1972).

Delbert Miller, *Handbook of Research Design and Social Measurement* (New York: Longman, 1983).

Chapter 17

1. Monty G. Marshall, "States at Risk," in Ted Robert Gurr, *Minorities at Risk: A Global View of Ethnopolitical Conflicts* (Washington, D.C.: United States Institute of Peace Press, 1993), p. 178.

2. A. Kirch and M. Kirch, "Ethnic Relations: Estonians and Non-Estonians," *Nationalities Papers* 23, no. 1 (1995):44.

3. Vello A. Pettai, "Russian Minority in Estonia," *Nationalities Papers* 23, no. 2 (1995):406.

4. Pettai:407.

5. Kirch and Kirch:50.

6. "Memorandum on the Violations of Human Rights in the Baltic Countries," *Nationalities Papers* 23, no. 2 (1995):451.

7. Kirch and Kirch:43.

8. *The Cyprus Problem* (Nicosia: Press and Information Office of the Republic of Cyprus, 1988), p. 49.

9. John McGarry and Brendan O'Leary, eds., *The Future of Northern Ireland* (Oxford: Clarendon Press, 1990).

10. McGarry and O'Leary:177, 209.

11. Rudolf Joó and Andrew Ludanyi, eds., *The Hungarian Minority Situation in Ceausescu's Romania* (Boulder, CO: Social Science Monographs; Highland Lakes, N.J.: Atlantic Research and Publications, 1994), p. 113.

12. John F. Cadzow, Andrew Ludanyi, and Louis J. Elteto, eds., *Transylvania: The Roots of Ethnic Conflict* (Kent, OH: Kent State University Press, 1983), p. 192.

13. Joó and Ludanyi:113.

14. Cadzow, Ludanyi, and Elteto:208.

15. Cadzow, Ludanyi, and Elteto:209.

16. *Keesing's Record of World Events,* News Digest for May 1989, p. 36662.

CONCLUSION

1. Benzion Netanyahu, *The Origins of the Inquisition in Fifteenth Century Spain* (New York: Random House, 1993).

2. Margaret Cruikshank, *The Gay and Lesbian Liberation Movement* (New York: Routledge, Chapman & Hall, 1992), p. 5.

3. Cruikshank:34.

4. Cruikshank:60; Dennis Altman, "My America and Yours: A Letter to U.S. Activists," *Outlook* 8 (Spring 1990), p. 64, in Cruikshank:60, note 1.

5. Dominique Arel, "Language Politics in Independent Ukraine: Toward One or Two State Languages?" *Nationalities Papers* 23, no. 3 (September 1995), p. 616, notes 3, 4.

6. Arel:619, note 45.

SELECTED BIBLIOGRAPHY

BOOKS

Barry D. Adam, *The Rise of a Gay and Lesbian Movement*, Boston: Twayne Publishers, 1987.

Ch. M. Ali, *The Emergence of Pakistan*, New York: Columbia University Press, 1967.

Christopher Allmand, *The Hundred Years War*, Cambridge: Cambridge University Press, 1988.

Benedict Anderson, *Imagined Communities*, London: Verso, 1983.

Th. P. Anderson, *The War of the Dispossessed*, Lincoln: University of Nebraska Press, 1981.

John A. Armstrong, *Nations before Nationalism*, Chapel Hill: University of North Carolina Press, 1982.

Abraham Ashkenasi, *Modern German Nationalism*, New York: John Wiley & Sons, 1976.

Earl Babbie, *The Practice of Social Research*, Belmont, CA: Wadsworth Publishing Co., 1986.

Francois-Xavier Bangamwabo et al., *Les relations interethniques au Rwanda à la lumière de l'agression d'octobre 1990*, Ruhengeri: Editions Universitaires du Rwanda, 1991.

Olive Banks, *Faces of Feminism*, New York: St. Martin's Press, 1981.

Fredrik Barth, ed., *Ethnic Groups and Boundaries*, Bergen: Universitets Forlaget, 1969.

I. Bell, *The Dominican Republic*, Boulder, CO: Westview Press, 1981.

Nicolas Berdyaev, *The Origin of Russian Communism*, Ann Arbor: University of Michigan Press, 1937/1960.

——, *The Russian Revolution*, Ann Arbor: University of Michigan Press, 1971.

Elez Biberaj, *Albania: A Socialist Maverick*, Boulder, CO: Westview Press, 1990.

E. A. H. Blunt, *The Caste System of Northern India*, Delhi: S. Chand & Co., 1969.

Elise Boulding, *The Underside of History: A View of Women through Time*, Boulder, CO: Westview Press, 1976.

Svetlana Boym, *Common Places: Mythologies of Everyday Life in Russia*, Cambridge: Harvard University Press, 1994.

Fernand Braudel, *L'identité de la France*, Paris: Arthaud-Flammarion, 1986.

John Breuilly, *Nationalism and the State*, New York: St. Martin's Press, 1982.

C. Brinton, J. Christopher, and R. Wolff, *A History of Western Civilization*, Englewood Cliffs, N.J.: Prentice-Hall, 1955.

E. H. Buschbeck, *Austria*, Oxford: Geoffrey Cumberlege, Oxford University Press, 1949.

J. K. Byrkit, *Forging the Copper Collar*, Tucson: University of Arizona Press, 1982.

Robert F. Byrnes, *Pobedonostsev: His Life and Thought*, Bloomington: Indiana University Press, 1968.

John F. Cadzow, Andrew Ludanyi, and Louis J. Elteto, eds., *Transylvania: The Roots of Ethnic Conflict*, Kent, OH: Kent State University Press, 1983.

Kenneth Neill Cameron, *Marxism: The Science of Society*, South Hadley, MA: Bergin & Garvey Publishers, 1985.

J. Chome, *La crise congolaise*, Brussels: Editions de Remarques Congolaises, 1960.

R. Clogg, *A Short History of Modern Greece*, Cambridge: Cambridge University Press, 1979, 1986.

S. Collinson, *Europe and International Migration*, London: Pinter Publishers, 1993.

Robert Conquest, *The Harvest of Sorrow*, New York and Oxford: Oxford University Press, 1986.

————, ed., *The Last Empire: Nationality and the Soviet Future*, Stanford: Hoover Institution Press, 1986.

————, *The Nation Killers*, London: Macmillan, 1970.

Dominick J. Coyle, *Minorities in Revolt*, Rutherford: Farleigh Dickinson University Press, 1983.

Oliver Cromwell Cox, *Caste, Class, and Race: A Study in Social Dynamics*, Garden City, N.Y.: Doubleday, 1948.

S. Cronin, *The Irish Nationalism: A History of its Roots and Ideology*, New York: Continuum, 1981.

Margaret Cruikshank, *The Gay and Lesbian Liberation Movement*, New York: Routledge, Chapman & Hall, 1992.

Robert A. Dahl, *Polyarchy: Participation and Opposition,* New Haven and London: Yale University Press, 1971.

B. Dahm, *History of Indonesia in the Twentieth Century,* London: Praeger, 1971.

J. Daigle, ed., *Les acadiens des Maritimes: Etudes thématiques,* Moncton: Centre d'études acadiennes, 1980.

R. Daniels, ed., *Anti-Chinese Violence in North America,* New York: Arno Press, 1978.

John Darby, *Conflict in Northern Ireland: The Development of a Polarized Community,* Dublin: Gill and Macmillan; New York: Barnes & Noble Books, 1976.

J. Davies, *From Charlemagne to Hitler,* London: Casell, 1948.

Lucy Dawidowicz, *The War against the Jews,* New York: Holt, Rinehart and Winston, 1975.

N.K. Deker and A. Lebed, eds., *Genocide in the USSR,* New York: Scarecrow Press, 1958.

John D'Emilio, *Sexual Politics, Sexual Communities: The Making of a Homosexual Minority in the United States, 1940-70,* Chicago and London: University of Chicago Press, 1983.

R. R. Denktash, *The Cyprus Triangle,* London: K. Rustem & Bro. and George Allen & Unwin, 1982.

K. M. De Silva, *A History of Sri Lanka,* London: C. Hurst & Company; Berkeley and Los Angeles: University of California Press, 1981.

Karl W. Deutsch, *Nationalism and Social Communication,* Cambridge: MIT Press, 1953.

George De Vos and Lola Romanucci-Ross, *Ethnic Identity: Cultural Continuities and Change,* Palo Alto, CA: Mayfield Publishing Company, 1975.

Ch. Dickens, *A Child's History of England,* London: J.M. Dent & Sons, 1907/1978.

Nadia Diuk and Adrian Karatnycky, *The Hidden Nations: The People Challenge the Soviet Union,* New York: William Morrow, 1990.

W. H. Durham, *Scarcity and Survival in Central America: Ecological Origins of the Soccer War,* Stanford, CA: Stanford University Press, 1979.

Lawrence Durrell, *Bitter Lemons,* New York: Penguin Books, 1991.

Abba Eban, *My People: The Story of the Jews,* New York: Behrman House Inc. and Random House, 1968.

Peter W. Edbury, *The Kingdom of Cyprus and the Crusades, 1191-1374,* Cambridge: Cambridge University Press, 1991.

Cynthia H. Enloe, *Ethnic Conflict and Political Development,* Boston: Little, Brown and Company, 1973.

Milton J. Esman, ed., *Ethnic Conflict in the Western World*, Ithaca and London: Cornell University Press, 1977.

T. R. Fehrenbach, *Fire and Blood: A History of Mexico*, New York: Da Capo Press, 1995.

Charles R. Foster, ed., *Nations without a State*, New York: Praeger, 1980.

Konstantin Fotić, *The War We Lost: Yugoslav Tragedy and the Failure of the West*, New York: Viking Press, 1948.

E. K. Francis, *Interethnic Relations*, New York: Elsevier, 1976.

P. Gates, ed., *The Rape of Indian Lands*, New York: Arno Press, 1979.

Clifford Geertz, *Old Societies and New States*, London: Free Press of Glencoe, 1963.

Ernest Gellner, *Nations and Nationalism*, Ithaca: Cornell University Press, 1983.

Hans Heinrich Gerth and Charles Wright Mills, eds., *From Max Weber: Essays in Sociology*, London: K. Paul, Trench, Trubner & Co., 1948.

M. Gilbert, *Jewish History Atlas*, New York: Collier Books, 1969.

J. F. Gotanegre, C. Prioul, and P. Sirven, *Géographie du Rwanda*, Brussels: Editions A. de Boeck; Kigali: Editions Rwandaises, 1974.

M. Grant, *History of Rome*, New York: Charles Scribner's Sons, 1978.

P. Green, *Alexander of Macedon*, Berkeley and Los Angeles: University of California Press, 1991.

Liah Greenfeld, *Nationalism: Five Roads to Modernity*, Cambridge: Harvard University Press, 1992.

R. D. Grillo, ed., *"Nation" and "State" in Europe*, London: Academic Press, 1980.

J. Gunther, *Inside Australia*, New York: Harper & Row, 1972.

Ted Robert Gurr, *Minorities at Risk: A Global View of Ethnopolitical Conflicts*, Washington, D.C.: United States Institute of Peace Press, 1993.

D. Gwyn, *Idi Amin: Death-Light of Africa*, Boston: Little, Brown and Company, 1977.

Lubomyr Hajda and Mark Beissinger, eds., *The Nationalities Factor in Soviet Politics and Society*, Boulder, CO: Westview Press, 1990.

H. Hall, *The Ancient History of the Near East*, New York: Macmillan, 1935.

Karl-Heinz Hausner and Beatrice Jezic, *Rwanda, Burundi*, Bonn: K. Schroeder, 1968.

H. Heger, *The Men with the Pink Triangle*, Boston: Alyson Publications, 1980.

R. D. Heinl, Jr. and N. G. Heinl, *Written in Blood*, Boston: Houghton Mifflin, 1978.

Aart Hendriks, Rob Tielman, and Evert van der Veen, eds., *The Third Pink Book: A Global View of Lesbian and Gay Liberation and Oppression,* Buffalo, N.Y.: Prometheus Books, 1993.

George C. Homans, *The Human Group,* New York: Harcourt, Brace & World, 1950.

Elemer Illyes, *National Minorities in Romania: Change in Transylvania,* Boulder, CO: East European Monographs, 1982.

Jill A. Irvine, *The Croat Question,* Boulder, CO: Westview Press, 1993.

G. Jackson, *The Spanish Republic and the Civil War, 1931-1939,* Princeton, N.J.: Princeton University Press, 1965.

Raja Jayaraman, *Caste and Class: Dynamics of Inequality in Indian Society,* Delhi: Hindustan Publishing Corporation, 1981.

Paul Johnson, *A History of the Jews,* New York: Harper & Row, 1987.

Rudolf Joó and Andrew Ludanyi, eds., *The Hungarian Minority Situation in Ceauşescu's Romania,* Boulder, CO: Social Science Monographs; Highland Lakes, N.J.: Atlantic Research and Publications, 1994.

George Kelling, *Countdown to Rebellion,* New York: Greenwood Press, 1990.

Joan Kelly, *Women, History and Theory,* Chicago and London: University of Chicago Press, 1984.

D. Kenrick and G. Puxon, *The Destiny of Europe's Gypsies,* New York: Basic Books, 1973.

Charles F. Keyes, ed., *Ethnic Adaptation and Identity,* Philadelphia: Institute for the Study of Human Issues, 1979.

D. George Kousoulas, *Modern Greece: A Profile of a Nation,* New York: Charles Scribner's Sons, 1974.

Viktor Ivanovich Kozlov, *Natsional'nosti SSSR,* Moscow: Statistika, 1975.

Jaroslav Krejčí and Vítězslav Velímský, *Ethnic and Political Nations in Europe,* New York: St. Martin's Press, 1981.

Eugene M. Kulischer, *The Displacement of Population in Europe,* Montreal: International Labor Office, 1943.

———, *Europe on the Move: War and Population Changes, 1917-47* (New York: Columbia University Press, 1948).

S. W. Kung, *Chinese in American Life,* Seattle: University of Washington Press, 1962.

R. Lafont, *Sur la France,* Paris: Gallimard, 1968.

M. L. W. Laistner, *Greek History,* Boston: D.C. Heath and Company, 1932.

David Marshall Lang, *The Armenians: A People in Exile*, London: Unwin Paperbacks, 1981.

John Lauritsen and David Thorstad, *The Early Homosexual Rights Movement (1864-1935)*, New York: Times Change Press, 1974.

Paul Lazarsfeld, Ann Pasanella, and Morris Rosenberg, eds., *Continuities in the Language of Social Research*, New York: Free Press, 1972.

J. Limbert, *Iran*, Boulder, CO: Westview Press, 1987.

Paul E. Lydolph, *Geography of the U.S.S.R.*, Elkhart Lake, WI: Misty Valley Publishing, 1990.

Nadezhda Mandelshtam, *Vospominaniia*, New York: Izdatel'stvo imeni Chekhova, 1970.

Ramadan Marmullaku, *Albania and the Albanians*, Hamden, CT: Archon Books, 1975.

Karl Marx, *Capital*, Moscow, Foreign Languages Publishing House, 1962.

John McGarry and Brendan O'Leary, eds., *The Future of Northern Ireland*, Oxford: Clarendon Press, 1990.

J. Metge, *The Maoris of New Zealand*, London: Routledge and Kegan Paul, 1967.

Delbert Miller, *Handbook of Research Design and Social Measurement*, New York: Longman, 1983.

R. J. Misiunas and R. Taagepera, *The Baltic States: Years of Dependence, 1940-1990*, Berkeley and Los Angeles: University of California Press, 1993.

Zaim M. Necatigil, *The Cyprus Question and the Turkish Position in International Law*, Oxford: Oxford University Press, 1989.

Benjamin Netanyahu, *A Place among the Nations*, New York: Bantam Books, 1993.

Benzion Netanyahu, *The Origins of the Inquisition in Fifteenth Century Spain*, New York: Random House, 1993.

Eric A. Nordlinger, *Politics and Society*, Cambridge: Harvard University Press, 1970.

J. Oates, *Babylon*, London: Thames and Hudson, 1979.

Pierre Oberling, *The Road to Bellapais: The Turkish Cypriot Exodus to Northern Cyprus* (Boulder, CO: Social Science Monographs; New York: Columbia University Press, 1982).

Dmitri Obolensky, *The Bogomils: A Study in Balkan Neo-Manichaeism*, Cambridge: Cambridge University Press, 1948.

M. B. Olcott, *The Kazakhs*, Stanford: Hoover Institution Press, 1987.

G. Osborne and W. F. Mandle, eds., *New History,* Sydney: George Allen & Unwin, 1982.

S. A. Pakeman, *Ceylon* (New York and Washington, D.C.: Frederick A. Praeger, 1964).

S. Payne, *A History of Spain and Portugal,* Madison: University of Wisconsin Press, 1973.

Anne Phillips, *Divided Loyalties: Dilemmas of Sex and Class,* London: Virago, 1987.

Richard Pipes, *Russia under the Old Regime,* New York: Charles Scribner's Sons, 1974.

R. Plant, *The Pink Triangle,* New York: Henry Holt and Company, 1986.

F. Prucha, *American Indian Policy in the Formative Years,* Cambridge: Harvard University Press, 1962.

H. D. Purcell, *Cyprus,* New York and Washington: Frederick A. Praeger, 1969.

Jose Ramos-Horta, *Funu: The Unfinished Saga of East Timor,* Trenton, N.J.: The Red Sea Press, 1987.

John Rex and David Mason, eds., *Theories of Race and Ethnic Relations,* Cambridge and New York: Cambridge University Press, 1986.

Audrey I. Richards, *Chisungu: A Girl's Initiation Ceremony among the Bemba of Zambia,* London and New York: Tavistock Publications, 1956.

J. Rickard, *Australia: A Cultural History,* London: Longman, 1988.

Jules Romains, *Montée des perils,* Paris: Flammarion, 1958.

Russell R. Ross and Andrea Matles-Savada, *Sri Lanka, a Country Study,* Washington: U.S. Government Printing Office, 1990.

Steven Runciman, *A History of the Crusades,* vol. 3, Cambridge: Cambridge University Press, 1951.

K. Rupesinghe, P. King, and O. Vorkunova, eds., *Ethnicity and Conflict in a Post-Communist World,* New York: St. Martin's Press, 1992.

Michael Rywkin, *Moscow's Muslim Challenge,* Armonk, N.Y. and London: M.E. Sharpe, 1990.

Howard M. Sachar, *Diaspora,* New York: Harper & Row, Publishers, 1985.

———, *Farewell España,* New York: Alfred A. Knopf, 1994.

K. S. Salibi, *The Modern History of Lebanon,* New York: Frederick A. Praeger, 1965.

Shmuel Sandler, *The State of Israel, the Land of Israel: The Statist and Ethnonational Dimensions of Foreign Policy,* Westport, CT: Greenwood Press, 1993.

R. Satz, *American Indian Policy in the Jacksonian Era*, Lincoln: University of Nebraska Press, 1975.

Joseph Schechtman, *The Arab Refugee Problem*, New York: Philosophical Library, 1952.

————, *Postwar Population Transfers in Europe, 1945-1955*, Philadelphia: University of Pennsylvania Press, 1962.

R. Schumann, *Italy in the Last Fifteen Hundred Years*, Lanham, MD: University Press of America, 1986.

Emile Senart, *Caste in India*, London: 1930.

Hugh Seton-Watson, *Nations and States: An Enquiry into the Origins of Nations and the Politics of Nationalism*, London: Methuen, 1977.

R. W. Seton-Watson, *A History of the Roumanians*, New York: Archon Books, 1963.

J. Shipps, *Mormonism*, Urbana: University of Illinois Press, 1985.

Fred Singleton, *A Short History of the Yugoslav Peoples*, Cambridge: Cambridge University Press, 1985.

Albion W. Small, *General Sociology*, Chicago: University of Chicago Press; London: T. Fisher Unwin, 1905.

Anthony D. Smith, *Nationalism in the Twentieth Century*, New York: New York University Press, 1979.

————, *The Ethnic Revival*, Cambridge: Cambridge University Press, 1981.

Eric Solsten, ed., *Cyprus: A Country Study*, Washington, D.C.: Library of Congress Federal Research Division, 1991.

O. H. K. Spate, *India, Pakistan and Ceylon: the Regions*, London: Methuen, 1972.

Graham Stephenson, *Russia from 1812 to 1945*, New York: Praeger, 1970.

Peter F. Sugar, Peter Hanak, and Tibor Frank, eds., *A History of Hungary*, Bloomington and Indianapolis: Indiana University Press, 1990.

S. J. Tambiah, *Sri Lanka: Ethnic Fratricide and the Dismantling of Democracy*, Chicago and London: University of Chicago Press, 1986.

M. Teich and R. Porter, eds., *The National Question in Europe in Historical Context*, Cambridge: Cambridge University Press, 1993.

Argus John Tresidder, *Ceylon: An Introduction to the "Resplendent Land,"* Princeton, NJ: D. Van Nostrand, 1960.

Barbara W. Tuchman, *A Distant Mirror*, New York: Alfred A. Knopf, 1978.

Marie Mitchell Olesen Urbanski, *Margaret Fuller's "Woman in the Nineteenth Century"*, Westport, CT: Greenwood Press, 1980.

S.L. Utchenko, ed., *Ancient Rome,* Moscow: State Pedagogic Publishing House of the Ministry of Education of the Russian Soviet Socialist Republic, 1950.

Pierre van den Berghe, *The Ethnic Phenomenon,* New York and Oxford: Elsevier, 1981.

Thorkil Vanggaard, *Phallos: A Symbol and its History in the Male World,* New York: International Universities Press, 1974.

Katherine Verdery, *Transylvanian Villagers,* Berkeley and Los Angeles: University of California Press, 1983.

Miranda Vickers, *The Albanians: A Modern History,* London and New York: I. B. Tauris, 1995.

Christopher J. Walker, *Armenia: The Survival of a Nation,* London: Croom Helm, 1980.

B. Wilkinson, *The Late Middle Ages in England,* New York: David McKay, 1969.

John B. Williamson, Linda Evans, and Lawrence A. Powell, *The Politics of Aging: Power and Policy,* Springfield, IL: Charles C. Thomas, 1982.

J. Yoors, *Crossing,* Prospect Heights, IL: Waveland Press, 1971.

Alfred M. de Zayas, *Nemesis at Potsdam: The Expulsion of the Germans from the East,* Lincoln and London: University of Nebraska Press, 1989.

Theodore Zeldin, *France, 1848-1945,* vol. 1, Oxford: Clarendon Press, 1973.

Alexandr Zinoviev, *My i Zapad,* Lausanne: Editions l'Age d'Homme, 1981.

ACADEMIC JOURNALS

American Anthropologist 67(1965):1222.

American Anthropologist 64(1962):919-28.

American Ethnologist 1, no. 2(1974):333.

Current Anthropology, 5(1964):288.

Ethnicity 3(1976):226.

Geographical Review, 70(1980):24.

International Journal of Comparative Sociology, 17, nos. 3-4:242.

Missouri Historical Review 68, no. 3(1974):280-398;

    4(1974):393-415.

Nationalities Papers, 22, no. 1(spring 1992):96;

    23, no. 3(September 1995):616, 619.

DISSERTATIONS

J. F. Shearouse, "Protestant Activities as Contributing Factors to the 1731 Expulsion of the Salzburg Lutherans: Viewed in Light of the 1648 Peace of Westphalia," Ph. D. diss., Northwestern University, 1985.

ENCYCLOPEDIAS

Yu. Bromley, ed., *Narody Mira*, Moscow: Sovetskaia Entsyklopediia, 1988.

Brig. Peter Young, ed., *Illustrated World War II Encyclopedia*, H.S. Stuttman.

NEWSPAPERS

Lidová Demokracie, 1945-47.

The New York Times, 1987, 1996.

RESEARCH PAPERS

Saul B. Cohen, *The Geopolitics of Israel's Border Question*, Jaffee Center for Strategic Studies, study no. 7, Boulder, CO: Westview Press, 1987.

Fabian Schmidt, "Kosovo: The Time Bomb that Has Not Gone Off," RFE/RL Research Report, vol. 2, no. 39, October 1, 1993.

R. Wixman, *Language Aspects of Ethnic Patterns and Processes in the North Caucasus*, University of Chicago, Dept. of Geography, Research Paper no. 191, Chicago:1980.

V. Žerjavić, "The Losses of Yugoslav Population in the Second World War," *Geographical Papers*, vol. 8, Institute of Geography, University of Zagreb, Zagreb, Croatia:1991, p. 96.

ATLASES

Country Atlas (Rand McNally, 1994).

World Atlas (Rand McNally, 1994).

MAGAZINES

Foreign Affairs, January 1942.

Midstream, October 1994.

Newsweek, April 1994.

Time, August 1992.

SPEECHES

Nicos Kranidiotis, "The Cyprus Problem," delivered at the International Symposium on Cyprus at the Panteios School of Political Science in Athens on March 10-14, 1975.

OTHER PUBLICATIONS

Crisis on Cyprus, Washington, D.C.: American Hellenic Institute, 1975.

Cyprus, Encyclopedia Britannica Year Book, 1995.

Cyprus, Nicosia: Republic of Cyprus Press and Information Office, 1990.

The Cyprus Problem, Nicosia: Press and Information Office of the Republic of Cyprus, 1988.

East Timor Violations of Human Rights, London: Amnesty International Publications, 1985.

Helsinki Watch, *Struggling for Ethnic Identity: Ethnic Hungarians in Post-Ceausescu Romania,* New York: Human Rights Watch, 1993.

Helsinki Watch, *War Crimes in Bosnia-Hercegovina,* New York: Human Rights Watch, 1992.

Hungarian Human Rights Foundation ("HHRF"), "International Protection of National Minorities: An Imperative for the Hungarians of Romania," Memorandum for the Copenhagen Meeting on the Human Dimension, Conference on Security and Cooperation in Europe, June 5-29, 1990.

————, "Romania's Policies and Practices toward National Minorities," Summary for the Geneva Meeting of Experts on National Minorities, Conference on Security and Cooperation in Europe, July 1-19, 1991.

————, Letter to the Representatives at the Parliamentary Assembly in the Council of Europe, September 24, 1993.

————, "An Unbroken Record of Broken Promises," October 18, 1993.

The Keesing's Record of World Events, London: Longman, 1994.

Richard F. Nyrop et al., *Area Handbook for Ceylon,* Washington, D.C.: The American University, 1971.

On The Cyprus Problem: 1964-88 (Resolutions adopted by the United Nations).

Peoples of the Soviet Union, Moscow: Novosti Press Agency, 1989.

Strany Mira, Moscow: Izdatel'stvo politicheskoi literatury, 1991.

U.S. Army Area Handbook for Algeria, Dept. of the Army, Pamphlet 550-44, Washington:1965.

Webster's New Collegiate Dictionary, Springfield, MA: G. & C. Merriam Company, 1976.

INDEX

100-1, 106-7, 109-10, 112
Brass, Paul, 80, 85, 87, 90, 110, 112
Brazil, 64, serranismo in, 88
Breton(s), 85, 232
Britain, 100, 137, 140, 203-9, 223, 267-
68; Foreign Office, 171; the Irish
question, 92; Palestine, 168-71
British, 203-9, identity of, 69
Budak, Milan, 45, 131
Budapest, 128, 130
Buddha, 191
Buddhism, 190
Buddhist(s), 76, 187-88, 191
Bukovina, 37, 238
Bulgaria, 46, 124, 126, 158, 196, 221, 225-
26, 255; minority in, 121; Turkish
expellees from, 266; Turkish victory over,
160
Bulgarians, 22; cleansing of, 31-32;
suppression of, 129
Burundi, 47, 181-86, 214, 243, 257, 274-
75, 279; emigration from, 181; ethnic
conflict in, 183, 185; under colonial
rule, 182-84;
Byzantium/Byzantines, 11, 13, 22, 55, 138,
145-46, 158, 175; forced conversions,
15; loss of African and Asian provinces, 145;
Byzantines, 77, 168

C
Canada, 18, 260; French minority in, 216
Carthage, 58; destruction of, 9-10; Second
Punic War, 10;
Carthaginians, 59
caste, 65, 61, 72, 79, 89-97, 190; Catalan
identity, 69; Catalonia, 85; hereditary
occupational, 110; hierarchy, 87-88. See
also Indian caste system
Catholicism, 76, 113, 129, 131; imposition
of (in Cyprus), 138
Catholic(s), 258; Albanians, 160; Church,
218; conversion to, 124; doctrine, 91;
dogma, 77; massacres of Roman
catholics, 16; rite, 77; Roman, 60-61,
69-71, 73, 77
Caucasus, 31-32; Russian advance into,
146. See also Transcaucasia
Ceausescu, 200-1
Celts, 59, 203; Celtic fringe (in Britain),
92
Central Asia, 26, 121, 174-79, 243, 255,
258
Central Committee of the League of
Communists of Yugoslavia, 162
Central Europe, 49, 71, 81-82
Ceylon, 187, 190-91. See Sri-Lanka
Chamberlain, Houston Stewart, 34, 61
Chechnya, 174, 261; cleansing in, 32
China, 29, 63; cleansing in, 54; Maoist, 62
Chinese, 76; expulsion of, 19-20

Christ, Jesus, 67
Christianity/Christendom, 13, 31, 51, 61,
65, 67, 75-76, 78, 129-31, 187; Latin,
11; spread of, 59; symbolism, 83;
world, 16
Christian(s), 146, 149, 168; Arabs, 23;
Byzantine, 11; capture of, 52; cleansing
of, 54; Jacobite, 25, 151; Lebanese, 22,
25; medieval, 281-82, missionaries,
182, Nestorian, 22, 25, 151, New
Christians, 15, Orthodox, 22-23
Churchill, Winston, 170, 206
Cilicia, 144, 146, 150
citizenship, definitions of, 224
civil rights, 215
class, 1, 3, 63, 71, 73, 80, 89-97, 103,
110-13, 182, 206, 281; as category, 62;
(category) ideological, 64, 67, 89-90;
(category) sociological, 64, 67, 89;
cohesiveness of, 91; consciousness, 67,
90, 96; divisions, 91, 96; class-based
entity, 22; class enemy, 28, 33, 62; as
ideology, 35; mobilized, 89; nationalism, 90, 96; oppression, 90; parasitic,
29, 34, 54, 63, 282; politicized, 89;
social, 90, 100, 108; solidarity, 94;
struggle, 91; underclass, 96; upper
class, 96; working class, 96
cleansing, 31, 48, 52, 57, 61, 66, 119-21,
135, 214, 217, 281-82, 286; by age, 56,
106; in antiquity, 7-11, 52, 55; of
aristocracy, 29, 54; of bourgeoisie, 29,
54; civilizational, 54, 59; class, 29, 40,
54, 63; colonial, 18-21, 52, contemporary, 21-49; definition of, 3; early
modern, 17-21; economic, 7-11, 55;
ethnic, 9, 11, 30, 32-33, 35, 40, 43-47,
52-53, 133; external/internal (self-), 54;
by gender, 55; ideological, 30, 32-33,
35, 43-44, 52; medieval, 11-17, 52;
mental patients, 56; modern, 52;
paradigmatic, 53; parameters of, 15;
permanent, 56; political, 7-11, 43, 52,
54; population, 1-3; postcolonial, 40-
41, 52; preemptive, 53; of prostitutes,
56; pseudoracial, 53; racial, 40, 44-45,
53; religious, 11-18, 40, 52-54, 60; by
sexual preference, 35, 55-56; social
(beggars), 56; as a state policy, 7;
strategic, 54; temporary, 56; typology
of, 51-56. See also expulsion, forced
emigration, deportation, removal
clergy, 93-94
Cluj, 199-201
collectivity, 49, 51, 73, 79, 91, 96, 113-14;
based on age, 109; creation of, 106;
lateral, 71-72; vertical, 71-72
colonialism, 41-42
commensality, 93-97
Communism, 77-78, 175; anti-Communism, 43; Chinese, 33; collapse of, 233,